BIBLICAL MASCULINITIES FOREGROUNDED

Hebrew Bible Monographs, 62

BIBLICAL MASCULINITIES FOREGROUNDED

edited by

Ovidiu Creangă and Peter-Ben Smit

SHEFFIELD PHOENIX PRESS

2017

Copyright © 2014, 2017 Sheffield Phoenix Press
First published in hardback, 2014
First published in paperback, 2017

Published by Sheffield Phoenix Press
Department of Biblical Studies, University of Sheffield
45 Victoria Street
Sheffield S3 7QB

www.sheffieldphoenix.com

A CIP catalogue record for this book
is available from the British Library

Typeset by Forthcoming Publications
Printed by Lightning Source

ISBN 978-1-907534-88-1 (hardback)
ISBN 978-1-910928-34-9 (paperback)
ISSN 1747-9614

CONTENTS

Part III
NEW TESTAMENT AND APOCRYPHA

Part IV
FINAL REFLECTIONS

LIST OF CONTRIBUTORS

Matthew Anderson (PhD McGill University) is Assistant Professor at the Department of Theological Studies and at Loyola College for Diversity and Sustainability at Concordia University, Montreal, Canada. His research interests include New Testament studies as well as pilgrimage as a religious and social phenomenon.

Susanna Asikainen is a PhD candidate at the University of Helsinki. Her doctoral dissertation is on the constructions of Jesus' masculinity in the early Christian gospels.

Ovidiu Creangă (PhD King's College London) teaches Hebrew Bible at Wesley Theological Seminary in Washington, DC, and is an Applied Researcher in the Center for Advanced Holocaust Studies, US Holocaust Memorial Museum. He maintains research interests in biblical gender, sacred literature as cultural memory, and the Holocaust. His publications include *Men and Masculinity in the Hebrew Bible and Beyond* (ed., Sheffield Phoenix Press, 2010) and *Ethical Thinking at the Crossroads of European Reasoning* (ed., with Parush Parushev and Brian Brock, IBTS Press, 2007).

Justin Glessner is an Instructor and PhD Candidate in the Department of Classical, Near Eastern, and Religious Studies at the University of British Columbia, Canada. His interests include social-scientific, gender-critical, and postcolonial approaches to the New Testament and the literature and culture of early Christianity.

Alan Hooker is a PhD candidate at the University of Exeter. His research concerns divine sexuality in ancient West Asia, with a specific focus on Yahweh's gender identity in the Hebrew Bible.

Milena Kirova (PhD University of Sofia) is Professor of Literature and Head of Department of Bulgarian Literature at the University of Sofia. She teaches and publishes in the areas of Bulgarian Literature and Gender

Studies of the Hebrew Bible. She has authored eleven books and edited twelve volumes, among which is the first *History of Bulgarian Literature Written by Women* (Altera, 2009). Her monographs include *Medusa's Dream: Towards A Psychoanalysis of Bulgarian Literature* (Sofia University Press, 1995), *Biblical Femininity: Mechanisms of Construction, Politics of Representation in the Hebrew Bible* (Sofia University Press, 2005), and *David, the Great: History and Masculinity in the Hebrew Bible* (Sofia: Ciela, 2009).

Björn Krondorfer (PhD Temple University) is Director of the Martin-Springer Institute at Northern Arizona University and Endowed Professor of Religious Studies in the Department of Comparative Cultural Studies. His research interests include religion and gender, (post-)Holocaust studies, and reconciliation studies. He has published *Male Confessions: Intimate Revelations and the Religious Imagination* (Stanford University Press, 2010), *Men and Masculinities in Christianity and Judaism* (SCM Press, 2009), and *Remembrance and Reconciliation* (Yale University Press, 1995).

Hilary Lipka (PhD Brandeis University) is an instructor in the Religious Studies Program at the University of New Mexico in Albuquerque, NM. She is the author of *Sexual Transgression in the Hebrew Bible* (Sheffield Phoenix Press, 2006) as well as several articles on issues related to sex and gender in biblical texts.

Marcel V. Măcelaru (DPhil University of Oxford) is Associate Professor of Old Testament at the Theological Pentecostal Institute in Bucharest, Romania. His research interests focus on constructions of identity in the Hebrew Bible and their hermeneutical translation within contemporary cultural, academic and faith contexts. His most recent monographs published in Romania are *Identity between Burden and Privilege: Representations of a Holy Nation in the Deuteronomistic Literature* (Cluj-Napoca: Risoprint 2012), and *Ethno-national Discourse in the Hebrew Bible: Methodological Insights Pertaining to the Interpretation of Old Testament Historiographic Narratives* (Bucharest: Editura Universitară, 2012).

Stuart Macwilliam (PhD University of Exeter) is an honorary research fellow in the Department of Theology at University of Exeter since 2011. His research interests are queer theory, masculinities and the Hebrew Bible. He is the author of *Queer Theory and the Prophetic Marriage Metaphor in the Hebrew Bible* (Equinox, 2011), and he has written journal articles and book chapters on male beauty, queer theory and Jeremiah.

Karin Neutel (PhD University of Groningen) is Lecturer in New Testament and Early Christianity at the University of Groningen, The Netherlands. Her research focuses on early Christianity as well as contemporary constructions of the past.

Martti Nissinen (PhD University of Helsinki) is Professor of Old Testament Studies at the University of Helsinki. His research interests include history of religion in the ancient Eastern Mediterranean, especially prophecy and gender-related issues. His publications include *Prophets and Prophecy in the Ancient Near East* (SBL, 2003); *Homoeroticism in the Biblical World* (Augsburg Fortress Press, 1998); *Sacred Marriages: The Divine–Human Sexual Metaphor from Sumer to Early Christianity* (ed., with R. Uro, Eisenbrauns, 2008); *Constructs of Prophecy in the Former and Latter Prophets and Other Texts* (ed., with L.L. Grabbe, SBL, 2011).

Peter-Ben Smit (PhD University of Bern) is Assistant Professor of New Testament at VU University Amsterdam, extraordinary Professor of Early Catholic Ecclesiology at Utrecht University, Research associate at the University of Pretoria, and assisting priest in the Old Catholic parish of Amsterdam. His research interests include masculinity in early Christianity, Anglican ecumenism, and Old Catholic theology. Author of articles on gender in the early Christian literature, he has recently published *Paradigms of Being in Christ: A Study of the Epistles to the Philippians* (New York: Bloomsbury T. & T. Clark, 2013) and, with Adriaan S. van Klinken, he edited *Jesus Traditions in the Construction of Masculinities in World Christianities* (special issue of *Exchange* 42.1; 2013).

Hans-Ulrich Weidemann (PhD University of Tübingen) is Professor of New Testament Theology in the Department of Catholic Theology at Siegen University, Germany. After studying Catholic Theology at the University of Tübingen and at the Pontificia Università Gregoriana in Rome, he completed his doctorate on the Johannine Passion Narrative in 2003 and his habilitation on the emergence of early Christian baptismal Eucharists in 2008, both in Tübingen. His research interests are asceticism in late antiquity, Masculinity studies, the rites of early Christian initiation, the Pastoral epistles, and Johannine theology.

ABBREVIATIONS

AB	Anchor Bible
ABD	David Noel Freedman (ed.), *The Anchor Bible Dictionary* (New York: Doubleday, 1992)
AFS	*Asian Folklore Studies*
AOAT	Alter Orient und Altes Testament
AR	*Archiv für Religionswissenschaft*
ARCA	ARCA Classical and Medieval Texts, Papers and Monographs
AwK	Altertumswissenschaftliches Kolloquium
BBR	*Bulletin for Biblical Research*
BCH	*Bulletin de Correspondance Hellénique*
BHM	*Bulletin of the History of Medicine*
BibInt	*Biblical Interpretation*
BibRev	*Bible Review*
BIS	Biblical Interpretation Series
BJOS	*The British Journal of Sociology*
BNTC	Black's New Testament Commentaries
BTB	*Biblical Theology Bulletin*
BWANT	Beiträge zur Wissenschaft vom Alten und Neuen Testament
BZAW	Beihefte zur *Zeitschrift für die alttestamentliche Wissenschaft*
CBQ	*Catholic Biblical Quarterly*
CBQMS	Catholic Biblical Quarterly Monograph Series
CH	*Church History*
CP	*Classical Philology*
CRRAI	Compte Rendu Rencontre Assyriologique Internationale
EKK	Evangelisch-katholischer Kommentar zum Neuen Testament
ELO	*Estudos de Literatura Oral*
ET	English translation
FCB	Feminist Companion to the Bible
FemTh	*Feminist Theology*
FOTL	Forms of Old Testament Literature
HBM	Hebrew Bible Monographs
HBS	Herders biblische Studien
HBT	*Horizons in Biblical Theology*
HeyJ	*Heythrop Journal*
Historia	*Historia: Zeitschrift für Alte Geschichte*
HR	*History of Religions*
HSM	Harvard Semitic Monographs
HTR	*Harvard Theological Review*
HTS	*Harvard Theological Studies*
HUCA	*Harvard Union College Annual*
HvTSt	*Hervormde teologiese studies*
ICC	International Critical Commentary
ISBL	Indiana Studies in Biblical Literature

JAC	*Jahrbuch für Antike und Christentum*
JACC	*Journal of American Culture*
JAOS	*Journal of the American Oriental Society*
JBL	*Journal of Biblical Literature*
JEA	*Journal of Egyptian Archaeology*
JECS	*Journal of Early Christian Studies*
JFI	*Journal of the Folklore Institute*
JFSR	*Journal of Feminist Studies in Religion*
JHistSex	*Journal of the History of Sexuality*
JMMS	*Journal of Men, Masculinity, and Spirituality*
JPS	Jewish Publication Society translation of the Tanakh
JR	*Journal of Religion*
JSJ	*Journal for the Study of Judaism in the Persian, Hellenistic and Roman Period*
JSNT	*Journal for the Study of the New Testament*
JSNTSup	Journal for the Study of the New Testament, Supplement Series
JSOT	*Journal for the Study of the Old Testament*
JSOTSup	Journal for the Study of the Old Testament, Supplement Series
JSQ	*Jewish Studies Quarterly*
JTS	*Journal of Theological Studies*
LCM	*Liverpool Classical Monthly*
LEC	Library of Early Christianity
LHBOTS	The Library of Hebrew Bible/Old Testament Studies
LSJ	H.G. Liddell, R. Scott, and H.S. Jones (eds.), *A Greek–English Lexicon* (Oxford: Clarendon Press, 9th ed. with revised supplement, 1996)
Mnemosyne	*Mnemosyne. Bibliotheca Classica Batava*
NCB	New Century Bible
NCBC	New Cambridge Bible Commentary
NICNT	New International Commentary on the New Testament
NICOT	New International Commentary on the Old Testament
NIGTC	New International Greek Testament Commentary
NIV	New International Version
NovT	*Novum Testamentum*
NRSV	New Revised Standard Version
NTS	*New Testament Studies*
OBT	Overtures to Biblical Theology
OTL	Old Testament Library
OTM	Oxford Theological Monographs
PRSt	*Perspectives in Religious Studies*
RSR	*Religious Studies Review*
RSV	Revised Standard Version
SBL	Society of Biblical Literature
SBLDS	Society of Biblical Literature Dissertation Series
SBLSP	*Society of Biblical Literature Seminar Papers*
SBLSymS	Society of Biblical Literature Symposium Series
SBS	Stuttgarter Bibelstudien
SemeiaSt	Semeia Studies
SNTSMS	Society for New Testament Studies Monograph Series
SPhilo	*Studia Philonica Annual*
StPatr	*Studia Patristica*

SVTQ	*Saint Vladimir's Theological Quarterly*
TBei	*Theologische Beiträge*
TDNT	Gerhard Kittel and Gerhard Friedrich (eds.), *Theological Dictionary of the New Testament* (trans. Geoffrey W. Bromiley; 10 vols.; Grand Rapids: Eerdmans, 1964–)
TDOT	G. Johannes Botterweck *et. al.* (eds.), *Theological Dictionary of the Old Testament* (Grand Rapids: Eerdmans)
TS	Texts and Studies
TSAJ	Texts and Studies in Ancient Judaism
TU	Texte und Untersuchungen
VC	*Vigiliae Christianae*
VT	*Vetus Testamentum*
Viator	*Viator: Medieval and Renaissance Studies*
WBC	Word Biblical Commentary
WMANT	Wissenschaftliche Monographien zum Alten und Neuen Testament
WSIF	*Women's Studies International Forum*
WUNT	Wissenschaftliche Untersuchungen zum Neuen Testament
YCS	*Yale Classical Studies*
ZAW	*Zeitschrift für die alttestamentliche Wissenschaft*
ZNT	Zeitschrift für Neues Testament
ZNW	*Zeitschrift für die neutestamentliche Wissenschaft und die Kunde der älteren Kirche*

Part I

INTRODUCTION

INTRODUCTION

Ovidiu Creangă

A critical and consciously male-gendered reading, then, assumes a *male difference* without claiming that men constitute a homogeneous whole. Put simply, but no less thorny in its implications: men are men, but not all men are equal; men become men by articulating their distinctiveness from women; men become "straight" by distinguishing themselves from "deviant" male behavior; men become heteronormative by mistaking *sameness* of discrete groups of men as *universal*; men become "real men" by reiterating the fictions they have helped to construe about the other (Krondorfer 2010: 4).

Biblical Masculinities Foregrounded, the first collection of studies dedicated exclusively to the representation of masculinities in the Hebrew Bible and the New Testament, cuts new ground in male gender readings of biblical texts. When its precursor volume *Men and Masculinity in the Hebrew Bible and Beyond* was published in 2010, I was convinced the exploration was still in its early days and that other volumes would quickly follow. That estimation was right. *Men and Masculinity in the Hebrew Bible and Beyond* arrived seven years after Stephen D. Moore and Janice C. Anderson's highly influential *New Testament Masculinities* (Moore and Anderson 2003) and one year after Björn Krondorfer's equally important, *Men and Masculinities in Christianity and Judaism* (2009). It provided what was missing from both studies, namely, an engagement with and an analysis of Hebrew Bible masculinities. But a volume bringing together studies of masculinity from the Hebrew Bible *and* the New Testament was still nowhere to be found. It therefore seemed entirely logical to me and my co-editor Peter-Ben Smit that *Biblical Masculinities Foregrounded* should focus on both Testaments and related literature, and keep within its covers the richness of insight that the study of masculinities currently generates in scriptural canons.

The advantage of asking two senior scholars to respond to the articles assembled in *Men and Masculinity* is that most of the necessary theoretical and methodological aspects that needed further unpacking in a subsequent publication have been carefully spotted and addressed (see the 'Final Reflections on Biblical Masculinity' by David J.A. Clines and Stephen D. Moore, 234-39 and 240-55, respectively). In this short introduction, I shall therefore only raise four elementary questions (I find those are often the most difficult to answer), and ask others along the way, to contour the ten new studies gathered in this collection. I hope this reflection will encourage even more studies which foreground masculinities embodied by men and women in biblical literature.

Let me proceed then by asking the following blunt questions, before turning to the contents of the volume and describing each article in the shortest of words.

What Is Biblical Masculinities?

Defining 'masculinity' and the field of 'biblical masculinities' is more difficult than it first appears,[1] but very simply put, biblical masculinities is the study of the representation/s of the male gender (what 'mans' a man or a woman, including what 'mans' God) in biblical and related literature. Biblical masculinities as distinct representations of the male gender is not about studying the Bible's male characters (as might appear if one looks at the table of contents inside this volume), though frequently a male personage becomes the focus of investigation. Rather, it is about studying male and/or female characters and their 'manly' acts. It is the multiple de- or re-constructions of the male gender in biblical literature that drives the investigation, not the sex of the character/s examined. Because the performance of gender is not limited to sex(uality) but encompasses one's entire life,[2] some of the places where the formulation of male gender can be seen with clarity are in societal *institutions* (marriage, family, religion, army, monarchy, priesthood); in *relationships* (some biological: paternal or maternal which develop into kinship relations; others social: friendship, courtships; and still other spiritual ties, binding people to each other and to the divine, though one can also include here people's ties to a particular place or space); in *roles* (that men play and are expected to play, like being a husband, a father, a leader, a soldier, a devout follower of God); in the social norms demarcating male *behavior* (sexual, non-sexual, religious, driven by honor and other virtues and by fear of being shamed or emasculated); in *emotions* (that one expresses, suppresses, or represses in order to gain something, or to maintain a particular image about oneself); and finally (though by no means exclusively) in discourses about the *body* (how it should be kept or dressed or fed to look healthy and 'manly', how physical and/or mental illness or being disabled

1. Cf. Connell 2005: 67: 'Masculinity is not a coherent object about which a generalizing science can be produced'. But this is not to say that no definitions can be attempted: '"Masculinity", to the extent the term can be briefly defined at all, is simultaneously a place in gender relations, the practices through which men and women engage that place in gender, and the effects of these practices in bodily experience, personality and culture' (71).

2. For gender as performance, see Butler 1990; and for the bodily aspects of that performance, see Butler 1993 and 2004.

redefines masculinity, and how it changes with the passing of time). To keep up, to perform their masculinity in any one or all of these areas, men or women also act and speak in a certain way, refraining from being emasculated or reduced to a 'womanly' state, a process which is also socially constructed.

Underlying this construction of the male gender are social norms, expectations, ideologies, and biases ingrained in each culture regarding what is an 'acceptable' or 'unacceptable' man or woman, what is a 'desirable' or 'rejectable' masculinity. Biblical writers and their readers/listeners internalized these norms (likely without being aware of it) and we and our contemporaries assimilate them too (and few are aware of it as well). Dominant ideas about what 'mans' someone always exist in competition with other gender scripts. Changes in historical circumstances, decline or rise of empires and their respective social and political institutions, emergence of new philosophies, or new encounters between peoples living apart, can sometimes alter or displace particular images of masculinity. A characteristic of masculinity that once was considered peripheral or opposite to a hegemonic gender ideal can gradually gain acceptance and even become the prevailing norm at other times. Despite appearance, gender hegemonies necessarily change across time and space to remain dominant, and any one group hardly ever adopts a single gender norm. A critical study of biblical masculinities works to interrogate and subvert an arranging of the world that 'naturalizes' a particular hierarchy of masculinity at the expense of, or over against, all other forms of being a 'man' or 'manly'. The critique of hegemonic masculinity is necessary not because a theory requires it, but because there are other legitimate forms of existing in the world that hegemony obscures and distorts.

Why Are We Today Studying Biblical Masculinities?

Or to put it differently: Isn't the moving away from the 'second sex', to play on Simone de Beauvoir's epic study, *Le Deuxième Sexe* (2011, orig. 1949), to the 'first sex' counter-productive in today's gender arena? But is biblical masculinities really an advocate for 'le premier sexe'? Moreover, should feminist biblical scholars be suspicious of the emergence of a field of study that puts masculinity at the center of its intellectual focus, especially when women are still fighting for equal rights and our society still privileges men over women (at least in strategic fields like politics and finance)? As I hope to show below, and as I trust *Biblical Masculinity Foregrounded* demonstrates, the answer is a triple no.

As a biblical feminist scholar myself (see Creangă 2007), I see the emergence of biblical masculinities as a critically important move in how we ought to read texts from a gender-sensitive standpoint. I believe the two fields partly overlap in their efforts to expose and deconstruct systems of male domination inscribed in biblical texts. This is not to say, of course, that the two fields are identical in every way simply because their goals sometimes align. For even if closely related, feminist and masculinity biblical criticism maintain, and rightly so, their own individual goals in respect to male ideologies, and each field maps, as it ought to, its own methodological or terminological paths for achieving those objectives. Yet this fact alone should not prevent scholars from cooperating. The hegemony of the 'first sex' is an issue for feminist and masculinity scholars alike. For feminist scholars, the major problem is the Bible's patriarchy and androcentrism; for masculinity scholars, it is the hegemony of certain expressions of masculinity that discriminate not only against women but also against other men who do not fit, or like, those images. A crisscrossing of concerns also exists between gender scholars, creating a degree of solidarity with each other's causes.

In *Men and Masculinity*, I suggested 'male logo-centricity'—the circular power and prestige that biblical men acquire through being institutionally privileged over women to speak in public gatherings, usually at critical moments in the life of the Israelite community—as an area of shared interest for feminist and masculinity biblical scholars alike (Creangă 2010: 88). The Bible's top men (I was thinking of Joshua, Moses' successor, when I made that proposition) are typically portrayed as speaking to/over/on behalf of women, but if we read carefully, we notice that they equally speak to/over/ on behalf of other men. Who are those 'other' men who are constantly spoken to? Are they the less prestigious, the ordinary, the masses from the point of view of hierarchy? The everyday man and the subaltern rarely emerge from the collective to make the news. In the Hebrew Bible, the 'Canaanites' and the 'people of the Land' are most of the time lifeless labels rather than flesh-and-blood entities. In the New Testament, there are the 'Jews', the 'Circumcisers', and other Christian heterodox sects that act merely as road-sign posts. The trouble with labels and road-signs is their impersonal nature, which closes us rather than opens us up to curiosity: 'curvy roads', 'bridge may be icy', 'speed limit 55mph', etc.—but you will never read a sign asking you to get out of the car and say hello. The diversity of biblical men and the many ways of being 'manly' are reduced in the holy script to a model that reflects little variation. Not unlike biblical women, biblical men too are defined by stereotypical appellation: son/s of so and so, brother/s of so and so, man/men of so and so tribe. In the Transylvanian village where I spent my summers as a boy, newcomers were usually asked when encountered alone on a street, 'whose are you?' When I was asked that question, I would say 'I'm of so and so...(usually my father's family name)', and the interlocutor seemed content that he/she could now place me somewhere in his/her mind. The question, however, missed *me* almost entirely. Who I was only mattered to that person because of my parents. In my interlocutor's eye, my identity was almost totally absorbed into my father's. Patriarchy can, therefore, be harmful to women as well as men.

I am not suggesting that 'other men' (young, old, womanized) and 'women', as embodiments of society's 'other' sexes, have similar experiences of discrimination, for they clearly do not. What I am saying is that male hegemonies inscribed in biblical texts can be effectively attacked from both directions. The spectrum of masculinities (complicit, subordinated, marginalized) existing in relation to a hegemonic type, besides hegemony's own internal instabilities, reveals tensions and fissures between types of man and masculinity that can be effectively exploited by feminist and masculinity scholars alike for their own respective goals. For an alliance against male domination to form, however, there has to be a sustained interest not only from feminist scholars but also from masculinity scholars in deconstructing male gender scripts that promote inequality between men, and between men and women.

The many studies about biblical men that do not tackle the question of masculinity/patriarchy/androcentrism will add little in this regard. The last decade, in the Hebrew Bible area for example, has seen the publication of new monographs on Abraham (Hendel 2005), Joshua (Hall 2010), and perhaps we could add here Walter Brueggemann's revised study on David (2000). All are excellent studies in their own right, but none attend to the analysis of the most basic aspect of their character of choice: that Abraham, Joshua, and David and their writers were, or were attempting to be, *men* before anything else. Feminist biblical scholarship has corrected this anomaly somewhat by providing studies that reflect critically on masculinity (rather than on men alone) while also maintaining a feminist agenda.[3] The more recent masculinity studies (including those collected in *Biblical Masculinities Foregrounded*) are further remedying the situation, but the task still remains enormous. As I write these lines I can think of only two Hebrew Bible monographs that employ masculinity as a central theme published since the appearance of *Men and Masculinity* in 2010, namely, Susan E. Haddox's *Masculinity and Metaphor in Hosea* (2011) and Stuart Macwilliam's *Queer Theory and the Prophetic Marriage Metaphor in the Hebrew Bible* (2011). These two monographs represent progress from where we were in 2010, when Moore could list only one book-length study that

---

3. See, for instance, Deborah W. Rooke's work on priestly breeches (undergarment) covering male genitalia (2009); Saul Olyan's work on the Leviticus's prohibition of male–male sexual relations (Olyan 1994), despite its exceptional quality and rigor, reflects only minimally on the issue of gender evoked by the legislation in question. Rooke's study on the same prohibition more clearly discusses masculinity as an integral component of the legislation (Rooke 2007).

examined biblical masculinity concepts (and that in the New Testament area, Conway 2008).[4] A couple of edited volumes published since 2010 spring to my mind and are an encouraging sign: Teresa J. Hornsby and Ken Stone's *Bible Trouble: Queer Reading at the Boundaries of Biblical Scholarship* (2011), an important contribution to queer biblical masculinity, and Jonathan Stökl and Corrine L. Carvalho's *Prophets Male and Female: Gender and Prophecy in the Hebrew Bible, the Eastern Mediterranean, and the Ancient Near East* (2013), the latter bringing a much-needed engagement with masculinity in prophetic literature in ancient Mediterranean and Near Eastern sources.[5] There remains much more to be excavated, however, and I hope the studies assembled in this volume will tantalize scholars to explore new topics in this field.

Who Should Biblical Masculinities Befriend?

All other critical biblical studies would be my answer. In the preceding section I made a case for why feminist biblical criticism is an appropriate companion in the study of masculinities. I also see queer studies making a suitable partner, but again, it is a matter of identifying common goals around heteronormativity to which we can strive together. Intersecting with historical studies (of the ancient Near East, of Mediterranean antiquities, but also with medieval and modern history), with postcolonial studies, with cultural studies (including memory, spatial, arts, and film studies), with social-cultural anthropology, with literary studies (traditional as well as new approaches), and with the study of ideologies, among other fields, will expand the theoretical base, necessary for producing new insights and keeping the field fresh. All the chapters in *Biblical Masculinities Foregrounded* showcase close readings of biblical texts, and all are interdisciplinary in method, but there is certainly plenty more that can be drawn from and employed as a critical tool in this emerging field.

Why Should Biblical Masculinities Matter?

This question has followed me like a shadow ever since David J.A. Clines imprinted the following thoughts in his response to *Men and Masculinities* (and because of their importance, I am going to cite a few paragraphs):

4. David J.A. Clines is preparing a volume, *Play the Man! The Masculine Imperative in the Bible* (HBM; Sheffield: Sheffield Phoenix Press, forthcoming), which contains some of his previously published articles (with some revision) on biblical masculinity.

5. An important new volume on masculinities is to appear soon: Ilona Zsolnay (ed.), *Being a Man in Antiquity: Negotiating, Legitimating, and Maintaining Ancient Constructs of Masculinity* (London: Routledge, forthcoming).

Especially by comparison with the beginnings of feminist biblical criticism, masculinity studies in the Hebrew Bible seem strangely lacking in passion. One gains no impression from the articles in this volume that masculinity studies is a *movement*, to which people have a commitment. Perhaps it is not. Perhaps there is no agenda in masculinity studies, other than intellectual curiosity.

If indeed that is so, I am disappointed. I regard the ubiquity of masculine thought and language in the Hebrew Bible as a problem, or rather an outrage. I regard its casting of the whole of the Hebrew Bible's contents, its poetry and its narratives, its ideas and its religious opinions, in the forms and dress of the masculine as a crime.

I want to urge that there is an injustice, damaging to women and men alike, in the Hebrew Bible's assumption of the normative masculinity. The people who should be noticing it, writing about it, and protesting against it, are biblical scholars. No one else [is] in such a good position to speak with under-standing and discernment about the situation. Our first task, as it was with feminist movement, is consciousness raising. Our second task as I see it, is apology; we are doing a lot in our professional lives to keep the biblical books alive, and it is our duty as academics to distance ourselves from the unlovely aspects of what we teach and research, and not to give the impres-sion that because we are experts on these texts we subscribe to them warts and all. Our third task is to constantly refine what it is about masculinity that is objectionable. Masculinity is not a vice, and it is no part of a proper study of the subject to smear all expressions of masculinity with the wrongs and excesses of some of its manifestations.

I want to urge, in short, that it should not be possible to remain 'objective' about the issue of masculinity in the Hebrew Bible. It is a political matter, and a refusal to speak about it is a dereliction of our moral duty. I want to urge a masculinity movement, not, as with feminism's project to assert the rights of women and to redress inequality, but to assess, critique and row back from the kind of unthinking masculinity that are spread all over the Hebrew Bible (Clines 2010: 238-39).

There is a lot packed in these paragraphs. That the study of biblical mascu-linities matters for biblical interpretation and that it helps scholars better understand biblical texts and their writers and readers—these are the easy answers. This and previous volumes of masculinity illustrate that. But if this is all we hope for (and who is to say it is not enough?), we will likely see biblical masculinities run its course in a few years from now. Should biblical masculinities have a social, political, and religious mandate for today, and if yes, what might it be? Are masculinity scholars (including the authors in this volume) writing just for the sake of intellectual curiosity? Can biblical masculinities become a 'movement'? What the agenda for such a movement should be may transpire from the tasks that Clines mentions in his manifesto cited above: raise consciousness about the dangers of upholding the Bible's normative masculinity uncritically, confess ('apology' is his word) that which is objectionable about biblical masculinity, and refine the search for unattractive male gender scripts within the Bible. But, if my assessment of Clines's words is correct, there is a 'political matter' involved in speaking, or refusing to speak, against certain expressions of biblical masculinity. Is it implicit that biblical masculinities, as a movement, should promote a fair/er society for all men and women (heterosexual, gay and lesbian, transgendered, transsexual)? Should we as a scholarly community stand (a scholarly 'occupy movement' of sorts?) against misogynist, racist, sexist ideologies (and their intersections) found in forums like politics, finance, religious institutions, learning institutions, and so on, which promote a type of masculinity or a vision of society that puts most men and women at a disadvantage? Whatever the answers may be, we should do more than critique and deconstruct. It is also our responsibility to offer viable models of masculinity that promote well-being, healthy relationships/marriages/unions, good parenting, peaceful conflict-resolution, and responsible living among all people and the creation.

At the time of composing these lines, the United States of America is going through a remarkable gender (r)evolution. Policies and every-day attitudes are changing on gender-matters that only a few years ago looked unmovable. The 'Don't Ask, Don't Tell' policy that used to prevail in the US military has been outlawed; as a result, openly gay and lesbian army soldiers can no longer be discriminated against because of their sexual preference. A majority (small, but growing) of Americans support same-sex marriage.[6] A short while ago, the US Supreme Court struck down as unconstitutional the 'Defense of Marriage Act' (DOMA), a Californian law according to which only heterosexual married couples were entitled to benefits. These accomplishments are listed here not to obscure the fact that opposition to gay men and lesbian women, and to same-sex liaisons, remains in some parts of the US (reflected both at the legislative level and in society more generally). I mention these only to say that, overall, it is undeniable that the United States, along with its President Barak Obama, is evolving to become fair/er on gender matters. These cultural shifts are shaping the way Westerners (and younger generations, in particular) read their respective Bibles. A changing culture also changes the world in which the Bibles are being read. If we, scholars of biblical masculinities in the West, are going to occupy a front seat in these and related changes in our own countries, we will have to be more assertive and outspoken.[7]

---

6. Fifty-two percent overall, according to a recent Gallup poll (conducted in July 2013): see http://www.gallup.com/poll/163730/back-law-legalize-gay-marriage-states.aspx. Accessed 12 August 2013.

7. I am aware that the gender r/evolution discussed above is particular to the United States and to an extent Western Europe (though even in the West is limited to certain groups) and it is not reflected globally. Analyzing the politics of masculinity at the level

The Foregrounding of Biblical Masculinities

And finally, a word about the contents of this volume. The essays gathered here foreground important theoretical and methodological aspects in the study of biblical masculinities across both Testaments and apocryphal literature. The program unit 'Biblical Masculinities' that exists within the Society of Biblical Literature, and which Peter-Ben Smit and I co-chair, was instrumental in gathering an active group of biblical scholars working on masculinity. The contributions inside this volume reflect the names and scholarship of some of the scholars associated with the program. The volume is divided into three parts. Part I focuses on Hebrew Bible masculinities, Part II on New Testament masculinities (and its related literature), and Part III contains short reflections by two senior scholars, Martti Nissinen (Hebrew Bible) and Björn Krondorfer (Comparative Cultural Studies).

Part I opens with Alan Hooker's essay on Yahweh's manifestation, his 'Glory', in the books of Exodus and Ezekiel, as instantiations of God's masculinity. Hilary Lipka discusses the representation of masculinity in the book of Proverbs, as an alternative to the hegemonic ideal inscribed in other parts of the Hebrew Bible. Marcel V. Măcelaru examines King Saul's masculinity in 1 Samuel 9–31, finding that Israel's first king falls short of traditional traits of hegemonic masculinity (which King David embodies more successfully). Milena Kirova treats the function of male weeping in the Torah and the Deuteronomistic History, highlighting its strategic usage in relation to God and other men. Stuart Macwilliam analyses Queen Athaliah's male gendering in 2 Kings 11 as a narrative technique that foretells her condemnation in the eyes of the male narrator.

In Part II, dealing with the New Testament, Susanna Asikainen writes on Matthew's use of 'eunuchs' as representatives of a subordinate masculinity essential to the Matthean community's identity. Hans-Ulrich Weidemann tests the limits of androcentrism in Matthew's Sermon on the Mount. Justin Glessner uncovers the literary makings of an 'average Joe' in the person of Joseph of Nazareth in Luke, Matthew, and the apocryphal *Infancy Gospel of*

---

of various faith-communities and state legislation among the African nations, the Middle East, Eastern Europe, and Asian countries is critically important for conversing globally about the constructed nature of gender and its rooting in networks of power (political, social, and religious) within national contexts. For constructions of biblical masculinity in African contexts, see Adriaan S. van Klinken and Peter-Ben Smit, 'Jesus Traditions and Masculinities in World Christianity' (2013), and the articles in the journal introduced by the two authors. For a discussion of the implementation of legislation partaking to gender and sexuality in the newly ascended Eastern European countries to the European Union, see Lavina Stan and Lucian Turcescu, *Church, State, and Democracy in Expanding Europe* (2011), and my review of the book in Creangă 2013.

James, also known as the *Protoevangelium of James* (PJ). The connection of masculinity to circumcision in the Greco-Roman sources and Paul's writings is the subject of the co-authored essay by Karin B. Neutel and Matthew R. Anderson. And finally, Peter Ben-Smit examines disciple-turned-apostle Thecla's 'cross-dressing' as a site of her gender change in the apocryphal *Acts of (Paul and) Thecla*.

In Part III, the two concluding responses by Björn Krondorfer and Martti Nissinen situate the volume within the larger biblical, social, and cultural contexts dealing with ancient and modern masculinities. Such situationing is vital to the development of the field of biblical masculinities.

Bibliography

Brueggemann, Walter
  2000 *David's Truth in Israel's Imagination and Memory* (Minneapolis, MN: Fortress Press).
Butler, Judith
  1990 *Gender Trouble: Feminism and the Subversion of Identity* (New York: Routledge).
  1993 *Bodies that Matter: On the Discursive Limits of "Sex"* (New York: Routledge).
  2004 *Undoing Gender* (New York: Routledge).
Clines, David J.A.
  2010 'Final Reflections on Biblical Masculinity', in Creangă (ed.) 2010: 234-39.
  forthcoming *Play the Man! The Masculine Imperative in the Bible* (HBM; Sheffield: Sheffield Phoenix Press).
Connell, R.W.
  2005 *Masculinities* (Berkley, CA: University of California Press, first published in 1995).
Conway, Colleen M.
  2008 *Behold the Man: Jesus and Greco-Roman Masculinity* (Oxford: Oxford University Press).
Creangă, Ovidiu
  2007 'The Silent Songs of Victory: Power, Gender and Memory in the Conquest Narrative of Joshua (Joshua 1–12)', in Rooke (ed.) 2007: 106-23.
  2010 'Variations on the Theme of Masculinity: Joshua's Gender In/stability in the Conquest Narrative (Josh. 1-12)', in Creangă (ed.) 2010: 83-109.
  2013 'Review of Lavinia Stan and Lucian Turcescu, *Church, State, and Democracy in Expanding Europe*', *Europe-Asia Studies* 65/8: 1680-81.
Creangă, Ovidiu (ed.)
  2010 *Men and Masculinity in the Hebrew Bible and Beyond* (BMW, 33; Sheffield: Sheffield Phoenix Press).
Beauvoir, Simone de
  2011 *The Second Sex* (trans. Constance Border and Sheila Malovany-Chevalier; Introduction by Judith Thurman; New York: Alfred A. Knopf [*Le Deuxième Sexe*, 1949]).

Hall, Sarah Lebhar
    2010   *Conquering Character: The Characterization of Joshua in Joshua 1–11*
            (LHBOTS, 512; London: T. & T. Clark).
Haddox, Susan E.
    2011   *Metaphor and Masculinity in Hosea* (Studies in Biblical Literature, 141;
            New York: Peter Lang).
Hendel, Roland S.
    2005   *Remembering Abraham: Culture, Memory, and History in the Hebrew
            Bible* (Oxford: Oxford University Press).
Hornsby, Teresa J., and Ken Stone (eds.)
    2011   *Bible Trouble: Queer Reading at the Boundaries of Biblical Scholarship*
            (Atlanta, GA: Society of Biblical Literature).
Klinken, Adriaan S. van, and Peter-Ben Smith
    2013   'Jesus Traditions and Masculinities in World Christianity', *Exchange:
            Journal of Missiological and Ecumenical Research* 42: 1-15.
Krondorfer, Björn
    2009   *Men and Masculinities in Christianity and Judaism: A Critical Reader*
            (London: SCM Press).
    2010   *Male Confessions: Intimate Revelations and the Religious Imagination*
            (Stanford, CA: Stanford University Press).
Macwilliam, Stuart
    2011   *Queer Theory and the Prophetic Marriage Metaphor in the Hebrew Bible*
            (London: Equinox).
Meyers, Carol
    2007   'Contesting the Notion of Patriarchy: Anthropology and the Theorizing of
            Gender in Ancient Israel', in Rooke (ed.) 2007: 84-105.
Moore, Stephen D.
    2010   'Final Reflections on Biblical Masculinity', in Creangă (ed.) 2010: 240-55.
Moore, Stephen D., and Janice Capel Anderson (eds.)
    2003   *New Testament Masculinities* (SemeiaSt, 45; Atlanta: Society of Biblical
            Literature).
Olyan, Saul M.
    1994   '"And with a Male You Shall Not Lie the Lying Down of a Woman": On
            the Meaning of Leviticus 18:22 and 20:3', *JHistSex* 5.2: 179-206.
Rooke, Deborah W.
    2007   'The Bare Facts: Gender and Nakedness in Leviticus 18', in Rooke (ed.)
            2007: 20-38.
    2009   'Breeches of the Covenant: Gender, Garments and Priesthood', in Deborah
            W. Rooke (ed.), *Embroidered Garments: Priests and Gender in Biblical
            Israel* (HBM, 25; Sheffield: Sheffield Phoenix Press): 19-37.
Rooke, Deborah W. (ed.)
    2007   *A Question of Sex? Gender and Difference in the Hebrew Bible and
            Beyond* (HBM, 14; Sheffield: Sheffield Phoenix Press).
Stan, Lavinia, and Lucian Turcescu
    2011   *Church, State, and Democracy in Expanding Europe* (Oxford: Oxford
            University Press)

Stökl, Jonathan, and Corrine L. Carvalho (eds.)
    2013   *Prophets Male and Female: Gender and Prophecy in the Hebrew Bible, the Eastern Mediterranean, and the Ancient Near East* (Atlanta, GA: Society of Biblical Literature).
Zsolnay, Ilona (ed.)
 forthcoming *Being a Man in Antiquity: Negotiating, Legitimating, and Maintaining Ancient Constructs of Masculinity* (London: Routledge).

Part II

HEBREW BIBLE

'SHOW ME YOUR GLORY':
THE KABOD OF YAHWEH AS PHALLIC MANIFESTATION?

Alan Hooker

Introduction

In Exodus 33, Moses goes to see Yahweh in the Tent of Meeting and asks him to reveal his divine glory (v. 18). Yahweh does not refuse, but we are told that Moses would not be permitted to see his face, only the godly backparts (v. 23). The text does not describe what this glory (כבוד) is, but many scholars understand it to be an aura of light around the deity. Frank Moore Cross, for example, describes כבוד as the 'refulgent aureole' which encompasses the god; he also writes that it is the 'hypostatization of the abstract "majesty" of the deity' (1973: 165-66; see also Eichrodt 1967: 31).

Words like נגה ('brightness') and אור ('shine') in conjunction with כבוד ('abundance, honour, glory') (Ezek. 10.4; 43.2; Isa. 60.1, 3) naturally suggest the connection between כבוד and light, while Taylor links it with Yahwistic solar imagery (1993: 158). In my opinion, the term 'hypostasis' should be used carefully due to its association with Trinitarian thought. Using the term implicitly connotes divine immateriality and transcendence, neither of which, I would argue, are explicitly found in the Hebrew Bible. Nevertheless, כבוד has been read as a nonmaterial and transcendent aspect of the deity, especially in relation to Ezekiel's portrayal of it. Eichrodt calls Yahweh's glory 'transcendent' and the means by which Yahweh 'declares his gracious presence' (1967: 32), and Daniel I. Block writes that 'the glory of Yahweh defies human description, verbally or visually' (1997: 106).

While I understand Ezekiel's כבוד theology as a response to the ambiguity surrounding the Temple's future at that time, I do not view this as transcendentalism: Ezekiel does not locate Yahweh in the heavenly realm (1.26-28) apart from the Temple to show his transcendence, but rather to ensure he/his cultic icon is not captured with the Temple's destruction. The notion that Yahweh is 'transcendent' suggests a philosophical privileging of mind over matter as well as their disjunction, a common motif in Western philosophy (Gersdorf 2000: 178) which does not have any particular resonance with ancient West Asian perceptions of materiality and personhood.

The inherited assumption with which we work as biblical scholars is that incorporeal mind is more befitting deity than 'base' corporeality—perhaps an idea which has come down to us from the sharp dichotomies we see between flesh and spirit in Christian traditions.

However, Yahweh's response to Moses' desire in Exod. 33.18 implies a correspondence between כבוד and the divine body. This identification has already been put forward and is a fairly standard interpretation of the כבוד theophanies. As M. David Litwa writes, '[w]hether or not one agrees that Yahweh *is* his Glory or is somehow co-extensive with it, it is nonetheless evident that Glory can represent God's physical manifestation' (2012: 125, emphasis his).

Ben Sommer too demonstrates by recourse to parallelism in Isa. 17.4 and Ps. 16.9 that כבוד 'in biblical Hebrew can simply mean "body, substance"' (2009: 60). From our starting text, Exodus 33, he also gathers that 'the *kabod* must refer to God's body… It moves, and it has a face (פנים), a hand (כף), and a back (אחור)' (2009: 60). כבוד *is* body, but Sommer maintains it is also more than body; abstractly, it is used to talk of God's 'righteousness, salvation, loyalty, or truth' (2009: 61). The strength of Sommer's position is that he can acknowledge both the anthropomorphic status of כבוד as well as other ways in which it is used. We must forgo the idea that the metaphorical is synonymous with the nonliteral or immaterial, since our embodied, material existence is the locus of metaphorical language.[1]

In the biblical corpus, sightings of the divine body are not unusual: in Gen. 32.30 Jacob meets with God and wrestles with him, Gideon sees (the angel of) Yahweh face-to-face (Judg. 6.22), Manoah and his wife see a divine figure (Judg. 13), and Isaiah also looks directly at the deity (Isa. 6.5). Additionally, Deut. 5.24 contains an account in which the people see the 'glory and greatness' of Yahweh when he reveals the Ten Commandments. I must add a caveat to this discussion: although sightings of the divine body are not unusual in the sense that they appear somewhat frequently in the text, the surprise accompanying these theophanies implies that something about them *was* considered out of the ordinary.

Jacob, Gideon, Manoah, and Isaiah all make statements about the deadly nature of Yahweh's presence/gaze. When they face God, Jacob speaks of the preservation of his life (Gen. 32.30), while Manoah worries that he and his wife will die (Judg. 13.22); in the case of Gideon, Yahweh himself reassures him that he will live despite seeing (the angel of) Yahweh (Judg. 6.23). As we can see, God's body is *not* the problem, that he has one is taken *prima*

---

1.   See further Jacob L. Mey (2006), who argues that metaphors do not reside solely in the mind, but are 'primarily pragmatic activities' (45) and 'originate in human *activity*' (58).

facie; the issue concerns the nature of this body. God's materiality can kill, and it is for that reason that we *need* to acknowledge God has a body, else these passages lose their force.

Like the biblical authors I will take Yahweh's body as given,[2] so that my question for the present study is not about the divine body per se but about the relationship of כבוד to it. Using the texts of Exodus and Ezekiel (for כבוד is a prominent feature of both), I intend to demonstrate that כבוד highlights Yahweh's masculinity, and that through כבוד theology Yahweh is constructed as the Most Masculine in accordance with those attributes of masculinity outlined by Clines and Hoffner, namely, military prowess, the production of offspring, and physical beauty (Clines 1995: 212-43; Hoffner 1966).

The Phallus and כבוד

In psychoanalysis, the phallus has had many incarnations: Freud took its genealogy back to the meaning it held for the ancients: that of sovereign power (Macey 2010: 529); although we do not see Freud evolve the concept of 'phallus' much beyond this (Evans 1996: 140). Lacan, who draws on and develops Freud's work, claims the phallus is the 'privileged signifier of the symbolic order', the realm of language (Moore 2007: 95); in other words, it is 'the signifier of signification, the very signifier that enables meaning to arise in the first place' (Moi 2004: 108).

Since the symbolic order is already operational before we enter it as children, we must accept the Name-of-the-Father which 'sustains the struc-ture of desire with the structure of the law' (Lacan 1994: 34) in order to enter into communication with others. This Law, says Althusser, 'has been lying in wait for each infant since before his [*sic*] birth, and seizes him before his first cry, assigning to him his place and role' (Silverman 1992: 33). In my understanding, the Name-of-the-Father inscribes identity and sets the boundaries in which the subject may act for it simultaneously names the child and 'call[s] a halt to uncertainty about the identity of the father' (Gallop 1982: 39). However, it must be borne in mind that the Name-of-the-Father is not to be taken as a biological father but is rather 'the patronym, patriarchal law, patrilineal identity, language as our inscription into patriar-chy' (1982: 47).

This very small and inadequate summary of the phallus in psychoanalysis draws on those points which I myself will use to read כבוד. While Lacan emphatically separated the phallus from the biological organ that is the

---

2. In the words of Lacan, 'if Javeh forbids the Jews to make idols, it is because they give pleasure to the other gods. In a certain register it is not God who is not anthropo-morphic, it is man who is begged not to be so' (1994: 113).

penis,[3] Freud did not (although Evans [1996: 140] maintains the distinction is implicit in his work), and I too will remain ambivalent about the division of the terms.

I will argue כבוד indexes Freud's sovereign power, and that it can uphold or expose the masculinity of those who appear in the narrative since it stands for an ideal masculinity. As (a manifestation of) Yahweh's body, Glory shares in the normative masculinity embodied by Yahweh and the ways in which Yahweh functions as the man *par excellence*. In this way, the Glory may be compared to the Lacanian phallus and Name-of-the-Father whose power and presence construct meaning, since it is by כבוד that presentations of masculinity are judged. If כבוד displays those attributes of masculinity outlined by Clines and Hoffner mentioned above then there is a good case for asserting its phallic nature since normative masculinity in the Hebrew Bible is often centred on how one uses one's penis—as in the case of siring a child. One may also see how military prowess links to the penis in ancient West Asia where, as we see in Assyrian iconography, a battering ram extends from the king's penis (Haddox 2010: 4-5); and furthermore, we should also not forget the discourses which concern rape in the context of war (Washington 1998: 203).

It is important to point out from the start that I do not suggest that penis = phallus = masculinity, but that these terms in relation to normative masculinity are at least correlated, however hazily or unstable that link might be. The instability of this equation permits masculinities to arise which do not conform to and which challenge the status quo of the hegemonic masculinity at work in any given moment.

Melammu and Pulḫu

כבוד has as its ancestors the Assyrian *melammu* and *pul(u)ḫ(t)u*. The *melammu* is the effulgence that surrounds Assyrian kings (Blenkinsopp 2003: 81), and there is an overlap between Akkadian terminology for divine radiance and Hebrew הוד and כבוד (Weinfeld 1995: 29-31). As well as a divine light inherent in deity, the *melammu* may be bestowed and taken away, as in *Enuma Elish* II.24. In this text, Tiamat clothes the *ušum-gallu* monsters with *melammu* so as to render them divine. In contrast, another episode has Mummu (Apsu's vizier) divested of his *melammu* and royal jewellery by Ea (Oppenheim 1943: 31).

---

3. Although note Evans discussion of the 'real phallus' (1996: 141) in which he states there are a few instances in which Lacan appears not to uphold the distinction between phallus and penis.

The *melammu* in these instances is a signifier of status and divine power. In royal ideology this power centres around warfare: for example, the Cylinder Inscription of Tiglath-pileser I contains the line: 'the brilliance (*melam*) of my valour overwhelmed them and they…embraced my feet' (III.2). The 'brilliance' to be feared by the king's enemies is frequently referred to as 'my royal terror' or 'my lordly terror', and in the Cylinder Inscription it has the form 'the glory of my heroism, military prowess' (ME-LAM QARDUTIJA).

Kingship and war become mediators of the divine *melammu* which therefore exemplifies normative masculinity. Not only does *melammu* appear in relation to persons, but it is also ascribed to ^{GIŠ}TUKUL, a weapon of war (Akk. *kakku*), in the *Angim dimma* epic. Moreover, the walls of the royal residence were covered by the *melammu* of kingship. The *melammu* which identifies gods and divinizes royalty also functions as a supernatural aide in warfare. Its purpose in this role is to force enemies to recognize the sovereignty of the king. This total submission is conveyed through a bodily metaphor: to embrace the feet is to do obeisance to the signifier of one's oppression. Not only that, but it is a direct acknowledgment of the divine (the king's) body.

The *pul(u)h(t)u* is often found with the *melammu* and is, like the *melammu*, another form of divine radiance. These radiances are closely connected with the god's body: the *melammu* is borne upon the head as a diadem, while *pulhu* is worn on the body as a garment (Haran 1984: 172 n. 19). The *pulhu* is fearsome and terrifying as well: 'I accomplished for all time the victory of Aššur, my lord, over Urartu and left there the fear (*puluhtu*) of him' (*CAD*, XII, 507). Divine creatures such as the *bašmu* dragon and the *lahmu* sea monsters also embody *pulhu* in various ways: the former has *pulhu* come forth from his mouth, while the latter are *malû pu-luh-ta*, 'full of terror' (as are the eleven creatures Tiamat forms in *Enuma Elish* IV.115 to battle Marduk). Rhetorically, the language of *puluhtu* supports kingship and the king's ownership of land: 'Marduk caused the *puluhtu* of my reign to cover the mountains of the (four) quarters like a heavy fog' (*CAD*, XII, 507). Of note here is the extent of the *puluhtu* which reaches the dwelling place of the gods: this is divine acknowledgment of the king's right to rule.

The motif of light-shrouded deities also finds prominence in Egypt which possessed winged sun disk iconography, and Michael B. Hundley associates the disk with the *pulhu* and *melammu* (2011: 42). Othmar Keel and Christoph Uehlinger write that at the end of Iron Age IIC, Yahweh's כבוד manifested to Ezekiel in this form, that is, like the Assyrian sun god, whose upper body rises from a winged sun disk (1992: 402). The disk denotes the 'name of the King' and is an 'image of the king himself' (Gardiner 1944:

51) and, like *pulḫu*, it manifests territorially, designating what comes under the auspices of the king (Sugi 2003: 515).

Thus the radiance of the deities principally denotes their power which manifests as (1) divinity, (2) military prowess, and (3) land subjugation. This visualized power is not abstract, but deeply embodied; these attributes inhere in the divine body and *melammu* and *pulḫu* signify material power: the power of the god-king's body, the strength he possesses as warrior, and the land he is able to subjugate by his might.

כבוד *in Exodus*

כבוד punctuates the narrative of Exodus in five places. In the first instance, ch. 16, the Israelites are situated in the wilderness between Elim and Sinai (where God will later reveal himself), while in the Glory's last appearance, ch. 40, it fills (מלא) the tabernacle. These Glory-narratives take us from a wandering group who are not assured of God's presence with them to a scenario in which God positively dwells among them. Through these narratives the reader comes closer and closer to the Promised Land, and כבוד functions as a sign of Yahweh's presence and his promise to conquer those who occupy the land he will give to his people.

Exodus 16 begins with the people, who complain to Moses and Aaron that they would rather have died as slaves in Egypt with their fill of bread, than be free with Moses and Aaron in the wilderness starving (v. 3). After he hears the people's complaint, Yahweh tells them that in the morning they will see the Glory (vv. 7, 10). This will reveal to the Israelites that it was Yahweh, and not Moses and Aaron, who brought them into the wilderness (vv. 6-8).

The Glory therefore operates to remind the people that it was Yahweh's actions which led Israel out of Egypt. In Exodus 7, this is accomplished by Yahweh's hand, his *yad* (יד) (see also, Exod. 15.6). As well as meaning 'hand', *yad* also designates the penis (Ackroyd 1986: 402), and is used to denote power/control (1986: 418-23). In Exod. 6.6 it is Yahweh's arm (זרוע), as well as his יד (v. 1), which redeems Israel and the similarity between זרוע and זרע ('seed') in this context should not go unnoticed.

In Exodus 16, when morning arrives, the Israelites find manna on the surface of the wilderness (Exod. 16.13). By heavenly intervention (v. 4), the land has provided, and I think it is safe to say that here is a prefiguration of the fertile land the Israelites will later occupy. The Israelites eat the manna *until* they come to the border of Canaan (Exod. 16.35) and in this way the manna serves as a reminder of the land to flow with milk and honey; the manna even tastes like honey (v. 31).

The next stage of the Glory-manifestation in ch. 24 is set at Sinai where the כבוד appears to Moses (v. 15). In the narrative preceding ch. 24, there is a promise on Yahweh's part that not only will the Israelites conquer Canaan, but that the land will be abundantly fertile (Exod. 23.26). When, in 23.20, Yahweh speaks to his people and tells them he will bring them to a prepared land (הכנתי), it evokes ch. 16 once more for here God commands the people to gather the manna and on the sixth day prepare it (והביינו). The sixth day in particular is marked by abundant plenitude, for the Israelites will gather twice as much as they have on any other day (Exod. 16.5).

Seen in this light, the כבוד theophany of ch. 24 may be considered a continuation of the Glory-motif in ch. 16 as well as the preceding land-narrative in Exodus 23. In Exodus 16, Yahweh's Glory comes to confirm the Israelites' future land possession in conjunction with Yahweh's fertile provisionary acts. It is Yahweh who can make bread appear in the chaotic מדבר ('wilderness'), a place associated with the netherworld and wastelands in ancient West Asian sources (Talmon 1997: 115). As Laura Feldt writes in her analysis of the מדבר-narratives in Exodus and Numbers, Yahweh 'is the donor of agricultural, "natural" fertility' (2012: 89-90). That Yahweh is able to feed his people in the sterile wilderness is, I would argue, indicative of his power over fertility, especially in a broader ancient West Asian context which links agricultural fertility with the powers possessed by fertility deities.

Yahweh's Glory appearance and provision of food for his people is in response to the community's cry in Exod. 16.3, 'you have brought us out into this wilderness to kill this whole assembly with hunger'. Yahweh acts in order to assert his masculinity, to prove that he can provide for his people, and essentially assert his power over Egypt and its produce (compare Exod. 12.12, in which Yahweh says he will execute judgments on all the gods of Egypt).

Thus I would argue we are able to read the continuation in the Glory-narrative from Exodus 16 to Exodus 24 mindful of the narrative's apogee, that is, the dwelling of Yahweh among his people (see Exod. 25.8; 40.34-38). The manna of Exodus 16 embodies the land which the Israelites have been promised, since they are said to eat it *until* they come into the land of Canaan (v. 35). This appearance of manna, a sign of Yahweh's Glory (16.6), discloses the fertility and abundance of the Glory itself and also shows the Israelites that Yahweh is concerned with their care.

Chapter 24 carries on these themes: before the revelation of Glory on Sinai, Yahweh commands Moses to begin the construction of the Ark so that God might 'dwell among them' (25.8). Before the Sinaitic theophany (24.15-18), Moses sets up twelve pillars by the foot of the mountain to represent the twelve tribes of Israel (24.4). Moses' actions recall Joshua's, who commands his men to take twelve stones from the Jordan river (Josh.

4.1-9). As with Exodus 24, Joshua 4 is preceded by Yahweh's promise to drive out the Israelites' enemies. The twelve pillars serve to remind the people of the group's identity as well as their hope for land.

Moses ascends Mt Sinai (Exod. 24.15) and does not return from the mountain until ch. 32. In the intervening time, the Israelites grow weary and beg Aaron to make gods who will go before them (32.1). He constructs a molten calf whom they take to be Yahweh (v. 5), and while this does rouse Yahweh's anger, it is Moses' appeal to Abraham, Isaac, and Jacob which changes God's mind. Moses petitions Yahweh to remember (זכר) his ancestors and what he spoke to them, that they would have descendants as numerous as the stars who would receive a land as an eternal inheritance (v. 12).

כבוד next appears in Exodus 28 when God commands Moses to make 'holy garments' for Aaron and his sons (vv. 2-5). These garments, Yahweh says (v. 2), are 'for glory and beauty' (לכבוד ולתפארת), and while this occurrence of כבוד is not the theophanic Glory, it nevertheless sheds light on Yahweh's masculinity. The word תפארת used in Exod. 28.2 also describes, for instance, the beauty of the Temple adorned with precious jewels (2 Chron. 3.6), and it is often used of (royal) headgear (Prov. 4.9; 16.31; Isa. 28.1, 5; 62.3; Jer. 13.18; Ezek. 16.12; 23.42). In ancient West Asian royal ideologies, kingship and beauty are very much associated: Psalms 45 and 72 are prime examples of this (Gerstenberger 1988: 187; Childs 2001: 248). Moreover, two kings of Israel, Saul and David, are both described as 'handsome' before they are chosen to lead (1 Sam. 9.2; 16.12), and in David's case it is explicitly his beauty which causes Yahweh to choose him.

The beautiful garments that Aaron wears are intended to legitimate him as a minister between Yahweh and the people. If glory and beauty are attributes of deities and kings, then Aaron's vestments are designed to divinize him in some respect, to allow him to interact with the divine realm. He is permitted access to God and to bear the names of the Israelite tribes on his breastplate before Yahweh so that Yahweh will remember (זכר) them (Exod. 28.11-12). This remembrance is closely associated with another meaning of זכר, that of maleness (see Gen. 1.27). Many Semitic languages share this association: Aramaic, Syriac, Akkadian, Arabic, Soqotri, and Old Ethiopic (Murtonen 1989: 165). The link between these two concepts—memory and maleness— is not far-fetched: Murtonen argues 'both the concept of memory…and masculinity share the salient characteristic of *active nature, virility*' (1989: 165).[4] Indeed, in the worldview of the biblical authors, virility ensured

---

4. Although זכר properly denotes males, there seems to be an idea within some strands of the biblical texts that maleness and masculinity are dependent on one another, and this is arguably the hegemonic assumption. This does not mean however that there are not narratives in the Hebrew Bible which subvert, challenge, and renegotiate this association.

memory, for the propagation of one's household guaranteed that one would possess ancestors who would (in theory) call upon his name after death, thereby safeguarding this postmortal existence. Aaron will certainly be remembered by God since his glory and beauty will be the centre of the divine attention. His beauty, like that of kings, gains divine support, and his glory demarcates the masculinity which Yahweh so favours. The relationship between Yahweh and his priest(s) may be read as male–male bonding, in which Aaron's garments act as a visual stimulus for Yahweh. In response, Yahweh 'males' (זכר) the men of Israel, that is to say, he virilizes them in accordance with hegemonic expectations of masculinity: he gives divine approval to their continued existence as a virile and fertile people.

Moreover, Aaron and the priests wear undergarments to cover their naked flesh (בשׂר ערוה) from Yahweh lest 'they bring guilt on themselves and die' (Exod. 28.42). That בשׂר and ערוה appear together implies the commandment specifically has penile exposure in mind, since בשׂר connotes to the genitals (Ezek. 16.26; 23.20; Lev. 6.3; 15.2-4). Although Aaron is beautified by his garments, Yahweh must not 'know' Aaron is male—it is a fact hidden before the altar; his בשׂר pollutes. Why his 'flesh' pollutes is another matter altogether. Is Aaron's uncovered flesh a challenge to Yahweh's own masculinity? For Deborah Rooke, the priestly breeches are 'an indicator that the masculinity of the priesthood in relation to God is very different from the masculinity of power and control that characterizes the patriarchal society in which the priests live' (2009: 35). She writes that the priest's confrontation with an omnipotent male god renders the phallus redundant; to cover the phallus, the symbol of 'power and respect' (2009: 33), is to express 'appropriate obedience, humility and devotion' (2009: 34) before their (hyper)masculine deity—the priests are put into a position of 'wifely submission' (2009: 35).[5] Yahweh cannot re-member, give the power of the phallus/member to Aaron and the priests if their sexual members are already on show. He must first set them apart for himself and dress them up.

Aaron's underwear will 'cover' (כסה) his exposed penis, an act similar to the incident in Genesis 9 in which Shem and Japheth have to 'cover their father's nakedness' (ויכסו את ערות אביהם) because he gets drunk and passes out unclothed (Gen. 9.21). Ham, the third son, looks upon his father's nudity

---

5. In her 'Notes on Camp' (1966), Susan Sontag defines the essence of Camp as 'its love of the unnatural: of artifice and exaggeration', and notes that 'Camp sees everything in quotation marks'. Turning to our narrative, then, is Aaron a man or a 'man'? Does the narrative represent the 'triumph of the epicene' (another aspect of Camp Sontag identifies)? Does Aaron have legitimate gender ambiguity here—is his penis deliberately veiled, 'castrated'? These questions and the possible Campness of this text may help us understand how a male deity can be seen to love his male worshippers within the arguably heteronormative cultural settings of the biblical texts.

(Gen. 9.22) and as a result Canaan (Ham's descendant) is cursed (v. 25). Genesis 9 speaks of the danger inherent in the possible sexual gaze within a familial environment; as Eilberg-Schwartz notes, '[t]he prohibition against seeing Noah's nakedness deals with this potential disruption', that is, the disruption caused by erotic relationships between fathers and sons (1994: 93).

Read from the point of view of Genesis 9, the exposure of Aaron's genitals in Exodus 28 would threaten the bond between Yahweh (father) and himself/the priests (sons). God's commandment in Exodus 28 for Aaron to cover his nether-regions might be intended to sustain the 'orthodox' construction of a good subject/object relationship. In this way, the priestly garments which are 'for כבוד and תפארת' simultaneously draw attention to the priests' masculinity, for only particular men can wear them, and hide masculinity insofar as the priests must cover up their phalluses. In Exodus 28, then, כבוד does function as a masculine marker for Aaron, but also as a confirmation of Yahweh's desire for men as they enact a masculinity in which they are not visibly manly.

Exodus 33 is the fateful meeting between Moses and Yahweh. It opens with the command to leave Sinai and head toward the land God promised his people, the fertile land 'flowing with milk and honey' (v. 3). The כבוד theophany of Yahweh on Mt Sinai occurs in response to Moses' petition that Yahweh accompany the people of Israel with his presence (פני) so that his people will be distinct from all others (v. 16). After Yahweh promises to go with them, Moses asks to see the כבוד. Yahweh does not explicitly deny Moses this request; instead Yahweh causes all his goodness (כל־טובי) to pass before him, but the divine face/presence is not to be seen since it is fatal (v. 20). Stephen Moore argues that it is not his face (the usual translation of פנים) that God tries to hide, since Yahweh reveals it elsewhere, even to Moses (Exod. 33.11), but rather his female physique (2010: 212).[6] While I agree that Yahweh attempts to hide his physical form here, I believe it is his male features he attempts to conceal, not his/any female ones. I take טוב to be a reference to God's beauty (cf. its use in Gen. 6.2; 24.16; Exod. 2.2; Est. 1.11) and as such Exodus 33 is a reversal of Exodus 28. Whereas Aaron

---

6. Moore's understanding of the androgynous Yahweh comes principally from Exod. 33 and the possible connection between the epithet אל שדי ('El Shaddai') and the word for 'breasts', שדים (2010: 212 n. 10). While Gen. 49.25 with its use of both terms lends strong support for the connection between El Shaddai and breasts, I find it more plausible that the term derives from Akkadian *šadû*, 'mountain' (see Day 2002: 32-34; Hamilton 1990: 462-63; Cross 1973: 52-56). Although these scholars do note the semantic link between 'mountain' and 'breast' (and visually, it is not difficult to see how they could be seen as the earth's breasts), in Exod. 33 the god Shaddai is not present, only Yahweh is (though note the redactional identification between the two in Exod. 6.3).

had to cover his penis before Yahweh, here Yahweh hides his own from Moses; in Exodus 28, Yahweh had to re-member Aaron, and in Exodus 33, Moses and his people must re-member Yahweh. To answer Eilberg-Schwartz's question ('how can male worshippers love a male God?'), Moses can love his male God because he is enticed by God's beauty without having to see that he is male—in this way the heterosexual ideal is maintained.

כבוד in Ezekiel

The first mention of כבוד in Ezekiel is certainly the most interesting:

> And seated above the likeness of a throne was something that seemed like a human form (כמראה אדם). Upward from what appeared like the loins (מתניו) I saw something like gleaming amber, something that looked like fire enclosed all around; and downward from what looked like the loins I saw something that looked like fire, and there was splendour all around. Like the bow (קשת) in a cloud on a rainy day, such was the appearance of the splendour all around. This was the appearance of the likeness of the glory (כבוד) of the LORD. (Ezek. 1.26-28, NRSV)[7]

Here is a reference to God's essentially human form. What is immediately noticeable is the focus on the loins (מתנים) of the deity; they form a reference point in Ezekiel's description of Yahweh. Roland Boer says מתנים 'refer to a man's marbles' (2011: 45), and if that is the case for Ezekiel 1, then God's own testicles become the foundation, the origin, of the splendour (נגה) which surrounds the divine person.[8] The divine gonads are accompanied by a bow in the clouds, which, as Sandra Jacobs demonstrates by recourse to ancient West Asian sources (2010: 146-49), is a symbol of masculinity, progeny, and sexual ability.

In Ezekiel 3, Yahweh's Glory and spirit raise Ezekiel and bring him to the exiles at Tel-abib (v. 15). It is here that God makes Ezekiel a sentinel for the house of Israel (v. 16), and gives him charge to warn the Israelites not to commit sin. Failure to do this could result in transgression, in which case the

---

7. Ezekiel constantly refers back to this monumental revelation of Yahweh's Glory at Chebar (3.23; 10.15, 20, 22; 43.3), and it is apparent that it forms the lens through which Ezekiel views the historical situation he is in. The Temple is unstable and Jerusalem is under threat of attack. Part of Ezekiel's rhetoric attempts to save Yahweh by distancing him from the then-current Temple. If he exists above it on the cherub throne then he is not bound to dwell fixedly in the Temple in his iconic manifestation. In fact, this Glory in Ezekiel in human form is evidently a relocation of Yahweh's cultic statue (Niehr 1997: 92-93), thus keeping it out of reach and unavailable for capture by foreign enemies.

8. While the word מתנים anatomically suggests 'hips and lower back', it also connotes 'strength and virility' and thence a man's 'reproductive parts' (Low 2011: 9). In choosing the term 'testicles', I want to bring attention to the connotations מתנים has, which are not present in today's English 'waist'.

righteous deeds of those people would be forgotten, not remembered (זכר).
The sins for which God chides the people of Jerusalem are outlined in ch. 8:
the image of 'jealousy' (סמל הקנאה) in the Temple, portrayals of 'creeping
things and loathsome animals' on the walls of the Temple, accusations that
'Yahweh has forsaken the land', mourning for Tammuz, and sun worship
(vv. 3-18). These features of Jerusalemite worship essentially rob Yahweh of
his identity as a fertile, life-giving god.

Susan Ackerman identifies Tammuz as the symbol of 'prosperity and
yield' in the season of harvest (1999: 26), and Meindert Dijkstra writes that
'[t]he bewailing of Tammuz is associated with the return of the rains and the
coming of a new agricultural season' (2001: 176). Tammuz's consort Ishtar
also acts within the sphere of human and animal fertility, for when she
descends to the underworld, human and animal procreation cease (Isaac
2006: 243). The bewailing of Tammuz takes place at the entrance of the
Temple's north gate (Ezek. 8.14); these cultic activities are a threat to Yahweh, who, at least according to Ezekiel, has no consort. In fact, the 'image
of jealousy' in Ezek. 8.3 is evocative of the *qnyt 'ilm* ('Creatress of the
Gods') title used of Asherah (see Lutzky 1996: 121-25). If these Jerusalem-
ites are worshipping the Creatress instead of the Creator, it undermines the
maleness of Yahweh, especially since the Creator has no consort; moreover,
the accusation that 'Yahweh does not see us, Yahweh has forsaken the land'
(8.12; 9.9) is a blow to a deity who claims control over it (11.15, 17). In
Ezekiel 36, the reader truly sees Yahweh's fertile power: fruit shall be
yielded to Israel when the exiles return home, the land will be sown, and
people and animals will multiply in abundance (vv. 8-13).

However, before the return to the land occurs the slaughter of the
'idolaters' (NRSV) must take place (Ezek. 9). 'Draw near', Yahweh says,
'you executioners of the city, each with his destroying weapon in his hand'
(v. 1). The slaughter is a means by which Yahweh reasserts his masculinity
to those who doubt it, for warriorhood is, as discussed above, a key component of ancient West Asian portrayals of masculinity. The declaration of
the slaughter is concomitant with the כבוד rising from its seat and coming to
rest on the threshold of the Temple (v. 3).

The Glory of Yahweh seemingly confuses the hegemonic understanding
of masculinity. The Glory commands the slaughter of Israelite idolaters, but
it comes at a price—the death of those from a nation promised fertility.
Ezekiel, however, envisions this slaughter in terms of שארית, 'remnant', as
does Jeremiah (Jer. 6.9; 23.3). While on the surface the slaughter may
appear detrimental to the nation, couching it in language of שארית allows the
prophet to evoke images of pruning which makes trees more fertile. Yahweh
is able to kill his people as a sign of masculinity without issue; indeed this is
a perfect way to combine discourses of masculinity without exposing the
tensions in them. Perhaps כבוד is the tension resolver.

In the description of Israel's restoration in Ezekiel 11 to be enacted by the Glory, Yahweh promises his people that he will remove their hearts of stone (לב האבן) and give them a heart of flesh (לב בשׂר) (vv. 19-22). In Ezekiel אבן is used to talk about the idolatry of the Israelites who 'served wood and stone (אבן)' (20.32; cf. Deut. 4.28; 2 Kgs 19.18). The hardness of Israelite hearts causes them to worship falsely; however, the new heart which Yahweh gives them is fleshy (בשׂר), giving them the capacity to hear and obey Yahweh's commandments. The word בשׂר is part of a semantic field which includes 'penis' (see Ezek. 16.26; 23.20; Lev. 6.3; 15.2-4), and I think the idea of a 'penised heart' (!) is useful in truly comprehending the rich and fertile organ which Ezekiel sees as the replacement of the sterile stone once there.

In another instance of this promise, Ezek. 36.26, the prophet writes that this בשׂר-heart will not only allow the people to follow Yahweh's statutes (as in Ezek. 11.19), but it will also bring them to the land of their ancestors (36.28), which Yahweh will make plentiful with grain and fruit (vv. 29-30, 35). This image of fertility correlates in my opinion with the heart of בשׂר, and also with the כבוד which will fill the Temple (43.1-7), one filled with images of fertile palm trees (41.17-20, 25-26).

Conclusion

In this study I have hopefully demonstrated that כבוד can be read as underscoring masculinity where it appears, and although I have only had space to touch upon two sets of texts, I hope their treatment here is able to uncover matrixes of masculinity in other Glory texts. In terms of Clines's and Hoffner's suggested criteria for masculinity in ancient West Asia, כבוד is foremost a manifestation of the divine for the purpose of conquering peoples and seizing land, which accords well with the presentation of *melammu* and *pulḫu* in other ancient sources. Psalms 24 and 29, as other telling examples, both use Glory imagery (24.7-10; 29.1-2) and are also strongly militaristic. The מלך הכבוד, the glorious king, is 'strong and mighty', 'mighty in battle', and has the epithet 'Yahweh of Armies' (יהוה צבאות). The deity of Psalm 29 breaks the strong cedars of Lebanon, shakes the wilderness, and thunders over the mighty waters with his majestic and powerful voice.

As regards offspring, though Yahweh does not beget in the texts discussed, there runs through the narratives a strong thread of fertility. In Exodus, כבוד presages the fertile land of inheritance and in Ezekiel signals the מתנים, the testicles, of Yahweh which envelop him in the fire and light they seem to produce. I would compare this with another Glory-text, Isaiah 6, and Isaiah's vision of the enthroned Yahweh, whose genitalia fill the Temple complex (reading שׁול in v. 1 as 'pudenda', following Eslinger 1995:

145-73). In Isaiah 6, the seraphs who attend on Yahweh, known here and elsewhere as 'Yahweh of Armies' (cf. Ps. 29.1-2), attest that the whole land is full of his Glory. In this one Isaian scenario there is the intersection of כבוד, military language, and extreme fertility (vv. 12-13).

Male beauty is also a bedfellow with כבוד, as we saw in Exodus 28. The beautification of Aaron with Glory appears to rouse the desire of Yahweh and equally Yahweh's Glory is intended to stir the yearning of his followers. In both cases, one party must hide the marker of his maleness: Aaron covers his with cloth, while Moses' eyes are covered by Yahweh's hand lest he see what he ought not to (Exod. 33.22). In this way, one party is 'feminized' and the heterosexual matrix of desire is satisfied. Yahweh's Glory is the consort of his people: the Glory makes the Israelites and their land fertile, protects them as a warrior, and creates space for remembrance (זכר), 'male-ing', virilizing, in order to help the Israelites propagate their seed and live now and forever.

At times the כבוד also challenges conventional portrayals of masculinity: principally in relation to offspring. Ezekiel's Yahweh has no goddess consort, and is therefore unable to produce divine children; the Glory, as a phallic manifestation of deity, renegotiates the concept of sonship: in Ezekiel, the כבוד encourages the growth of the Israelites and their land, and in light of Ezek. 23.4 ('they [Samaria/Israel and Jerusalem/Judah] were mine, and they bore sons and daughters'), we may say that if the lands function here as God's consorts (Eilberg-Schwartz 1994: 112), then the Israelites' growth is analogous to child birth.[9]

Finally, כבוד is a site of desire and functions in relation to זכר (male/ penis): in the rituals of the priests, the people are re-membered, virilized, by Yahweh because Aaron is made beautiful before Yahweh, and (like David's or Saul's handsomeness) it arouses the deity to act and preserve his people. Terrance MacMullen writes that the phallus 'marks sites of power, authority, and, perhaps most importantly, desire' (1992: 7); this being so, the Glory, the כבוד יהוה, *is* phallic: he is powerful and authoritative in battle, and Yahweh's people desire him and he them because of his Glory.

---

9. Howard Eilberg-Schwartz notes there is an important distinction between 'the idea of Zeus having sex with Hera' and 'God cohabiting with Israel' since 'Zeus and Hera are imagined in human form, and since their coupling does not stand primarily for a conceptual idea' (1994: 112). While the difference between these two images is mainly, in my opinion, the way in which כבוד challenges notions of conventional masculinity, since the intercourse between Yahweh and the lands in Ezek. 23 is seemingly metaphorical, since a goddess consort does not birth the Israelites, we must always question *why* the metaphor works. In this case, the metaphor works because in an ancient West Asian milieu the gods are seen to be sexual beings.

Bibliography

Ackerman, S.
> 1999   '"And The Women Knead Dough": The Worship of the Queen of Heaven in Sixth-Century Judah', in Alice Bach (ed.), *Women in the Hebrew Bible: A Reader* (New York: Routledge): 21-32.

Ackroyd, P.R.
> 1986   'יד', in *TDOT*, V: 397-426.

Blenkinsopp, J.
> 2003   *Isaiah 56–66* (AB, 19; New York: Doubleday).

Block, D.I.
> 1997   *The Book of Ezekiel: Chapters 1–24* (NICOT; Grand Rapids: Eerdmans).

Boer, R.
> 2011   'The Patriarch's Nuts: Concerning the Testicular Logic of Biblical Hebrew', *Journal of Men, Masculinities and Spirituality* 5: 41-52.

Childs, B.S.
> 2001   *Isaiah* (OTL; Louisville, KY: Westminster/John Knox Press).

Clines, D.J.A.
> 1995   *Interested Parties: The Ideology of Writers and Readers of the Hebrew Bible* (JSOTSup, 205; Sheffield: Sheffield Academic Press).

Creangă, O. (ed.)
> 2010   *Men and Masculinity in the Hebrew Bible and Beyond* (The Bible in the Modern World, 33; Sheffield: Sheffield Phoenix Press).

Cross, F.M.
> 1973   *Canaanite Myth and Hebrew Epic: Essays in the History of the Religion of Israel* (Cambridge, MA: Harvard University Press).

Day, J.
> 2002   *Yahweh and the Gods and Goddesses of Canaan* (JSOTSup, 265; London: Sheffield Academic Press).

Dijkstra, M.
> 2001   'Women and Religion in the Old Testament', in B. Becking and M. Dijkstra (eds.), *Only One God? Monotheism in Ancient Israel and the Veneration of the Goddess Asherah* (The Biblical Seminar, 77; London: Sheffield Academic Press): 164-88.

Eichrodt, W.
> 1967   *Theology of the Old Testament* (OTL; 2 vols.; Philadelphia: Westminster Press).

Eilberg-Schwartz, H.
> 1994   *God's Phallus: And Other Problems for Men and Monotheism* (Boston: Beacon Press).

Eslinger, L.
> 1995   'The Infinite in a Finite Organical Perception', *VT* 45: 145-73.

Evans, D.
> 1996   *An Introductory Dictionary of Lacanian Psychoanalysis* (London: Routledge).

Feldt, L.
    2012   'Wilderness and Hebrew Bible Religion: Fertility, Apostasy and Religious Transformation in the Pentateuch', in L. Feldt (ed.), *Wilderness in Mythology and Religion: Approaching Religious Spatialities, Cosmologies, and Ideas of Wild Nature* (Berlin: W. de Gruyter): 55-94.

Gallop, J.
    1982   *The Daughter's Seduction: Feminism and Psychoanalysis* (Ithaca, NY: Cornell University Press).

Gardiner, A.H.
    1944   'Horus: The Beḥdetite', *Journal of Egyptian Archaeology* 30: 23-60.

Gersdorf, C.
    2000   'Ecocritical Uses of the Erotic', in G. Carr (ed.), *New Essays in Ecofeminist Literary Criticism* (Cranbury, NJ: Associated University Presses): 175-91.

Gerstenberger, E.S.
    1988   *Psalms: Part I, with an Introduction to Cultic Poetry* (FOTL, 14; Grand Rapids: Eerdmans).

Haddox, S.E.
    2010   'Favoured Sons and Subordinate Masculinities', in Creangă 2010: 2-19.

Hamilton, V.P.
    1990   *Genesis: Chapters 1–17* (NICOT; Grand Rapids: Eerdmans).

Haran, M.
    1984   'The Shining of Moses' Face: A Case Study in Biblical and Ancient Near Eastern Iconography', in W.B. Barrick and J.R. Spencer (eds.), *In the Shelter of Elyon: Essays on Ancient Palestinian Life and Literature in Honour of G.W. Ahlström* (JSOTSup, 31; Sheffield: JSOT Press): 159-73.

Hoffner, H.A.
    1966   'Symbols for Masculinity and Femininity: Their Use in Ancient Near Eastern Sympathetic Magic Ritual', *JBL* 85: 326-34.

Hundley, M.B.
    2011   *Keeping Heaven on Earth* (Tübingen: Mohr Siebeck).

Isaac, J.R.
    2006   'Here Comes This Dreamer', in J.R. Wood, J.E. Harvey and M. Leuchter (eds.), *From Babel to Babylon: Essays on Biblical History and Literature in Honour of Brian Peckham* (LHBOTS, 455; New York: T. & T. Clark): 237-52.

Jacobs, S.
    2010   'Divine Virility in Priestly Representation', in Creangă 2010: 146-70.

Keel, O., and C. Uehlinger
    1992   *Gods, Goddesses, and Images of God in Ancient Israel* (Minneapolis: Fortress Press).

Lacan, J.
    1994   *The Four Fundamental Concepts of Psychoanalysis* (London: Penguin Books [first published 1973]).

Litwa, M.D.
    2012   *We Are Being Transformed: Deification in Paul's Soteriology* (Berlin: W. de Gruyter).

Low, K.
  2011   'Implications Surrounding Girding the Loins in Light of Gender, Body,
             and Power', *JSOT* 36: 3-30.
Lutzky, H.C.
  1996   'On the "Image of Jealousy" (Ezekiel VIII 3, 5)', *VT* 46: 121-25.
Macey, D.
  2010   'Phallus', in M. Payne and J.R. Barbera (eds.), *A Dictionary of Cultural
             and Critical Theory* (Malden, MA: Wiley-Blackwell): 529.
MacMullen, T.
  1992   'What Is Male Embodiment?', in N. Tuana (ed.), *Revealing Male Bodies*
             (Bloomington: Indiana University Press): 1-16.
Mey, J.L.
  2006   'Metaphors and Activity', *DELTA* 22: 45-65.
Moi, T.
  2004   'From Femininity to Finitude: Freud, Lacan, and Feminism, Again', in
             Iréne Matthis (ed.), *Dialogues on Sexuality, Gender, and Psychoanalysis*
             (London: H. Karnac): 93-136.
Moore, H.L.
  2007   *The Subject of Anthropology: Gender, Symbolism and Psychoanalysis*
             (Cambridge: Polity Press).
Moore, S.D.
  2010   *The Bible in Theory: Critical and Postcritical Essays* (Atlanta: Society of
             Biblical Literature).
Murtonen, A.
  1989   *Hebrew in its West Semitic Setting: A Comparative Survey of Non-
             Masoretic Hebrew Dialects and Traditions: Part One: A Comparative
             Lexicon* (Leiden: Brill).
Niehr, H.
  1997   'In Search of YHWH's Cult Statue in the First Temple', in K. van der
             Toorn (ed.), *The Image and the Book: Iconic Cults, Aniconism, and the
             Rise of Book Religion in Israel and the Ancient Near East* (Leuven:
             Uitgeverij Peeters): 73-96.
Oppenheim, A.L.
  1943   'Akkadian *pul(u)ḫ(t)u* and *melammu*', *JAOS* 63: 31-32.
Rooke, D.W.
  2009   'Breeches of the Covenant: Gender, Garments and the Priesthood', in
             D.W. Rooke (ed.), *Embroidered Garments: Priests and Gender in Biblical
             Israel* (HBM, 25; Sheffield: Sheffield Phoenix Press): 19-37.
Silverman, K.
  1992   *Male Subjectivity at the Margins* (New York: Routledge).
Sommer, B.D.
  2009   *The Bodies of God and the World of Ancient Israel* (New York: Cambridge
             University Press).
Sontag, S.
  1966   'Notes on Camp', in *Against Interpretation and Other Essays* (New York:
             Farrar, Straus & Giroux): 275-92.

Sugi, A.
    2003   'The Iconographical Representation of the Sun God in New Kingdom
                Egypt', in Z. Hawass and L. Brock (eds.), *Egyptology at the Dawn of the
                Twenty-first Century: Proceedings of the Eighth International Conference
                of Egyptologists, Cairo, 2000* (3 vols.; Cairo: American University in
                Cairo Press): II, 514-21.
Talmon, S.
    1995   'מדבר', in *TDOT*, VIII: 87-118.
Taylor, J.G.
    1993   *Yahweh and the Sun: Biblical and Archaeological Evidence for Sun
                Worship in Ancient Israel* (JSOTSup, 111; Sheffield: JSOT Press).
Washington, H.C.
    1998   '"Lest he die in the battle and another man take her": Violence and the
                Construction of Gender in the Laws of Deuteronomy 20–22', in V.H.
                Matthews, B.M. Levinson, and T. Frymer-Kensky (eds.), *Gender and Law
                in the Hebrew Bible and the Ancient Near East* (JSOTSup, 262; London:
                T. & T. Clark): 185-213.
Weinfeld, M.
    1995   'כבוד', in *TDOT*, VII: 22-38.

WHEN REAL MEN CRY:
THE SYMBOLISM OF WEEPING IN THE TORAH AND THE DEUTERONOMISTIC HISTORY

Milena Kirova

Research on biblical masculinity still has no specific theoretical and methodological foundation of its own. As such, to recourse for help to the older and better developed field of Masculinity Studies seems the easier—and 'natural'—way of coping with this lack. In doing this, however, we grow more and more aware of getting into a Procrustean bed: of getting a service which can easily turn to disservice. While it helps to structure observations, it also entails the application of standards to the biblical text that do not always prove adequate to the social and historical practices of the ancient Hebrew world. An example in point is the widespread use of a dichotomous conceptual tool: the opposition *hegemonic vs. subordinate masculinities*. It implies that the main figures of biblical narratives—patriarchs, kings and prophets, should be assumed to belong in hegemonic masculinity. This clarity, however, vanishes as soon as one imagines cramming into the same mould the trickster Jacob, the merciful Joseph, the heroic David and the weeping Jeremiah. Hypothetically, I see two reasons for the difficulty in applying the 'hegemonic vs. subordinate' model. The first is that in the world of the Hebrew Bible we should better talk of *hegemonic masculinities*, rather than of a hegemonic masculinity, the way Raewyn Connell does in her attempt to define the new gender situation in the post-modern world.[1] The second is that biblical[2] hegemonic masculinity is a category much wider and inherently variable in a way that is unfamiliar to the modern Western world. Further on in this study I will try to give preference to the second reason by studying the persona of the weeping man and the symbolic usages of male weeping in the narrative of the Torah and the Deuteronomistic History.

---

1. See, e.g., Connell 2005: 76-77. See also Seidler 2006; Whitehead and Barrett 2001: 18.
2. The word 'biblical' is used throughout the present study with reference to the 'Hebrew Bible'.

To begin with, it should be noted that in the Hebrew Bible weeping is rather a collective act, an act of the entire community of Israel—and that is how it occurs in the Torah or in books like Joshua and Judges. There are two paradigmatic situations where the plot requires collective weeping. In the first one, the entire community is in a situation of dire crisis, suffering and univocally complaining to God as the highest instance of power and order. Such is, for example, the behaviour of Israel in Egypt or on the long way through the desert after the Exodus. And because 'The Lord is slow to anger, and abounding in steadfast love' (Num. 14.18),[3] he is expected to understand the suffering of his children; weeping in this case is a voice of suffering which is to arouse compassion and turn human destiny to a new path. The second case is ritualistic in character: the community is lamenting somebody already dead or destined to die (like Jephthah's daughter who has to be sacrificed in Judg. 11).

From the archaic functions of weeping as a collective ritualistic practice types of individual weeping have developed worthy of inclusion in the plot of the ancient epic narrative. The first weeping character in the Torah is a woman—Hagar, abandoned with her son in the desert. Her behaviour is a minimized replica of the big collective model of *weep-as-appeal for help and salvation*. After Hagar the next one to cry is Esau, and though he seeks no direct contact with Elohim, it is yet another case of *weep-as-complaint of great injustice*; later, the weeping of Jacob and that of Hannah, the mother of Prophet Samuel, fit the same typology. It is difficult to notice any gender specifics of the weeping character within the framework of this model: both man and woman seek protection from God, the very source of justice.

The first characters who weep for 'inter-human' reasons are Esau and Jacob; their tears are caused by their joy and relief at their first meeting after the long separation since Jacob stole Esau's primogeniture. With this weeping similar feelings are shared between two men; the narrator apparently finds nothing strange in the situation he is describing. This situation, however, is not unique to men in biblical narratives: women are also capable of crying when overpowered by mutual feelings. Naomi's daughters-in-law twice weep aloud while taking leave from her (Ruth 1.9, 14). Soon after the story of Esau and Jacob we get to the first great figure of male weeping: Joseph. For nine chapters (starting at the moment he meets his brothers in Egypt) Joseph cries eight times. Weeping is among the most typical features of his behaviour: we can even speak of a model with specific characteristics, of which he is (the first, greatest and most perfect) representative in the biblical narrative. I will point out several of the most typical characteristics of this model as they are manifested in the Egyptian part of Joseph's story.

---

3.   All quotations from the Bible are from the NRSV.

The weeping of that Hebrew patriarch is personal; it is an intimate experience, without any ritualistic and/or public theatrical effect. He often attempts to weep in secret: turns aside ('he turned away from them and wept', Gen. 2.24), hides ('So he went into a private room, and wept there', 43.30), makes efforts to hide his face and control himself ('Then he washed his face and came out; and controlling himself, he said…', 43.31). In moments of particularly overpowering emotion his weeping is accompanied with kisses on other men's bodies: 'And he kissed all his brothers and wept upon them' (45.15); 'Then Joseph threw himself on his father's face and wept over him and kissed him' (50.1). As Robert Alter says, he is 'a man of powerful spontaneous feeling' (Alter 2008: 292). Neither weeping, nor mercy, nor kisses, however, prevent Joseph from being a resourceful crook, at the very moments when he feels mercy, and cheat the very people he loves. The narrative does not hesitate to show him as a typical trickster, scheming in cold blood. It seems that to the narrator those characteristics of the man chosen by God—mercy and cheating—do not contradict each other: rather they complement each other to make an entity, which differs from present-day concepts of heroic male character.

Still, the highest point in the depiction of Joseph is his ability to feel 'with his guts'. The first time a verbal sign of this ability appears is the moment when he meets Benjamin: 'Joseph hurried out because he was overcome with affection for his brother' (43.30), literally 'because his insides (רחמים) yearned (כמר) for his brother', רחמים being the plural form of the noun רֶחֶם, 'womb', used with the meaning *compassion, mercy*, and *love*. The symbolic meaning in the use of רחמים can be made clear by comparing it with another similar case.[4]

In 1 Kings 3 Solomon, who has recently chosen to be granted 'an understanding mind' by God, and has become 'able to discern between good and evil' better than anyone else, offers an unusual solution to the argument between two harlots, each of whom claims she is the mother of a newborn baby. The moment the king passes his verdict—'Divide the living boy in two'—the woman who is the real mother gives up her claim 'because compassion for her son burned within her' (3.26), or 'because her rahamim (compassion) grew warm, grew tender, or yearned [*kmr*] for her son' (Trible 1980: 33). Only then did the king respond: 'Give [her] the living boy… She is his mother', thus building a symbolic connection between motherhood, the ability to feel 'with one's womb' and the fairness of the law.

Actually, the moment these three things come together—the ability to give life, the capacity for empathy, and higher justice—the realm of the transcendent and the divine has been reached. Indeed, both the verb כמר

---

4. I owe this comparison to Phyllis Trible, who considers the womb metaphor and its symbolic meanings in Trible 1980: 33-57.

('to show mercy') and its cognate adjective *merciful* are among the distinctive features of the Hebrew God.[5] There are also other cognates of the verbal
root כמר, adjectives and nouns, mostly common nouns, with the potential to
be turned into proper nouns. Thus, for example, from the marriage of the
prophet Hosea and the harlot Gomer a daughter is born, whom God orders
to be named Lo-ruhamah ('not loved' or 'unpardoned') 'for I will no longer
have pity on the house of Israel or forgive them' (Hos. 1.6).

Going back to Joseph and his רחמים, it becomes clear that in the Benjamin
episode the biblical narrator is trying to convey a symbol of exceptional
moral integrity, a mode of godliness in humans. This is the ability to be in
the world through love and compassion, an experience that is transitory
(mercy upon somebody) and intransient (visceral affect) at the same time.
'To the responsive imagination', writes Phyllis Trible, 'this metaphor suggests the meaning of love as selfless participation in life'; and defines it as
'a semantic movement…from the wombs of women to the compassion of
God' (Trible 1980: 33-34). Trible, an already classical author of feminist
biblical exegesis, traces the meaning of the womb metaphor to the erstwhile
significance of women and their experience in the archaic world, but her line
of thinking could be continued, applying a gender studies methodology
emancipated from its traditional fusion with women's studies.

A womb without doubt belongs to the female body but to the archaic
mind it functioned as a metaphor of inner fertility which any human being
possessed. And because in the Hebrew Bible the ultimate figure capable of
giving life is God, God is also seen as possessing a womb. The man-with-
womb is therefore an identification of the generic human being (*adam*, as in
Gen. 2.7) with Yahweh in one of his most important functions; this is a case
of *imitatio Dei* that marks the behaviour of very few chosen men.

Here is another case in which the prominent man must have a womb
according to the task he was given by God himself. In Num. 11.12 Moses
finds it harder and harder to bear the burden of the responsibility of a fickle
and whimsical people, so when he hears the Israelites demand meat instead
of manna, he raises a desperate voice/weep to God, saying: 'Did I conceive
all this people? Did I give birth to them that you should say to me: Carry
them in your bosom, as a nurse carries a suckling child…' Now we have a
whole series of metaphors based on feminine behaviour but what they really
mean is God's ability to give and nurture life. Moses gives up the chance to
resemble God but behind the explicit complaint the narrative clearly implies

---

5.   Most often the adjective *merciful* belongs to a ritualistic formulation, which may
appear in an extended form ('The Lord is merciful and gracious, slow to anger and
abounding in steadfast love', Exod. 34.6; Neh. 9.7; Ps. 103.8), or in a concise form ('for
you are a gracious and merciful God', 2 Chron. 30.9; Neh. 9.31; Ps. 116.5).

that, yes, he does resemble God because of the task he has been given. The prophet leader has become God-like and is unable to give up 'the compassionate womb', which he acquired the moment he made his choice. To summarize: the womb metaphor appears in male behaviour because the ancient imagination tries to identify it with the divine; it is doubtlessly derived from the biological functions of the female body (the way other metaphors make use of natural phenomena); however, what it implies is not femininity but almost-divinity, which ontologically precedes the division between male and female. For the biblical narrator there is no problem in principle if women, too, think with the womb (as in the case with the mother prostitute) but the narrative of the history of Israel is simply not interested in their experience. It is focused on the behaviour of men for it is men who perform the roles in which the historical process takes place. Thus men turn out to be 'greater' owners of wombs, or more similar to God than women. Mercy/womb and weeping out of mercy fall on their side of the gender boundary but this does not make men women-like; rather, it makes them more male.

Having said all this, it is hardly any wonder that the second great weeper is also the greatest male hero in Israel's history—King David. The very first time David cries—on his separation with Jonathan in 1 Samuel 20, his behaviour follows one of the most ancient Middle-Eastern patterns of heroic behaviour. Here is this moving scene, worthy to be part of any epic saga: 'David rose from behind the stone heap and prostrated himself with his face to the ground. He bowed three times, and they kissed each other; David wept the more' (20.41). The reader is left with the impression that the two heroic males are outweeping each other; the winner of this contest ('David wept the more') will also prove to be the 'manlier' man.

It is again Jonathan who begets David's cry—this time with his death. The news of how the king and his son died makes David perform in a public spectacle in which all of Israel is the audience and all of Israel witnesses his ability to weep well, to show compassion (to feel with his guts). He sets the example and starts the ritual by tearing his clothes, then all 'mourned and wept, and fasted until evening' (2 Sam. 1.12) together. The culmination of the performance is the moment when David performs a funeral song over Saul and Jonathan and orders this song to 'be taught to the people of Judah'. David's elegy over Jonathan and Saul is a good piece of poetry. Alongside the entire performance, the elegy has symbolic functions, so rich in consequences that today's researchers of the Hebrew Bible are still unpacking its meaning.

For instance, all the episodes narrating the relationship between Jonathan and David, when seen as an entity in gradation, place the elegy at the top of the scale in an ancient model of treasured friendship between two male heroes. This scenario can be found in the ancient epic sagas of the ancient Near East and the Mediterranean region, starting with the oldest among them, *The Epic of Gilgamesh.* Numerous comparisons have been made between the stories of Gilgamesh and Enkidu, David and Jonathan, Achilles and Patroclus.[6] In all those cases the love between two great men ends with the death of one (the less heroic one); this makes the survivor lament the death of his beloved friend in heart-rending poetry accompanied by excessive gestures of anguish and despair: for seven days Gilgamesh will not leave the dead body until worms begin to crawl out of its mouth; tearing his hair out, moaning 'like a lioness', Achilles claims that he would not have suffered so much even if his father had died. Along this line of symbolically functional weeping David's behaviour is inscribed into a very prestigious matrix of male heroism. The implication of this pattern in the plot is an important moment of the apologetic strategy of the Deuteronomistic Historian.

In the second place, weeping gives David the chance to perform as a poet; the narrator implies a connection between the ability to feel with one's womb/guts and the gift of speaking in beautiful verses. The combination of the two abilities enhances the hero's exceptionality, as well as his resemblance to God—not only because God has the habit of talking in verses,[7] but also because each unusual skill in a human being could only come from him.

In the third place the excessive and publicly spectacular lament on the death of Saul and Jonathan has a practical political effect: it legitimizes the ambition of David to impose himself as the legal king of Judah. People weep the hardest for their closest loved ones (especially those of same blood); thus Joseph was moved 'in his womb' only when he saw Benjamin, a brother born of 'his mother's womb', and Jacob's weeping on learning about the alleged death of his son was long and disconsolate. Lamenting over Saul as his son, David symbolically becomes the son the king cannot (any longer) have once he has lost Jonathan. Though made public post factum, this is also the way love between David and the king's son works. Mark K. George writes about this: 'On the basis of his relationship with Jonathan, on this second step David declares himself son of his "brother's father", and as son he carries out the appropriate actions expected of a good son by lamenting for his patrilineal "father"' (George 1997: 171). Besides a patrilineal blood connection, the male lament also contains a strong homosocial aspect: it has the capacity to constitute a community of equal (worthy of being wept upon) men. After the grand scale funeral ritual which David stages and acts in, he joins the club of regal men.

6. See, e.g., Hammond and Jablow 1987; Nissinen 1995; Halperin 1990.
7. Two of the numerous examples are Gen. 9.6 (God speaks to Noah) and Gen. 16.11-12 (the angel speaks to Hagar).

There may be other symbolic consequences to David's poetic lament but it would be more important to say that the Deuteronomistic narrator was completely aware of the story-telling potential of this situation of mourning for he applies it beyond the *love-between-two-heroic-men* pattern so persistently that it becomes a narrative *leitmotif* in the story of David.

Only two chapters after the episode with the funeral of Jonathan and Saul, the mourning-in-eulogy situation unfolds to even vaster dimensions when David's chieftain Joab kills Abner of the house of Benjamin (2 Sam. 3). This seems to be the gala-performance staged by David: here his artistry comes to perfection. He orders everyone to tear their clothes, to put on sackcloth and mourn over Abner, while he himself was following the bier, weeping aloud. At the funeral site the king recites another one of his laments with everyone around in tears (3.33). The performance, however, does not end here. He refuses to eat as a sign of his grief, all the people are concerned with their king's health and beseech him to have some food, but he heroically refrains until nightfall. That strongly impresses the people: 'All the people took notice of it, and it pleased them just as everything the king did pleased all the people' (3.36).

David's ability to manipulate people through his weeping is unconcealable. The narrator makes no effort to hide this; on the contrary, he never fails to keep it in focus, with a strong apologetic accent, just as Genesis emphasizes the trickery of the merciful Joseph. Coming from David, weeping is a powerful tool for moral and political influence over the others. When a group of Amalekites raid Ziklag, taking captives the wives and children of his people, what saves him from their anger is loud weeping (1 Sam. 30). The narrator believes that strong feelings can only be overpowered by stronger feelings, so David outweeps all the men; only then does he make a reasonable offer—leading 600 men he tracks down the Amalekitian gang, defeats it and everyone gets back what they had lost.

The culmination of David's ability *to weep for profit* is the episode with the death of the firstborn child of Bathsheba. The king weeps, prays and fasts while the baby is ill; after the baby's death he stops grieving abruptly, washes and sits down to have a meal. When his servants, rightly amazed, ask him about the reason for this strange behaviour, he answers: 'While the child was still alive, I fasted and wept; for I said, "Who knows? The Lord may be gracious to me, and the child may live." But now that he is dead; why should I fast? Can I bring him back again?' (2 Sam. 12.22-23). It is difficult to overstate the moral practicality of this behaviour, which is reminiscent of patriarch Abraham's custom of bargaining with the Lord. Once it fails to work, the deal no longer exists; besides, it is no use crying over spilt milk.

It would seem that in 2 Samuel the narrator himself is tired of the hero's pragmatism, therefore he tries to introduce a delicate alternative of masculine weeping. Just before Abner's death there is a meaningful episode:

David claims and gets back from the house of Benjamin his first wife Michal, who has been given to another man and already has five children with him. Michal's husband—Paltiel, the son of Laish, 'went with her, weeping as he walked behind her all the way to Bahurim' (2 Sam. 3.16); he returns only when Abner rudely drives him away. The two episodes correlate in meaning precisely through the symbolism of male weeping; the unusually ample details which present a marginal character Paltiel confirm his significance in the biblical narrator's design. It would be easiest to read the comparison in Paltiel's favour: his weeping is personal and sincere, unlike David's ostentatious performance. This explication is tempting but only from a present-day Western perspective, not so for the ancient historian, who could hardly see anything wrong with David's ability to manipulate people (and God himself) by crying. We can interpret the narrator's position by paraphrasing John Austin: the male hero needs to know how to do things with weeping. The use of tears in this case is analogous to David's use of madness.

In 1 Sam. 21.13, having left Saul's court, David makes an attempt to find employment at the court of the Philistine king Achish. The men at the court, however, quickly recognize him as the Israelite hero, who killed 'ten thousand Philistines', as the song says; he needs to save himself urgently. David, accordingly, resorts to madness: he scratches marks on the wooden gate and lets his spittle run down his beard (21.13). In both cases (the weeping and the madness) the narrative focuses on extreme displays of affection—the kind that is known to be beyond control. They happen unexpectedly, leaving the body helpless. David, however (unlike King Saul who lets himself be tormented by the evil spirit of God) is in control of his body and of the psychological states that can be expressed through it; this capacity of his makes him different from other people, a 'superman' who can be the master of his own fate. The narrator not only displays his skills, he seems deliberately to create plot-turns and situations where they can be highlighted with particular clarity. The 'superhuman' and the regal work co-operate to shorten the distance that separates man from God (though David is perfectly aware of how far he can go in his relationship with God, which is yet another of his unusual skills).

So here is the difference between Paltiel and David: Paltiel weeps the way an (ordinary) man does, David weeps the way a King does. The weeping of the former is private, personal, intimate: it is of no consequence except to the weeping man himself. The weeping of the latter is always public, effective, and eloquent; it generates consequences that affect many people. It is precisely *the performative function of weeping* that distinguishes God's anointed man from the other people and constitutes an important part of the apologetic strategy of the Deuteronomistic narrative about David.

The episodes which have the king crying in public with serious effect upon other people continue to the end of 2 Samuel: when Absalom kills Amnon (13.36), during David's flight from Jerusalem at the time of Absalom's rebellion (15.30), when Joab kills Absalom (18.33). Without being identical they all fit the model I already delineated so I will not go into any more details. I will make use of them, however, to point out yet another symbolic feature of the ability to weep well.

In my comments on David so far I seem to have neglected the connection between his weeping and the weeping of Joseph in Genesis: the tears of the patriarch appear to be personal, like those of Paltiel, and David's tears are public and politically effective, a manifestation of his 'royal body'.[8] A position like this seems suspiciously rational and is hardly valid for the ancient epic narrator but it was present in the early Common Era, as proved by the writings of Josephus Flavius. His manner of retelling the books of the Bible contains meaningful deviations aimed at updating 'the Jewish antiquities' to suit the moral expectations of the Roman readers from the first century CE. Thus, for example, when describing the relationship between David and Jonathan, he carefully 'expurgates' the amorous rhetoric of the biblical narrator motivated by the fear of unwanted homoerotic associations with his own reality. However, when talking of David's weeping, Josephus never omits even the details and sometimes additionally stresses its power and duration. What is more, he even adds invented weeping episodes to David's behaviour when they appear to suit the narrative's general message.[9] At the same time, Josephus totally omits the episode with Paltiel, whose crying he apparently thought insignificant. All of this implies that in the first century CE male weeping had still not acquired a negative ('anti-masculine') connotation, at least not in the Mediterranean world.

What was Josephus' purpose, which features of David's personality was he trying to foreground to make the character unequivocally appealing to his audience? The answer can be seen in the comments he several times inserts between the facts of the biblical story. His words after the episode of Abner's death could serve as an example: 'the entire nation rejoiced at the king's gentleness and mildness of disposition, every one being ready to

8. 'The successful kings, most notably David, can display their bodies in ways that serve higher purposes, ultimately divine ones, and these displays deserve the emulation of Israelites' (Hamilton 2005: 30).

9. This is what he does, for example, when recounting the conversation of Saul and David after following what happened in the cave in the wilderness of En-gedi (1 Sam. 24). According to the Deuteronomistic historian, the only one who cries is the moved Saul. In the behaviour of the elderly man who recognizes David as his son there is something of Joseph's mercy—it is the ability to feel with the male womb. Josephus, however, will not let the 'real' hero be surpassed in mercy, so he makes him cry no less hard and no less sincerely than Saul.

suppose that the king would have taken the same care of them in the like circumstances which they saw be showed in the burial of Abner'.[10] This comment is worth being analyzed in detail for it contains the ideal of a man and king in Roman history and philosophy from the beginning of the new Common Era. However, what we are interested in is the strong didactic accent the writer put on David's gentle nature and his mercy. The character portrayed by Josephus Flavius is reminiscent of both Joseph and Solomon: he connects mercy to the fairness and democratic disposition in the king's behaviour. A ruler like this is a real father, *pater familias* to his people.

The second comment on David's personality is placed immediately after the announcement of his death. It is a succinct psychological portrait, which contains a wealth of character traits and moral characteristics. Having mentioned features like bravery, insight, and the ability to give the right orders at the right moment Josephus adds: 'He was prudent and moderate, and kind to such as were under any calamities; he was righteous and humane, which are good qualities, peculiarly fit for kings'.[11] It matters neither that a single person cannot have all those qualities at the same time, nor that many of them go against the upbringing a hereditary king was likely to get. What Josephus wrote is not a biography but a passionary: or, to put it in Christian terms, he is painting an *icon of the Good King*. He has no individual king as a prototype, but the *King of Kings* himself, Elohim. All other figures of great men—patriarchs, kings, judges, priests—originate here: each of them gets some kind of combination of sacred features but David is the only one who can have it in its (relative) entirety for he stands closest (his capacity to cheat and manipulate included) to God.[12]

The narrative of David is the unrivalled climax of the Deuteronomistic plot about royal weeping, but not its end. Let us follow what happens after David 'went to sleep with his ancestors' and was buried in his city (1 Kgs 2.10). In spite of the great number of kings appearing in 1 and 2 Kings, very few of them can weep. The first is Ahab, king of Israel and husband of the evil Queen Jezebel. Frightened by the prophecy of Elijah, he 'tore his clothes, and put sackcloth over his bare flesh; he fasted, lay in the sackcloth, and went about dejectedly' (1 Kgs 21.27). This appears to be the entire royal grieving pattern, complete with all the details familiar from David's behaviour. Yet, in the Masoretic text there is a symptomatic gap: the verb

---

10. Josephus, *Ant.* 7.1.6.

11. Josephus, *Ant.* 7.15.2

12. Like the Deuteronomistic historian, Josephus never hides these characteristics, either. After the story about the lament of Abner's death, for example, we can read: 'And indeed David principally intended to gain a good reputation, and therefore he took to do what was proper in this case, whence none had any suspicion that he was the author of Abner's death' (Josephus, *Ant.* 7.1.6).

weep is never used in it.[13] Still, God takes pity on Ahab and mercifully promises him not to bring disaster in his own days, but in the days of his son.

We do not see the next grieving king until 2 Kings. Another ruler of Israel, seeing the famine in his land and the women eating their children to survive, tears his clothes apart in such a way that 'the people could see that he had sackcloth on his body underneath' (2 Kgs 6.30). Here, as in the previous case, no form of the verb *weep* is used. The verb does not appear until the very end of 2 Kings where Hezekiah, king of Judah, is lying on his deathbed. Anticipating the nearing end he prays to the Lord while weeping bitterly (20.3). And God responds through the prophet Isaiah: 'Thus says the Lord, the God of your ancestor David: I have heard your prayer, I have seen your tears; indeed, I will heal you' (20.5). As soon as the tears have sprung, the name of David has also turned up. The two seem to go together in the mind of the Deuteronomistic writer; to him they express two elements of the same construction. Indeed, Hezekiah proves to be a relatively good king: he at least takes care of his people by bringing water to the city.

The same story is also told in Isaiah 38. What is interesting here is that the author puts in the mouth of the dying-and-crying Hezekiah a self-lament, a good piece of poetry, which is mainly a prayer for salvation but ends with gratitude to God expressed in advance. The mentioning of David and his house motivated a later author to make even shorter the distance between Hezekiah and his royal ancestor, to develop the semblance in detail, in the first place through the ability to weep in beautiful poetry. Weeping has already turned into a signifier of the positive traits that a Judean king should have.[14] From this point there is only a short distance to Josephus, who insisted on David being a personage that combines all the positive qualities a universal king can have.

The last hero of the Deuteronomistic history who weeps is Josiah; as could be expected, 'He did what was right in the sight of the Lord and walked in all the way of his father David' (2 Kgs 22.2). He starts crying at the most suitable and sublime moment: when he touches the sacred Book of the Covenant that had been found during repair works in the Temple. Because of his tears and because his 'heart was penitent', and he 'humbled himself before the Lord' (2 Kgs 22.19), Yahweh promises to let him live in peace to the end of his days. Josiah is the most righteous Judean king after David; even if his deeds had not been described in detail, one could surmise it from the phrases 'you wept', 'your heart was penitent', 'you humbled

---

13. The Septuagint, though, takes the formula literally and adds new details to Ahab's behaviour, including the key verb: 'he was walking about and *weeping*'.

14. Isaiah is, generally speaking, a firm believer in the sacred redeeming role allotted to David's dynasty.

yourself'. Though very succinctly, the Deuteronomist reproduces certain features of the good, righteous king. The restraint of the description comes to express the conviction that in spite of his reforms Josiah can no longer change anything. Judah's fate has already been sealed.

Having already discussed the symbolism of royal weeping and being aware of the social structure of male roles in the Torah and the Deuteronomistic history, one would expect at least one more model—that of prophetic weeping. It turns out, however, that prophets here almost never cry. It takes some imagination to insert at least some of the episodes with prophetic protagonists in the male crying plot; yet, the usual words signifying weeping are not explicitly used in the text.

The prophet who has perhaps the strongest propensity for weeping seems to be Moses; sometimes he raises his voice to cry out in front of God at the unbearable weight of the mission imposed upon him. The great prophets of the Deuteronomistic history—Eli, Samuel, Elijah, and Isaiah—are not explicitly presented as weeping: their crying could be only guessed in a few situations. Samuel for example 'grieved over Saul' so long that God had to ask him: 'How long will you grieve over Saul?' (1 Sam. 15.35). To save the breathless child of the woman, who offered him shelter in her own home, Elijah 'stretched himself upon the child three times and cried out to the God: O Lord my God, let this child's life come into him again' (1 Kgs 17.20). It could be surmised that the performance of this magical ceremony also included some ritualistic crying, typical in cases when a man was trying to obtain something from God by means of prayer.

Those fragments, however, are not enough to construct the persona of the weeping prophet, not the one we see in Lam. 3.48-49:

> My eyes flow with rivers of tears
> because of the destruction of my people.
> My eyes will flow without ceasing…

Rather than parts of a whole, the fragments above seem more like self-sufficient, symbolically meaningful instances of male behaviour applicable to different narrative situations and characters. If we go back to the two figures previously discussed—the man who feels with his guts and the Good King—we could see that these figures are also composed of self-sufficient, symbolically meaningful features, some of which they tend to exchange. But let me go back to the question posed at the very beginning: Are we talking about *hegemonic masculinity* or about *hegemonic masculinities* in the Hebrew Bible? And can we talk at all about hegemonic masculinity/masculinities?

From everything we have seen so far, it could be concluded that there is only one big and internally diverse model of 'hegemonic' masculinity; its matrix is the concept of the divine character. The various types of heroic men in the biblical narrative are depicted through a variety of combined features which can be found in the behaviour of God; the combinations suit the plot essentials as well as the symbolic functions of each specific hero. The one who seems capable of possessing the greatest variety of heroic male features (being thus closest to the divine prototype) is David.[15] To bring this resemblance home to their audience, the commentators of later times stress the variety in question by adding new features or by enhancing the presence of old but not sufficiently manifest ones. One typical way to do this is the expansion of the character towards charity and compassion. These qualities are not so clearly expressed in the character of the Deuteronomistic hero, but are a must in mythologizing his messianic role, not least to match the words pronounced by the Lord in Isa. 49.10: 'for he who has pity on them will lead them'.

At the beginning of this essay I wrote about *hegemonic masculinities*, but we should be careful when applying modern concepts to the biblical images of masculinity. Beyond any doubt, the Hebrew Bible represents an entity of masculine traits which could be articulated by a classical definition of hegemonic masculinity as a 'culturally exalted form of masculinity' (Carrigan, Connell, and Lee 1987: 92); the biblical books testify that these traits have been promoted as a norm by the institutionalized means of literary writing. At the same time, the entity is very large, much larger, diverse and internally contradictive than the one, on the basis of which modern researchers defined the terminology of masculinity studies. This large-scale diversity stems from the religious ideas of human existence that underlie biblical writing: human beings exist by practicing the divine image and likeness; God is an all-encompassing matrix of human behaviour. As a result the pattern of normative masculinity embraces many pairs of conflicting features: honesty and trickstery;[16] honour and slipping out of it when needed;[17] mercy and cruelty; simplicity of heart and competence of bargaining; frank bravery and unfair

15.   The wealth of traits in his character is demonstrated very convincingly by David Clines, who formulates and analyzes six 'leading male characteristics in the figure of David'. For more details see Clines 1995.

16.   Biblical researchers sometimes define the trickster traits of some male characters (Jacob and Joseph among the patriarchs for example) as a slip from the position of hegemonic to the position of subordinate masculinity (Haddox 2010: 16). Anthropology teaches us otherwise. In many primitive mythologies (South American for instance) the trickster (he may be human or a cunning animal, most often the Rabbit) is a prominent figure of creative masculinity. The same attitude to tricksters and trickery persists in such Near Eastern folk tales as the popular comic stories of Nastradin Hodzha. As a matter of fact, God also plays the trickster advising, 'his chosen people' to borrow gold and silver ornaments from their neighbours when leaving Egypt.

17.   David at the court of the Philistine King Achish is an example in point (1 Sam. 21.10-15).

manipulativeness,[18] to name just a few pairs. Once again, the best example is the literary character of David. King David as the Deuteronomist conceptualizes him could stand for no real man's figure for the very reason that his personality is burdened with an impossible multitude of conflicting characteristics. This makes him 'beyond-human' and serves well the messianistic ideas implicit in his literary presence. All this points again to the necessity to be cautious when using modern concepts of hegemonic and subordinate masculinities;[19] it also highlights the urgency to initiate a debate on the traps of effortlessly applying terminology of modern social sciences to the biblical representations of gender without theoretical reflection and detailed elaboration.

Finally, I would like to go back to my title: male weeping and its symbolism in the Torah and the Deuteronomistic history. Literary weeping probably stems from an important, perhaps the most important, ritualistic function of weeping in the ancient world: the human being or the whole community weeps to obtain mercy from the gods, or merely to gain access to the gods' attention. There are many descriptions of this function in biblical books, and the shortest way of formulating is: 'When the righteous cry for help, the Lord hears and rescues them from all their troubles' (Ps. 4.17), or 'Give ear to my words, O Lord, give heed to my sighing' (Ps. 5.1). In biblical philosophy weeping holds a position of exceptional importance; it is an ability that has been granted to some of the greatest heroes. In the face of God a mortal being ought to cry, this is what could be termed 'the human situation', and an expression of the equilibrium human–divine. Sorrow is the best way to represent human existence: short, agonizing and uncertain. That is why Ecclesiastes, the wise man, says:

> Sorrow is better than laughter
> for by sadness of countenance
> the heart is made glad.
> The heart of the wise is in the house
> of mourning (Eccl. 7.3-4).

He who cries best will see the day when he can say, like the Judean king Hezekiah, 'Surely it was for my welfare that I had great bitterness' (Isa. 38.17).

18.   The competence of bargaining with God included, just as Abraham does in Gen. 18.23-32.

19.   A theoretical elaboration on non-hegemonic masculinities exists in the work of Ovidiu Creangă. Following a four-types model of masculinity constructed by R.W. Connell (2005), he differentiates between subordinate and marginalized masculinities in the Conquest Narrative of Joshua (Creangă 2010: 101-103). Subordination is defined as 'that which is wholly rejectable from the hegemonic point of view', while 'marginalized men are within the hegemonic framework, but outside its privileges' (Creangă 2010: 101).

Bibliography

Alter, Robert
  2008   *The Five Books of Moses: A Translation with Commentary* (London: W.W. Norton).
Brod, Harry (ed.)
  1987   *The Making of Masculinities: The New Men's Studies* (Boston: Allen & Unwin)
Carrigan, Tim, Bob Connell, and John Lee
  1987   'Toward a New Sociology of Masculinity', in Brod (ed.) 1987: 63-100.
Clines, David J.A.
  1995   'David the Man: The Construction of Masculinity in the Hebrew Bible', in *Interested Parties: The Ideology of Writers and Readers of the Hebrew Bible* (JSOTSup, 205, Sheffield: Sheffield Academic Press): 212-43.
Connell, Raewyn W.
  2005   *Masculinities* (Berkeley: University of California Press, 2nd edn).
Creangă, Ovidiu
  2010   'Variations on the Theme of Masculinity: Joshua's Gender In/stability in the Conquest Narrative (Josh. 1-12)', in Creangă (ed.) 2010: 83-109.
Creangă, Ovidiu (ed.)
  2010   *Men and Masculinity in the Hebrew Bible and Beyond* (Bible in the Modern World, 33; Sheffield: Sheffield Phoenix Press).
George, Mark K.
  1997   'Assuming the Body of the Heir Apparent', in Timothy K. Beal and David M. Gunn (eds.), *Reading Bibles, Writing Bodies: Identity and the Book* (London: Routledge): 164-74.
Haddox, Susan E.
  2010   'Favoured Sons and Subordinate Masculinities', in Creangă (ed.) 2010: 2-19.
Halperin, David
  1990   *One Hundred Years of Homosexuality: And Other Essays on Greek Love* (London: Routledge).
Hamilton, Mark W.
  2005   *The Body Royal: The Social Poetics of Kingship in Ancient Israel* (Leiden and Boston: E.J. Brill).
Hammond, Dorothy, and Alta Jablow
  1987   'Gilgamesh and the Sundance Kid: The Myth of Male Friendship', in Brod (ed.) 1987: 241-58.
Josephus Flavius
  n.d.   *Antiquities of the Jews* (trans. William Whiston). Online: http://www.ccel.org/j/josephus/works/ant-7.htm.
Nissinen, Martti
  1995   *Homoeroticism in the Biblical World: A Historical Perspective* (Minneapolis: Fortress Press).
Seidler, Victor Jeleniewski
  2006   *Transforming Masculinities* (London: Routledge).

Trible, Phyllis
    1980   *God and the Rhetoric of Sexuality* (Philadelphia: Fortress Press).
Whitehead, Stephen, and Franc J. Barrett
    2001   'The Sociology of Masculinity', in Stephen Whitehead and Frank J. Barrett (eds.), *The Masculinities Reader* (Cambridge: Polity Press): 1-26.

SAUL IN THE COMPANY OF MEN:
(DE)CONSTRUCTING MASCULINITY IN 1 SAMUEL 9–31

Marcel V. Măcelaru

1. *Saul in the Narrative of 1 Samuel: The Problem*

The somewhat ambiguous portrayal of Saul in the first book of Samuel has created a bit of a riddle in Hebrew Bible scholarship. Different views regarding Saul's historical and literary functions have been put forward and the interpreter endeavouring to study the relevant biblical material will also unavoidably deal with a sizable stack of secondary literature. In it, one will discover, when regarded as a protagonist in Israel's history, Saul is seen as either an institutionalized version of the charismatic type of leader commonly associated with the book of Judges (Alt 1966: 173-237; cf. Czövek 2006: 41-99); or as a self-appointed military protector (Miller 1974); or as a pre-monarchic type of ruler (chieftain), who coexisted and competed with David (Flanagan 1981); or as a king with limited prerogatives, subject to Samuel's prophetic charismatic authority and the old tribal socio-political arrangements (Bright 1981: 187-95; cf. Măcelaru 2012: 54 n. 5); or as the founder of monarchic Israel proper (Edelman 1991). Nevertheless, differences between such roles seem minuscule, or of no consequence, when the discussion focuses on Saul's characterization in the narrative. To explain, it seems to me that historical hypotheses such as those listed above say more about socio-political leadership models than about the character 'Saul' and give therefore an incomplete picture of this literary personage.

In all fairness, however, it must be said that this variety of opinions about a historical Saul is, to a large extent, a consequence of the literary complexity of the text of 1 Samuel, both in terms of its formation[1] and in terms of ideological underpinnings identifiable in its presentation of the beginnings of kingship in Israel.[2] It is widely assumed in Hebrew Bible scholarship that in the books of Samuel represent a compilation of originally independent

---

1. The beginnings of historical-critical work on 1 Samuel can be traced back to Wellhausen (1871) and Rost (1926). Following in their footsteps, a whole host of scholars has undertaken to examine the literary history of this material; McKenzie (2000: 286-314) provides an excellent summary of this work.

2. On ideological polemic in the story of Saul, consult Amit 2000: 168-88.

sources, which were brought together and subsequently edited in several stages to generate the narrative as it now stands. Particularly, 1 Samuel 9–31,[3] which is the segment that interests us here, combines two distinctive blocks of material. The first, commonly called the 'Saul Cycle' (9.1–10.16; 10.17-27a; 10.27b–11.15; 13.2-7a, 15b-23; 14.1-46),[4] is a collection of short stories that recount the beginnings of the Israelite monarchy and the rise and rejection of Saul as Israel's king. Specific within this section are the existence of three versions of Saul's election as king (9.1–10.16; 10.17-27; 11.1-15), presumably evidencing that at the origin of chs. 8–15 stand three independent literary sources, and a related thematic tension that sets in opposition pro- and anti-monarchy views throughout the narrative, possibly indicating that such differences of opinion regarding the suitability of kingship as Israel's model of governance were part of the ideological milieu within which the Israelite kingship emerged (Halpern 1981: 59-96; Brueggemann 2003: 133-35). As a narrative feature, however, this tension serves to set in opposition two leadership models: that of Samuel, who epitomizes the old order, and that of Saul, the symbol of the new order (cf. Măcelaru 2012: 51-94). The purpose of this contrast within the larger context of the Deuteronomistic material is to subtly undermine human kingship as the model of governance in Israel.[5] Within the narrative of 1 Samuel, however, the ambiguity characterizing the beginning of kingship reflects negatively on Saul and serves to prepare the way for the anointing of David as Israel's king.

An unequivocal fondness for David is the most prominent feature of the second block of material, a narrative which has accordingly been called the 'History of David's Rise' (1 Sam. 16.14–2 Sam. 5.10). It is usually argued that its purpose is to explain and legitimize David's ascension to the throne and to present Davidic kingship as the divinely endorsed alternative to Saul's rule. Various literary features in the narrative seem to be designed to do just that. For instance, the Spirit of God departs from Saul (16.14) and comes upon David (16.13; cf. 17.37; 18.12); YHWH ignores Saul's requests for divine guidance (14.37 and 28.6) but gives prompt answers to David (on this, see Craig 1994); David keeps acquiring clothing while Saul is losing it, which may be symbols alluding to David's rise and Saul's fall (on this, see Prouser 1996, 1998). In such-like fashion, throughout the story, David's qualities, success and election are emphasized and contrasted with Saul's weaknesses, failures and rejection. As a literary feature, the juxtaposition of the characters Saul and David results in a story-line within which the first

3. Unless otherwise noted, Bible references from here onwards are to 1 Samuel.
4. Here I follow McCarter's (1980: 12-20) division.
5. On the 'Deuteronomistic History' hypothesis (Noth 1943) as it applies to the material in view, see Kratz 2005: 153-221.

character and the model of leadership he embodies function as a negative point of reference against which the second character and the model *he* represents shine more brightly (Grottanelli 1999: 91-104).

In a literary reading as employed below, these two blocks of material—the 'Saul Cycle' and the 'History of David's Rise'—are brought together and regarded as a coherent narration that tells the story of Saul's life and career as Israel's king in a plot that progresses according to a 'rise–fall' or 'success–failure' pattern (e.g. Miscall 1986; Polzin 1989; Brueggemann 1990; Jobling 1998; Green 2003a, 2003b). The turning point of the plot is commonly placed in chs. 13–15, and the motif of rejection is associated with Saul's shortcomings as leader due to his moral and psychical deterioration (e.g. Esler 1998).

Furthermore, some have endeavored to redeem the image Israel's first king and have argued that, especially in chs. 13–15, but also in the later part of the narrative, he is a victim of God's jealous rejection of kingship, or perhaps a victim of the writer's ideological stance, and that his story should be read as a tragedy.[6] However, it seems to me that neither a 'guilty' nor a 'victim' verdict fully applies in Saul's case. My reading will reveal that Saul fulfils more than one literary function in the narrative. He is the 'protagonist' of the story, for he sits at the centre of much of the telling—out of 23 chapters that make the narrative, 17 chapters refer to Saul. Yet, he is also the 'antagonist', for as soon as David makes his appearance (ch. 16 onward), David, whom the narrative favours, takes a leading role, while Saul becomes David's counterpart. Moreover, because he is portrayed as a negative character, Saul may be regarded as the 'foil', especially in the narrative parts describing his encounters with David. However, his attempts, at points, to do the 'right thing' may also earn him a place as an 'ambivalent' character, for clearly there is a tendency in the story to interlace positive and negative qualities and attitudes in his portrayal. Needless to say, all these make Saul a complex, multifaceted literary personage whose characterization may open more than one interpretive possibility.

So, whether a consequence of anti-monarchic and/or pro-Davidic ideologies, or the result of some kind of narrative logic, it seems from the summary discussion given here that the rejection of Saul is commonly associated in biblical scholarship with his shortcomings as leader; and indeed, that appears to be a point the narrative itself makes strongly.[7] Such an inference may then

---

6. The most prominent proponent of this view has been Gunn (1980). On this regard, see also Humphreys (1978, 1980, 1982; 1985: 23-66), who puts a historical spin on the argument by suggesting that the tragic tones within Saul's story are remnants from an earlier form of the material, Exum (1992), who treats the tragic aspects of Saul's story as elements in a larger pattern of tragedy available in the Hebrew Bible, and Nicholson (2002), who reassesses the story in light of two extra-biblical works of literature.

7. On this, see Măcelaru 2009 and 2012: 51-94.

lead to the conclusion that in 1 Samuel it is not Saul as an individual, but his office and what he represents, that is, a human alternative to divine kingship, that are rejected. I propose, however, that there is an additional 'measuring rod' that applies to Saul in this narrative that has been neglected by scholars. Since Saul's inadequacy is 'accomplished' in the text by setting him in continuous contrast with other (male) characters (e.g. David, Samuel, Jonathan), it seems plausible to proceed with the assumption that Saul is not measured here only as a leader vis-à-vis other leaders but also as a man vis-à-vis other men. This being the case, I suggest that an examination of Saul 'the man', that is, of how masculinity, or the lack of, is expressed in Saul's story, is called for.

2. Research Context

The study of masculinity in Hebrew Bible narratives is an endeavour that hardly needs justification. Most interpreters nowadays will accept that there is no such thing as gender-free texts (Brenner and van Dijk-Hemmes 1993; Brenner 1997), for neither authors nor readers can escape being 'socialized into their gender roles according to the norms prevalent in or aimed at in their communities' (Brenner 1997: 1). Adding to this the presumption that most, if not all, of the Hebrew Bible is the work of an elite class of (unsurprisingly!) men,[8] it seems logical to conclude that assumptions of masculinity are embedded in the text. This being the case, undertaking an analysis of such assumptions becomes a must.

The investigation proposed here is closely connected with the work of David Clines. His analysis of David's masculinity in the books of Samuel (Clines 1995a) is the text that has established a framework for undertaking such an analysis with reference to the portretization of other characters in the same biblical material,[9] such as Saul in this study.

Although some variation is present, in his works Clines has identified five basic traits that seem to describe the portrayal of masculinity in the Hebrew Bible: (1) prowess in battle expressed via such notions as strength, bravery and capacity for violence, the end aim being to exert dominance over other men; (2) powerful and persuasive speech visible in one's capacity to convince others to a certain course of action; (3) womanlessness seen in the lack of male–female bonding in one's life and also in the ability to use

---

8. The 'patriarchal' nature of the biblical text has been discussed in the past several decades by an entire host of feminist biblical scholars. To exemplify, see the works of Trible (1978, 1984) and Schüssler-Fiorenza (1983).

9. Clines has applied the initial insights of his study on David to other texts and characters in both the Hebrew Bible and the New Testament; see, e.g., Clines 1995b, 2003, 2010.

relationships with women to one's personal advantage; (4) male bonding seen in one's capacity to attract and maintain relationships with other males; (5) and beauty, seen as personal appearance that is out of ordinary. Taking the repetitive occurrence of these characteristics as an indication of their broad applicability, I would venture to suggest that we consider Clines's description of masculinity as a norm with regard to the Hebrew Bible and therefore use it as the rod against which biblical portrayals of masculinity can be measured. Thus, I will ask below to what extent Saul's description conforms to Clines's categories and to what extent it challenges those analytical categories.

3. *Methodological Framework*

The analysis that follows makes no direct claims in regard with the historical reality behind the text. It is however assumed that the narrative is strongly connected to both the context in which it emerged, as a witness to its ideological milieu, and to the contexts of its reception, in which it helps shape beliefs and attitudes; and since such contexts unavoidably include notions pertaining to gender identity, examining representations of masculinity in the biblical text may come to be for the interpreter an act of self-exploration and self-analysis. This brings in view the equally important fact that the perspective of the reader, that is, the interpreter's own understanding of masculinity, plays a crucial role in the interpretive process. By this I do not refer primarily to how one sees oneself or others as 'men', for such assumptions are not always consciously defined. Rather, what I have in mind is the particular research milieu influencing the interpreter's choices.[10] In this regard, it should be indicated that a constructivist understanding of masculinity is favoured in this essay.[11]

---

10. Naas (2003: xvii) rightly observes that 'we are always preceded, that we always think, read, and write within a certain history and from a certain origin, within a unique and irreplaceable tradition that exerts an almost unthinkable and inescapable influence over us'. Doherty (2001: 37) provides a definition of gender which incidentally describes the research milieu, or perhaps the 'tradition', informing the analysis of masculinity undertaken below: 'a gender system is a nexus of ideas, images, and practices, functioning at a given time and place in the "real world". People can live within it and follow its rules while remaining largely unconscious of it. It changes over time, but it must be reproduced from generation to generation and thus has important conservative elements. The mode of its reproduction within the family helps to account for its unconscious dimension, as well as its relationship to the individual's sense of identity. Yet it is not monolithic, for it contains internal contradictions, and those who live within it can disagree about its apportionment of roles and power'.

11. The constructivist approach is also the preferred methodological framework for the study of masculinity in the religious studies arena. See, in this regard, Lofton 2004.

Two specific implications result from such a perspective. First, the study of masculinity is the study of gender (as opposed to the study of one's sexual anatomy, which is implied in a positivist approach); and since gender represents an important element in the depiction of one's identity, it follows then that an analysis of masculinity unavoidably is an analysis of identity. As such, masculinity does not and cannot exist in a vacuum, by itself. Rather it is the result of a process of interconnectedness in which one is *like* and at the same time *different* than another.[12] Applied to the case in view, this opens the possibility that more than one version of masculinity may emerge from the same text and it indicates the inevitability of comparison—that is, comparison between alternative versions of masculinity as well as comparison between masculinity and other gender models.[13]

Second, masculinity is a socio-cultural construct: it consists of assumptions and beliefs, it is practiced in social interaction (relationships) and it finds expression in attitudes, behaviour, actions and speech. From these it follows that an inquiry which has 'masculinity' as its object will take into account observable features such as one's appearance, the manifestation of assumptions in one's actions and relationships, and elements of self-definition revealed by one's speech. Thus, the realms of masculinity: Saul's Appearance; Saul's Military Actions; Saul's Relationships; and Saul's Speech.[14]

4. *Saul the Man*

As identified earlier, the scope of the analysis undertaken below is the account pertaining to Saul's life and career in 1 Samuel 9–31. Taking ch. 9 as the beginning of the narrative is an obvious choice because that is where

12.   I follow here Ricoeur's (1990) description of identity in terms of sameness and selfhood.

13.   Although due to the limited scope of the present essay such comparison here is limited to measuring Saul against Clines's description of masculinity in the books of Samuel, I suggest that, generally speaking, the definition of masculinity in biblical texts need include comparison on a larger scale, with both masculine and non-masculine (e.g. female) gender identities.

14.   Incidentally, appearance, actions, relationships and speech belong to a list of narrative elements Alter (1981: 116-17) also suggests as significant in the study of literary characters: 'Now, in reliable third-person narrations, such as in the Bible, there is a scale of means, in ascending order of explicitness and certainty, for conveying information about the motives, the attitudes, the moral nature of characters. Character can be revealed through report of actions; through appearance, gestures, posture, costume; through one character's comments on another; through direct speech by the character; through inward speech, either summarized or quoted as interior monologue; or through statements by the narrator about the attitudes and intentions of the personages, which may come either as flat assertions or motivated explanations'.

Saul makes his appearance in the biblical story for the first time. Placing its end in ch. 31, however, is not the only option, for one could argue that David's lament over the loss of Saul and Jonathan available in 2 Samuel 1 is the true conclusion to the tale. Nevertheless, since *Saul* is the focus of the analysis below, it seems logical to conclude the story with the account of his death rather than with its aftermath.

a. *Saul's Appearance*

Under the rubric of 'appearance' I discuss references to Saul's handsome-ness as well as remarks pertaining to elements in his portrayal that challenge that image. As one may conclude from the work of David Clines, male beauty is a recurring component in the portrayal of masculinity in the Hebrew Bible; and although Creangă (2010: 87-88) has shown that this is not as prevalent a notion as it may be implied from Clines's analysis, in the books of Samuel, where physical appearance is an important part of charac-terization, it is to be expected that Saul's description includes references to his exceptional appearance. Nevertheless, subverting that image, I suggest, is also one of the purposes of this narrative; as such, the ambiguity regarding Saul's portrayal as leader noted above is present in his portrayal as man as well.

(i) *Saul's beauty*. Saul is a good-looking man; in fact, he is the best-looking Israelite of his time. The narrative specifically points this out in 9.2 and the superlative 'there is no one like him among all people' reinforces that description in 10.24. Admittedly, the term טוב alone, used in 9.2 to describe his looks, is ambiguous when used to refer to one's appearance; it may be translated as 'impressive' (so NIV) and as such is not necessarily an indica-tion of handsomeness (cf. Macwilliam 2009: 278). However, seen in the context (e.g. 1 Sam. 16.12—David is טוב ראי, 'good-looking'), it is most likely a reference to a pleasant appearance (cf. Clines 1995a: 221-23). Furthermore, the notable thing about Saul is his height—he stands 'head and shoulders above everyone else' (9.2b). In contemporary contexts, where height is associated with one's strength, authority and capacity for domi-nance (Gawley, Perks and Curtis 2009), physical parameters such as these are an asset in the portrayal of one's masculinity. One could assume that this is also the implication in the description of Saul, for stature is apparently associated by Samuel with one's physical suitability to become king (cf. 16.6), that is, to assume the highest position of power and authority in Israel. However, it should be noted that in the same narrative context height is what makes Israel's enemy noticeable (cf. 1 Sam. 17.4). Thus, in an incipient state, a 'subtle indictment' of Saul may already be present in his description (Bergen 1996: 120). In fact, it does not take long and the depreciation of the value of one's height becomes more straightforward. In 1 Sam. 16.7 we learn that stature and good looks are not as important as they may seem, at least not in the eyes of the Lord. Admittedly, the depreciation here could be regarded as part of the rhetoric of rejection that has Saul's kingship as subject. However, considering the fact that that which is specifically belittled in 1 Sam. 16.7 pertains to physical parameters traditionally associated with masculinity, the decline is not only of Saul 'the king' but also of Saul 'the man'. This is confirmed at the end of the story when Saul's stature comes once again in view. In 1 Sam. 28.20, hearing Samuel's pronouncement of impending doom, Saul, the man who is remarkable because of his stature, loses his advantage and becomes less than ordinary as he falls down to the ground 'in the fullness of his stature'.

(ii) *Saul's illness.* One may of course argue that, strictly speaking, the devaluation of Saul's height noted above does not imply an actual deterioration of his appearance. Therefore, the question remains whether the undermining of Saul's masculinity observed thus far includes the reference to his good-looks (טוב). I argue that this is the case, for one should take note in this context of other elements available in the characterization of Saul that suggest changes in his appearance. The first of these is Saul's sickness. This has been described either as an anxiety syndrome coupled with acute panic attacks (Esler 1998) or as 'paranoia with homicidal and suicidal tendencies accompanied by severe depression and other psychotic components' (Sussman 1992: 13). Nevertheless, as Vartejanu-Joubert (2000) shows, such diagnosing is wanting for it does not encompass the complexity of Saul's situation; and in the context of the argument being made here it is also unnecessary for that which interests us is how Saul's countenance is affected by the symptoms of his condition and not what that condition might have been. The text (1 Sam. 16.14-16, 23; 18.10; 19.9) associates Saul's condition with the coming of a harmful spirit (רוח רע) upon him and records but one visible symptom: raving in a state of prophetic ecstasy (נבא—18.10). Grottanelli (1999: 92-95) rightly observes that this description echoes the other two occasions in which Saul prophesies and concludes that the negative connotation of 18.10 applies to the other two instances as well (10.10-11 and 19.23-24); and if in the first case only Saul's reputation seems to be affected (cf. 10.11),[15] in the second the effect prophesying has on his appearance is clear—he strips himself naked and lays down like this for a considerable period of time (19.23-24). Elsewhere in the Hebrew Bible,

---

15.   Grottanelli (1999: 92) takes the question posed by the people who see Saul prophesying—'Is Saul also among the prophets?' (10.11)—as a statement of disapproval that a man of 'certain nobility', the 'high-profile personality' that Saul is, is 'mixing and associating' with people without a genealogy such as the prophets (if the question 'who is their father?' in 10.12 bears such implications). Cf. also Sturdy 1970.

nudity results in derisive contempt and discredits the one without clothes (Exod. 32.19-25). Moreover, his instances of ecstatic prophesying, which involve loss of composure, could be taken at least as deteriorations of Saul's appearance if not as indications of loss of self-mastery, and therefore as diminished masculinity on his side.[16]

(iii) *Saul's attire.* The mention of Saul's nakedness in the instance examined above leads to a further point in the discussion pertaining to Saul's appearance, that is, his attire. In several occasions throughout the narrative Saul disposes of, or loses, clothing (1 Sam. 17.38-39; 19.24; 24.4; 31.9). As shown by Prouser (1998: 30), in the Hebrew Bible the lack and/or loss of garments has clear negative connotations: it is an attack on one's dignity as it brings shame and humiliation (2 Sam. 10.4-5; cf. Gen. 3.7-11) and it is a sign of poverty (cf. Exod. 22.25-26). On the positive side, when given away, clothes are used to show friendship (18.3-4) and love (Gen. 37.3; 1 Sam. 2.19). Even more, clothing may also be used to add to one's beauty and honour (cf. Exod. 28.2, 40). In light of all these, the possibility of a connection between Saul's loss of attire and a deterioration of his appearance seems plausible. In 17.38-39 Saul willingly gives his armour, that is, the symbol of his kingly power, authority and glory, to David. Although not explicitly identified as such, the armour is associated with Saul's kingly superiority: in 13.22 it is only the king and his son out of all the Israelites that possess armour. Therefore, giving it away seems to be more than providing for David's safety. It is also a gesture that lessens Saul's appearance, for he is now lacking that which has previously singled him out. The loss of attire is continued and even intensified in 24.4 and 31.9 for in both instances Saul is no longer the subject of the action but the one acted upon. Therefore, the symbolic deterioration of his robe in the first case and the removal of the armour off his lifeless body in the second belong in the same category of narrative elements which indicate a worsening of Saul's appearance.

b. *Saul's Military Actions*
In ancient times, the issue of mastery was decided on the battlefield; it was there that one's physical and spiritual resources were put to test. No wonder then that violence, particularly militarily motivated violence, is a prominent characteristic of men in biblical narratives. The portrayal of Saul seems to conform fully to this image, for waging war is the activity that occupies most of his time. Out of seventeen chapters that specifically talk about him in 1 Samuel (chs. 9–15, 17–20, 22–24, 26, 28, 31), ten chapters (chs. 11, 13–15, 17, 22–23, 26, 28, 31) show Saul engaged in some sort of military

---

16. On self-mastery as a measure of one's masculinity in the ancient Near Eastern world, see Satlow 1996; Moore and Anderson 1998.

exploit. There are two types of battles Saul wages: wars against Israel's enemies and conflicts with his real or perceived personal enemies. This shows that the story is not only about Saul the king doing the job he was appointed to do but also about Saul the man doing the job of a man—that is, fighting for his own upper ground, fighting to dominate other men that are perceived as threats.

It comes as a surprise, therefore, to discover that the image of Saul's might and prowess suggested by this general concern with war, upon closer scrutiny, is blurry. The diminishing of Saul's image is accomplished narratively by setting his exploits in contrast to other male characters' actions and by showing that the attitude which defines Saul throughout the narrative is antagonism, bordering on paranoia, towards Samuel, David, and even Jonathan—that is, antagonism towards other mighty men whom he fails to dominate.

Note, for instance, his fear or inability to take charge of extreme situations. In his first battle against the Philistines (ch. 13–14) it takes for Jonathan to engage in an insane act of courage before Saul begins to move. The narrative suggests this by delaying at maximum the moment of Saul's intervention in the battle. In fact, even when Saul intervenes it seems that he only manages to diminish the scope of the victory by forcing the Israelites into an oath which was uncalled for (cf. Jonathan's comment that the slaughter among the Philistines was not great, or not as great as expected 14.30), an oath in which he assumes responsibility for a battle that is evidently out of his control (14.24). The contrast between Saul's diminished masculinity and the 'ideal man' is brought even more strongly in view in the conclusion of this story, where Saul, after failing to subdue the Philistines completely, is (perhaps ironically?) presented as the one who fought valiantly against Israel's enemies.

In ch. 15 Saul fails yet again. He is afraid to complete the *ḥerem* and denies responsibility for keeping some of the spoils. This comes in sharp contrast with Samuel's fearlessness, who does not hesitate to kill Agag, the Amalekite king, even though Saul had informed him that 'the people' wanted Agag alive.

Furthermore, beginning with ch. 16, after David appears on the scene, the deterioration of Saul's image becomes more open, more intentional. In any comparison with David, Saul comes second. He does not have the courage to confront Goliath while David engages the giant in battle and kills him (ch. 17). The song sung by the Israelite women gives David tens of thousands of kills as opposed to only thousands in Saul's case (ch. 18). Even the stories of David escaping Saul's chasing after him (chs. 24 and 26) seem to point out to David's superiority as a man.

As for the end of Saul's story, it is true that our modern sensibilities may prompt, and indeed have prompted, readings that restore Saul's image (see n. 6 above) by portraying him as a hero who accepts his fate and goes into battle in spite of the fact that he knows he will die in it. However, in light of the pattern of deterioration traced thus far, a less romantic interpretation may be closer to the authorial intention behind the narration. This seems evident when considering that in the middle of the story of Saul's end, that is, in between the moment he finds out that he will die and the battle in which this take place, the narrator placed two episodes meant to bring David and his success back in view—the mention that the Philistines are afraid of David even as he is apparently in their service and do not want his participation in the upcoming battle; and the story of David's victory over the Amalekites. These evidently serve to contrast David's prowess in battle and fame as a warrior with Saul's loss of battle and loss of life.

c. *Saul's Relationships*

Closely connected to Saul's actions in war are his dealings with other characters in the story. The standards of a hegemonic masculinity are particularly challenged under this rubric, for as we will see, relationships show Saul's fall, from being the one who dominates to becoming the one who is dominated.

(i) *Saul and women.* Saul's relationship with women conforms to the general picture of masculinity as defined by David Clines. There is no romance or anything of the sort in Saul's life. He has no problem using his own daughters as means to entrap David and achieve his political goals. What attracted my attention in particular, however, is the episode with the spirit medium from ch. 28. There the image of masculinity is once again challenged. It is not only that Saul depends entirely on a woman's capacity to perform her function as a medium, but she ends up tending to his physical needs as well. In fact, the unnamed woman in this episode shows more characteristics associated with masculinity than Saul himself—she shows courage and resourcefulness after hearing Samuel's announcement while Saul falls to the ground in fear, and she is persuasive enough to convince Saul to eat even though he initially refuses to do so.

(ii) *Saul and men.* As one would expect, Saul spends more time with men than with women. As early as ch. 13 we are told that he spent most of his time with the permanent army he created and throughout the narrative he is shown to be together with men who are either his servants or his army. However, there is no indication of a close male friendship. This comes as a surprise considering the fact that one would expect a certain emotional bond between Saul and his son. In fact, one gets the impression from the story that, although permanently surrounded by men, Saul is a loner. Even the two relationships that come prominently in view, the relationship with Samuel and the relationship with David, never have a chance to develop into what could be considered 'bonding', and this, the narrative makes clear, is because of Saul's sinful disobedience in one case and paranoia in the other.

(iii) *Saul and YHWH.* A further point which should be made here regards Saul's relationship with YHWH. Differently than other men in the narrative, who enjoy direct access to the divinity, Saul seems to be cut off from YHWH at all times. He does not get responses to his questions and his relationship with YHWH is mediated by Samuel, although not for lack of trial on his side to deal directly with God. In fact, the attention he receives seems to be a negative one, for he is tormented by an evil spirit sent by YHWH and he is rejected without the 'right to appeal'. All these become obvious shortcoming Saul has as a man when we notice that his 'opponents' succeed in obtaining from YHWH what they want: Jonathan enjoys God's protection as he leads Israel in victory against the Philistines (chs. 13–14), Samuel 'orders' successfully a theophany (ch. 12), and David receives answers and guidance from God in more than one occasion throughout the story. Thus, it may appear that 'true' men in this narrative can access divine power and wisdom at will, something Saul cannot and does not do, thus remaining at a disadvantage.

d. *Saul's Speech*
On the whole, Saul's voice is not heard much in the narrative. For the most part, his interventions are short and scarce—the minimum necessary in order to create the dialogue. Judging from what little speech is available, the characterization of Saul continues the ambiguity that has by now become familiar.

(i) *Saul's persuasiveness.* In the words of Sternberg (1983: 71), 'the final end of persuasion consists in aligning the addressee's view point with the speaker's'. Seen from this perspective there are only four occasions in which Saul's remarks seem to fulfil the norm by producing the expected effect on his audience. The first instance appears in ch. 11, where Saul's victory against the Ammonites is framed by two utterances, the first (v. 7) being Saul's successful call to arms (although one may argue that the gesture of cutting the oxen in pieces has helped his persuasion) and the second (v. 13) being Saul's intervention on behalf of the Israelites who previously did not recognize his kingship (10.27). Both utterances seem to have the desired effect.

The second instance appears in ch. 14, where Saul utters an oath (v. 24) that binds the people to fasting throughout the day. This, we have seen, was an unfortunate initiative on Saul's part and although in the beginning the priest and the people obey and follow Saul into taking the oath, as the situation draws to a conclusion Saul looses authority to the point that the oath breaker gets a free pass, therefore nullifying the impact of Saul's persuasion.

In the third instance (15.6) Saul asks the Kenites to leave their home. However, since the alternative for these would have been the prospect of a war, it is not clear whether their leaving is the result of Saul's speech or of concern for their lives.

The fourth instance is in 28.7-25. Here Saul convinces the frightened female medium to divinate, even though such action was endangering her life. Interestingly, however, the passage shows that in the end it is the one persuaded that becomes the persuader, for at the end of the story it is the woman that speaks and Saul obeys her.

Clearly Saul's persuasiveness is not what it should be. In each instance above the result of his speech is shadowed and diminished by subtle nuances in the story that allow for questioning the motivations behind the action of those presumably responding to Saul's interventions.

(ii) *Saul's confessions.* In several instances throughout the narrative Saul's speech turns into confession. Interestingly, in all such cases Saul speaks in order to point out his failures, weaknesses and errors. There are four such confessions. First, in 1 Sam. 15.24-25 Saul admits his fear of the Israelites and recognizes his disobedience in front of Samuel. Second, in 23.21-23 Saul speaks of his incapacity to capture David. Third, in 24.16-21 Saul recognizes that David is better than him and accepts David's mastery over him as he confirms something everyone already knows—that David will succeed him on the throne of Israel. Finally, in 26.21, 25 the same message is repeated as Saul explicitly admits that David is the victor. All these show Saul as weak and fallible—an image unsuitable for a man—and could be interpreted as Saul's gradual unmanning.

4. Conclusion

The analysis presented here has revealed that Saul's characterization does not conform to the parameters highlighted by Clines as features defining the portrayal of David's masculinity in the narrative of 1 Samuel. Saul's masculinity is consistently undermined in the narrative; so much so, in fact, that one should feel justified to ask: Is Saul a 'man'? The right answer, I suggest, is neither a strong 'yes' nor a weak 'no'. Rather, it is to admit, together with deconstructionists such as Derrida (e.g. Derrida 1978 and

1979) that in the narrative studied here, like in any other text, we are faced with irreconcilably contradictory meanings placed side by side. As such, a definition of masculinity that is specific to 1 Samuel will neither be found in the search for a unifying logic that brings contradictory characterizations together nor in the choosing of a preponderant model over against other, secondary, models. It is in fact the very interplay of opposites, that is, the interchange of different characterizations, that provides the full view on masculinity available in the text under scrutiny.

Given the above, it would seem then that a conclusion in which Saul's characterization is simply seen as an alternative model of masculinity, one that should exist alongside the model identified by Clines in the same text, will not suffice. Undoubtedly, such an interpretation is a strong, valid, possibility, which reflects conclusions reached by previous research regarding the fact that masculinity is a fluid concept and variations of its parameters are likely and indeed available (e.g. Creangă 2010). However, I suggest that the examination undertaken here also raises the question of why would the author of the Samuel narrative be so intent on deconstructing a romanticized image of masculinity that is the prevailing depiction of Israel's heroes in this story (thus the idealized, almost hegemonic, 'male' persona discovered by Clines in the books of Samuel). Is the downplaying in Saul's characterization of superlatives applicable to David just another way in which Saul's unsuitability as king is suggested? Or could the contrast drawn between Saul and other men in the story, although clearly governed by an anti-Saul pro-David ideology, be regarded also as a subtle indictment of the prevailing image of masculinity, undertaken in order to create space for a more realistic depiction of maleness, one that would fit the multifaceted, complex reality, of real-world men and their penchant for acting out varied male identities? Undoubtedly, such indictment is not the primary purpose of the narrative. However, the very fact that a contrast at this level is drawn between Saul and David, the two men in the story who are similarly chosen by God and anointed by the prophet as kings, serves as a pointer to the fact that the different versions of masculinity presented are not to be pitched against each other but rather placed side by side in order to depict together a more balanced image of male identity in 1 Samuel.

Bibliography

Alt, Albrecht
    1966   *Essays on Old Testament History and Religion* (trans. R.A. Wilson; Oxford: Basil Blackwell).
Alter, Robert
    1981   *The Art of Biblical Narrative* (London: Allen & Unwin).

Amit, Yairah
  2000   *Hidden Polemics in Biblical Narrative* (trans. J. Chipman; Leiden: E.J. Brill)
Bergen, Robert D.
  1996   *1, 2 Samuel* (The New American Commentary, 7; Nashville, TN: Broadman & Holman).
Brenner, Athalya
  1997   *The Intercourse of Knowledge: On Gendering Desire and 'Sexuality' in the Hebrew Bible* (Biblical Interpretation, 26; Leiden: E.J. Brill).
Brenner, Athalya, and Fokkelien van Dijk Hemmes
  1993   *On Gendering Texts: Female and Male Voices in the Hebrew Bible* (Leiden: E.J. Brill).
Bright, John
  1981   *A History of Israel* (London: SCM Press, 3rd edn).
Brueggemann, Walter
  1990   *First and Second Samuel* (Interpretation Bible Commentary; Louisville, KY: John Knox Press).
  2003   *An Introduction to the Old Testament: The Canon and Christian Imagination* (Louisville, KY: Westminster/John Knox Press, 2nd edn).
Clines, David J.A.
  1995a   'David the Man: The Construction of Masculinity in the Hebrew Bible', in *Interested Parties: The Ideology of Writers and Readers of the Hebrew Bible* (JSOTSup, 205; Gender, Culture, Theory, 1; Sheffield: Sheffield Academic Press): 212-41.
  1995b   'Ecce vir: Or, Gendering the Son of Man', in J. Cheryl Exum and Stephen D. Moore (eds.), *Biblical Studies/Cultural Studies: The Third Sheffield Colloquium* (JSOTSup, 266; Gender, Culture, Theory, 7; Sheffield: Sheffield Academic Press): 352-75.
  2003   'Paul, the Invisible Man', in Stephen D. Moore and Janice Capel Anderson (eds.), *New Testament Masculinities* (Semeia Studies, 45; Atlanta: SBL): 181-92.
  2010   'Dancing and Shining at Sinai: Playing the Man in Exodus 32–34', in Creangă (ed.) 2010: 54-63.
Craig, Kenneth M., Jr
  1994   'Rhetorical Aspects of Questions Answered with Silence in 1 Samuel 14:37 and 28:6', *CBQ* 56: 221-39.
Creangă, Ovidiu
  2010   'Variations on the Theme of Masculinity: Joshua's Gender In/stability in the Conquest Narrative (Josh. 1–12)', in Creangă (ed.) 2010: 83-109.
Creangă, Ovidiu (ed.)
  2010   *Men and Masculinity in the Hebrew Bible and Beyond* (The Bible in the Modern World, 33; Sheffield: Sheffield Phoenix Press).
Czövek, Tamás
  2001   *Three Seasons of Charismatic Leadership: A Literary-Critical and Theological Interpretation of the Narrative of Saul, David and Solomon* (Regnum Studies in Mission; Oxford: Regnum).

Derrida, Jacques
  1978   'Structure, Sign, and Play in the Discourse of the Human Sciences', in
          Writing and Difference (trans. Alan Bass; Chicago: University of Chicago
          Press): 278-94.
  1979   'Living On: Borderlines', in *Deconstruction and Criticism* (trans. James
          Hulbert; New York: Continuum): 75-176.
Doherty, Lillian E.
  2001   *Gender and the Interpretation of Classical Myth* (London: Duckworth).
Edelman, Diana Vikander
  1991   *King Saul in the Historiography of Judah* (JSOTSup, 121; Sheffield:
          Sheffield academic Press).
Esler, Philip F.
  1998   'The Madness of Saul: A Cultural Reading of 1 Samuel 8–31', in J. Cheryl
          Exum and Stephen D. Moore (eds.), *Biblical Studies/Cultural Studies: The
          Third Sheffield Colloquium* (JSOTSup, 266; Sheffield: Sheffield Academic
          Press): 220-62.
Exum, J. Cheryl
  1996   'Saul: The Hostility of God', in *Tragedy and Biblical Narrative: Arrows of
          the Almighty* (Cambridge: Cambridge University Press): 16-44.
Flanagan, James W.
  1981   'Chiefs in Israel', *JSOT* 20: 47-73.
Gawley, Tim, Thomas Perks and James Curtis
  2009   'Height, Gender, and Authority Status at Work: Analyses for a National
          Sample of Canadian Workers', *Sex Roles* 60: 208-22.
Green, Barbara
  2003a   *How Are the Mighty Fallen? A Dialogical Study of King Saul in 1 Samuel*
          (JSOTSup, 365; Sheffield: Sheffield Academic Press).
  2003b   *King Saul's Asking* (Interfaces; Collegeville, MN: Liturgical Press).
Grottanelli, Cristiano
  1999   *Kings and Prophets: Monarchic Power, Inspired Leadership and Sacred
          Text in Biblical Narrative* (Oxford: Oxford University Press).
Gunn, David M.
  1980   *The Fate of King Saul: An Interpretation of a Biblical Story* (JSOTSup,
          14; Sheffield: JSOT Press).
Halpern, Baruch
  1981   *The Constitution of the Monarchy in Israel* (HSM, 25; Atlanta, GA:
          Scholars Press).
Humphreys, W. Lee
  1978   'The Tragedy of King Saul: A Study of the Structure of 1 Samuel 9–31',
          JSOT 6: 18-27.
  1980   'The Rise and Fall of King Saul: A Study of an Ancient Narrative Stratum
          in 1 Samuel', *JSOT* 18: 74-90.
  1982   'From Tragic Hero to Villain: A Study of the Figure of Saul and the
          Development of 1 Samuel', *JSOT* 22: 95-117.
  1985   *The Tragic Vision and the Hebrew Tradition* (OBT, 18; Philadelphia:
          Fortress Press).
Jobling, David
  1998   *1 Samuel* (Berit Olam; Collegeville, MN: Liturgical Press).

Kratz, Reinhard Gregor
  2005   *The Composition of the Narrative Books of the Old Testament* (trans. John
          Bowden; London: T. & T. Clark).
Lofton, Kathryn
  2004   'The Man Stays in the Picture: Recent Works in Religion and Mascu-
          linity', *RSR* 30: 23-28.
Măcelaru, Marcel V.
  2009   'Israel in Transition: Liminality and Status Change in 1 Samuel 8–15', in
          C. Constantineanu and M.V. Măcelaru (eds.), *Bible, Culture, Society:
          Postgraduate Explorations* (Osijek: Evanđeoski teološki fakultet): 39-64
  2012   *Identitatea între povară şi privilegiu: reprezentări ale poporului sfânt în
          literatura deuteronomistă* (Cluj Napoca: Risoprint).
Macwilliam, Stuart
  2009   'Ideologies of Male Beauty and the Hebrew Bible', *BibInt* 17: 265-87.
McCarter, P. Kyle, Jr
  1980   *I Samuel: A New Translation with Introduction, Notes and Commentary*
          (AB, 8; Garden City, NY: Doubleday).
McKenzie, Steven L.
  2000   'The Trouble with Kingship', in Albert de Pury, Thomas C. Römer and
          Jean-Daniel Macchi (eds.), *Israel Constructs its History: Deuteronomistic
          Historiography in Recent Research* (JSOTSup, 306; Sheffield: Sheffield
          Academic Press): 286-314.
Miller, J. Maxwell
  1974   'Saul's Rise to Power: Some Observations Concerning 1 Sam 9:1–10:16;
          10:26–11:15 and 13:2–14:46', *CBQ* 36: 157-74.
Miscall, Peter D.
  1986   *1 Samuel: A Literary Reading* (Indiana Studies in Biblical Literature;
          Bloomington: Indiana University Press).
Moore, Stephen D., and Janice Capel Anderson
  1998   'Taking it Like a Man: Masculinity in 4 Maccabees', *JBL* 117: 249-73.
Naas, Michael
  2003   *Taking on the Tradition: Jacques Derrida and the Legacies of Decon-
          struction* (Stanford, CA: Stanford University Press).
Nicholson, Sarah
  2002   *Three Faces of Saul: An Intertextual Approach to Biblical Tragedy*
          (JSOTSup, 339; London: Sheffield Academic Press).
Noth, Martin
  1943   *Schriften der Königsberger Gelehrten Gesellschaft* (Geisteswissen-
          schaftliche Klasse, 18; Halle: Max Niemeyer): 43-266 (reprinted as *Über-
          lieferungsgeschtliche Studien. I. Die sammelnden und bearbeitenden
          Geschichtswerke im Alten Testament* [Tübingen: Max Niemeyer, 1957]:
          1–110; ET *The Deuteronomistic History* [trans. Jane Doull *et al.*; JSOTSup,
          15; Sheffield: JSOT Press, 1981]).
Polzin, Robert
  1989   *Samuel and the Deuteronomistic: A Literary Study of the Deuteronomy
          History.* Part Two. *1 Samuel* (San Francisco: Harper & Row).

Prouser, Ora Horn
    1996   'Suited to the Throne: The Symbolic Use of Clothing in the David and Saul Narratives', *JSOT* 71: 27-37.
    1998   'Clothes Maketh the Man: Keys to Meaning in the Stories of Saul and David', *Bible Review* 14: 22-27.
Ricoeur, Paul
    1990   *Soi-méme comme un autre* (Paris: Editions du Seuil).
Rost, Leonhard
    1926   *Die Überlieferung von der Thronnachfolge Davids* (BWANT, 3/6; Stuttgart: W. Kohlhammer).
Satlow, Michael L.
    1996   '"Try to be a man": The Rabbinic Construction of Masculinity', *HTR* 89: 19-40.
Schüssler-Fiorenza, Elisabeth
    1983   *In Memory of Her: A Feminist Theological Reconstruction of Christian Origins* (London: SCM Press).
Sternberg, Meir
    1983   'The Bible's Art of Persuasion: Ideology, Rhetoric, and Poetics in Saul's Fall', *HUCA* 54: 45–82.
Sturdy, John
    1970   'The Original Meaning of "Is Saul also among the prophets?" (1 Samuel X 11, 12, XIX 24)', *VT* 20: 206-13.
Sussman, Max
    1992   'Sickness and Disease', in *ABD*, VI: 6-14.
Vartejanu-Joubert, M.
    2000   'Madness and its Social Background in the Old Testament', *Bulletin du Centre de recherche français de Jérusalem* 6: 175-82.
Trible, Phyllis
    1978   *God and the Rhetoric of Sexuality* (Philadelphia: Fortress Press).
    1984   *Texts of Terror: Literary-Feminist Readings of Biblical Narratives* (Philadelphia: Fortress Press).
Wellhausen, Julius
    1871   *Der Text der Böcher Samuelis untersucht* (Göttingen: Vandenhoeck & Ruprecht).

ATHALIAH: A CASE OF ILLICIT MASCULINITY*

Stuart Macwilliam

2 Kings 11 traces the later career of Queen Athaliah. Those unfamiliar with the story may expect this introductory sentence to herald the celebration of a rare event in ancient Western Asia,[1] an account of a woman in a position of authority and power, and they may be delighted to be told that a whole chapter of Kings is devoted to this the only woman to be sole monarch of Judah or Israel. But they will be disappointed: the picture we are given of Athaliah is curiously hollow; she merely tops and tails the detailed description of the plot to oust her.

Athaliah has not received abundant scholarly attention: apart from the standard commentaries on 2 Kings, she features in two monographs,[2] and a handful of articles.[3] For the feminist commentator, she presents a challenge. She cannot easily be represented as an innocent female victim. She is, after all, a mass murderer. Perhaps this difficulty explains her absence from Alice Bach's 'lists of stories about women' (1999: xxi-xxii); she fails to make it even into the list of 'bad girls',[4] and she appears only sporadically in the ensuing pages of *Women in the Hebrew Bible*.[5] Outside the bastions of academic feminist scholarship, popular commentary frankly condemns her. An online search for the name Athaliah, for instance, will speedily find uncritical acceptance of the biblical account. A flavour can be tasted, for instance, from a blog by the Reverend D.H. Jenkins. In a section called *Devilish Plan* he comments:

*   I am grateful once again to Francesca Stavrakopoulou for her help and encouragement. This paper is dedicated to her and to Geoff Urwin with love.

1.   Other examples of regnant queens in Western Asia include several from Egypt, notably Hatchepsut. Hatchupset is indeed an interesting case; although not a sole monarch—she co-reigned with Tuthmosis III—she is described and depicted as both male and female (Tyldesley 1998: 99-128).

2.   Barré 1998; Dutcher-Walls 1996.

3.   E.g. Barrick 2001; Solvang 2003: 154-71; Branch 2004.

4.   Perhaps because her portrayal does not include the colourful personal details that can be found in that of, say, Jezebel.

5.   Athaliah has had a reasonably distinguished afterlife, notably in Handel's oratorio (*Attalia*) and Racine's play (*Athalie*)

> So Athaliah gave orders that they should all be killed—her own grandsons. Remember: this is a woman who in her youth had seen her husband kill all his brothers because they were a possible threat to his throne. You can see why I say she is the most wicked woman in the Bible. What kind of woman will kill her own baby grandchildren for the sake of her own personal ambition? This woman is much worse than Jezebel—for all her faults, *she* never did anything like this (Jenkins 2013: n.p.; emphasis original).

Coming from an entirely different perspective, Jackie Kestner in *Alabaster Jars* attempts to counter the idea that women in the Bible 'could all be categorized by features such as "married", "reserved", "obedient", "quiet", "stay at home"'. Kestner seems to be employing a rescue strategy familiar from feminist theology. But the section 'Women of the Bible' tells another tale. Athaliah may be restored, but it is certainly not to grace; for it is God, not Athaliah, who is let off the hook:

> God's silence in this story seems telling. Not once does he criticize her for assuming the throne due to her gender, though many preachers have. Instead her faults are the same as many other rulers in Judah; she was wicked (Kestner 2013: n.p.).

There can be no doubt that in the language of *1066 and All That* Athaliah was not a Good Thing, at least to judge from what her narrator tells us. Although she is introduced to the reader as a mother—and there can be no more satisfactorily feminine behaviour than maternal devotion—at the same time the reader will recall that her son was himself not a particularly Good King (he having been ignominiously despatched by Jehu).[6] But the main description of her in ch. 11, though sparse, is telling: she is a mass murderer, and she usurps the throne; moreover, we are to infer from v. 18—as though, given her family background we had not already guessed it—that she was not an aficionado of the Yahwistic cult.[7] Indeed, an important feature in the hostility towards her on the part of the narrator is the fact that she is a 'foreigner' from the Northern Kingdom, with all that that implies as regards dubious religious practices.

---

6. Examples of such devotion can be found in 1 and 2 Kings, for instance, at 1 Kgs 3.16-28; 17.17-24 and 2 Kgs 4.8-37. The alarming case of the cannibalistic mothers at 2 Kgs 6.26-30 seems to me to underline, rather than undermine, the belief that maternal devotion is an inevitable concomitant of gender performativity: the behaviour of the two mothers serves to demonstrate that the effects of famine at Samaria were so extreme that the strongest of human bonds was abandoned. For further discussion, see Stone 2006: 241-41.

7. Presumably we are to infer something similar from the description of her influence over her son at 2 Chron. 22.3.

Patricia Dutcher-Walls comments on the use of 'multiple condemnations' against Athaliah: 'foreign, female, apostate' (1996: 112).[8] It is upon the second of these 'condemnations' that I should like to focus in this study. Dutcher-Walls's inclusion of gender as one of the 'condemnations' of Athaliah has not won unanimous support. Carol Smith directly challenges Dutcher-Walls's position, citing Bathsheba, who, 'also female, and possibly foreign...apparently suffered no such condemnation' (1998: 158). More robustly, Robin Branch states:

> Significantly, the biblical texts offer no condemnation of Jezebel and Athaliah because of their gender above what their sins of murder and idolatry merit (Branch 2004: 556).

And, broadening out her argument, she continues:

> A principle throughout the Bible is that while the writers consistently condemn sin, their condemnation is gender-neutral... While women writers are few and far between in the Hebrew Bible, the text gives no indication that women are ineligible for or incapable of leadership and authority. Furthermore, the biblical writers give no indication that the leadership of women over men is somehow alien to nature (Branch 2004: 556-57).

If explicit statements in the texts are the sole criteria for assessing a narrator's attitudes, then Branch has to be considered justified in her pronouncement. But a broader analysis of literary and rhetorical devices may demonstrate that Dutcher-Walls is indeed justified in giving Athaliah's gender such prominence. And just to make a small start with the comparison between Bathsheba and Athaliah, upon which Smith sets such great store, what is the significant difference between the two women? Smith seems to forget that Bathsheba, however influential, remained a royal wife and mother, and a classic *gebirah*; Athaliah, in contrast, went beyond the contemporary conventions of her gender and sought kingship for herself. And it is this last point that forms one preoccupation of the present study: what does Athaliah's gender tell us about kingship and masculinity in ancient Judah? Another preoccupation is the (presumably) male narrator's presentation of Athaliah: how does he cope with a female king? These two preoccupations overlap to such an extent that it is not possible always to disentangle them. We know of Athaliah only through this text,[9] and it may be difficult to decide at any one point whether the account is impartial or the

---

8. It should be noted, however, that the choice of the word 'apostate' may indicate that its user is herself a victim of the narrator's propaganda, since Athaliah's non-Yahwistic practices, if indeed they are implied in the text, may well be better thought of not as apostasy but loyalty to long-held allegiance.

9. Along with its counterpart in 2 Chron. 22.10–23.21.

product of a masculine or masculinist stance; indeed, it is hardly possible for the narrator not to perform *his* gender along accepted norms when he is describing someone else's gender performance.

Gender and Athaliah

How then does Athaliah's gender contribute to the case against her? From the point of view of queer theory, Athaliah pays the price not only of her supposed non-Yahwistic allegiance and foreignness, not to mention her being on the wrong side in dynastic competition, but also of her way of 'being' a woman. I want to show that Athaliah attempts to resist the necessity to perform her gender correctly and is punished for doing so. Judith Butler is famously/notoriously ambiguous about the possibility of resistance to the demands of gender performativity; indeed, she seems to draw a distinction between the necessity of attempting resistance in terms of political activism, on the one hand, and, on the other, in terms of philosophical theory, the apparent impossibility of subverting a system that dictates the terms in which we think, talk, act and desire.[10] Athaliah offers us an example of the consequences of transgressing gender performativity. She is certainly not the 1990s queer activist, busily subverting the boundaries of heteronormativity by means of drag shows and other transgressive performances. Her resistance is in terms of gender roles rather than irregular sexual desire. Her offence is that she acts as a man beyond her gender, exaggeratedly so, in that she kills *en masse* and takes on the role of king.

Contrasting Performativities 1: Athaliah and Jehosheba

Commentators have emphasized the contrast between Athaliah and Joash: the upstart, foreign queen-usurper vs. the rightful king. Dutcher-Walls, for instance, in her rhetorical analysis of the text, summarizes the opening verses of ch. 11:

> [T]he author has established a case that Athaliah, queen and only Omride survivor, is evil and rules illegitimately. A threatened but legitimate son of the king, the only Davidide survivor, backed by agents representing both the royal house and the temple, stands in opposition to her (Dutcher-Walls 1996: 73).

This too is what one might infer from Mario Liverani's schema, in which the crucial distinction is made between 'la première usurpation' and 'la deuxième usurpation' (1974: 440-41), and this is broadly developed over chs. 11 and 12. Others have concentrated on the contrast between Athaliah

---

10.   For further discussion of this point, see Macwilliam 2011: 18-22.

and Jehoiada, Yahwistic priest vs. Baalistic monarch; in contrast to Athaliah's fleeting appearance and relative silence, Jehoiada's voice is heard through-out these verses—the planning of the coup against Athaliah takes up half of the chapter—and, as Burke O. Long points out,

> Not only does the writer accord to Jehoiada the commanding presence in these scenes, but he defines the temple as the dominant space within which the really significant actions gain their authority and power (Long 1991: 150).

But while I agree that Athaliah is portrayed, even defined, by contrast with the people around her, it is not only males who effect this contrast; there is another comparison within ch. 11 that more aptly demonstrates Athaliah's misplaced, or, rather, misplayed gender performativity. As if to underscore Athaliah's outrageous masculinity, we are presented with the picture of the perfect femininity of Jehosheba: in vv. 2-3, the writer describes how Joash is secretly rescued from the slaughter of his fellow princes by his aunt Jehosheba (2 Kgs 11.2-3); Athaliah's gender behaviour is placed in implicitly unfavourable contrast with that of another woman. Long notes the contrast between the two women, but characterizes it as their reactions to two opposite instincts; for him,

> [Verse 2] simply depicts two women thrown into conflict. One gives in to ambition and denies the biological urge to nurture the young; the other surrenders to the opposite—Jehosheba selflessly offers protection to the child... (Long 1991: 148).

Long has spotted the contrast but sees it as that between an essentialist biological drive and socio-culturally derived temptation. But from the point of view of queer theory, the contrast is between 'natural' and 'unnatural' behaviour, between performing one's gender along the prescribed lines and making an attempt to break out. Robert L. Cohn, perhaps, comes nearer to a performative stance:

> But here the drama pits one woman against another: a mother who slaughters children against an aunt who saves her nephew (Cohn 2000: 78).

Jehosheba performs her gender in exemplary fashion: she puts herself out on behalf of a male; she displays tenderness towards a baby and ensures his nurture (literally so, by saving his wet nurse along with him[11]); having ensured/safeguarded the boy's masculine destiny (*he* at least will be well placed to perform his gender role appropriately), she then gradually retires from the foreground with due modesty. The masculine task of organizing the practical details of the plot to overthrow Athaliah and to place Joash on the

---

11.   The word for nurse at v. 2, מֵינֶקֶת, has its roots in the verb יָנַק, 'to suck'; see Gruber 2000: 277.

throne is handed over to her husband, and she herself withdraws from the reader's view, back to the usual publicly silent role of wife.

It is interesting that the MT displays some gender confusion over this matter of withdrawal. After she has snatched her nephew from death, we are told that a hitherto unknown 'they' hid the baby (masculine plural ויסתרו). This may be simple textual corruption—in the corresponding version at 2 Chron. 22.11, the concealment is firmly attributed to Jehosheba (ותסתירהו, feminine singular, with a masculine singular object suffix); and LXX has the third singular ἔκρυψεν. But perhaps the *difficilior lectio* of 2 Kings is after all more authentic: 'they' are familiar anonymous attendants in the royal household.[12] Dutcher-Walls argues that the masculine plural form here may be 'proleptic for the wider conspiratorial circle to come' (1996: 30-31), the inference being that though the conspiracy had feminine beginnings, it evolved into something very masculine indeed. Perhaps, too, these anonymous males suggest a certain discomfort with any prolongation of this feminine/female initiative—it is surely time to turn to a safer masculinity.[13]

Contrasting Performativities 2: Athaliah and the Queen of Sheba
Athaliah's political circumstances make her performance of gender unique in the Hebrew Bible. The only other reference to a queen as sole monarch seems to be to the Queen of Sheba (1 Kgs 10.1-10; 13; cf. 2 Chron. 9.1-9; 12). A comparison between the two is instructive, if complex. A start might be made with the straightforward observation that Athaliah's foreignness is a source of condemnation, whereas that of the Queen of Sheba presents no problem to the narrator: after all, she is the monarch of a country whose inhabitants were, according to the writer of Joel (4.8 [EVV 3.8]), גוי רחוק, and Israel was under the rule of its (very) male king—she presents no threat to *his* masculinity. Her very exoticism, then, distances her from explicit hostility. But is the narrator making some implicit point by juxtaposing this tale of a foreign queen with the account in the next chapter of Solomon's amatory exploits with foreign women and his consequent slide into non-Yahwistic practices? Marvin A. Sweeney cogently argues for a process of editorial recycling. According to him, a Hezekian Deuteronomistic historian originally used the account of the queen's visit as a means of portraying Solomon 'as the ideal monarch of all Israel and model for Hezekiah's rule'; a post-exilic reworking, or perhaps re-setting, of the account 'portrayed

---

12.   See, e.g., 1 Kgs 1.1: 'King David was old and advanced in years; and although they covered him with bedclothes (ויכסהו בבגדים) he could not get warm'.

13.   Another uncertainty lurks in v. 2 with the word מינקתו; it is Athalya Brenner who causes the confusion with her assumption that it is Jehosheba herself who is Joash's nurse (1985: 30). But her assumption is very unlikely given the specialist and, indeed, ritualistic role performed by nurses.

Solomon as an errant monarch whose misdeeds were set right by Josiah' (Sweeney 2007: 149). The Queen of Sheba, then, is condemned not by her conduct but for her company. To enrich this mixture still further, one is prompted by the presence of the word חידה in v. 1 to add the speculation that the original version used a traditional trope of a young hero proving his masculinity by successfully answering the riddles of a female repository of wisdom—it is, of course, the masculinity not of physical prowess but of mental cunning.[14]

Whatever the origins of the account, if we assess the narrator's presentation in terms solely of the core account in 1 Kings 10, it is difficult to find much hostility towards her.[15] It is true that she comes across as a flat figure: we may reasonably infer that she is intellectually curious and appreciative of Solomon's talents. But she remains undeveloped as a character and we are not even told her name. Her personal relationship with Solomon is left unclear: he may take her breath away,[16] but there is no hint of more intimate feelings. This is the case, at least for the Hebrew version, even if we take seriously Alice Ogden Bellis's surmise that the LXX reading of αἱ γυναικες σου for אנשיך in v. 8 suggests 'that Sheba finds Solomon attractive in ways that go beyond wisdom and wealth' (1994: 18).

Sara Japhet takes a different tack. In her commentary on the parallel account in 2 Chronicles, she argues that 'the literary protagonist is the queen, whose movements open and conclude the story, and who is the subject of most of the verbs'. She concludes:

> Moreover, in spite of the reference to Solomon's perspicacity (v.2), it is the queen alone whose words are actually quoted, and quoted generously so. Solomon is certainly the object of the wisdom tale, but he is merely a secondary character in the story (Japhet 1993: 633).

Yet it is difficult to escape the more traditional view of this account, namely, that all the Queen's considerable presence is there 'to laud Solomon', as Sweeney puts it (2007: 149). The queen may have all the words, but the

---

14. An extra-biblical parallel might be Oedipus's encounter with the Sphinx. While the circumstances are very different, the theme of proving superior to a female source of wisdom is there, as is the trope of the riddle; the LXX uses the word αἴνιγμα to translate חידה in 1 Kings, and this is the word used to describe the Sphinx's riddle in Sophocles' *Oedipus Tyrannus*. See, for instance, line 1525, where there is a splendidly concise correlation between Oedipus's solution of the riddle and his masculine power:
ὅς τὰ κλειν' αἰνιγματ' ἤδει και κρατιστος ἦν ἀνηρ.

15. This is, of course, to ignore the queen's vigorous post-biblical life, for which see, for instance, Bellis 1994: 18-24.

16. Amazement seems to be the force in v. 5 of losing one's רוח; Japhet, commenting on the parallel passage in 2 Chron. 9.4, aptly compares Josh. 5.1 (Japhet 1993: 636).

focus is on the king. Hers is an entirely orthodox and, in Butler's terminology, 'natural' performance of her gender—her function is to underscore
his superior masculinity.

Athaliah: Silences

Just as narrators can achieve their desired effects by including details in
their accounts, so they can convey meaning by what they chose to omit.
Omissions can be insidious silences, sleights of hand that convey an impression by default. 'Treason! Treason!' are Athaliah's last words. Indeed, they
are her only words; otherwise, unlike the Queen of Sheba, she is not
permitted to address the reader,[17] and this enforced silence was perhaps
intended to distance her from the reader's sympathy. But it can be argued
that, despite this literary device, Athaliah had the last word in more than one
way. The noun קֶשֶׁר is significant. Cohn draws our attention to the fact that a
related form of the word is used to describe Jehu's plot against Joram (2 Kgs
19.14); and he argues that its 'repetition here suggests a link between this
conspiracy and the one which launched Jehu, and by extension, Athaliah,
into power' (2000: 79). This echo may very well be intentional, but it is
perhaps of more significance that the noun קֶשֶׁר is used consistently in 1 and
2 Kings (and in two parallel passages in Chronicles) to refer to a conspiracy
against a legitimate king, including that later one against Joash himself,
Athaliah's apparently very legitimate successor, which is why at the beginning of this paragraph I translated קֶשֶׁר as 'treason'.[18] קֶשֶׁר, then, can reasonably be read as Athaliah's last despairing[19] assertion of her own legitimacy as
Queen of Judah. She is making a vain protest against a plot to unseat a
legitimate monarch. One might have expected the narrator to make her cry
מִרְמָה, as Joram cried to Ahaziah when he recognized Jehu's plot against him
(2 Kgs 9.23).[20] If the portrayal of Athaliah is thought to be propagandist,

---

17.   The Queen of Sheba, by contrast, is given four verses of speech in her eleven-
verse appearance (1 Kgs 10.6-9)

18.   So 1 Kgs 16.16, 20; 2 Kgs 12.21 (treason against Athaliah's successor, Joash),
14.19; 15.15, 30; 17.4 (a case of treason by King Hoshea against King Shalmaneser of
Assyria whose vassal he had become). Elsewhere in the Hebrew Bible it appears rarely:
at Amos 7.10 it refers to an alleged conspiracy against the king; at Jer. 11.9 to a
conspiracy against the covenant with Yhwh; at Isa. 8.12 and Ezek. 22.25, however, its
meaning is more difficult to gauge.

19.   'Despairing', of course, because, as the action of tearing her clothes conveys,
she foresees the likely success of the plot and her own death as the inevitable outcome.

20.   מִרְמָה is used elsewhere to denote deceit, usually translated in LXX as δόλος. As
such it describes a moral failing, often referring to verbal deceit (e.g. Pss. 10.7; 50.19;
Prov. 12.17; 14.25); perhaps the deceit of Jacob's son as practiced on Shechem and

then it may be surprising that the word קשׁר has survived the masculinist filter, and perhaps it is a certain discomfort with this verbal weakness that impels the narrator to use the word המלך twice in v. 14. Most readers would agree with Cohn here that at this point 'the scene...is... described from [Athaliah's]... perspective opening with [הנה]' (2000: 79); but, in view of what I have just said about קשׁר, her 'perspective' is that it is she who is queen and not Joash king; so that it is strange that she is so emphatically described as seeing the king. Perhaps we must take this oddity as some sort of prolepsis—she sees acted out before her eyes the impending usurpation of her power.[21] Alternatively, what we are presented with here is the narrator's over-enthusiastic loyalty towards the Davidic dynasty intruding itself into Athaliah's own perspective and in contradiction to, perhaps also in compensation for, her own words—he is not going to let a woman's perspective alter *his* view of the situation. I should like to delay Athaliah's death for a short while in order to compare this, her last, unerased, assertion of her regal status with an earlier acknowledgment of it, this time in the mouth of the narrator himself. At v. 3, she is described as מלכת על־הארץ. The verb מלך means 'to be a king'. It is used fairly frequently in the Hebrew Bible, often in the Hiphil and Hophal forms, in the sense of making, or being made, a king. It is not surprising that it is rarely used in the feminine—exceptions are in the book of Esther (2.4 and 2.17). The feminine participle at 2 Kgs 11.3, however, is not only rare, but significant in the context. This is not an instance of Athaliah claiming regal legitimacy, as I have argued with regard to קשׁר, but of the narrator himself implicitly conceding Athaliah's legitimacy as ruler. This is of course to an extent disguised in most English translations, since there is no one-word verb 'to king', let alone 'to queen', in common contemporary English usage.[22] Most modern translations use the verb 'to reign' or 'to rule', neither of which is exclusively regal. Long, indeed, in an otherwise helpful paraphrase of this verse, sums up her political position with a verb that, to an even greater extent, distorts her regal status:

Hamor is tempered by circumstance, at least as far as the narrator is concerned (Gen. 34.13). Another idiomatic usage refers to false weights (e.g. Prov. 11.1). מרמה at 2 Kgs 9.23, then, is perhaps better translated in terms of trick rather than of treason.

21.   Long may be hinting at such a prolepsis in his comment: '...she discovers what we already know, that her power has flowed to others' (1991: 151).

22.   The *OED* lists historic verbal forms of both these nouns, but they are rare; it is perhaps more significant that the *Concise Oxford Dictionary* (10th edn), under *queen* as a verb, apart from a technical usage in chess, notes only the sense 'to queen it', that is 'to act in an unpleasantly superior way'

> Within the temple's bounds the scion of David survives; outside these
> protective courts, in the palace, Athaliah *presides* over Judah (Long 1991:
> 148; my emphasis).

Judah has become a republic! And yet, in what other terms than those of
kingship can the narrator describe Athaliah's status? Perhaps he could have
used the word שׁפט. He would have thereby provided the authors of the
Theological Dictionary of the Old Testament with yet another example of
the use of שׁפט to connote leadership or sovereignty, in contrast to its other,
perhaps better-known meaning of judgment.[23] But can we imagine the
narrator describing Athaliah with the word that was so closely associated
with the magisterial and charismatic Yahwistic personalities of pre-
monarchical Israel? No, he is stuck with describing her in terms of a status
he otherwise denies her. He prefigures Derrida by putting (Queen) Athaliah
under erasure. In her life, Athaliah is a queen who is not a queen.

But it is time to return to the end of Athaliah's life. In the Hebrew Bible a
woman's death is a private matter; we should hear nothing of it. There are
occasional exceptions, some of them portrayed with the narrator's approval
of the woman concerned. Perhaps the most elaborate is the description of
Sarah's death and burial (Gen. 23.1-20);[24] other women of the times of the
Patriarchs whose deaths rate a mention include Deborah, the nurse of
Rebecca (Gen. 35.8) and Rachel (Gen. 35.16-19). At a later period, there is
a brief mention of Miriam's death and burial (Num. 20.1). Otherwise,
mention of a woman's death is an indicator of misfortune or misdeed. Lot's
wife, for example, famously pays the price of disobedience (Gen. 19.26).
But the woman whose death may be uppermost in our minds at this point is
Athaliah's own putative mother, Jezebel. Both women are the objects of
narratorial condemnation, and both, to one extent or another, pursue their
careers in an unwomanly fashion. Jezebel is the manipulative power behind
the throne; she unduly influences her husband's actions (1 Kgs 21.25), and
in doing so can be said to have unmanned him.[25] There is a certain resonance
too in their post-mortem annihilation: Jezebel's body is left to be eaten by
dogs; she is deprived of burial and remembrance (1 Kgs 9.36-37). As for

---

23.   For a discussion of the range of meanings of שׁפט, see Niehr 1993. For examples of its use in the sense of sovereignty, see 1 Sam. 8.5-6, 20.

24.   Although even in Sarah's case the actual death is briefly described; the rest of
the account deals with Abraham's arrangements for her burial.

25.   In this respect her behaviour is mirrored by Athaliah's: at 2 Kgs 8.18,
Athaliah's husband, King Jehoram of Judah, is accused of walking 'in the way of the
kings of Israel, as the house of Ahab had done, for the daughter of Ahab was his wife'.
As Elna K. Solvang comments, she 'is charged with causing kingship in Judah to become
like the "house of Ahab"' (2003: 154).

Athaliah, it is the narrator himself who effects the disappearance of her body—we hear nothing of her burial, and she is forgotten as soon as she is dead. There are, however, one or two significant differences between mother and daughter. Jezebel never wholly abandons her femininity: in her life she stops short of taking regal power for herself; and it is from her private quarters, surrounded by her eunuchs, that she is propelled to her death. Moreover, her preparations for the meeting with Jehu are described with such an emphasis on her femininity that some commentators have assumed that she was planning to seduce him.[26] Athaliah, on the other hand, is already in the public space, and we have no record of the femininity or otherwise of her appearance—although the tearing of her clothes may be seen as the performance of a role that is usually a masculine practice.[27] As for the extended description of her death, Dutcher-Walls makes an interesting comparison with that of Joash, her successor (his death is described in 2 Kgs 12.21), and notes the great contrast between the elaborate portrayal of her demise to the single sentence afterword of his:

> Little rhetorical shaping is seen and the assassination seems to carry little ideological weight. It seems to be included in the regnal closing formula as a [*sic*] annalistic notation only (Dutcher-Walls 1996: 156).

The narrator's silence about Athaliah's words and burial is matched by his silences about her life in general. The most obvious silence, pointed out by most commentators, is the absence of the usual formulae that begin and end a king's reign; at one end, typically they state the king's age at succession, the length of the reign and the name of his mother; at the other, they give the place of burial and the name of the successor; they often add a statement about the king's virtues or otherwise, from the point of view of the editor.[28] Between the regnal formula that ends Ahaziah's reign (2 Kgs 9.27-28) and the one that begins Joash's (2 Kgs 12.1-4), there is a gap of six or seven years unmarked by any formal statement. Commentators are generally agreed that this narratorial silence implies the illegitimacy of Athaliah's tenure of power: John Gray, for instance, notes that her 'reign…is not intro-duced or rounded off with the usual editorial notes and comments; this shows that it was regarded as a usurpation' (1970: 569; cf. Sweeney 2007: 342). But how can the editor make a formal statement? Athaliah was nobody's son; who would know her age? And would it not be very odd to

---

26. See, for instance, Sweeney (2007: 335) and Cohn (2000: 69-70), both of whom argue that Jezebel is making the usual preparations for a royal woman to be seen in public. It is also possible that Jezebel is being portrayed in terms of the cult.

27. I owe this last point to Francesca Stavrakopoulou.

28. As an example the regnal formulae for Athaliah's son Ahaziah are presented at 2 Kgs 8.25-27 and 9.28-29.

say that a royal woman slept with her fathers? Does not the fact of her gender alone, never mind her religious practices or her nationality, preclude regnal formulae?[29]

And what is in between these absent formulae? Already, before the death of her son, we have read of her family background (confusingly), her marriage (2 Kgs 8.26), her undue influence over her husband (hinted at in 2 Kgs 8.18), and then we learn about the ruthless steps she takes upon learning of her son's death (2 Kgs 11.1). But as to the reign itself, we are told only that it lasted for six years until one day she left the palace and was assassinated. With other monarchs, even those who meet with the narrator's disapproval, we are at least given some statement about their actions and behaviour—consider, for instance, the coverage of Ahaziah's reign at 2 Kgs 8.27-29. It is brief, even terse, but it gives us some indication of the course of his reign. With Athaliah, on the other hand, we might infer from v. 18 that she promoted the Baal cult, but that is all. Otherwise there is complete silence about what she did or how she behaved during her six years of power. There is a silence too about her power base. The narrator gives the impression that Athaliah acts entirely alone, not only in the way she meets her death, but also in her single-handed campaign of slaughter.[30] It is inconceivable, however, that she could secure power and retain it for six years without significant Judahite support. But for the narrator to allow mention of such support would significantly weaken the charge that her reign was a foreign imposition upon Judah, and give credence to the ridiculous notion that *men* could support a *woman* in power.[31]

Moreover, her absence from the core of ch. 11 is an effective narrative device, which, as Dutcher-Walls points out, 'represents her ignorance of the opposition arising to her rule' (1996: 41).[32] What is most significant about this core is that, apart from the scene of femininity played out by Jehosheba (in contrast, as I have argued, to Athaliah's own unnatural behaviour), the major focus is on the traditional masculine preserves of military organization and engagement; the tense scene bristles with weapons and warriors, and there is manly noise: we imagine the tramp of troops as they take up their positions and we are told about their shouts of acclamation, which finally

29.   Branch may be right to see the silence here (she calls it 'omission') as a reference to foreign intrusion; she characterizes it as 'an unfortunate interlude in the Davidic dynasty' (2004: 544). Yet it is also the case that Athaliah's gender would make the traditional formula nonsensical.

30.   In v. 1 there is a succession of third person singular feminine verbs.

31.   So Dutcher-Walls: 'That her wickedness could have had any support in Judah might have been anathema to the Deuteronomist and thus impossible to mention' (1996: 155).

32.   Dutcher-Walls discusses in some detail the ideological significance of the regnal formulae, and of their absence in ch. 11 (1996: 135-39).

alert Athaliah to what is going on; above all, there is the voice of Jehoiada himself: efficiently business-like and determined, it is his voice, not that of Athaliah, that dominates the chapter and that finally silences the queen.

Of Hubris and Death

2 Kings 11 presents a double game of gender performativity, that of Athaliah herself and that of her narrator. Both can tell us something about how masculinity is performed in the Hebrew Bible. The biblical man performs his gender publicly. Some queer theorists may focus aetiologically on the internal psychological reactions to that nexus of stimuli and taboos that confront and surround the developing infant; in the biblical texts, however, we are invited for the most part to observe, and react to, the consequences of that developmental process in the way adults outwardly interrelate with each other. A man performs his gender in terms of both rivalry with other men and contrast with women. With regard to the second aspect, one might state, if a little baldly, that a man must maintain the clear distinctions that 'naturally' exist between men and women.[33] He does so in conjunction with women themselves, who have their part to play in maintaining these distinctions. The woman's ideal pattern of performativity vis-à-vis a man is to be a Jehosheba—to support men without in any way challenging their superiority. She can do so actively—and indeed Jehosheba is an example of active support—but just how active a woman can be without transgressing boundaries is a matter of delicate judgment. The question of the *gebirah* is an interesting case in point.[34] Smith offers a lively feminist debate when she challenges Athalya Brenner's argument that 'outside motherhood and family politics, women appear to have had almost no rôle open to them in ancient Israel's and Judah's political and religious life' (Brenner 1994: 15). Smith replies that the *gebirah* is an example of a woman with real power and influence, although the 'value' of this power is questionable, in her opinion, since it is male-dependent (1998: 148). But, as Maacah shows us, it can be a difficult role to maintain,[35] and Jezebel demonstrates what can happen when a woman overplays her hand and resorts to 'unnatural' behaviour.[36] Athaliah, however, outshines them both in gender hubris. It may be that the

33.   The word 'naturally' is in quotation marks to imply that the process of gender performativity is not natural at all and that a key part of the process of performativity is to disguise its own unnaturalness (for more on this feature of queer theory, see, for instance, Macwilliam 2011: 13).

34.   For discussions, see, for instance, Ackerman 1993; Smith 1998; Spanier 1998; Bowen 2001.

35.   1 Kgs 15.13, a verse gives some support to the suggestion that the *gebirah* had an official position in the royal court.

36.   In her case, as a queen consort rather than as a queen mother.

divine sonship of the kings of Israel and Judah, if we accept the case for this concept put forward by scholars,[37] aggravated the scale of her offence, set in the context of what for the editors of the biblical texts was an exclusively male godhead. How can a *woman* be the divine son of Yahweh?[38]

Given her outrageous behaviour, can we be surprised at the handling of her story by the male editor? If a man has to ensure the maintenance of gender boundaries, how will he cope when trying to describe a woman who so blatantly challenges them? One way, as I have noted, is by silence. But another may be seen in the way he tells us how she dies. For there is a puzzle here—why is her death mentioned twice (11.16 and 20)? Various solutions have been offered. Certainly for many biblical scholars, from Bernhard Stade (1885) until the later part of the twentieth century, the double mention of Athaliah's death was one piece of evidence for hypothesizing that in 2 Kings 11 there is a priestly and a popular source (priestly: vv. 1-12, 18b-20; popular: vv. 13-18a). Gray, while supporting the hypothesis, nevertheless seems to discount the value of the double mention as support-ing evidence, 'since vv. 16 and 20 agree on the death of Athaliah in the palace, and either v. 16 may be proleptic of v. 20 or v. 20 may be a circum-stantial amplification of v. 16' (1970: 566).[39] Burke O. Long offers a different explanation:

> The mention of Athaliah's death in v.20 seems less a second report than a summarizing statement of circumstances to conclude the narrative (Long 1991: 147).

And perhaps this is what versions are trying to convey when they translate the verb into the English pluperfect.[40] Yet these attempts to explain away the oddity of the double mention do not quite succeed. Some doubt lingers about the location of the death scene. Both verses agree that it takes place outside the Temple, and perhaps this is the crucial information they wish to convey. In v. 20 it seems clear that despite both a minor blip in the textual tradition and the omission of the location altogether in the parallel verse in Chronicles

---

37.   For discussions of this issue, see, for instance, Widegren 1951; Johnson 1955; Wyatt 2005 and 2010.

38.   Interestingly, Hatchupset seems to have had no such problems. According to Joyce Tyldesley, by Year 7 of her regency her titles included the terms 'Female Horus of Fine Gold, King of Upper and Lower Egypt...' (1998: 99). It may be relevant to note that there was no separate word for 'queen' in ancient Egyptian.

39.   Yet a little later he does see a discrepancy in that in 'vv. 13-18a the death of Athaliah is after the anointing of Joash, but before the covenant with God and the people; in vv. 4-12, 18b-20 it is after these events, when the excitement had died down' (1970: 567).

40.   So NRSV, NIV and JPS. The Hebrew verb can indeed convey the pluperfect; equally it can convey the simple past.

(2 Chron. 24.21), the location is within the palace area (בחצר בית המלך, 'at/in the court of the house of the king'). But at v. 16 the location is less clear. The ambiguity is captured well by NRSV: '...she went through the horses' entrance to the king's house, and there she was put to death'. Did she die *in* the palace or *at* the gate? In other words, does 'the king's house' belong syntactically to the horses' entrance or her verb of motion? This ambiguity in the English reflects, whether accidentally or not, an ambiguity in the Hebrew.[41] Commentators vary in their treatment of the phrase. Gray's translation, for instance, removes the ambiguity and prefers Athaliah to go 'into the palace' (1970: 576). Sweeney, on the other hand, translates, '...and she came to the entryway of the horses at the house of the king...' (2007: 341). Lloyd M. Barré's position is odd: on the one hand, he sides with Gray's statement that vv. 16 and 20 agree on the palace as the location of the death (1988: 26); on the other, his own translation of v. 16 does not bring Athaliah quite into the palace itself: 'And when she had gone as far as the entrance where the horses enter the palace grounds, there she was executed' (1988: 35).[42] To place Athaliah's death outside the palace is attractive on purely literary grounds: it conveys the impression that Athaliah does not belong either in the temple or in the palace. She dies, therefore, as she lived, in no-(wo)man's-land.

The puzzle of Athaliah's death is difficult to resolve: the narrative presents the reader with two separate, and possibly contradictory, descriptions. But perhaps the double death should be read not as some by-product of the editorial process but as a reflexion on gender; as such it echoes the overall tenor of the chapter. Athaliah's career threatens to reveal the artificiality of gender: if a woman can survive for six years in power, what does that say about masculinity; what is the point of a man? Further, in his study of Judges 9 Ken Stone argues that 'when the manhood of [Israel's] kings is represented so often at risk, the manhood of Israel itself is seen to be uncertain' (Stone 2007: 199). The masculinity of every Israelite man, including that of the narrator, is compromised if Athaliah can be seen as a successful queen/king. The narrator of 2 Kings 11 responds manfully: to emphasize Athaliah's unnatural presumption he has recourse to judicious silences and omissions, and lingers on the very masculine plot to overthrow her; finally, he ensures that the reader knows she really has failed and really is dead by killing her twice, as though stamping with needless, frightened repetition on some strange and repugnant insect.

41. בית המלך, of course, cannot be a part of the construct chain דרך־מבוא הסוסים, but it could 'belong' to it less formally as a quasi-prepositional phrase.

42. It is interesting that Barré sees v. 20 as an expansion based on v. 16b, which is concerned to convey the 'proper location' of Athaliah's death (1988: 35). The interpolator, then, did not feel that the original narrator had made it sufficiently clear where the death had taken place.

Bibliography

Ackerman, Susan
 1993 'The Queen Mother and the Cult in Ancient Israel', *JBL* 112: 385-401.
Bach, Alice
 1999 *Women in the Hebrew Bible: A Reader* (New York: Routledge).
Barré, Lloyd M.
 1988 *The Rhetoric of Political Persuasion* (CBQMS, 20; Washington, DC: Catholic Biblical Association of America).
Barrick, W. Boyd
 2001 'Another Shaking of Jehoshaphat's Family Tree: Jehoram and Ahaziah Once Again', *VT* 51: 9-25.
Bellis, Alice Ogden
 1994 *Helpmates, Harlots, and Heroes: Women's Stories in the Hebrew Bible* (Louisville, KY: Westminster/John Knox Press).
Bowen, Nancy R.
 2001 'The Quest for the Historical Gebira', *CBQ* 63: 597-618.
Branch, Robin
 2004 'Athaliah, a Treacherous Queen: A Careful Analysis of her Story', *In die Skriflig* 38: 537-59.
Brenner, Athalya
 1985 *The Israelite Woman: Social Role and Literary Type in Biblical Narrative* (Sheffield: JSOT Press).
 1994 *A Feminist Companion to Samuel and King* (Feminist Companion to the Bible, 5; Sheffield: Sheffield Academic Press).
Butler, Judith
 1990 *Gender Trouble: Feminism and the Subversion of Identity* (London: Routledge [1999 reprint with rev. preface]).
Cohn, Robert L.
 2000 *2 Kings* (Berit Olam: Studies in Hebrew Narrative and Poetry; Collegeville, MN: Liturgical Press).
Dutcher-Walls, Patricia
 1996 *Narrative Art, Political Rhetoric: The Case of Athaliah and Joash* (JSOTSup, 209; Sheffield, Sheffield Academic Press).
Gray, John
 1970 *I & II Kings: A Commentary* (OTL; London: SCM Press, 2nd edn).
Gruber, Mayer I.
 2000 'Nurse of Joash', in Carol Meyers (ed.), *Women in Scripture: A Dictionary of Named and Unnamed Women in the Hebrew Bible, the Apocryphal/ Deuterocanonical Books and the New Testament* (Grand Rapids: Houghton Mifflin): 277.
Japhet, Sara
 1993 *I & II Chronicles: A Commentary* (London: SCM Press).
Jenkins, David Haydn
 2013 *Athaliah: Revdhj's Weblog*. Cited 11 May 2013. Online: http://revdhj. wordpress.com/2011/02/12/atheliah/.
Johnson, Aubrey Rodway
 1955 *Sacral Kingship in Ancient Israel* (Cardiff: University of Wales Press).

Kestner, Jackie
  2013   *Alabaster Jars*. Cited 8 January 2013. Online: http://www.alabaster-jars.com/womenindex.html.
Liverani, Mario
  1974   'L'histoire de Joas', *VT* 34: 438-53.
Long, Burke O.
  1991   *2 Kings* (FOTL, 10; Grand Rapids: Eerdmans).
Macwilliam, Stuart
  2011   *Queer Theory and the Prophetic Marriage Metaphor in the Hebrew Bible* (BibleWorld; Sheffield: Equinox).
Niehr, H.
  1993   'שׁפט', in *TDOT*: XV, 411-31.
Smith, Carol
  1998   '"Queenship" in Israel? The Cases of Bathsheba, Jezebel and Athaliah', in John Day (ed.), *King and Messiah in Israel and the Ancient Near East: Proceedings of the Oxford Old Testament Seminar* (JSOTSup, 270; Sheffield: Sheffield Academic Press): 142-62.
Solvang, Elna K.
  2003   *A Woman's Place Is in the House: Royal Women of Judah and their Involvement in the House of David* (JSOTSup, 349; Sheffield: Sheffield Academic Press).
Spanier, Ktziah
  1998   'The Northern Israelite Queen Mother in the Judaean Court: Athalia and Abi', in Meir Lubetski (ed.), *Boundaries of the Ancient Near Eastern World: A Tribute to Cyrus H. Gordon* (JSOTSup, 273; Sheffield: Sheffield Academic Press): 136-49.
Stade, Bernhard
  1885   'Anmerkungen zu 2 Kö. 10–14', *ZAW* 5: 275-97.
Stone, Ken
  2006   '1 and 2 Kings', in Deryn Guest (ed.), *The Queer Bible Commentary* (London: SCM Press): 222-50.
  2007   'Gender Criticism: The Unmanning of Abimelech', in Gale A. Yee (ed.), *Judges and Method: New Approaches in Biblical Studies* (Minneapolis: Fortress Press, 2nd edn): 183-201.
Sweeney, Marvin A.
  2007   *I & II Kings: A Commentary* (OTL; Louisville, KY: Westminster/John Knox Press).
Tyldesley, Joyce
  1998   *Hatchepsut: The Female Pharaoh* (London: Penguin Books).
Widegren, G.
  1951   *The King and the Tree of Life in Ancient Near Eastern Religion* (Uppsala: Lundequistska).
Wyatt, Nicolas
  2005   *'There's such divinity doth hedge a king': Selected Essays of Nicolas Wyatt on Royal Ideology in Ugaritic and Old Testament Literature* (London: Ashgate).
  2010   'Royal Religion in Ancient Judah', in F. Stavrakopoulou and J. Barton (eds.), *Religious Diversity in Ancient Israel and Judah* (LHBOTS, 422; London: T. & T. Clark): 61-81.

MASCULINITIES IN PROVERBS:
AN ALTERNATIVE TO THE HEGEMONIC IDEAL

Hilary Lipka

Masculinity is a performance upon which men are judged, both by themselves and by others. Yet while in all societies there are notions of what masculine performance ideally should be, there is a lot of variation as to what is considered most important in regards to excelling in the art of performing masculinity. When one reads the Hebrew Bible with an eye towards ideals of masculine performance, one finds that there is a hegemonic masculine ideal that pervades many biblical texts. Yet at the same time, there are many glimpses of other views towards masculinities, and in some biblical texts, a model of masculinity presented that is quite different from the hegemonic ideal. In this study I will consider the model of manhood presented in the book of Proverbs, which in some aspects overlaps with the hegemonic masculine ideal found in other parts of the Hebrew Bible, but in other ways represents quite a departure from it.

By now there is widespread scholarly consensus that when we talk about the construction of masculinity within a given culture, we are really talking about multiple masculinities and, in fact, a whole spectrum of relative masculinities. At one end of the spectrum is what is termed hegemonic masculinity, the predominant cultural ideal within a given culture at a particular time, and then there is something of a sliding scale of other masculinities whose relationship with the hegemonic model can generally be characterized as one of complicity, subordination, or marginalization.[1] The

---

1. While hegemonic masculinity at one end of the spectrum is the form that embodies the current, predominant cultural ideal of masculinity, complicit masculinities include those who cannot quite perform at the level of hegemonic ideal, but support the ideal and benefit from its predominance. Subordinated masculinities are those that are stigmatized, considered inadequate or inferior, and sometimes oppressed by those who support and benefit from the hegemonic ideal. Men whose masculinity falls into this part of the spectrum are sometimes viewed as having qualities associated with femininity. At the far end of the spectrum are marginalized masculinities, which are often associated with certain racial or ethnic minorities within a particular culture, those with severe physical disabilities, or those possessing a stigmatized sexuality. Marginalized masculinities are subverted and de-legitimized by the socially dominant masculinities, and thus those who

relationship between hegemonic masculinity and other masculinities on the spectrum is not fixed, and the continuing predominance of the current hegemonic ideal at any given point is never a given. In order to retain dominance, the hegemonic ideal will often have to evolve over time, changing as society changes, reflecting evolving societal norms and mores, the effects of shifting politics, and changes in socio-economic conditions. It will have to adapt to new circumstances by reconfiguring itself, sometimes appropriating and incorporating aspects of other, relative masculinities in order to do so effectively. A hegemonic ideal that does not evolve to reflect new social realities will not remain hegemonic for very long.[2]

The Hegemonic Masculine Ideal in Biblical Texts

The biblical evidence indicates that ancient Israel was no exception in its construction of masculinity,[3] and in fact there was a rather wide spectrum of relative masculinities whose relationship with the hegemonic ideal spanned the entire range from complicity to subordination to marginalization.[4] While

fall at this end of the spectrum often have the least authority and social status. On the idea that each culture has multiple masculinities and for a discussion on the interrelationships between them, see Carrigan, Connell, and Lee 1997; Connell 2005: 36-37, 76-81; Connell and Messerschmidt 2005; Howson 2006: 55-79; Aboim 2010: 2-5, 41-50; and Buchbinder 2012: 90-95. Anthony Synnott (2009: 11-24) expands upon the idea of multiple masculinities, contending that the construction of masculinity within a given culture should be viewed as a continuum. Virginia Burrus (2006: 1-8) makes a similar assertion about masculinities in the ancient Mediterranean world, contending that they should be seen as comprising a dynamic spectrum of relative masculinities. As we shall see, the same can also be said for ancient Israel.

2. Connell 2005: 37-39, 76-81; Buchbinder 2012: 94-95; Aboim 2010: 54-60; and Synnott 2009: 12.

3. This section on the hegemonic masculine ideal in ancient Israel was first presented in slightly different form as part of a paper entitled 'Shaved Beards and Bared Buttocks: Shaming through Emasculation in Biblical Texts', presented at the *Mapping Ancient Near Eastern Masculinities* conference, Penn Museum, University of Pennsylvania, Philadelphia, Pennsylvania, March, 2011.

4. Several excellent studies have examined different aspect of the masculinities spectrum to be found in biblical texts. Martti Nissinen, in a paper entitled 'Relative Masculinities in the Hebrew Bible', presented at the *Mapping Ancient Near Eastern Masculinities* conference (see n. 3), focuses on some of these relative masculinities that comprise other parts of the spectrum of the biblical construction of masculinity, demonstrating how complex and multi-faceted the spectrum of masculinities was in ancient Israel. Several articles in *Men and Masculinity in the Hebrew Bible and Beyond* (Creangă 2010) also address the wide range of masculinities on the spectrum. Susan E. Haddox (2010: 15-16) compares how Abraham, Isaac, Ishmael, Jacob and Esau stack up in terms of hegemonic standards of masculinity, and finds that the those favored by God in the Genesis narratives often were not exemplars of the hegemonic masculine ideal. Mark K.

fully acknowledging the wide variety of masculinities present in the Hebrew Bible, and that what was considered hegemonic was to an extent fluid and did gradually evolve over time as societal circumstances changed, one particular masculine ideal appears to be predominant in the majority of biblical texts, which would seem to indicate that it was the mainstream hegemonic masculine ideal in ancient Israel for a considerable length of time.[5]

Hegemonic masculinity in biblical texts is tied to the notion of strength, as expressed by terms such as גבורה, חיל, זרוע, כח, and עז, all of which denote strength,[6] almost exclusively male strength.[7] In order to perform the ideal masculine role, an Israelite man needed to demonstrate several different kinds of strength, including physical strength, virility and dominance in sexual matters, and what can be termed inner strength.

George (2010: 81) discusses representations in Deuteronomy of several lesser masculinities in addition to the hegemonic ideal. Ovidiu Creangă (2010: 101-103) discusses the depiction of marginalized and subordinated masculinities in Josh. 1–12.

5.   This is not to say that all men were expected to live up to this ideal of masculine performance. It was understood that most men could not live up to it, which is generally the case with the hegemonic ideal of masculinity in a given society. The majority of men living in ancient Israelite society fell into the complicit range of the spectrum. While not being able to sustain an ideal masculine performance consistently themselves, they supported the ideal, promoted it, and benefited from it.

6.   There are also several verbs that mean 'to be strong' in Biblical Hebrew, including חזק and אמץ, in addition to the verbal forms of the nouns listed above. There are also other terms that are part of what could be called the vocabulary of masculinity. און can mean either sexual vigor or physical strength, depending on the context; in both usages it always refers to male vigor or strength.

7.   In the few cases where terms of strength are used in the context of women in biblical texts, they generally have a more limited meaning than when used in the context of men. For example, while an איש חיל is a man who possesses strength in every sense, the אשת חיל in Prov. 31.10-31 is a woman of strong character who has the makings of an excellent wife. She is industrious, capable, efficient, virtuous, generous, and wise, and thus worthy of respect, as is the husband who is lucky enough to have her. Nowhere is she described as possessing much in the way of physical strength, much less ability in warfare or sexual vigor, another form of strength often associated with males in biblical texts. Christine Roy Yoder (2003: 427 n. 1) makes a strong case for translating אשת חיל as 'a woman of substance', since this expression conveys all of the qualities associated with the אשת חיל. Other terms of strength are used to describe the אשת חיל in Prov. 31, including the noun עוז and the verb אמץ in v. 17, both of which appear to refer in this context to the high level of industriousness, enthusiasm and vigorous energy with which the אשת חיל approaches her household tasks. עוז appears again in v. 25a, where the term of strength is used metaphorically, and v. 29, where חיל occurs again in reference to the woman's strength of character. Proverbs 12.4 contrasts an אשת חיל with a מבישה, a woman acting shamefully. The former is the crown of her husband, while the latter is like rot in his bones In Ruth 3.11, חיל is similarly used to denote a woman's strength of character.

A man's physical strength was often perceived as tied to his ability and courage in warfare; a man who epitomized this masculine ideal was expected to be strong, brave, good with a weapon, and skilled in battle.[8] The ideal of masculine performance in ancient Israel was so integrally connected to displays of physical strength and ability in warfare that even when Judah no longer had much in the way of an army (or any army, for that matter), the importance of physical strength and prowess in combat continued to be upheld in several biblical texts as part of the hegemonic masculine ideal.[9]

In terms of sexual virility and power, a man who successfully performed the hegemonic ideal was supposed to produce many children as evidence of his potency.[10] He was also expected always to be the active and dominant partner, who had control over the sexuality of both his wife and his household, in addition to, of course, sexual control over his own body.[11] In several biblical texts, displays of physical strength and battle prowess are interconnected with imagery related to sexual virility, revealing that there was a

8. See, for example, the usage of חיל in Deut. 3.18; Judg. 21.10; 1 Sam. 16.18; 18.17; 2 Sam. 2.7; 1 Chron. 5.24; 8.40; 11.22; זרוע in Ezek. 22.6; Jer. 17.5; Ps. 44.4; Job 22.8; כח in Judg. 16.5, 6, 9, 15, 17; Isa. 44.12; Lev. 26.20; and גבורה in Judg. 8.21; Isa 3.25; 28.6; Jer. 9.22; 49.35; 51.30; Ezek. 32.29; 32.30; Mic. 7.16.

9. See, for example, Harold C. Washington's discussion of the laws in Deut. 12–26 as largely a utopian construction in 'Violence and the Construction of Gender in the Hebrew Bible: A New Historicist Approach' (1997: 344-45). By the time Deuteronomy reached its the present form, most likely during the Josianic period, many of its laws had no practical juridical application. Rather, the laws in Deuteronomy reflect an attempt at promoting certain values and creating a national identity. Washington points to the war code as a primary example of this utopian vision, since, as he points out, there was no situation in reality where it would be applicable at the time it was written. He also observes that from the time of the death of Josiah in 609 BCE until the Maccabean period, Judah had no army to speak of, so clearly the laws of war were defunct, and yet they were promulgated all the same. Of course, in time the masculine ideal in ancient Judea did change in order to reflect the new social reality, but it appears to have been a very gradual process, perhaps in part because as long as there was still hope for renewed Judean independence and restoration of the army, a masculine ideal emphasizing physical strength and ability with a weapon could be sustained.

10. See, for example, the use of חיל in Prov. 31.3: 'Do not give your strength (חילך) to women', meaning do not waste your semen on women other than your wife; the use of און in Deut. 21.17, in which a man's son is referred to as ראשית און, 'the first (fruit) of his vigor'; and the use of both און and זרוע in Gen. 49.3 in reference to a first-born son. In Ps. 127.3-5, the connection between masculinity and male fertility is made when the poet compares a man surrounded by multiple offspring to a גבור with a bow full of quivers, and 'happy is the man who has his quiver full of them' (v. 5).

11. See Matthews 1998; Frymer-Kensky 1998: 84-86; Stone 1996: 41-46; and Brenner 1997: 136-39. The following texts from the legal collections demonstrate this connection between a man's honor and his sexual control over the females in his household: Deut. 22.13-21; Lev. 21.9; and Gen. 34.31.

perception at least among some that these two forms of masculine performance were closely associated with one another.[12]

Another quality that was associated with the hegemonic masculine ideal
could be described as possession of inner strength, demonstrated by display
of virtues such as courage, fortitude, self-discipline, and dignity.[13] A large
part of the performance of this aspect of the masculine ideal involved the
display of measured control over one's passions and emotions in potentially
overwhelming situations, such as facing the enemy in battle or confronting
the prospect of immanent military defeat. Men who successfully perform the
hegemonic masculine ideal in biblical texts are supposed to maintain their
dignity and self-control at all times, no matter what adversity and devasta-
tion they are facing.[14]

The epitome of hegemonic masculinity was the גבור,[15] who was noteworthy for his exceptional strength, usually exhibited on the battlefield
and/or through his leadership ability, for his bravery, and for his ability to

---

12. For more on this, see Washington 1997: 330, and especially Hoffner 1966: 327-
29, who points out that sometimes the same image will represent both. For example, the
bow or its arrows is used both as a symbol of masculine physical prowess and sexual
potency (see, e.g., 2 Sam. 1.22; 22.35; 2 Kgs 13.15-19; Hos. 1.5; Ps. 127.4-5).

13. See, for example, the use of גבורה in Isa. 11.2; 30.15; and Mic. 3.8. The term חיל
is used to denote qualities related to inner strength in Exod. 18.21; 1 Kgs 1.42 and 52;
and Hab. 3.19. There are also depictions of men who fail to live up to this aspect of the
hegemonic ideal of masculinity. For example, one of the charges against the defiant and
wayward son in Deut. 21.18-20 is that he has no control over his physical appetites, and
is thus labeled a glutton and a drunkard. See George 2010: 69-70, 81.

14. Thus a man's performance of the hegemonic masculine ideal is often depicted in
biblical texts as being undermined by displays of fear or cowardice at the prospect of
battle (see, e.g., Deut. 20.5-8, in which certain categories of men are excused from fighting, including, in v. 8, any man who is afraid and faint-hearted at the prospect of battle,
lest he 'cause the hearts of his comrades to melt like his'. Judges 7.3 presents a similar
scenario), succumbing to fear when facing the enemy in battle (see, e.g., Jer. 50.36-37;
51.30; Nah. 3.13; Isa. 19.16, all prophetic oracles against the enemy that describe men
becoming so afraid when facing the enemy that they turn into women), or losing self-
control by being overwhelmed by panic, terror and despair when facing a devastating
military loss (see, e.g., Isa. 13.7-8; 21.3-4; Jer. 6.24; 30.6; 48.41; 49.22; and 50.43, in
which such men, overwhelmed by emotion, rather than being described as turned into
women, are likened in their terror and distress to women in the throes of labor or writhing
in the unbearable agony of childbirth). For a discussion of prophetic use of these motifs,
see Kamionkowski 2003: 85-91; Chapman 2004: 64-65; Washington 1997: 346; and
Magdalene 1995.

15. גב, which occurs 159 times in biblical texts, is an intensive form of גבר and
denotes, as Kosmala (1977: 373) puts it, 'a particularly strong or mighty person who
carries out, can carry out, or has carried out great deeds, and surpasses others in doing
so'. גבור often refers to experienced and skilled soldiers (e.g. Joel 4.9; 2 Chron. 13.3;
25.6), elite troops (e.g. 2 Sam. 20.7; 1 Kgs 1.8; Isa. 21.17; Jer. 26.21; and Cant. 3.7-8), or

produce many offspring.[16] As an exemplar of hegemonic masculinity, the
גבור was expected to retain constantly a flawless masculine performance,
which included displays of physical strength, ability in battle, sexual virility,
and courage.[17]

a man who has distinguished himself in military service through brave deeds, exceptional
fighting skills, or exemplary leadership (e.g. Judg. 6.12; 11.1; and 2 Sam. 23.8-9, 16-17).
גבור appears several times in construct with חיל, usually (though see below) denoting a
man of great strength and courage either in regard to fighting in the military or generally,
as in 1 Kgs 11.28; Neh. 11.14; and 1 Chron. 5.24; 7.2, 5, 7, 9, 11. While the vast majority
of the uses of גבור have to do with strength and might, as Kosmala notes, the span of the
term is broader than that, also encompassing those who have a heightened degree of
physical strength or authority, a very high station or position, or have demonstrated
excellence in a particular area, usually one associated with masculine virtues (for examples of these usages of גבור, see Gen. 10.8-9; 1 Kgs 15.20; Ruth 2.1; 1 Chron. 9.13; Ezra
7.28). In Isa. 5.22 there is an ironic use of גבור, in that men who distinguish themselves
in drinking are termed 'mighty (גבורים) at drinking wine and valorous (אנשי חיל) at
mixing strong drink'.

16. In 1 Chron. 8.40 a direct connection is made between the might and valor of
גבורי חיל and their ability to produce many offspring. In Cant. 3.7-8, a looser connection
seems to be made between גבורים and fertility. The Solomon of the Song of Songs is the
lover of many women, and in this passage his bed, perfumed with spices and presumably
ready for love, is guarded by sixty גבורים.

17. I am hardly breaking new ground here. Several authors have already offered
excellent studies on various aspects of the hegemonic masculine ideal in biblical texts.
See, for example, Hoffner 1966; Washington 1997; Haddox 2010: 4-7; DiPalma 2010:
36-39; George 2010: 67-81; and Creangă 2010: 87-88. David J.A. Clines has been the
most prolific author so far on this topic (see the bibliography for a list of Clines's articles
on masculinity in biblical texts). In his articles, Clines identifies several components of
masculinity in the Hebrew Bible based on a combination of character studies of iconic
figures such as David, Job, and Moses, and more general studies on the construction of
masculinity in the book of Psalms and the prophets. In these studies he has included
qualities such as strength, violence, male bonding, detachment from women, powerful
and persuasive speech, honor, and beauty as attributes of masculinity in biblical texts.
While I do see some of these qualities as attributes of hegemonic masculinity in biblical
texts, others are more questionable. Clines seems to be making broad generalizations
from only a few pieces of evidence for beauty as a quality associated with the hegemonic
masculine ideal. I also see little biblical evidence that powerful and persuasive speech is
an attribute of the general masculine ideal. While there is evidence that persuasive speech
was important for leaders, military and otherwise, there is little evidence that is was a
quality expected of the general male population aspiring towards a successful performance of hegemonic masculinity; it was more important that they performed well in battle.
As for violence as a trait of masculinity, while males certainly commit a lot of violent
acts in the Bible, that does not necessarily mean that it was considered an attribute of
hegemonic masculinity. In fact, biblical texts often depict male violence negatively,
especially when it is committed outside of the context of legitimate warfare. For a similar
critique of Clines, see Creangă 2010: 87-88.

Masculinity is a social achievement, in that it is defined by the observation, perception and judgment of other people. As such, it is a performance that must be constantly maintained, and successful performance of masculinity is an accomplishment. One of the results of a successful performance of masculinity in each of these areas was honor within the community, which in the biblical construction of masculinity is very highly prized.[18] A man had a strong sense of honor when his behavior, both as perceived by himself and by others, was seen as conforming to the masculine ideal. Once one or more of these qualities of strength was perceived as lacking, either because a man undermines his own masculine performance through his own behavior or because the actions of another undermines his performance, a man was vulnerable to attacks calling his honor into question.[19]

Yet even while one masculine ideal may be predominant in a particular society at a given time, at any point another model of masculinity may be emerging or even dominant within a particular sub-culture or sub-group of society, reflecting differing cultural perspectives. It is quite common for alternative models of masculinity to exist and flourish among one or more subcultures at the same time that a different, hegemonic masculine ideal is held up by the majority culture. When that occurs, one sometimes sees the phenomenon of competing masculinities within a culture.[20] One example of

18.   While several scholars include honor among the attributes of masculinity, I think it is more that successful performance of the hegemonic masculine ideal results in honor. Clines (2002: 316-18) discusses the relationship between honor and successful performance of masculinity in similar terms, contending that honor is the recognition by the group of a status of a male. On the nature of various aspects of honor in ancient Israel and how it was considered to be achieved and maintained, see also Stone 1996: 37-49; Olyan 1996; and Stansell 1996.

19.   The result in such cases was shame. On the nature of shame, see Lemos 2006: 227-29, who emphasizes the two most important aspects of shame: that it involves how others perceive one and that it is related to honor, in that shame involves the lack of honor. She notes (p. 228) that shame, like honor, is inextricably linked to both what others think of one and to one's own perceptions of what others think of one. See also Kamionkowski 2003: 60-65. Nissinen (1998: 43-52) discusses loss of honor and resulting shame associated with men taking (or being forced into) the passive sexual position during intercourse in biblical texts, since men were expected to be the penetrators, not the penetrated, in matters of sexual performance. Brenner 1997: 138-40, and Stone 1996: 43, 75-81, and 117-18, both discuss loss of honor that results when either a man takes (or is forced into) the passive sexual position or a women under his sexual control is taken without his consent (whether the woman is a willing participant or raped is not relevant, since the man's honor is hurt, either way). See also Olyan 1994: 183-86; Boyarin 1995: 340-48; Stone 1995: 96-98; and Brenner 1997: 140.

20.   See Connell 2005: 76-82; Buchbinder 2012: 91-95, and Aboim 2010: 42-60, on the fluid nature of the relationship between the hegemonic ideal and other masculinities, the idea of competing masculinities, and the way evolving societal circumstances

an alternative model of masculinity promulgated within a particular sub-culture of ancient Israel at the same time that the majority culture was still supporting the hegemonic masculine ideal can be found in the book of Proverbs.

Yet before we begin to discuss the content of Proverbs, we must consider the nature of the text. Proverbs is a collection of material that includes both compilations of folk wisdom and popular sayings,[21] and longer, more deliberately composed pieces. The content in the collection comes from various sources, including probably several earlier collections that were later combined, and the material likely spans a considerable time period and a variety of social contexts.[22] Proverbs 1–9 functions as an introduction to the rest of the collection, providing a context in which to view the proverbs in chs. 10–31, namely that of providing wisdom[23] to inexperienced young men in order to shape their characters so that they make good choices in life.[24] The final form of Proverbs appears to be the result of much editing and redaction, possibly reflecting an intent on the part of the editors to impart a certain unified world view.[25]

can change the relation between hegemonic and other masculinities within a culture. Buchbinder (2012: 158-79) also discusses the notion of emergent masculinities (mascu-linities that move up the spectrum from marginalized to more central roles in relation to the hegemonic ideal) and their potential impact on the hegemonic ideal, in part by presenting socially viable, often competing, alternatives to it.

21. That is, proverbs. On the nature, usage, and purpose of proverbs in biblical times, see Crenshaw 1981: 67-99 and Clifford 2009: 242-44.

22. See Dell 2006: 188-200, for an overview on the complexity and difficulty of dating the content of Proverbs, especially given that there was likely an oral as well as a written stage, and likely several different written stages, for much of the material. Stuart Weeks (1999: 5) theorizes that some of the material in Proverbs might date to as early as the tenth century BCE, and others as late as the fourth century BCE, which seems under the circumstances to be a realistic time frame.

23. Wisdom in the sense it was understood in regard to proverbs in ancient Israel meant knowledge that could be applied to practical situations. On the nature of wisdom in this sense (sometimes called didactic wisdom), see Scott 1964: xvi-xix and 22-23; Clifford 2009: 249; and Fox 2011: 1, 4, who also emphasizes the importance of develop-ment of character in wisdom instruction.

24. The audience for which this didactic wisdom collection is intended is depicted in Prov. 1–9 as young adult males who have not experienced enough yet to have acquired much in the way of wisdom on their own, and who now must choose which path in life they are going to follow—how they are going to live their lives. Many scholars view Prov. 1–9 (and Prov. 30–31, for that matter) as a later composition than Prov. 10–29. See, e.g., Clifford 2009: 244-46; Fox 2011: 4-5; and Scott 1964: xxxvii- xxxviii and 9-17. But some have called this later dating into question, such as Dell 2006: 18-50, and Weeks 1999: 1-5.

25. Thus the consistency of message that one sees in Proverbs, which perhaps one would not expect in a completely random collection. On the development of the book of

Masculinities in Proverbs:
An Alternative Model of Manhood

A recurring theme running throughout Proverbs is the importance of wisdom, along with virtues such as prudence, judiciousness, diligence, integrity, modesty, self-discipline, humble piety and moderation in all things, and of the positive consequences of employing these virtues in one's daily life and staying on the right path, and, conversely, the negative consequences of falling onto the wrong path.[26] Related to this theme, there is a model of manhood provided by Proverbs, offering an alternative, and perhaps even a challenge, to the hegemonic ideal in terms of how a man should ideally perform masculinity.[27] By examining (1) the passages in Proverbs that address the factors that lead to victory in military contexts, (2) the passages that contend that wisdom and strategy are superior to physical strength and ability with a weapon, and (3) the way that passages in Proverbs dictate that male honor is achieved, we can discern a definite consistency in message throughout the book regarding masculine performance.

If one looks at verses in Proverbs that either give advice about warfare or address how military victory or deliverance from the enemy[28] is achieved,

---

Proverbs as involving a long process of collection, collation, editing, redacting, and careful shaping on the part of editors, see Blenkinsopp 1983: 16-31; Fox 2000: 6-12; 2007: 675; 2009: 499-506; and Dell 2006. Proverbs does provide a pretty unified view on many issues, including those discussed in this study, which seems to provide evidence of some careful shaping and redacting on the part of the editors. What cannot be known is how much this unity of world view in Proverbs reflects the actions of the editors and how much reflects a unified world view found in the general wisdom tradition that was present in ancient Israelite society. It is a possibility that the collection in Proverbs in part reflects a wisdom tradition in ancient Israel in which views on many matters were consistent.

26. On this aspect of Proverbs, see, among many, Scott 1964: 24-26; Clifford 2009: 242-53.

27. The emphasis in Proverbs is on performance—how one acts determines one's path in life. On the emphasis in Proverbs on actions, see Clifford 2009: 243, 246-48. Proverbs describes different behaviors and the varying consequences that result from those behaviors. How one acts is what will place one on either the right path or the wrong path.

28. Usually expressed by תשועה. The term generally means salvation or deliverance. It is often used in contexts of war, in which case it can either refer to military victory (see Judg. 15.8; 1 Sam. 11.13; 19.5; 2 Sam. 19.3; 23.10, 12; 2 Kgs 5.1; 13.17; Isa. 45.17; 46.13; 1 Chron. 11.14); or being saved or delivered from the enemy (e.g. 1 Sam. 11.9; Jer. 3.23; Ps. 33.17; 1 Chron. 19.12). In both usages, the victory or salvation is often (though not always) described as either an act of God or done with the help or backing of God (see such a sentiment, for example, in Prov. 21.31). However, in this study we will be focusing on descriptions of military victories and military advice that focus on human actions.

one sees a pattern beginning to develop.[29] Proverbs 11.14 advises, 'Without strategy,[30] a people[31] falls, but victory comes with an abundance of counselors'. Proverbs 20.18 also emphasizes the importance of relying of wise counsel and the centrality of use of clever strategy to succeed in war: 'Plans are established by counsel; so by strategy wage war'.[32]

Not only is the use of wise counsel, careful planning, and clever strategy deemed an essential element in achieving a military victory, but in some Proverbs it is seen as trumping the power of mighty warriors. Proverbs 24.5-6 counsels, 'A wise man is mightier than a strong one,[33] and a knowledgeable man [mightier] than one physically powerful.[34] For by strategy you wage war and victory comes with an abundance of counselors.' In essence, this proverb asserts that brains are superior to brawn in matters of warfare, the implication being that even if an army is made up of the strongest warriors, it will not matter if there is no sage counsel providing clever stratagems. Proverbs 21.22 takes the same sentiment a step further: 'A wise man scaled a city of warriors and brought down its mighty stronghold'. Here again we see emphasized that wisdom is superior to physical strength. A wise man can devise the tactics necessary to scale a city that is seemingly impossible to penetrate, and thus defeat it, despite the presence of the strongest warriors.[35]

The merits of physical strength are also downplayed elsewhere in Proverbs. Proverbs 16.32 asserts: 'He who is slow to anger is better than a warrior, and he who has control over his temper [is better] than one who

29. All translations that follow are my own unless otherwise noted.

30. תחבלות occurs several times in Proverbs, and appears to be a term used exclusively in wisdom literature. It can mean guidance (e.g. Job 37.12; Prov. 1.5) or strategy (e.g. Prov. 12.5). In the context of war (Prov. 11.14; 20.18; 24.6), the latter is the logical choice. On its meaning, see McKane 1970: 429 and Fox 2009: 536.

31. Fox (2009: 536) notes that עם, translated here as people, can also refer specifically to an army or military force. See, e.g., Judg. 20.10; 1 Sam. 14.17; 2 Sam. 10.10; and 2 Kgs 13.7.

32. Similar advice is given in Prov. 15.22, though with a more general context, placing emphasis on the importance for planning and listening to wise counsel for all endeavors: 'Plans are frustrated for want of counsel, while with a multitude of advisors they succeed'.

33. Following the suggested reading of *BHS*, and reading גְּבַר בחם מעז along with the Septuagint and the Syriac (and for מעז, also the Targum).

34. Following the suggested reading of *BHS*, and reading מֵאַמִּיץ כּח with the Septuagint, Syriac and Targum. The MT reading could work, rendering the second part of the verse: 'and a knowledgeable man secures power', but it does not provide the parallelism one would expect.

35. A similar sentiment is expressed by Qoh. 9.13-18, though in Qohelet the situation is reversed: a wise man could have saved a city when it was under siege, but no one thought to ask him. In both cases, wisdom is described as superior to an army's might.

captures a city'.[36] Prudence, sound judgment, and self-mastery demonstrated by a display of control over one's passions are depicted as more valuable for a man and superior in fact to strength and physical ability in battle, and possessing these qualities as better than achieving military victory. Somewhat similarly, Prov. 25.15 emphasizes the power of persistence and the ability to persuade without force: 'Through patience a ruler may be persuaded, and a gentle tongue can break a bone'. The emphasis here is on the power of persuasive speech,[37] which, when used to its fullest potential, can accomplish significant ends. Words are a powerful and, apparently, a potentially dangerous, force to be reckoned with.[38]

It is noteworthy that there are only three verses in Proverbs where the term גבור, depicted as the epitome of the hegemonic masculine ideal in many other biblical texts, appears. The first one is not relevant to this discussion, since it is not used in the context of a person.[39] The other two are Prov. 16.32 and 21.22, both of which, as discussed above, make it a point to downplay the merits of the גבור and his great strength and/or ability in war. The one time that גבורה appears in Proverbs, ironically, the term of strength is put in the mouth of Wisdom, who is personified as a female in Proverbs 1–9. The context is Wisdom's speech about all of the beneficial qualities that she gives those who embrace her, including discipline, prudence, and foresight. In Prov. 8.14-16, Wisdom talks specifically about the qualities she gives kings, rulers, officials and judges that make them judicious rulers who

36. The merits of achieving enough self-mastery to have control over one's temper also comes up in Prov. 14.29; 15.18; 19.11; 25.15 (discussed below) and 25.28, and is a frequent theme in wisdom literature generally. See Fox 2009: 623 and Clifford 2009: 251.

37. Clifford (2009: 247-48) observes that the theme of the power of speech runs throughout Proverbs. The mouth (along with the tongue and lips) is considered the most important organ in Proverbs, and the power of words and their potential both to impart wisdom and to harm through deception is repeatedly emphasized (see, for example, Prov. 6.19; 12.17; 14.5, 25; 17.4; 19.5, 9, 22, 28; 21.28; 30.6). He also points out that both Wisdom and the Strange (and Foolish) woman use speech to attract men, but while Wisdom's words are true (8.6-11), the words of her deceptive rivals are crooked (Prov. 5.3; 9.17) and slick (Prov. 2.16; 6.24; 7.5).

38. Very similar to this is a line from 'The Words of Ahiqar', an Aramaic wisdom text found at Elephantine that likely dates to the fifth century BCE: 'Soft is the tongue of a king, but it breaks a dragon's ribs; like a plague, which is not seen' (105; trans. Ginsberg 1958: 246). Both express the potentially dangerous power that can come with gentle speech. Ben Sira (Sirach) 28.17 also has a somewhat similar statement about the potential danger of words: 'The blow of a whip raises a welt, but a blow of the tongue crushes the bones' (NRSV translation).

39. In Prov. 30.30, גבור is used in the context of describing a lion, which is called mightiest among the beasts.

provide fair laws and make wise decisions,[40] opening in v. 14 with: 'I have counsel and deliberation;[41] I am insight; strength (גבורה) is mine'. Wisdom is not talking about physical strength, but stating that she possesses all of the qualities associated with inner strength.[42]

We see the merits of wisdom over physical strength also in Prov. 30.24-28, which extols the virtues of small animals, who though lacking power or strength, demonstrate great wisdom: 'There are four things that are little upon the earth, yet they are very wise: (v. 25) the ants are a folk without strength, yet they prepare their food in the summer; (v. 26) the badgers are a folk not mighty, yet they make their homes in the rock; (v. 27) the locusts have no king, yet all of them go forth in formation; (v. 28) the lizard can be grasped in the hand, yet it is in the palaces of kings' (vv. 25-28). All of these creatures are small and physically weak, and yet the accomplish great feats, overcoming their vulnerability through wisdom or cleverness and, in the ant's case, hard work. The message is that lack of physical strength need not present a hindrance to accomplishment. Through the use of wisdom and diligence, one can achieve great feats. Here again we see the downplaying of the virtues of physical strength in favor of virtues such as wisdom and industriousness.

Obtaining and maintaining honor seems to be a subject of some concern in Proverbs, given how often the theme comes up. Since honor is integrally connected with performance of the hegemonic masculine ideal in many other biblical texts, it is worth considering what behaviors are described as resulting in honor in Proverbs, and how terms of honor are used in the

---

40. There are quite a few references to kingship and what makes an ideal king in Proverbs, and the message is always consistent: demonstration of the possession of wisdom, having the benefits of wise counsel (Prov. 14.35), and demonstrating judiciousness (Prov. 16.10) and righteousness (Prov. 16.12; 20.8, 26). Never once is masculine performance demonstrating physical strength or battle prowess mentioned. Fox (2000: 273-74) contends that Prov. 8.14-16 are not actually claiming that all kings rule wisely or make righteous laws (since obviously that was not the case in reality) but that effective governance depends on wisdom, since wisdom results in a ruler exercising power effectively and justly. He observes that the assertion in this verse that wisdom is central to righteous rule is unusual in the Bible. Even in Isa. 11.2, where wisdom is one of several qualities that will be bestowed upon the king, it is not depicted as more important than other qualities.

41. תושיה, which Fox (2000: 272) observes 'denotes clear, efficient thinking as an intellectual act'.

42. While there are other biblical texts in which גבורה is used to refer to qualities associated with inner strength (e.g. Isa. 11.2; 30.15; Mic. 3.8; and Judg. 8.21), in the majority of biblical texts in which it is used in the context of the actions of people it denotes individual physical strength (e.g. Jer. 9.22; 51.30) or military power (e.g. Jer. 49.35; Ezek. 32.29, 30; Mic. 7.16), and is often associated with military triumph (e.g. 2 Kgs 18.20; Isa. 36.5; Ps. 20.6). See Kosmala 1977: 369-73.

context of masculine performance. Several Proverbs contrast the negative consequences that result from excessive pride with the honor that will come from displays of modesty and humbleness. Proverbs 29.23 asserts: 'A man's pride will cause his abasement, but a man humble in spirit will obtain honor'. Similar views are expressed in Prov. 18.12: 'Before destruction the heart of a man is haughty, but humility precedes honor'; and Prov. 22.4, 'The reward of humility is fear of Yahweh, wealth, and honor, and life'. In addition to displays of humility, displays of wisdom are also associated with honor. Proverbs 3.16 says of Personified Wisdom: 'Length of days is in her right hand, and in her left hand are wealth and honor'.[43] Proverbs 3.35 expresses a similar sentiment: 'The wise will inherit honor, but fools give rise to disgrace'. In Prov. 26.1 lack of wisdom is depicted as resulting in loss of honor: 'Like snow in summer or rain during the harvest, so honor is not fitting for a fool'.[44] Proverbs 15.33 ties together the notions of displays of humility and wisdom as resulting in honor: 'Fear of Yahweh is the instruction of wisdom, and before honor comes humility'.

Other qualities that result in honor according to Proverbs are displaying self-control by not letting anger overtake one when provoked and by staying out of quarrels and fights. Proverbs 20.3 advises: 'Honor goes to the man avoiding[45] conflict, but every fool will quarrel'. Proverbs 19.11 similarly advises: 'Prudence makes a man slow to anger, and his glory is overlooking an offense'. According to Prov. 21.21, one also obtains honor through performing acts of righteousness and kindness.[46]

In all of these cases, honor is earned through a performance of virtues related to inner strength: self-control, humility, judiciousness, and righteousness. This is quite different from the construction of honor one sees interconnected with the hegemonic masculine ideal, where display of inner strength certainly matters, but no more than successful performance of other aspects of the hegemonic masculine ideal, such as successful performance in battle and maintaining sexual control over the women in one's household. Proverbs focalizes displays of inner strength and mastery over one's self as performances that result in honor.

The sentiment we find repeatedly expressed in the book of Proverbs reflects a model of manhood in which virtues such as wisdom, judiciousness, integrity, humble piety, self-discipline, industriousness, and perseverance are extolled. Moreover, several times these personal qualities are described

43. Similarly, Prov. 8.18.

44. Similarly, Prov. 26.8, which states 'Like one who binds a stone in a sling is he who gives honor to a fool'.

45. Taking שבת as deriving from ישב, thus the sense is 'sitting away from' or 'sitting out' a dispute. Similarly, Scott 1964: 121 and Fox 2009: 664.

46. I am disregarding the second צדקה in the b part of the verse, which seems to have been repeated accidentally.

as more powerful than physical strength and ability with a weapon. This downplaying of the advantages and even the worth of physical strength and prowess with a weapon seems to be in part a response to and perhaps even a reaction against the hegemonic masculine ideal.[47] In this, Proverbs encourages a certain type of masculine performance that is quite different from that found in many other parts of the Bible.

Conclusions

The model of manhood provided by Proverbs appears to have co-existed with the hegemonic masculine ideal, providing, perhaps for several centuries, an alternative ideal of masculine performance for at least a sub-group or a sub-culture within the population. Proverbs does not seem to be trying to usurp the hegemonic masculine ideal that places so much emphasis on performances of feats of physical strength and ability to physically wield a weapon. Rather, it reflects the belief by some in ancient Israelite society that there was another option. By emphasizing and expanding upon the virtues of one aspect of the hegemonic masculine ideal, namely the display of qualities associated with inner strength, and downplaying the importance of the others, namely displays of physical strength, Proverbs presents a viable alternative for men who do not feel affinity for the hegemonic ideal.

When one looks at later Jewish writings, one sees the model of masculinity reflected in Proverbs becoming more predominant in society as a whole, likely reflecting evolving societal norms, mores, and expectations. Once long stretches passed where Judea did not have political independence, much less an army, this model of masculinity started to emerge more fully into the general population as a viable alternative to the hegemonic ideal.[48] Then,

47. As far as displays of sexual virility are concerned, there is a unified message through Proverbs that a man should solely take pleasure in his own wife, since seeking out sexual partners among married women or among prostitutes will lead to grief.

48. We see an example of this shift in *4 Maccabees*. Stephen D. Moore and Janice Capel Anderson (1998: 249-73) discuss in their analysis of *4 Maccabees* how tortured boys, their mother and a feeble old man are all shown as exemplars of masculine performance for demonstrating control over their passions and bravely enduring suffering. In comparison, their torturer, Antiochus Epiphanes, is depicted as weak for letting his passions gain control over him, and yielding to rage, thus compromising his masculine performance. For the author, successful performance of masculinity lies in disciplined self-mastery, the ability to use temperance and rationality to master one's passions. In part the masculine ideal found in this text is a reflection of a larger shift in the hegemonic ideal of masculine performance in Hellenistic society at the time, where self-mastery was gaining emphasis over mastery of others, but it also reflects specifically Jewish notions at the time of ideal masculine performance. The shift in expectations regarding masculine performance, focusing on displays of self-discipline and mastery over one's passions and emotions, was in part a reflection of the reality of Judea's political situation.

with the destruction of Jerusalem and the Diaspora of 70 CE, there was another shift in societal expectations, as any hope for a restored Judean nation, kingship or army was essentially dashed. At that point, the hegemonic ideal of manhood based so heavily on displays of physical strength and battle prowess was no longer viable, and it only made sense for the ideal of masculine performance to shift heavily to a focus on inner strength, something that Proverbs advocated all along.

Bibliography

Aboim, Sofia
    2010   *Plural Masculinities: The Remaking of the Self in Private Life* (Burlington: Ashgate).
Blenkinsopp, Joseph
    1983   *Wisdom and Law in the Old Testament* (Oxford Bible Series; Oxford: Oxford University Press, 1983).
Boyarin, Daniel
    1995   'Are There Any Jews in "The History of Sexuality"?', *Journal of the History of Sexuality* 5: 333-55.
Brenner, Athalya
    1997   *The Intercourse of Knowledge: On Gendering Desire and 'Sexuality' in the Hebrew Bible* (Biblical Interpretation Series, 26; Leiden: E.J. Brill).
Buchbinder, David
    2012   *Studying Men and Masculinities* (London: Routledge).
Burrus, Virginia
    2006   'Mapping as Metamorphosis: Initial Reflections on Gender and Ancient Religious Discourses', in *Mapping Gender in Ancient Religious Discourse* (ed. Todd Penner and Caroline Vander Stichele; Leiden: E.J. Brill): 1-10.
Carrigan, Tim, Bob Connell, and John Lee
    1997   'Toward a New Sociology of Masculinity', in *The Making of Masculinities: The New Men's Studies* (ed. Harry Brod; Boston: Allen & Unwin): 63-100.
Chapman, Cynthia R.
    2004   *The Gendered Language of Warfare in the Israelite–Assyrian Encounter* (HSM, 62; Winona Lake, IN: Eisenbrauns).
Clifford, Richard J.
    2009   'Reading Proverbs 10–22', *Int* 63: 242-55.
Clines, David J.A.
    1995   'David the Man: The Construction of Masculinity in the Hebrew Bible', in *Interested Parties: The Ideology of Writers and Readers of the Hebrew Bible* (ed. David J.A. Clines; JSOTSup, 205; Gender, Culture, Theory, 1; Sheffield: Sheffield Academic Press): 212-43.
    2002   'He-Prophets: Masculinity as a Problem for the Hebrew Prophets and their Interpreters', in *Sense and Sensitivity: Essays on Reading the Bible in Memory of Robert Carroll* (ed. Alastair G. Hunter and Philip R. Davies; JSOTSup, 348; London: Sheffield Academic Press): 311-28.

2010 'Dancing and Shining at Sinai: Playing the Man in Exodus 32–34', in Creangă 2010: 54-63.

Connell, R.W.
2005 *Masculinities* (Berkeley: University of California Press, 2nd edn).

Connell, R.W., and James W. Messerschmidt
2005 'Hegemonic Masculinity: Rethinking the Concept', *Gender and Society* 19.6: 829-59.

Creangă, Ovidiu
2010 'Variations of the Theme of Masculinity: Joshua's Gender In/stability in the Conquest Narrative (Josh. 1–12)', in Creangă (ed.) 2010: 83-109.

Creangă, Ovidiu (ed.)
2010 *Men and Masculinity in the Hebrew Bible and Beyond* (The Bible in the Modern World, 33; Sheffield: Sheffield Phoenix Press).

Crenshaw, James L.
1981 *Old Testament Wisdom: An Introduction* (Atlanta: John Knox Press).

Dell, Katherine J.
2006 *The Book of Proverbs in Social and Theological Context* (Cambridge: Cambridge University Press).

DiPalma, Brian Charles
2010 'De/constructing the Masculinity in Exodus 1–4', in Creangă 2010: 36-53.

Fox, Michael V.
2000 *Proverbs 1–9: A New Translation with Introduction and Commentary* (AB, 18A; New York: Doubleday).
2007 'The Epistemology of the Book of Proverbs', *JBL* 126: 669-84.
2009 *Proverbs 10–31* (Anchor Yale Bible, 18B; New Haven: Yale University Press).
2011 'Ancient Near Eastern Wisdom Literature (Didactic)', *Religion Compass* 5: 1-10.

Frymer-Kensky, Tikva
1998 'Virginity in the Bible', in Matthews, Levinson and Frymer-Kensky 1998: 79-96

George, Mark K.
2010 'Masculinity and Its Regimentation in Deuteronomy', in Creangă (2010) 64-82.

Ginsberg, H.L.
1958 'The Words of Ahiqar', in *The Ancient Near East*. I. *An Anthology of Texts and Pictures* (ed. James B. Prichard; Princeton, NJ: Princeton University Press): 245-49.

Haddox, Susan E.
2010 'Favoured Sons and Subordinate Masculinities', in Creangă 2010: 2-19.

Hoffner, Harry A., Jr
1966 'Symbols for Masculinity and Femininity: Their Use in Ancient Near East Sympathetic Magic Rituals', *JBL* 85: 326-34.

Howson, Richard.
2006 *Challenging Hegemonic Masculinity* (London: Routledge).

Kamionkowski, S. Tamar
2003 *Gender Reversal and Cosmic Chaos: A Study on the Book of Ezekiel* (JSOTSup, 368; London: Sheffield Academic Press).

Kosmala, H.
    1977   'גבר', *TDOT*, II: 267-382.
Lemos, T.M.
    2006   'Shame and Mutilation of Enemies in the Hebrew Bible', *JBL* 125: 225-41.
Lipka, Hilary
    2011   'Shaved Beards and Bared Buttocks: Shaming through Emasculation in Biblical Texts' Bible' (paper presented at the *Mapping Ancient Near Eastern Masculinities* conference, Penn Museum, University of Pennsylvania, Philadelphia, PA, March 2011).
Magdalene, F. Rachel
    1995   'Ancient Near Eastern Treaty-Curses and the Ultimate Texts of Terror', in Athalya Brenner (ed.), *A Feminist Companion to the Latter Prophets* (The Feminist Companion to the Bible, 8; Sheffield: Sheffield Academic Press): 327-52.
Matthews, Victor H.
    1998   'Honor and Shame in Gender-Related Legal Situations in the Hebrew Bible', in Matthews, Levinson and Frymer-Kensky (eds.) 1998: 102-12.
Matthews, Victor H., Bernard M. Levinson and Tikva Frymer-Kensky (eds.)
    1998   *Gender and Law in the Hebrew Bible and the Ancient Near East* (JSOTSup, 262; Sheffield: Sheffield Academic Press).
McKane, William
    1970   *Proverbs: A New Approach* (OTL; Philadelphia: Westminster Press).
Moore, Stephen D., and Janice Capel Anderson
    1998   'Taking It Like a Man: Masculinity in 4 Maccabees', *JBL* 117: 249-73.
Nissinen, Martti
    1998   *Homoeroticism in the Biblical World: A Historical Perspective* (Minneapolis: Fortress Press).
    2011   'Relative Masculinities in the Hebrew Bible' (paper presented at the *Mapping Ancient Near Eastern Masculinities* conference, Penn Museum, University of Pennsylvania, Philadelphia, PA, March 2011).
Olyan, Saul M.
    1994   '"And with a Male You Shall Not Lie the Lying Down of a Woman": On the Meaning and Significance of Leviticus 18:22 and 20:13', *Journal of the History of Sexuality* 5: 179-206.
    1996   'Honor, Shame and Covenant Relations in Ancient Israel and its Environment', *JBL* 115: 201-18.
Scott, R.B.Y.
    1964   *Proverbs and Ecclesiastes* (AB, 18; Garden City, NY: Doubleday).
Stansell, Gary
    1996   'Honor and Shame in the David Narratives', *Semeia* 68: 55-79.
Stone, Ken
    1995   'Gender and Homosexuality in Judges 19: Subject—Honor, Object—Shame?', *JSOT* 67: 87-107.
    1996   *Sex, Honor, and Power in the Deuteronomistic History* (JSOTSup, 234; Sheffield: Sheffield Academic Press).
Synnott, Anthony
    2009   *Re-Thinking Men: Heroes, Villains and Victims* (London: Ashgate).

Washington, Harold C.
1997   'Violence and the Construction of Gender in the Hebrew Bible: A New Historicist Approach', *BibInt* 5: 324-63.
Weeks, Stuart
1999   *Early Israelite Wisdom* (OTM; Oxford: Oxford University Press).
Yoder, Christine Roy
2003   'The Woman of Substance (אשת חיל): A Socioeconomic Reading of Proverbs 31:10-31', *JBL* 122: 427-47.

Part III

NEW TESTAMENT AND APOCRYPHA

BEING A MALE DISCIPLE OF JESUS ACCORDING TO MATTHEW'S ANTITHESES*

Hans-Ulrich Weidemann

1. *The Problem:*
Is the Sermon on the Mount a Text for Men (Only)?

Current research has shown that just like most New Testament texts, the Sermon on the Mount is an 'androcentric' passage, a text written from an entirely male point of view. As this assertion has recently evolved into an exegetical consensus,[1] one can consider the Sermon on the Mount to be a text written 'by and for men'.

Linguistic evidence for this assertion can be found throughout the text. It starts with the initial 'Beatitudes' (Mt. 5.3-12) promising the peacemakers to be called 'sons of God' (υἱοὶ θεοῦ, 5.9). In a similar manner, those men who love their enemies, pray for their pursuers and greet them are to become 'sons of your father who is in heaven' (5.45) according to the last of the six 'antitheses'. This analogous promise is made because they imitate their heavenly father in the way they treat their enemies. Although the 'gender-neutral' word τέκνα ('children') also belongs to the vocabulary' of the Sermon on the Mount (7.11; cf. 21.28), and despite the evangelist's occasional mentioning of 'brothers and sisters' (12.50; 19.29), Matthew opts for the definitely male variant here.[2]

Jesus clearly addresses men and touches upon a series of situations in which men both interact and interfere with other men. The repeatedly used keyword 'brother' (ἀδελφός), for instance, unmistakably indicates another man—at least in the Sermon on the Mount (cf. 5.22, 23-24, 47; 7.3-5).[3] The

* The present study is a revised version of Weidemann 2012. I am grateful to Lena Clemens for her translation of the text into English. Thanks too are due Timothy B. Sailors for his comments on the text.

1. On that point, see Anderson and Moore 2003: 71; Schottroff 1994: 170-79; Leutzsch 2000: 4; 2004: 614-17.
2. Cf. Leutzsch 2000: 4.
3. See Leutzsch 2004: 614.

same holds true for 'your neighbor' (5.43), 'your enemies' (5.43-44), 'the evil man' (ὁ πονηρός, 5.39), 'your adversary' (ὁ ἀντίδικος σου, 5.25; cf. 5.40), the supplicant and the debtor (5.42), the 'hypocrites' (6.2, 5, 16).

Furthermore, only men serve as examples in the Sermon on the Mount. We note, for example, especially the wise and the foolish builders with their houses at the end of the first Matthean Discourse (7.24-27: ἀνὴρ φρονιμός and ἀνὴρ μωρός)—the ten wise and foolish virgins are deployed outside the framework of the Sermon on the Mount in 25.1-13 (παρθένοι... μωραὶ καὶ... φρόνιμοι). Even luxuriant clothing, which does however lag behind the 'lilies of the field', is illustrated by a male figure, namely King Solomon in all his splendor (6.29). Therefore, the preferred translation of the text should normally be the distinctly 'male' one.[4]

Women, by contrast, appear only as *objects* in the Sermon on the Mount, particularly as objects of men's lustful glance (5.28) and of male intentions either to marry or to divorce (5.31-32). Unlike in Mark, the possibility for women to apply for a divorce is neither provided for in Mt. 5.31-32 nor in 19.9 (other than in Mk 10.12). The female realm of experience is almost completely neglected.[5]

The insight that most (!) situations provided in the Sermon on the Mount are distinctly inter-*male* situations and that its demands are primarily addressed to men has important consequences for a proper interpretation of the text in terms of historical as well as ethical-normative standards. Luise Schottroff has therefore justifiably pointed out that, for instance, the three model situations referred to in the fifth antithesis stringently imply *the role of men in society* that required them to repay injustice and, if necessary, to defend themselves forcefully against assaults.[6] Hence, turning the other cheek can only be regarded an offensive response to a punch in the face if the assaulted person is usually expected to fight back. According to

---

4. The term ἡλικία in 6.27, for instance, has to be translated '(men of) fighting age' or 'manhood'; it certainly does not designate general terms such as 'lifespan' or 'body height' in this context, but rather the time of active manhood. In 5.39 τῷ πονηρῷ indicates the 'evil man' (Neyrey 1998: 204), and also the aggressor in 5.39-41 is unambiguously male (ὅστις). Therefore, the translation should always be 'If a man...'

5. There is only exception: the 'flowers' in the field in 6.28 are denied both male and female labor (νήθουσιν = spinning wool, as contrasted with labor in the field: κοπιῶσιν). As opposed to this, the birds in 6.26 are only denied male labor (sowing, harvest, storing in barns). For the few exceptions outside of the Sermon on the Mount (e.g. the parable of the *sourdough* in Mt. 13.33, which belongs to Q), see Melzer-Keller 1997: 127-35, and for Jesus' partisanship for women in Mt. 15.21-28 and 21.31-32; see pp. 142-53.

6. Schottroff 1994: 172 (following W. Wink). She argues that counterviolence was socially considered a 'proper' male behavior and that turning the other cheek meant refraining from ones right of violence and resistance.

Schottroff, the same holds true for the demand to undress oneself in the event of a garnishment or to deliberately accompany a Roman soldier. In a similar vein, L. Sutter Rehmann considers the language of the second antithesis (5.27) androcentric, because the text presumes the patriarchal imbalance in power between men and women and because it concretely addresses the problem of men's assaulting behavior towards women by criticizing their 'lustful glance'.[7] If those demands, which were primarily addressed to a male audience, are transferred to women unreflectively, they will stabilize patriarchal hegemonic structures rather than challenge them provocatively.

Once the androcentric character of the Sermon on the Mount is detected, its relevance for women is critically called into question. Just like with other male-focused biblical texts, strategies are implied to make the text receivable for contemporary women. Concealed female stories are highlighted, for instance, and whole passages are censored by translating them into 'gender-inclusive language'.

2. The Thesis: Jesus's Male Disciples
in the Ancient Public Sphere

In contrast to the positions described above, I will take the irrefutable fact of the Sermon on the Mount's androcentric stance as a *starting point* to grasp the intention of the Matthean text more precisely. Clearly, Matthew's Gospel neither wants to contribute directly to ancient male discourses, nor is it a coincidence that 'the standard terminology associated with masculine virtue' is almost completely missing.[8] The Sermon on the Mount rather—and that is my hypothesis—deals with norms and rules of conduct in a realm which is inevitably considered to be dominated by men in antiquity, namely the *public sphere*, and that is why a number of topics also occurring in Graeco-Roman masculinity discourses are treated: for example, control of anger and lust, revenge, violence, honor challenges and other topics. Therefore, I will first focus on two programmatic passages of the Sermon on the Mount that explicitly correlate the behavior of *Jesus' male disciples* with the *public sphere* (Sections 2.1 and 2.2). I will then analyze the carefully designed *audience* of Jesus' speech (Section 2.3). These and other sensitive passages within the framework of Matthew 5–7 do not refer to 'men' (ἄνδρες), but to

---

7. See Sutter Rehmann 2004: 341-42.

8. See Anderson and Moore 2003: 71. The following terms are in particular missing: ἀνδρεία κτλ., ἐγκράτεια, and σωφροσύνη. Also, Matthew does not contain any explicit reflection on reason as master of the passions. In addition, the term ἀνήρ is rarely used ('man/husband'); cf. p. 76: 'Instead fatherhood and brotherhood dominate male kinship categories'.

'people' (ἄνθρωποι) who form a certain 'forum'. Both the actions of the (male) disciples (5.16 cf. 5.13) and the individual religious top performances of the 'hypocrites' (6.1, 2, 5, 16) take place in view of that audience.

2.1. *The Publicly Visible 'Good Works' of the Disciples (Matthew 5.16)*

5.16   a   In this way your light shall shine before the people (ἔμπροσθεν τῶν ἀνθρώπων),
     b   that they may see (ἴδωσιν) your good works (deeds)
     c   and glorify (δοξάσωσιν) your Father who is in the heavens (τὸν πατέρα ὑμῶν τὸν ἐν τοῖς οὐρανοῖς).

This verse closes the sequence 5.13-16, which has been composed by Matthew out of older *logia*, and draws a conclusion (οὕτως). It proposes to derive consequences for the disciples' actions according to the images developed in the preceding verses ('salt', 'city', 'light'). The disciples are the ones who are persecuted for Jesus' sake and they are the ones to whom the attributes apply. Salting is part of the nature of salt, just as visibility is characteristic for a city on a hill and luminosity is the essence of light.[9] At the same time, the relation between small and large is crucial both for the imagery and for the disciples as well: a small amount of salt needs a 'host' to take effect.[10] In this case, the earth (γῆ) or the world (κόσμος) serves as a 'host', which implies that the disciples are relevant to the whole world. Both genitive attributes are on the same level as the framing recourses to 'people' (5.13/16).[11]

Matthew has deliberately subdivided this sequence into two 'stanzas' and a conclusion. Two *logia*, probably deriving from Q (Q 11.33; 14.34-35), provide the basis for the stanzas—one concerning the salt, the other concerning the light metaphor. The former is also mentioned in Mk 4.21 and the latter in 9.49-50, but as opposed to Luke, Matthew seems to have ignored the Markan versions. In addition, the image of the city on a hill probably belongs to the material unique to the Gospel of Matthew.[12] Matthew pointedly puts the application to the disciples, who are *persecuted* according to 5.10-12, in front of the salt as well as the light metaphor: ὑμεῖς ἐστε τὸ

---

9.   Translated from Strecker 1984: 54. He further argues that 'V. 16 therefore is an interpretation and application of the verses 13-15' (author's translation).

10.   Cf. Zeilinger 2002: 59-60. Zeilinger emphasizes that salt itself remains ineffective: 'It can only take effect if, just like a virus, it encounters a "host". Hence, the metaphor suggests a movement geared towards the world' (author's translation). The fact that not food, but 'the inhabited land' or 'the world' serve as a 'host', is part of the metaphoric strategy alienation.

11.   See Deines 2004: 237.

12.   In contrast to Luz 2002a: 295, who claims that it derives from Q^Mt. Unfortunately, I have not been able to get hold of the English translation of Luz's commentary in the Hermeneia series.

ἅλας τῆς γῆς / ὑμεῖς ἐστε τὸ φῶς τοῦ κόσμου. With this strategy, he creates two stanzas (5.13/14-15)[13] and makes Jesus address his disciples twice. The formulation corresponds with 5.11-12, since (only) the ninth macarism is also formulated in the second person plural (μακάριοί ἐστε). The followers of Jesus are relevant to the whole world, as it is a 'community of perse-cutees' at the same time.[14]

Compared to the Q version, Matthew puts a different emphasis on his first stanza concerning the salt-*logion* (5.13): while the Q-*logion* already mentions the expulsion of the salt which has lost its flavor (βάλλειν ἔξω) and thereby hints at judgment, Matthew adds that the salt will be '*trodden under the feet of men*' (καταπατεῖσθαι ὑπὸ τῶν ἀνθρώπων).[15]

The keyword ἄνθρωποι functions as an inclusio for the whole sequence (5.13/16), yet Matthew shifts the emphasis away from the divine Last Judgment towards the disciples' rejection *by society*—in front of whom their light no longer shines if they will not correspond to their true nature (5.16). Thus, the inclusio is vital also in terms of its content: if the disciples do not perform their duty to do good in public, not only the glorification of God will fade (5.16), but also their rejection by society will indicate the failure of their discipleship.[16]

The subject of the persecution discussed in 5.10-12 and 5.44 is not society, but, according to 5.44, 'your enemies'. This *persecution of the ecclesia* has to be distinguished from the disciples' *rejection by society*, because their failure to accomplish the mission of Jesus seems to justify that they are met with refusal. R. Heiligenthal nicely encapsulates that they who lose their power are doomed to be defeated by those for whom they should be there for according to 5.13a.[17]

---

13. Cf. Deines 2004: 184. The fact that salt and light represent the disciples 'is beyond doubt, but the question is: Do they live and act according to their true nature, or are they "saltless salt" and "lightless light" trying to hide rather than shine?' (author's translation).

14. Cf. Heiligenthal 1983: 115-16: 'According to the macarism, communal identity is established if the community suffers the same fate as the prophets, namely persecution. The community hence exists as a community of persecutees (5.11-12). It reaps heavenly rewards by keeping its identity' (author's translation).

15. Cf. Mt. 5.13 with Q 14.35 (ἔξω βάλλουσιν). The verb 'to expel' used in the context of legal terminology can further be found in Mt. 8.12; 22.13; 25.30.

16. Betz 1995: 160, is right to distinguish between the *persecution* of the ecclesia and the disciples' (self-inflicted) *rejection* by society: 'If the disciples of Jesus fail in their mission, the people will throw them out like garbage... At any rate, such miserable failure is qualitatively different from persecution and other forms of harassment that are signs of strength. Being thrown out and trampled down by the people could also be a sign of true martyrdom and thus strength, but this passage does not consider this possibility.'

17. Translated from Heiligenthal 1983: 116. He aptly refers to the 'lapse into ineffectiveness' (author's translation).

The main focus is on the second 'stanza' (5.14-16). The *logion* of the city on a hill precedes the actual saying concerning the light, and the stanza finally results in v. 16. This includes a shift of emphasis: the disciples are 'the light of the world' (τὸ φῶς τοῦ κόσμου) provided that their 'light' shines 'before people'. To illustrate this, the phrase τὸ φῶς ὑμῶν is immediately elucidated by ὑμῶν τὰ καλὰ ἔργα: people should observe 'your good works' and thereby be incited to 'glorify your Father who is in heaven". The light imagery, which is transferred from the disciples to their actions, primarily serves to make this *public*. This applies in particular if one considers 5.16 the 'theme of the Sermon on the Mount', as Christoph Burchard argues, and that everything which follows merely illustrates concretely how the disciples have to behave if they want to be the light of the world.[18] While the expression 'your good works' is concretized in the passages immediately following, it is at the same time modified by ἔμπροσθεν τῶν ἀνθρώπων: the disciples must perform their actions 'before people', that is, *visibly* and, above all, *publicly*.[19]

2.2. *The Disciples' Concealed Righteousness (Matthew 6.1)*
The three-part 'cult-didache'[20] succeeding the antitheses is introduced with a introductory verse:[21]

6.1   a   Beware [however],
      b   of practicing your righteousness before the people (ἔμπροσθεν τῶν ἀνθρώπων)
      c   to be seen by them (πρὸς τὸ θεαθῆναι αὐτοῖς).
      d   For then
      e   you have no reward from your Father who is in the heavens (τῷ πατρὶ ὑμῶν τῷ ἐν τοῖς οὐρανοῖς)

First of all it is obvious that the two verses 5.16 and 6.1 are aligned with one another. Their common phrases (ἔμπροσθεν τῶν ἀνθρώπων / ὁ πατὴρ ὑμῶν ὁ ἐν τοῖς οὐρανοῖς), as well as the mutual semantic field of vision (ὁράω / θεάομαι), confirm this hypothesis. The expression 'to do your righteousness' (τὴν δικαιοσύνην ὑμῶν ποιεῖν, 6.1) corresponds with the expression 'your good works' (ὑμῶν τὰ καλὰ ἔργα, 5.16). Furthermore, both verses contain the three dimensions of the *disciples* ('you'), *people* (ἄνθρωποι), and the *Father* in heaven.

18. Burchard 1998: 38. According to Burchard, 5.3-16 is superordinate to the whole (!) corpus 5.17–7.12 not only as a prelude, but in terms of relevance. More cautious, but heading in the same direction, is Luz 2002a: 295.
19. Cf. Schenk 1987: 239.
20. Cf. Betz 1995: 351-52.
21. See Luz 2002a: 421; Deines 2004: 436; Strecker 1984: 101. According to Strecker, the 'headline' consists in the evangelist's deliberate integration of the following 'examples of Christian piety' (author's translation) into the topic of righteousness.

The impression of their similarity is further enhanced by the elements of the Matthean redaction in both verses.[22] As they both lack synoptic parallels, one has to assume that both verses can be traced back to Matthew who has probably correlated them from the start.

If that were the case, however, the contradictory message of the two verses would be all the more striking.[23] In 5.13-16 the followers of Jesus are assured of their purpose as 'the salt of the earth' and 'the light of the world' and at the same time encouraged to act according to their 'nature', that is, publicly visible. Therefore, the whole sequence which Matthew composed on the basis of preexisting *logia* aims at the *visibility* of the disciples 'before people', that is, the public performance of their actions.[24] While the sequence 5.13-16 amounts to an *ecclesia visibilis*,[25] the disciples should virtually remain *invisible* when 'doing their righteousness" in 6.1.

This contrastive character goes beyond the two programmatic verses 5.16 and 6.1. ὁρᾶν and δοξάζειν, for instance, are not only connected in 5.16, but also in 6.2. In either case, 'seeing' is supposed to lead to glorification, and 'people' are the subject of either verb. The object of δοξάζειν, however, is significantly different: as stated in 5.16, people should 'glorify your Father who is in heaven' when observing the good works of the disciples. The vociferously proclaimed and publicly visible almsgiving of the 'hypocrites', by contrast, aims at *their* glorification by society. In this respect, 6.2 forms a negative contrast to 5.16.[26]

Just like in 6.1, the keyword 'your righteousness' (δικαιοσύνη ὑμῶν) also occurs in a polemic context in 5.20: according to the latter, the disciples' righteousness needs to exceed that of the scribes and Pharisees for them to enter into the Kingdom of Heaven and according to 6.1-18, the followers of Jesus differ from the 'hypocrites' exactly by doing their righteousness secretly.

Of course, 6.2-18 also includes that righteousness, that is, charity, prayer, and fasting should be completely directed at the 'Father who is in secret'.[27] The Matthean Jesus does not criticize these performances themselves; rather,

22. See Luz 2002a: 295 n. 4, and 419 n. 9. The expressions common to both verses belong to the list of Matthew's preferred vocabulary on pp. 57-77: ἔμπροσθεν τῶν ἀνθρώπων and πατὴρ ὑμῶν ἐν τοῖς οὐρανοῖς.

23. Concerning this problem, see also Betz 1995: 164. According to Schenk 1987: 239, 6.1 is an 'intentional, delimiting, and refining resumption of 5.16' (author's translation).

24. Neyrey 1998: 215: '"Before men" clearly means that the deeds are done in public. Actions done in public are intended to be observed and evaluated, hence they are done "so that they [observers] may see your good works"'.

25. See Strecker 1984: 54.

26. See Deines 2004: 254.

27. See Deines 2004: 438.

he takes them for granted. At this point, the 'twofold audience' of the Sermon on the Mount must be taken into consideration. The crowd is told on the one hand that the disciples of Jesus cannot be *recognized* by publicly visible charity, prayer, and fasting—although they do practice all of them. On the other hand, the disciples are requested to attract public attention by meeting the demands of the antitheses. It is by so doing that they are supposed to incite people to glorify their Father in heaven, and not by performing the ritual examples illustrated in 6.2-18. With his staging of the Sermon on the Mount as a 'public speech' that Jesus addresses to his disciples, but before the forum of the crowd, the evangelist ensures that Jesus' demand towards his disciples is publicly proclaimed and hence *known* to the public. Therefore, the central question is: *Where* and *in what way* are, or are not, the followers of Jesus publicly 'visible'?

Conclusion: The two programmatic passages 5.16 and 6.1 illustrate that the *androcentrism* frequently noticed in the Sermon on the Mount serves the *public role* of discipleship.

2.3. In View of the Public of Israel: The Audience of the Sermon on the Mount
The carefully designed 'audience' of the Sermon on the Mount corresponds with the findings from Mt. 5.16 and 6.1. As stated in the introductory note on 5.1-2, the Sermon on the Mount is primarily addressed to the *disciples* concretely approaching Jesus in this scene. If one takes the narrative logic of the Gospel seriously, the *two Galilean pairs of brothers*, Simon and Andrew as well as James and John, must be meant by that (Mt. 4.18-22). They are, however, labeled with the term 'disciples' (μαθηταί) for the first time in 5.1. One can therefore assume that Matthew probably had in mind a broader group which exceeds the four disciples mentioned by name in the previous chapter.[28] Be that as it may, the two pairs of brothers as the primarily addressed audience are in conformity with the androcentric character of the Sermon on the Mount as developed above. Jesus particularly turns to *male disciples*, because he establishes requirements concerning their behavior in the social realm which is, according to what was generally accepted, reserved for men: the ancient *public*.

The uniquely Matthean presentation of Jesus as a public speaker should also be interpreted on the basis of ancient gender roles: 'the role of public speaker/teacher was a decidedly masculine one in the ancient world'.[29]

---

28.   Cf. Lohfink 1993: 33: According to Matthew, the community of disciples is constituted by Jesus' call to follow him (4.18-22) as well as by the Sermon on the Mount (5.3–7.27).

29.   Conway 2008: 114. She continues in line with J. Neyrey: 'Jesus in the role of a public speaker highlights his ideal masculine identity'. Cf. also Neyrey 2003: 60-65. On the male body in Roman rhetoric, cf. Gunderson 2000.

Furthermore, the 'great *multitudes* (ὄχλοι πολλοί) from Galilee, Decapolis, Jerusalem, Judea and from beyond the Jordan' already mentioned in 4.25 are part of the audience *as well* (7.28-29). By means of the distinctly altered location compared to Mk 3.7-8, Matthew indicates that Jesus addresses his disciples *before the audience of Israel*.[30] Hence, the People of God (4.23: ὁ λαός) is the broader audience overhearing the words Jesus addresses to his disciples.[31]

This implies that Jesus' address to his disciples is a *public speech* and certainly not an esoteric instruction.[32] In contrast to the main part of the so-called Parabolic Discourse (13.1-35 with the exception of the instruction of the disciples in vv. 10-23) as well as the warning against the Pharisees and scribes (23.1-39), Jesus does *not* address the Sermon on the Mount directly to the Jewish multitudes. Neither does he *solely* address his disciples, like in the Missionary Discourse (10.5-42), the Discourse on the Church (18.1-35), or the Discourse on the End Times (24.1–25.46). Jesus addresses those *Israelites called to his discipleship before the forum of Israel*. By instructing them publicly, he acts as a teacher of Israel simultaneously and, vice versa, he teaches Israel while he openly instructs the fellow Israelites who follow him.[33]

This in turn has the consequence that the people are aware of Jesus' claims and the demands on his disciples. Its reaction is characterized by consternation. Everything Jesus demands of those he calls to discipleship, be it Israelites or Gentiles who will be made disciples and baptized by the first missionaries after Easter (28.19, see below), is by no means an internal instruction—and for that reason different from the content of, for instance,

---

30. So, convincingly, Lohfink 1993: 107-109 (and *passim*). Matthew erases the Gentile territories Idumaea, Tyre, and Sidon from the list as found in Mk 3.7-8. He only adopts the territories of ancient Israel (to which Decapolis used to belong). The great multitudes assembled around Jesus 'represent the whole of Israel which was to be gathered by Jesus (author's translation, p. 29). At the same time, the community of disciples indicates a 'prefiguration of Israel' (author's translation, p. 56).

31. Cf. Davies and Allison 1991: 725: 'We are apparently to think of Jesus addressing his disciples in the midst of a crowd that overhears'.

32. This distinction becomes particularly obvious in the parable passages of Mt. 13. Their first part (13.1-35) takes place in the open air: Jesus addresses the multitudes from a boat on the lake. Later, he instructs his disciples esoterically in a private house (13.36-52). However, an instruction of the disciples is embedded in the speech to the crowd, which is not indicated by a change of location, but a change of addressees.

33. According to 7.29, the teachings of Jesus are (also) addressed to the people (ἦν γὰρ διδάσκων αὐτούς; cf. 4.23; 9.35, and 5.1 as well). With his doctrine, Jesus enters into competition with the scribes. Luz 2002a: 266, therefore argues: 'The Sermon on the Mount is ethically relevant to the disciples, but it applies as well to the entire crowd which is listening' (author's translation).

the other discourses. The crowd *knows* that it is to be encouraged to glorify the Father in heaven by the works of the disciples illustrated in the Sermon on the Mount. It also knows that the disciples are not recognizable by public almsgiving, visible individual prayer, or ostentatious fasting, and that they can be distinguished from their Jewish environment with the help of these criteria.

Strikingly, the restriction of the audience to the (restored) Israel made in the *frame sections* of the Sermon on the Mount has *no* parallel in the teachings of Jesus. The frequently and pointedly mentioned ἄνθρωποι, who form the forum for the disciples' works, *also* occur in synagogues according to Mt. 6.2, 5. The term hence includes Jews *as well*. Restricting the ἄνθρωποι to Jews, however, would neither do justice to the contextual evidence, for the ἄνθρωποι mentioned twice in 5.13 and 5.16 have to be interpreted in the context of the genitive attributes γῆ and κόσμος, claiming the universal orientation of the disciples in the gospel of Matthew.[34] This conclusion can also be drawn from 28.16-20[35] and from the light imagery in 5.14-16 as well.[36] The ἄνθρωποι mentioned in the Sermon on the Mount are thus not, or only partially, identical with the ὄχλοι, the Israelite audience—which can be regarded as alluded to Mt. 28.16-20 (see below).

3. *Disciples in Public—Men 'in the open air' (Philo)*

With programmatic reference to the ἄνθρωποι as a forum in front of which the required actions of the disciples take place and with the purposeful use of the semantic field of vision, Matthew signals that he wants the reader to understand central passages of the Sermon on the Mount on the basis of the disciples' behavior in public. This touches upon a realm which is *clearly associated with particular gender roles in antiquity*. Jerome Neyrey puts it this way: 'The ancients perceived the cosmos as totally gender-divided, and so they describe parallel male and female worlds, in which certain places, roles, tasks, and objects are deemed appropriate to each gender'.[37] Ancient realms of experience are divided into the categories 'indoors/outdoors' or 'private/public'.[38] It is necessary to outline this observation in the following.

---

34. See Deines 2004: 237.

35. See Davies and Allison 1991: 478.

36. Compare Mt. 5.14-16 and 28.18-19, as well as Isa. 42.6 (καὶ ἔδωκά σε εἰς διαθήκην γένους, εἰς φῶς ἐθνῶν); 49.6 (ἰδοὺ τέθεικά σε εἰς διαθήκην γένους εἰς φῶς ἐθνῶν τοῦ εἶναί σε εἰς σωτηρίαν ἕως ἐσχάτου τῆς γῆς); 60.3 (LXX: καὶ πορεύσονται βασιλεῖς τῷ φωτί σου καὶ ἔθνη τῇ λαμπρότητί σου). Cf. also Rom. 2.19.

37. Neyrey 2003: 44.

38. On that point, see Zoepffel 2006: 314-20. Cf. also Neyrey 2003: 44-53.

The Jewish philosopher *Philo of Alexandria* emphasizes that the following realms are suitable for men only (ἀνδράσιν ἐφαρμόζουσι): market-places (ἀγοραί), council-halls (βουλευτήρια), law-courts (δικαστήρια), cult associations (θίασοι), gatherings and meetings of large crowds (σύλλογοι πολυανθρώπων), as well as *open-air life* (ὁ ἐν ὑπαίθρῳ βίος) with full scope for discussion and action both in war and in peace. Women, by contrast, are supposed to look after the house (οἰκουρία) and stay inside (καὶ ἡ ἔνδον μόνη).[39]

Philo distinguishes between πόλις (city) and οἶκος (household): men are responsible for the statesmanship (πολιτεία) and women provide the house-hold management (οἰκονομία). They are to confine themselves to the life indoors and avoid other men's glances (ἐν ὄψεσιν ἀνδρῶν ἑτέρων) 'outside' in the streets.[40] Among other things, Philo argues that nature (φύσις) has laid down different statutes for each section of our race (τοῦ γένους ἡμῶν).[41]

One has to keep in mind, however, that the sharp distinction of the spheres along the gender differences does not necessarily mirror the *real* conditions. It is rather an ideal-typical differentiation reflecting norms, expectations, and ideologies.[42] This observation also holds true for the Gospel of Matthew: on the one hand, the Sermon on the Mount, as well as other passages, testify to the view of the public sphere as a male sphere; on the other hand, several parts of the Gospel quite naturally document the presence of women in public and, what is more, the presence of women without husbands or other male family members.[43] The best example of this is Jesus' encounter with the woman 'who for twelve years had a flow of blood' (Mt. 9.20-22).[44] Furthermore, Matthew takes it for granted that 'many

---

39. Philo, *Spec. leg.* 3.169 (LCL, ed. F.H. Colson).

40. Philo, *Spec. leg.* 3.170-71: 'There are two sorts of organized communities (δίττὸν γὰρ πόλεων εἶδος), greater and smaller ones. The greater ones are called cities (ἄστη), the smaller ones *households* (οἰκίαι)'. Cf. also Philo, *Virt.* 19 (LCL, ed. F.H. Colson): since the bodily shapes (τύπους σωμάτων) of men and women are different, so 'each of the two has a different life assigned to it, to the one domestic (ὁ κατοικίδιος), to the other a civic life (ὁ πολιτικός)'. That is why 'the true man' should 'maintain his masculinity' (ἡρρενῶσθαι) by not wearing unmanly (ἀνανδρίας) clothing.

41. Philo, *Spec. leg.* 3.176.

42. Philo, *Spec. leg.* 3.172, harshly reproaches women who interfere in a dispute or fight between men. This in turn presupposes the general possibility of such incidents.

43. Stressed by Levine 2012: 135.

44. On that point, cf. Levine 2012: 137, who emphasizes the mobility of women and who adds further examples on this aspect in the Gospel of Matthew. She concludes (p. 139): 'The Gospel of Matthew appreciates unmarried women, mobile women and women who voluntarily join the followers of Jesus in order to start a new family' (author's translation).

women...had followed Jesus from Galilee, serving him' (27.55).[45] This observation is related to the fact that Matthew does not presuppose an urban, but a rural milieu and that his protagonists do not belong to the upper class.[46]

However, we will at first stick to the norm (i.e. the ideology) as representing the ideal in order to classify the Sermon on the Mount correctly.

With his remarks cited above, Philo clearly resumes a tradition tracing back to Aristotle and Xenophon. While in Plato's ideal state the οἶκος has disappeared in favor of state institutions of reproduction and daily sustainment, and while Plato therefore argues for the equality of women and men, Aristotle emphasizes the polarity of πόλις and οἶκος. For him, this implies that women have to be excluded from the realm of the πόλις.[47] According to Aristotle, the πόλις is generally egalitarian and the οἶκος is structured hierarchically. He considers the conduct of the household a monarchy—'for every house is under one head'—and state leadership, by contrast, a government of free and equal men.[48] As compared to Plato, Aristotle emphasizes the differences between women and men more sharply and aligns them with hierarchical structures.[49] In line with Aristotle, the

45.   Wengst 2010: 26-27, justifiably points out that Matthew deprives these women of the title 'disciples'. Melzer-Keller 1997: 118-19, therefore only considers them companions of Jesus and portrayed in a traditional female role. However, this view might be underestimating. Cf. Luz 2002b: 374. Following Luise Schottroff, Luz hints at the connection of διακονέω with the term ἀκολυθέω, which indicates discipleship, and he also points out the references to Mt. 20.26-28.

46.   Cf. also Ilan 1995: 122-34 ('Preserving a Woman's Chastity') and 176-90 ('Women in Public'). Ilan repeatedly notes (pp. 128-29, 186 and *passim*) that the ideal of a public excluding women, which is captured in the Jewish sources, does *not* reflect the reality of an agricultural society, especially since these texts are usually written by male members of the upper middle class or the upper class. Cf. p. 229: 'Thus the requirement that men and women be kept separate comes from social circles whose members had means to put this into practice'.

47.   Cf. the overview by Heinz 2002: 10-14 and 94-98. '*Polis* and *oikos* are sovereign entities. While the *polis* is defined as a community of free and equal citizens, the authority relations within the house are principally relations between unequal people who are all dominated and governed by a superior male head of the household, the *oikodespotes*' (p. 95). 'To think of the *polis* as an egalitarian community also means to think of the exclusion of unequal and hence inferior members from the *polis*' (p. 98) (author's translations).

48.   Aristotle, *Pol.* 1.7 (1255b19f.): ἡ μὲν οἰκονομικὴ μοναρχία (μοναρχεῖται γὰρ πᾶς οἶκος), ἡ δὲ πολιτικὴ ἐλευθέρων καὶ ἴσων ἀρχή. Aristotle's works are cited according to the Scriptorum classicorum bibliotheca Oxoniensis (*Rhet.* and *Pol.* ed. W.D. Ross; *Eth. nic.* ed. I. Bywater).

49.   Aristotle, *Pol.* 1.5 (1254b10ff.). The male is by nature superior, and the female inferior; and the one rules, and the other is ruled. Accordingly, the virtue of a man is shown in *commanding*, of a woman in *obeying*, and so on (1260b20ff.). For a different view, cf. Plato, *Politeia* 5.455D and elsewhere.

tasks of men and women differ from one another within the household: for the duty of men is to acquire (particularly 'outside'), and of women to preserve (especially 'inside').[50]

This indicates the theoretical basis which was developed further and structured gender-specifically in ancient economics. Some crucial evidence concerning the characterization of the 'inside' and 'outside' based on gender differences can be found in Xenophon's *Oeconomicus*. The work narrates a conversation between Socrates and Ischomachus which deals with the 'education' (παιδεία, rather 'training') of married couples. Ischomachus assures Socrates that he does not spend any time 'inside' (ἔνδον), because his wife is much better suited to maintain 'my house'. The key sentence is: 'And since both the indoor and the outdoor tasks demand labor and attention, God from the first adapted the woman's nature, I think, to the indoor (τὰ ἔνδον) and man's to the outdoor (τὰ ἔξω) tasks and cares'.[51] And shortly after that: 'Thus, to the woman it is more honorable to stay indoors than to abide in the fields, but to the man is shameful (αἴσχιον) rather to stay indoors than to attend to the work outside'. To act differently would be 'against nature'![52] However, Xenophon is primarily concerned with agricultural work in the open air as well as warfare, because a male body and mind are better suited for these activities. As opposed to Aristotle, the distribution of roles is balanced with statements regarding equality. The ideal of 'self-control' (σωφροσύνη, ἐγκράτεια), for instance, should be aimed at by both spouses.[53] It is moreover striking that these two terms are used as counter-concepts for anger (ὀργή, θυμός) in different contexts.[54]

One last example: in the (pseudo-)Aristotelian treatise *Oikonomika*, the author interprets the different spheres of activity as a result of the bodily difference between men and women: 'The former has to acquire from the outside whatever may be necessary, and the latter has to protect the things inside'.[55]

Let us now return to Philo. Not only does he provide us with the theory of gender distribution to the realms of 'inside' and 'outside', but from his male point of view he also outlines an impression of men's life 'in the open air', the life which women should avoid: the male realm is characterized by the

---

50. Aristotle, *Pol.* 3.4 (1277b23ff.).

51. Xenophon, *Oec.* 7.22 (LCL, Xenophon IV, ed. O.J. Todd).

52. Xenophon, *Oec.* 7.30. Note the striking opposition of κάλλιον/αἴσχιον.

53. Xenophon, *Oec.* 7.6: 'this sort of training (παίδευμα) is, in my opinion, the most important to man and woman alike'; cf. 7.14-15 (σωφρόνων), 27: 'And God also gave to both impartially the power to practice due self-control (τὸ ἐγκρατεῖς)'. Aristotle, by contrast, distinguishes between male and female temperance and courage (*Pol.* 3.4 1277b17ff.).

54. For an elaborate analysis, see Harris 2001: 80-128.

55. Ps.-Aristotle, *Oik.* 1.3 (1343b30-1344a7).

male *glance* (see above), but also by *disputes, acts of violence* and *fights* between men, by *cursing* and *diatribes*.[56] It is not farfetched to think of the situations depicted in the Sermon on the Mount in this context (see below, Section 5). Remember: life in the open air particularly by means of communication is a male preserve!

By leaving the house, women enter the male realm of verbal and physical aggression. From a male perspective, women should not have anything to do with all this. By leaving the house, however, they risk getting involved.[57] But also sports competitions (where a female audience must be excluded) are worth considering. It is quite interesting that, according to Philo, a woman who tries to interfere in such events—unlike men!—risks her honor.[58]

Philo underlines that the public space is a male space associated with *agonistic* behavior.[59] One key term for this assertion is 'honor'. Men can attain honor by means of attribution or challenge (*challenge and riposte*) and must defend it publicly.[60]

For Aristotle, honor (τιμή) is closely linked to a good reputation (εὐδοξία)[61] and must therefore be understood in terms of appreciation and recognition.[62] Young men loving honor (φιλότιμοι) love victory still more (φιλόνικοι), because φιλοτιμία can be considered a competition.[63] Honor and victory are thus closely related for Aristotle.[64] In his *Nicomachean Ethics*, Aristotle refers to honor both as an 'award for eminent actions' and as an 'award for virtue' which is only adjudged to good people.[65] A man striving

---

56.   Philo, *Spec. leg.* 3.172 (τὸ δὲ λοιδορουμένων ἢ συμπλεκομένων ἀνδρῶν), 173 (ὑβρίζεσθαι τὸν ἄνδρα), 174 (κακηγοροῦντος, πληγαῖς καὶ ὕβρεσι).

57.   The involvement of women in fist fights (outside the home) is a particularly shocking image for Philo (*Spec. leg.* 3.175). He urges severe punishment (i.e. cutting off hands) for women who catch hold of male genitals during such a fight.

58.   Philo, *Spec. leg.* 3.173.

59.   On the agonistic, honor-and-shame-based Mediterranean societies, see Malina 2001: 27-57.

60.   Cf. Malina 2001: 35: 'As a rule, challenger and receiver are men, although elite women could and did challenge men… Moreover, men may be challenged by actions directed to the women or other men for whom they are responsible.'

61.   Aristotle, *Rhet.* 1.5 (1361a28): τιμὴ δ' ἐστὶν μὲν σημεῖον εὐεργετικῆς εὐδοξίας; accordingly, the opposite of honor, shame (αἰσχύνη), especially consists in losing one's reputation (ἀδοξία, *Rhet.* 2.5 [1383b11f.]).

62.   Aristotle, *Rhet.* 1.7 (1365a7f.): ἡ γὰρ τιμὴ ὥσπερ ἀξία τίς ἐστιν.

63.   On that point, cf. Aristotle, *Rhet* 2.12 (1389a11-13): καὶ φιλότιμοι μέν εἰσιν, μᾶλλον δὲ φιλόνικοι, etc.

64.   Cf. Aristotle, *Rhet.* 1.9 (1367a23): καὶ νίκη καὶ τιμὴ τῶν καλῶν. That is because both are desirable, although they do not instantly bear fruit.

65.   Aristotle, *Eth. nic.* 4.3: τὸ ἐπὶ τοῖς καλλίστοις ἆθλον (1123b19f.) and τῆς ἀρετῆς ἆθλον (1123b35).

for honor (ὁ φιλότιμος) is not reprimanded automatically, because for Aristotle it is all about the right measure.[66] There can be too much as well as too little striving for honor (τιμῆς ὄρεξις). Witty and vigorous people therefore tend to choose honor as the 'goal of their political life', that is, life in the public of the city state. Aristotle, however, points out that honor strongly depends on those who bestow honor, that is, other people, rather than on him, who receives it.[67] He thus argues that it is unimportant what kind of honor or fame one receives from socially subordinate fellows.[68]

These notions constitute the background of the Sermon on the Mount which is to a great extent clearly aimed at *male* followers of Jesus *in the public*. We will now try to reconstruct the 'public' and therefore also 'male' situations presumed in the text in two steps (Sections 4 and 5).

4. Retreat of the Disciples into the Private Sphere?
Exegesis of Matthew 6.1-18

We first have to consider the passage of the Sermon on the Mount in which Jesus seems to tell his disciples to *retreat* from the public: in Mt. 6.1-18, the Matthean Jesus asks his disciples *not* to practice their 'righteousness in front of others'. They should not perform it publicly, or else they must not expect any reward from their Father concealed in heaven. This principle (6.1) is illustrated by the examples of almsgiving (6.2-4), prayer (6.5-6), and fasting (6.16-18). Old Testament traditions serve as an example for this series of three.[69] As regards content, Jesus' statement concerns religious practices in a strict sense, namely, the 'performance' (ποιεῖν) of 'cultic rituals'.[70]

4.1. Reward by the Concealed God
First of all, the concept of God within this passage is quite remarkable. While the other parts of the Sermon on the Mount also stress that God is the 'Father in heaven', here the emphasis is put on the *hiddenness* of God.[71]

---

66. Aristotle, *Eth. nic.* 4.5 (1125b8-12). Both the ambitious (φιλότιμος) as well as the non-ambitious man (ἀφιλότιμος) are rebuked. The former strives too much for honor, the latter too little. The ambitious man, however, can be praised for his *manfulness* (τὸν φιλότιμον ἐπαινοῦμεν ὡς ἀνδρώδη).

67. Aristotle, *Eth. nic.* 1.5 (1095b23-25).

68. Aristotle, *Rhet.* 1.11 (1371a13-17).

69. On that point, cf. Tob. 12.8 (including variants of the text); Sir. 7.10-11.

70. Betz 1995: 351-52; he therefore considers 6.1-18 a 'cultic *didache*'.

71. The phrase (τῷ πατρί σου) τῷ ἐν τῷ κρυπτῷ and τῷ πατρί σου τῷ ἐν τῷ κρυφαίῳ in 6.6, 18 is not adverbial, but adjectival: it concerns the *hidden Father*. Individual almsgiving, prayer, and fasting must match this concept of God and hence take place in secret. The reach of his glance 'into hiddenness' corresponds to the hiddenness of God in heaven (6.4, 6: ὁ βλέπων ἐν τῷ κρυπτῷ; 6.18: βλέπων ἐν τῷ κρυφαίῳ).

Exaggerating, one could say that public life in the synagogues and in the streets is being 'secularized' by this notion. Whoever stands out against the collective by individual religious performances, places him/herself before the forum of other men (and women) and *not* before the concealed God.[72]

Furthermore, the concept of *reward* (μισθός) or retaliation (ἀποδιδόναι) plays an important role for 6.1-18.[73] Everybody will receive their expected reward from the authority to which they dedicate their religious performance to: If people are the object of their endeavors, piety leads to 'honor' in terms of being honored by the people (δοξασθῆναι). Only if one's 'cultic performance' corresponds to the concealment of God (which is the crucial notion of God within this passage), can heavenly reward be obtained. The motif of the reward, however, also connects this passage with Mt. 5.10-12. Here, those who are persecuted for Jesus' sake are promised great reward in heaven (5.12), and also those who are 'persecuted for righteousness' sake' are promised the kingdom of heaven in the eighth macarism (5.10).

4.2. *Does the Matthean Jesus Tell his Disciples to Retreat from the Public?*
Until recently, Jesus' demands have often been interpreted as requiring his disciples to retreat from the public or from Israel's religious life. To illustrate this, let us consider the following two examples:
1. Jerome H. Neyrey puts his exegesis of 6.1-18 under the pro-grammatic headline 'Vacating the playing field'. He addresses the ancient distinction between public vs. private sphere which is gender-related: the 'public' sphere is characterized by the fact that men are being seen by other men.[74] According to Neyrey, Jesus prohibits (!) his disciples from operating in certain public places (synagogues, streets) and, by contrast, demands they retreat to 'private', that is, 'female' realms.[75] He puts it pointedly: 'Jesus proscribes "public" and prescribes "private" rituals for his male disciples'.[76] As a consequence, Neyrey argues that 'the disciple must vacate the playing field, at least in regard to deeds of piety'. That means: 'Jesus mandates that his disciples stay away from the

72.   Cf. Betz 1995: 353: 'The point here is not whether the people are present, but whether the intention of the performer is to be seen by them or by God'.

73.   According to Deines 2004: 437-38, the keyword μισθός indicates that it is not about the membership in the *basileia*, but rather—like in 5.19—about a promotion within its realms.

74.   Neyrey 1998: 214: 'Being seen by others is an essential element for earning a good reputation, worth, and honor'; cf. Neyrey 2003: 63.

75.   Neyrey 1998: 214.

76.   Neyrey 1998: 218. He continues: 'It is, then, no minor matter for Jesus to tell males to quit the "public" world for the "private" one'. Cf. p. 227: 'The public forum for seeing and being seen is denied them'.

synagogues and refrain from joining other Judean males in their customary acts of piety. Moreover, he informs them that the honorable place to practice piety is the household, not the synagogue.'[77]

2. Jacob Neusner goes even further.[78] He interprets Mt. 6.1-18 as Jesus' criticism of 'public piety', but not only as—justified!—criticism of an excess of public piety, but also as 'a rejection of the life of Israel, the community'. This is a fundamentally different interpretation as it implies a *general rejection of the public and communal Jewish service altogether*. According to Neusner, the Matthean Jesus only accepts prayer in secret as true and valid prayer and, in doing so, he challenges a principle of the Torah: Israel is supposed to serve God 'not one by one but all together and all at once'. Just like with several other statements, the Matthean Jesus thereby 'places a wall between himself and other Israelites, whom he calls hypocrites'. This includes not addressing the people of Israel as a whole, but only individuals within Israel—precisely that part of Israel which belongs to him.

Despite their different foci, Neusner and Neyrey both agree that the disciples of Jesus have to withdraw from the Jewish public, especially from liturgical services. The question now is whether the interpretations outlined above correspond to the wording of 6.1-18.

Concerning the form of Mt. 6.1-18, the following observations must be noted: the text following the 'headline' in 6.1 is clearly structured in three parts, although this is obscured by the 'insertion' of the Our Father as well as the verses introducing and summarizing this prayer (6.7-8, 9-13, 14-15). The remarks on almsgiving (6.2-4), prayer (6.5-6) and fasting (6.16-18) are structured analogously in two parts each. The first part (introduced with ὅταν) contains a prohibition (formulated with οὐκ or μή + imperative) which is combined with the deterrent comparison to 'hypocrites'. Their (wrong) ambition is described with ὅπως-sentences in which 'people' appear as the actual objects of the hypocrites' devotional practice. Stereotypically, this part concludes with the phrase 'Amen, I tell you, they have received their reward in full'.[79] The second part begins with an instruction introduced by σύ/σοῦ δέ and is thus addressed to the second person singular. It ends in the stereotypical phrase 'and your Father, who sees what is done in secret (ἐν τῷ κρυπτῷ/κρυφαίῳ), will reward you'.

---

77. Neyrey 1998: 219. He continues: 'Jesus effectively challenges his disciples to break their social and ceremonial ties with their neighbors, ties that functioned to confirm their identity and gave them honor'. Cf. Betz 1995: 343.

78. On the following, see Neusner 1993: 32-34.

79. On ἀποδιδόναι, 'payment (of wages)' (2 Clem. 20.4; Barn. 11.8); see Strecker 1984: 106.

At first, it must be emphasized that Mt. 6.1-18 is *not* concerned with the question *whether* alms have to be given, *whether* prayers have to be said, or *whether* fasting has to be adhered to. Rather, the passage exclusively deals with the *manner of performing* these rituals. The readers of the Sermon on the Mount hence are told *that* the followers of Jesus give alms, pray, and fast indeed. But at the same time they are told that the disciples *cannot be publicly recognized* by their way of almsgiving, prayer, and fasting.

To assess this properly, we have to take a closer look at the behavior of the so-called hypocrites. The double mentioning of the synagogues (6.2, 5) underlines that these 'hypocrites' are *Jews*. However, the Matthean Jesus clearly identifies them with scribes and Pharisees only in ch. 23. In this respect, the Sermon on the Mount is much more open and, because of that, also applicable within the *ecclesia*. Matthew 23, by contrast, is a clearly outward-facing text.

In all three cases, another group is mentioned in Mt. 6.1-18 next to the 'hypocrites': 'people'. From them, the 'hypocrites' expect honor (6.2: ὅπως δοξασθῶσιν ὑπὸ τῶν ἀνθρώπων) and prestige (6.5, 16: ὅπως φανῶσιν τοῖς ἀνθρώποις). They are not specified any further, but as they *also* appear in the synagogues, we can at least assume that Jews are *also* among this group. Thus, the 'hypocrites' are by no means identical with 'the Jews' or 'Israel' (contra Neusner)! In mentioning alleys and street corners (6.2, 5), Matthew apparently wants to include Gentiles. Just like in 5.13/16 (see above), the term comprises both Jews as well as Gentiles.

Jesus criticizes the hypocrites' way of almsgiving, prayer, and fasting, because it is aimed at *public visibility*. But principally—and both Neusner as well as Neyrey overlook this—they perform their actions in a manner that *distinguishes* them from and makes them stand out against the 'collective' of Israel, which is especially present in the synagogues. The 'hypocrites' are portrayed as performing their piety that *contrasts* them to and *elevates* them above Israel. They are *criticized* for setting themselves apart from the others and for having a *different* spirituality, otherwise they would not be visible as pious examples in their environment.

By no means can one say that the Matthean Jesus asks his Jewish followers to retreat from the synagogues, to break with the praying community of Israel, or to withdraw into their private spheres. And he does not say, 'that the only (!) valid prayer is offered up in secret' and consequently dismisses 'as null the practice of public worship'.[80] Collective and public Jewish practices, such as the care of the poor, communal prayer and liturgy as well as communal fasting (e.g. before Jewish feasts), are not addressed at all! Jesus does not worry about leaving the praying community of Israel (on the contrary, Matthew apparently still has in mind Jewish followers of

80. Neusner 1993: 33.

Jesus). What he wants his disciples to do is not to attract human attention by *publicly announcing* their almsgiving, *extensively* praying *on their own*, and *ostentatiously displaying* their fasting practices. The male followers of Jesus are publicly *neither to be recognized by performing nor by withdrawing from this.*

But how can they be recognized then? This question has already been answered within the Sermon on the Mount, precisely in the passage following 5.16, that is, in the so-called 'antitheses'. Let us now turn to this passage.

5. The Shining Light of Jesus' Disciples:
The Matthean Antitheses (Matthew 5.21-48)

According to Mt. 5.16 the light of the followers of Jesus should shine before people, that they may see their good works and glorify their Father who is in heaven. There is consensus that this sentence serves as a declaration of the subject for the following remarks.[81] If so, the following so-called antitheses consequently have to be interpreted not only in the light of 5.17-20,[82] but primarily as an explication of 5.16: in the antitheses, the Matthean Jesus gives examples of 'good works' by means of which his male disciples should be publicly visible and cause others to glorify God.

We hence approach the diverse *situations* presumed in the six antitheses, which Matthew only secondarily formulated as such.[83] As we saw earlier, the evangelist narrates male and public situations.

5.1. *Anger Towards One's Brother (Matthew 5.21-22)*
The first situation evoked by the Matthean Jesus is a verbal insult: in 5.22, a man is called an 'airhead' and a 'fool'. The insult is spoken by a man who is angry with 'his brother' (ὁ ὀργιζόμενος τῷ ἀδελφῷ αὐτοῦ).[84] The situation itself is not specified any further; it remains open whether or not the insult takes place publicly, but on the basis of 5.16, a public accusation is most

---

81. See Burchard 1998: 38.

82. On the relation of 5.17-20 to 5.21-48, see Broer 1980: 124-25: Matthew consciously put *both* contradictory conceptions of law next to one another, 'because apparently he believed that put together, both conceptions interdependently and thus adequately represent Jesus' perception of law' (author's translation).

83. On the problematic term 'antitheses', cf. the digression in Section 5.10.

84. Luz 2002a: 337, argues convincingly that v. 22a ('Everyone who is angry with his brother will be liable to judgment') is the major premise, while the two verbal insults in v. 22bc are pointed concretizations. Similarly, Betz 1995: 220: 'two illustrative examples...climactically arranged and parodistic in nature'. On the Matthean concept of a masculinity in which Jesus' followers are spiritual brothers (but not spiritual fathers), see Anderson and Moore 2003: 82-87.

likely. Furthermore, the implied audience of the Matthean *ecclesia* might primarily relate the keyword 'brother' to brothers within the community; however, the term itself is not limited at all in this context. Some components of the text (Sanhedrin, altar) even point in the direction of the 'Jewish comrade'.[85]

Obviously, 'the angry man' plays a key role here which exceeds the two following examples as well as the first antithesis in general. To capture the Matthean intention at this point, it is necessary to take a closer look at the ancient concepts of anger (ὀργή as well as θυμός). For that purpose, it is necessary to consider Aristotle's works, because more than any other ancient author, Aristotle dealt with the notion of anger and has therefore been nicknamed the 'defensor irae' by Seneca.[86]

For Aristotle, anger (ὀργή) is a passion or an emotion (πάθος).[87] In his *Rhetoric* he defines anger as a 'desire for visible revenge accompanied by pain' (ὄρεξις μετὰ λύπης τιμωρίας φαινομένης). It emerges due to public contempt (διὰ φαινομένην ὀλιγωρίαν), either towards ourselves or towards one of us, and is implemented by those who are generally not allowed to do so.[88] According to Aristotle, anger results from issues concerning ourselves and—as opposed to hate—it is always directed at individuals.[89] Usually, it is addressed to those individuals not having a big advantage over us in terms of power, which is why exacting vengeance is a real option.[90] Anger hence emerges when our mind or imagination proclaim an insult (ὕβρις) or disdain (ὀλιγωρία).[91] David Konstan puts it this way:

> Anger for Aristotle, then, is anything but a reflex to pain or harm, even when the cause is intentional. Aristotle envisages a world in which self-esteem depends on social interaction: the moment someone's negative opinion of your worth is actualized publicly in the form of a slight, you have lost credit, and the only recourse is a compensatory act that restores your social position. Anger is just the desire to adjust the record in this way—the internal correlative to the outward loss of respect.[92]

---

85. Cf. Davies and Allison 1991: 512-13, who also include the walk to the court, although the adversary in 5.25-26 is precisely not labeled as 'brother'.

86. Seneca, *De ira* 3.3.1 (ed. M. Rosenbach, Schriften I, Darmstadt: Wissenschaftliche Buchgesellschaft 1999). In his work on anger, Seneca deals with Aristotle thoroughly (cf. 1.3.3; 1.9.2; 1.17.1 and elsewhere).

87. On Aristotle's conception of anger, cf. Harris 2001: 93-98, and Konstan 2003: 99-120.

88. Aristotle, *Rhet.* 2.2 (1378a30-32).

89. Aristotle, *Rhet.* 2.2 (1378a32-35) and 2.4 (1382a1-7).

90. Aristotle, *Rhet.* 1.11 (1370b13-15).

91. Aristotle, *Eth. nic.* 7.6 (1149a30ff.). Cf. *Rhet.* 2.2: 'We get angry with those who slight us'.

92. Konstan 2003: 114.

Moreover, it is important that anger is connected with both pleasure (ἡδονή) and pain (λύπη), with pleasure especially arising from the expectation of revenge.[93]

Aristotle, therefore, is far away from criticizing anger itself. Just like with lust and other passions, there is 'too much', 'too little', and the right measure (τὸ μέσον).[94] The man who justifiably rages against something and who is rightly angry with someone in a correct manner, at the right moment and for the right amount of time, is praised (ἐπαινεῖται).[95] A moderate attitude, in particular with regard to anger, is considered praiseworthy (ἡ μὲν μέση ἕξις).[96]

Indifference, by contrast, is a defect in the passion of anger (ἀοργησία) and must be reprimanded according to Aristotle. A man who does not get angry makes a fool of himself (ἠλίθιοι) and is considered unable to defend himself (οὐκ εἶναι ἀμυντικός). It is a sign of an unmanly slave mentality (ἀνδραποδῶδες) to accept insults (τὸ προπηλακιζόμενον ἀνέχεσθαι) both against oneself and against one's family.[97] Thus, anger is closely linked to manliness and fortitude (ἀνδρεῖα), respectively.[98]

These considerations show that an angry man has *reason* to be angry. In most cases, anger is a *reaction*, and not an arbitrary aversion. The angry man in Mt. 5.22 therefore is a man who has been *provoked*.[99] The revenge resulting from passion/lust and anger is primarily *retaliation*.[100] As illustrated by the examples of classical epics, a man's anger usually has a history and is strongly connected with the ancient Mediterranean code of honor and shame. Anger originates when honor is refused, challenged or offended, it is

93. Aristotle, *Rhet.* 2.2 (1378b1f.): καὶ πάσῃ ὀργῇ ἕπεσθαί τινα ἡδονήν, τὴν ἀπὸ τῆς ἐλπίδος τοῦ τιμωρήσασθαι. Cf. also *Rhet.* 1.11 (1370b10f.) with reference to Homer. Also revenge itself is connected with pleasure (1370b30). Cf. *Eth. nic.* 3.8 (1117a5ff.): Angry people may feel pain, but as soon as they take revenge, they will feel pleasure (καὶ οἱ ἄνθρωποι δὴ ὀργιζόμενοι μὲν ἀλγοῦσι, τιμωρούμενοι δ' ἥδονται); 4.5 (1126a23ff.): Revenge puts an end to anger and turns pain into pleasure.

94. Aristotle, *Eth. nic.* 2.6 (1106b16ff.) and 2.7 (1108a2ff.), cf. 4.5.

95. Aristotle, *Eth. nic.* 4.5 (1125b30ff.).

96. Aristotle, *Eth. nic.* 4.5 (1126b5ff.).

97. Aristotle, *Eth. nic.* 4.5 (1126a1ff.).

98. Aristotle, *Eth. nic.* 3.8 (1116b23f.): καὶ τὸν θυμὸν δ' ἐπὶ τὴν ἀνδρείαν φέρουσιν.

99. For that reason, Aristotle, *Rhet.* 2.2, refers to the angry *Achilles* (1378b31-35)! Cf. also *Rhet.* 2.4 (1382a14f.): whoever is angry desires that he whom he is angry at *suffers in turn* (ἀντιπαθεῖν), whoever hates desires that the object of his hate no longer exists (μὴ εἶναι). On that, cf. also Neyrey 1998: 192: 'But in 5.22, the man who is angered (ὀργιζόμενος) has been challenged or provoked by another'. Wis. 10.3 speaks of ὀργή and θυμός as the reason for Cain's murder of Abel, and Wis. 10.10 refers to Esau's ὀργή on Jacob.

100. So, rightly, Harris 2001: 57: 'The implication is clear that while *orgē* is an emotion, it is only *orgē*, if it leads to action or comes close to leading to action'.

'a response to a slight, that is, an attack upon one's social standing or honor, entailing a desire to restore one's position by a compensating act of retribution'.[101] When contempt and insult cause anger, one can justifiably speak of ὀργή as 'active anger'.[102]

Hence, Mt. 5.22 effectively addresses a male *victim* of a slight ready to *strike back* verbally. All the more shocking seems Jesus' equation of anger (ὀργίζειν) and murder,[103] as well as his statement: every man who is angry with his brother will be liable to judgment. The question of the reason for anger does not even arise and Jesus' command has nothing to do with repressing one's feelings.[104] Rather, anger is penalized here as a *reaction to* an insult, because it is assumed to lead to *retaliation* at once.

For Aristotle as well as for the Matthean Jesus, the opposite of anger is *gentleness* (or calmness: ἡ πραότης κτλ). Aristotle defines it as an interruption and easing of anger.[105] More precisely, gentleness is the opposite of *excessive, exorbitant* anger.[106] For Aristotle, the problem is not anger itself (see above), but rather being angry with somebody one should not be angry with, something one should not be angry about, or generally being too angry altogether.[107] The one who, on the other hand, has a proper reason for their anger and only rages for a limited amount of time, is gentle just as well.[108] For Jesus, by contrast, *anger* and *gentleness* are diametrically opposed, because *retaliation* is the criterion.

Jesus' condemnation of anger hence refers back to the third beatitude: The πραεῖς blessed in 5.5 are 'gentlemen' who do not rage, that is, those who do not react to a provocation by insulting their opponents verbally. Whoever acts this way, will inherit the land (Mt. 5.5 = Ps. 37.11 LXX).

It would be erroneous, however, to assume that Jesus challenges 'the' ancient ideal of masculinity. Just like him, a whole range of ancient authors, both pagan as well as Jewish, consider anger to be negative.[109] Not least

---

101.　Konstan 2003: 115. Extensively, Aristotle, *Rhet.* 2.2 (1379a30-80a5).

102.　Harris 2001: 401, and *passim*.

103.　Jewish parallels are legion; see Wengst 2010: 84-91, and Luz 2002a: 338ff. with his conclusion: 'As regards content, the first antithesis is by no means novel' (author's translation).

104.　Harris 2001: 392: 'But none of these imperatives [of Mt. 5.39] was specifically about emotions'.

105.　Aristotle, *Rhet.* 2.3 (1380a6f.): ἐπεὶ δὲ τὸ ὀργίζεσθαι ἐναντίον τῷ πραΰνεσθαι καὶ ὀργὴ πραότητι...

106.　Aristotle, *Eth. nic.* 4.5 (1126a29): τῇ πραότητι δὲ μᾶλλον τὴν ὑπερβολὴν ἀντιτίθεμεν.

107.　Extensively, Aristotle, *Eth. nic.* 4.5 (1125b26-1126b9).

108.　Aristotle, *Eth. nic.* 4.5 (1125b30ff.).

109.　Pagan texts comparable to Mt. 5.21-22 are especially Plutarch, *De cohibenda ira* (= *Mor.* 452F-464D) and Seneca, *De ira*. The latter considers anger 'the biggest evil'

Jewish-Hellenistic sapiential literature formulates the ideal of the 'prudent and patient man' for young male Jews, which is often contrasted with the 'irascible man' as its negative counterpart.[110] For example, Prov. 15.1[111] also proves that an offending statement provokes anger, and shortly afterwards it is said. 'A man who rules his anger (ὁ δὲ κρατῶν ὀργῆς) is better than he who takes a city' (Prov. 16.32 LXX).

Notably, large parts of contemporary literature, pagan as well as Jewish, regarded anger as a loss of control, or even as a sign of *effeminacy*![112] According to R. Harris, one of the things that was wrong with anger was that it was feminine,[113] and this of course has much to do with self-control. Men who master their emotions and control their anger are not at all 'softies'—in fact, the opposite is the case. Jesus' position belongs to this context in demanding of his disciples rather masculine self-control, although he neither argues philosophically nor develops any kind of training or therapy, but rather imposes tough sanctions against anger by means of his divine power.

(2.12.6: *maximum malum*), which has to be completely abolished (2.13.3). He rejects the perception that a *vir bonus* must be able to rage (*De ira* 1.12 and elsewhere); anger does *not* support manfulness (*in adiotorium virtutis*), it rather *replaces* it (*sed in vicem*) (II.13.4-5). For other treatises on the emotions and on anger, cf. the list in Harris 2001: 127-28.

110.   Cf., e.g., (LXX versions!) Prov. 14.17 (ὀξύθυμος vs. ἀνὴρ φρόνιμος); 15.1 (anger also kills reasonable persons: ὀργὴ ἀπόλλυσιν καὶ φρονίμους); 15.18 (ἀνὴρ θυμώδης vs. μακρόθυμος); 22.24-25 (warning against friendship with an ἀνδρὶ θυμώδει and φίλῳ ὀργίλῳ). The comparison of 'anger' and 'patience' can also be found in Sir. 1.22-24 and elsewhere. Josephus praises the Essenes in *Bell.* 2.135 as 'righteous masters of anger and conquerors of wrath' (ὀργῆς ταμίαι δίκαιοι, θυμοῦ καθεκτικόι) before mentioning their refusal to swear an oath (see below).

111.   Prov. 15.1 LXX: λόγος δὲ λυπηρὸς ἐγείρει ὀργάς.

112.   For Seneca, anger is a sign of mushiness and self-pitying; thus he infers in *De Ira* 1.20.3: 'In the first place, anger is a female and childish vice' (*ita ira muliebre maxime ac puerile uitium est*). At II.13.5 he notes that 'children, old and sick persons' are most likely to get angry. Anger is a result of 'delicate and pampered education' (*educatio mollis et blanda*, 2.21.6). Also for Plutarch anger is neither noble nor masculine (οὐκ εὐγενὴς οὐδ' ἀνδρώδης), but is a sign of littleness and weakness (μικρότητα...καὶ ἀσθένειαν)—and that is why women are more prone to anger (ὀργιλώτεραι) than men (*Cohib. Ira* 8). Anger even was transferred from the women's quarters to the men's (*Cohib. Ira* 9)! Plutarch's deterring description of intemperately angry men is striking as well, in particular the account of their shrill voices and their red swollen faces (*Cohib. ira* 6-7). Cf., in the Old Testament, the contorted face of King Nebuchadnezzar filled with rage in Dan. 3.19. See also Conway 2008: 26-29, and the illuminating chapter, 'A Thesis on Women and Anger', in Harris 2001: 264-82.

113.   Harris 2001: 406. Cf. p. 264: 'The angry emotions were feminine'. For Harris, the ancient critique of anger and the ideology of anger control 'thus came to be, among other things, an instrument of male domination'.

5.2. *A Brother's Anger (Matthew 5.23-24)*

The situation changes in 5.23-24. During the offering at the Temple—in fact, *prior to* putting the gift on the altar[114]—the addressee ('you') remembers 'that your brother has something against you (ἔχει τι κατὰ σοῦ)'. The very general formulation is striking; neither the cause of the thought nor the reason for the conflict with the brother is mentioned. It is, however, obvious that, in contrast to 5.21-22, the *offender*, who insulted and dishonored his 'brother' in some way, is addressed here.[115] In effect, the brother is 'angered' (ὀργιζόμενος) now, but Matthew avoids labeling him as such, or else the audience could refer back to the maxim condemning anger altogether in 5.21-22. The addressed follower of Jesus is supposed to be proactive: he is encouraged to break the offering and reconcile with his brother *first* (πρῶτον). Only *then* (τότε) is he allowed to perform the offering. This order implies that the reconciliation with the brother is a precondition for the offering. Reconciliation (διαλλάσσομαι) in turn might include redemption, but again the text remains open.[116]

It is striking how often Aristotle mentions anger (ὀργή as well as θυμός) in the same breath as desire (ἐπιθυμία).[117] Moreover, he particularly associates *young men* (οἱ νέοι) with these two emotions, namely, anger (ὀργή) and desire (ἐπιθυμία).[118] Young men especially follow them (ἀκολουθεῖν τῇ ὀργῇ), since they cannot bear contempt (ὀλιγωρούμενοι) due to their desire for honor (διὰ φιλοτιμίαν). Rather, they rebel when they feel treated unjustly. On the one hand, young men are manly and brave (ἀνδρειότεροι); on the other, they can be embarrassed easily (αἰσχυντηλοί). In general, emotions such as love, hate, and desire are much more pronounced among them (φιλοῦσι γὰρ ἄγαν καὶ μισοῦσιν ἄγαν καὶ τἆλλα πάντα ὁμοίως) and integrated into their agonal behavior, because youth strives for superiority. Hence, the *young* man (ὁ νέος) is most likely to follow his affects (τοῖς

114. This assumption results from the fact that the addressee is supposed to lay down his offering *before* the altar (ἔμπροσθεν τοῦ θυσιαστηρίου). See Betz 1995: 223: 'The moment is crucial. The thought interferes at the precise moment when the gift is to be placed on the altar, when it leaves human hands and becomes the property of God'.

115. Rightly so Neyrey 1998: 193 (in line with Betz 1995: 223): 'the person who "has something against you" is the victim of a challenge and that "you" is the aggressor or challenger' (with reference to Mk 11.25; 1 Cor. 6.1; Rev. 2.4). Cf. Davies and Allison 1991: 517: 'The subject of ἔχω is clearly the innocent party'.

116. Cf. Strecker 1984: 70; Neyrey 1998: 193: 'some balance is restored where there was damage or loss'. LSJ: 401, aptly translate: 'change enmity for friendship'.

117. E.g. *Rhet.* 2.2 (1103a17). In the enumeration of the πάθη in 2.4, ἐπιθυμία and ὀργή are in the first positions. Cf. primarily 7.7 (the lack of self-control regarding anger is less reprehensible than regarding desire).

118. On the following, cf. the characterization of young men in *Rhet.* 2.12 (1388b31-89b12).

πάθησιν ἀκολουθητικός).[119] So, in regard to anger and desire, men in their prime will be manful as well as temperate and temperate as well as manful.[120]

One could (!) regard this as a hint at the primarily addressed audience of the Sermon on the Mount. The situations discussed here are relevant not least for *young men* in antiquity; however, Jesus' examples also refer to husbands, debtors, creditors, and so on. Instructions aimed at *fathers* are lacking.[121] The exclusive restriction to men at a certain age, that is, male adolescence, works best for parts of the first, second and fifth antithesis, as they presume agonal situations (challenges of honor).

In addition to that, Aristotle explicitly denies young men greed (φιλοχρή-ματοι),[122] because adolescents (at least those of the upper class) strive for honor, and even more so, for victory instead (φιλότιμοι μέν εἰσιν, μᾶλλον δὲ φιλόνικοι). Matthew, by contrast, confronts his readers in Mt. 19.16-22 with a *young man* (ὁ νεανίσκος) who, although he kept the Decalogue as well as the commandment of love, fails to follow Jesus because of his vast fortune which he is not willing to sell for the benefit of the poor. Similarly, the Matthean Jesus warns his male disciples against the accumulation of earthly treasures in 6.19. As opposed to Aristotle, the young men's greed seems to be an issue for Matthew, which also typifies the social position of his addressees.

5.3. *Bonding with the Adversary (Matthew 5.25-26)*

The next situation is a trial. The addressed 'you' is unmistakably charac-terized as a *debtor* threatened by custody 'until you have paid the last penny'. It is not clear whether the culprit borrowed money from his adversary (ὁ ἀντίδικος) which he cannot pay back, or whether he caused him any harm which can only be compensated by monetary payment (e.g. an injury).[123] Just like in the preceding scene, the protagonist is addressed as an *offender* or *tortfeasor* who is now in a very *unfavorable* situation himself, as he is

---

119.   Aristotle, *Eth. nic.* 1.3 (1095a2-6), this also holds true for men with an immature character.

120.   Aristotle, *Rhet.* 2.14 (1390b3f.): σώφρονες μετ' ἀνδρείας καὶ ἀνδρεῖοι μετὰ σωφροσύνης.

121.   On the affirmation of the male role of brotherhood and the rejection of literal and metaphorical fatherhood in the Gospel of Matthew, see Anderson and Moore 2003: 84-87.

122.   Aristotle, *Rhet.* 2.12 (1389a13-16). The fact that he considers young men non-greedy because they have never been in need, underlines that Aristotle solely bears in mind young men of the *upper class*.

123.   Compensatory payments were required for some delinquencies avenged according to the talion principle; cf. Josephus, *Ant.* 4.8.35. Neyrey 1998: 193, states decisively: 'Thus, we identify the man addressed as the challenger who has injured another person'. See also Malina 2001: 43.

threatened by dishonoring custody, a result which Matthew seems to have interpreted as an allegory to the menacing reprobation in the Last Judgment.

Both men, the debtor addressed as 'you' as well as his adversary, are on their way (ἐν τῇ ὁδῷ) to court. In effect, this only makes sense presuming a rural perspective where people need to cover a distance to reach the next town with a courthouse.[124] It is likely, but not said, that their destination is a pagan court and that the adversary is a Gentile.[125] Jesus hence suggests making use of the common path to become friends with the adversary. If this is realized by means of a financial agreement or any other arrangement prior to the trial, the possibility of a gesture of reconciliation, restoring honor, and so on, remains open. What is clear, though, is that the *initiative* must be taken by the *offender* (just like in 5.23-24).

Generally, the surface of the text aims at the *prevention* of the trial altogether, but the crucial point is to not even begin the domino effect connected with the trial by the initiative of the εὐνοεῖν. Therefore, the reconciliation with the adversary is located *ahead of* the trial (metaphorically: on the way to court). For Matthew, the emphasis is not so much on the threat of judgment, but rather on the relentless progress of the trial (κριτής—ὑπηρέτης—φυλακή). This sequence of events might be the reason for the evangelist's interest in the passage and his decision to place it into the context of the first antithesis.

The first 'antithesis' has been composed redactionally from distinctive Matthean material (5.22, 23-24) and material from the Sayings Source (cf. Mt. 5.25-26 with Q 12.57-59). More specifically, the short parable on the walk to court deriving from Q has been revised by Matthew.[126] Instead of the Lukan expression ἀπαλλάχθαι ('to get away'), Matthew makes use of the imperative ἴσθι εὐνοῶν ('be well-disposed!') in order to connect to the preceding demand for reconciliation (5.24). It should be suggested that Matthew probably wanted to display the Last Judgment behind the surface of the trial depicted in Q and emphasize the threat of judgment by the 'amen'.[127]

The phrase ἴσθι εὐνοῶν τῷ ἀντιδίκῳ σου ταχύ, redactionally inserted by Matthew, is particularly striking. Εὐνοεῖν is by no means a 'Greek hackneyed word'.[128] It can rarely be found in the LXX (Est. 8.13; Dan. 2.43;

---

124.   See Ebner 2003: 121.

125.   Luz 2002a: 345, points to the horror of a pagan trial, because custody was unknown in Jewish law.

126.   See Strecker 1984: 71-72.

127.   Cf. the Matthean phrase παραδιδόναι τῷ κριτῇ (instead of κατασύρῃ). The expression τῷ ὑπηρέτῃ (instead of τῷ πράκτορι) might be indicative of the angels; cf. Mt. 13.41-42, 49-50; 25.31.

128.   As opposed to Luz 2002a: 345. Nevertheless, it is by no means right to comprehend εὐνόω in the context of διαλλάγηθι.

3 Macc. 7.11), but it is closely linked to the ancient ethics of *friendship*, as can be seen in Aristotle's *Nicomachean Ethics*.

According to Aristotle, someone is 'well-meaning' (εὔνους) if he wishes his friend well just for the sake of his friend. Friendship (φιλία) and benevolence (or goodwill: εὔνοια) are not the same, because benevolence can also be directed at a *stranger* (πρὸς ἀγνῶτας) and thereby remain unrecognized. Furthermore, it can emerge *suddenly* (ἐκ προσπαίου). Nevertheless, friendship and benevolence correlate closely for Aristotle, because the latter precedes the former. He therefore defines benevolence as a form of a 'beginning of friendship' (ἀρχὴ φιλίας) and still 'idle friendship' (ἀργὴ φιλία), which only develops into true friendship over time and by practice.[129] Thus, he regards friendship as 'reciprocal benevolence'.[130]

Someone who received benefactions will give benevolence in turn according to Aristotle's concept,[131] and it might also emerge if someone appears beautiful or brave, for example, in a competition.

Here, the Matthean Jesus clearly puts emphasis on different aspects. Instructing his disciples to meet their adversaries with benevolence, he asks them to take a first step towards ancient *male bonding* (φιλία), although the proceeding remains unspecific.[132]

Again, we can observe obvious references to the macarisms unique to the Gospel of Matthew. The 'peacemakers' are blessed (5.9) as well as those not using violence although they could.

5.4. *The Lustful Glance at another Man's Wife (Matthew 5.27-30)*
This passage deals with the encounter of a man and another man's wife. Although the term γυνή ('woman') is used in 5.28 instead of the precise term γαμητή ('wife'), the keyword ἐμοίχευσεν ('to commit adultery') indicates that the *glance has to be darted at a married* woman.[133] Jesus prohibits

---

129. Aristotle, *Eth. nic.* 9.5 (1167a1ff.).

130. Aristotle, *Eth. nic.* 9.5 (1167a1ff.).

131. Aristotle, *Eth. nic.* 9.5 (1167a14f.): ὁ μὲν γὰρ εὐεργετηθεὶς ἀνθ᾽ ὧν πέπονθεν ἀπονέμει τὴν εὔνοιαν.

132. A very surprising, though inverse, linguistic parallel can be found with Aristotle, who claims that one can get away with injustice if one is *friends* (φίλοι ὦσιν) either with the victims of one's deeds (τοῖς ἀδικουμένοις) or with the judges, because friends do not recognize injustice and they are more likely to reconcile (προσκαταλλάττονται) (*Rhet.* 1.12 [1372a15-20]).

133. Matthew probably makes use of γυνή because of its relatedness to the ninth commandment of the Decalogue (οὐκ ἐπιθυμήσεις τὴν γυναῖκα τοῦ πλησίον σου, Exod. 20.17/Deut. 5.21). Cf. also Lev. 20.10 (γυνὴ ἀνδρός and γυνὴ τοῦ πλησίον) as well as Sir. 41.22 (ὁράσεως γυναικὸς ἑταίρας). On the grammatical analysis of the tricky phrase πρὸς τὸ ἐπιθυμῆσαι αὐτήν, see Zerwick and Grosvenor 1993: 12, who assume a Semitic Constructus-Compound: 'with force of gerund (lusting) = with lust'. The connection of

glancing at another man's wife by referring to the ninth commandment of the Decalogue with the keyword ἐπιθυμεῖν.[134] Hence, he does *not* want to prohibit every form of contact between men and women or fan fear of dirty thoughts.

What happens on the part of the woman, on the other hand, is left out completely.[135] Also, the presumed situation is not specified any further: Does the encounter take place in public, for example, in the agora, in the street, at the theatre or the temple precincts? Or is it supposed to take place in private, for example, during a visit? Could it even concern the imminent danger of intimate contact between men and women living together in a confined space, as they are itinerantly following Jesus?[136] Jesus' prohibition of the male lustful glance can be applied to all these and many other situations. Matthew 5.16, however, presupposes that refraining from staring at another man's wife distinguishes the followers of Jesus from other men in public.

The underlying ancient conception of the process of vision as well as its gender-specific accentuation can be traced once again in the works of Philo of Alexandria:[137] According to Philo, the senses of hearing and sight are superior to the other ones, but the ears are 'in a way more sluggish and *womanish* (βραδύτερα δέ πως καὶ θηλύτερα) than the eyes', because ears are only activated by an external stimulus (τι τῶν ἔκτος) and hence function *passively*. Therefore, Philo awards royal dignity to the eyes, because they dominate the other senses and actively, boldly reach towards that which is visible (ἐπὶ τὰ ὁρατὰ φθανόντων ὑπὸ εὐτολμίας). Eyes do not wait— passively and thus femininely—'to be acted on' by the objects, 'but antici- pate the meeting and seek to act upon them instead' (προϋπαντιαζόντων δὲ καὶ ἀντικινῆσαι γλιχομένων). Their activity and sustained occupation[138] constitute the 'male' character of the open and shifting eyes, although we have to acknowledge that in contrast to its female counterpart which occurs in connection with the ears, the term ἀρρενικός (or ἀρρενωπός, respectively) is not mentioned explicitly.

'seeing' (ἰδόντες) and 'desiring' (ἐπιθυμήσαντες) can also be found in Sus. 7–8 LXX, cf. also Prov. 6.24-25 (γυναικὸς ὑπάνδρου—ἐπιθυμία—σοῖς ὀφθαλμοῖς), Sir. 23.4-5, but also Job 24.15 (the eye of the adulterer).

134.   The two commandments were often combined in Judaism; see Luz 2002a: 347, in line with K. Berger.

135.   Duff 2001: 64: 'The woman plays a passive role. In fact, her role in the interchange goes virtually unnoticed except for the fact that her presence has provided stimulus for the male's lust.' This feature fundamentally distinguishes Mt. 5.28 from texts such as Sir. 26.9-12; Prov. 5; 7 etc.

136.   See Ebner 2003: 151.

137.   On the following, cf. Philo, *Abr.* 147-55 (LCL, Philo VI, ed. F.H. Colson).

138.   Philo, *Abr.* 154: 'the eyes when open are constant an uneasing in their activities (αἱ δὲ ὀφθαλμῶν ἀναπεπταμένων ἐνέργειαι συνεχεῖς καὶ μηδέποτε πληρουμένων εἰσί)'.

The background to the allocation of the male gender role to the eyes is the ancient conception of vision as an *active* process: the eye is not a passive, receptive sensory organ. It contains an inherent power which is emitted to the objects the gaze touches upon.[139] According to Plato's *Timaios*, the eye itself contains light or fire, and vision hence originates when the 'stream of vision' (τὸ τῆς ὄψεως ῥεῦμα) emerges from the eye and then merges with the sunlight.[140] It is important, however, that this fusion generates its own 'body' (σῶμα) or a part of the body, which conveys to the body and soul of the seeing subject the movements (κινήσεις) of the items it encounters. One can therefore argue that, according to this theory, the human gaze resembles an extended body part with which the seeing subject accesses objects in its surroundings.

For Plutarch, the human gaze is a form of 'emanations or effluences of bodies' (ἀπόρροια τῶν σωμάτων), comparable to smell, voice, and breathing, or even more than them.[141] According to him, the gaze radiates a miraculous power, because it is strongly moved (cf. above, Philo) and emitted by means of a fire-like breeze.[142] Due to the substance emitted through the gaze, Plutarch pointedly claims that neither through touch nor audible messages can lovers suffer more pain than through gazing or being gazed at.[143] He thus compares the gaze with an injury caused by a *stroke* or poisoned *arrows*.[144]

According to Jesus, the marriage of the other man is broken by the *gaze* (not by lustful thoughts!). The man who looks at another man's wife with

---

139.   Cf. Rakoczy 1996: 20. Despite several distinctions in the details, all ancient theories of vision share this common notion, except for the Epicureans and Aristotle (whose remarks are inconsistent, however).

140.   On the following, cf. Plato, *Timaios* 16 (45A-46C). Plato speaks of φωσφόρα ὄμματα (45B), as the eyes contain a 'fire' (πῦρ) congeneric with the sunlight. Therefore, two similar substances merge with each other in the process of vision (ὅμοιον πρὸς ὅμοιον, 45C). Vision is hence regarded a merging of the inner and outer fire (ἐκ γὰρ τῆς ἐντὸς ἐκτός τε τοῦ πυρὸς ἑκατέρου κοινωνίας ἀλλήλοις, 46A). See Rakoczy 1996: 23-24.

141.   On the following, cf. Plutarch, *Mor.* 680F-681F (= *Quaest con.* 5.7.2-3) (LCL, Plutarch, *Mor.* 8, ed. P.A. Clement and H.B. Hoffleit).

142.   Plutarch, *Mor.* 681A: 'For vision, being off enormous swiftness and carried by an essence that gives off a flame-like brilliance, diffuses a wondrous influence' (πολυκίνητος γὰρ ἡ ὄψις οὖσα μετὰ πνεύματος αὐγὴν αὐτὴν ἀφιέντος πυρώδη θαυμαστήν τινα διασπείρει δύναμιν).

143.   *Mor.* 681B: 'Neither by touch nor by hearing do they suffer so deep a wound as by seeing and being seen' (οὔτε γὰρ ἁπτομένοις οὔτ' ἀκούουσιν οὕτω τιτρώσκεσθαι συμβαίνει καὶ πάσχειν, ὡς προσβλεπομένοις καὶ προσβλέπουσι).

144.   *Mor.* 681D: 'as if by a blow (ὥσπερ ὑπὸ πληγῆς τιτρωσκόμενοι)'; *Mor.* 681E: 'as if with a poisoned arrows; (ὥσπερ πεφαρμαγμένα βέλη προσπίπωσιν). Further examples (the gaze as a 'missile', 'lance' etc.) are to be found in Rakoczy 1996: 34-36.

lust destroys *her* marriage, not his own.[145] Hence, the passage is actually about the preservation of the man's vested rights,[146] that is, the husband of the woman who is gazed at. By means of the adjunct ἐν τῇ καρδίᾳ αὐτοῦ, the offence of adultery is located in the heart of the *man* with the lustful glance, and not on the part of the wife.[147]

According to Mt. 15.19, the heart is the source of evil thoughts, murder, adultery (μοιχεῖαι), fornication (πορνεῖαι), theft, false testimony, and blasphemies. Matthew 15.17-19 is primarily concerned with the connection of heart and mouth; Mt. 5.27, by contrast, is about the relation of heart and mind.[148] Nevertheless, both passages are comparable: adultery originates in the man's heart and then emerges either from the mouth (15.17-18) or from the eye (5.27). Just as in the case of verbal insult, the penalty for adultery recoils entirely on the man with the 'lustful' glance.

As the lustful male glance at another man's wife can be interpreted as an 'act of bodily violence' (see above), Matthew combines Jesus' application of Old Testament adultery laws to the male gaze with a sequence deriving either from Q or Mark. This sequence, which speaks of the torn out *eye* and the chopped off *hand*, is arranged differently in Matthew as compared to Mark. Matthew puts the eye first and does not transmit the third example mentioned in Mk 9.45, namely the foot (other than in Mt. 18.8-9).[149] What connects eye and hand is the possibility of violence towards another man's wife, because both can 'cross the line' towards another person.[150]

It should also be noted at this point that, in contrast to today, excessive sexual interest in women was precisely *not* a proof of masculinity in many Roman sources. On the contrary, it was rather considered *effeminate*.[151] So,

145. See Strecker 1984: 73, furthermore Duff 2001: 72-73. Cf. also the warning directed at young Jewish men in Sir. 41.22-23: (αἰσχύνεσθε) ἀπὸ ὁράσεως γυναικὸς ἑταίρας... καὶ ἀπὸ κατανοήσεως γυναικὸς ὑπάνδρου. In addition, cf. 9.9.

146. See Melzer-Keller 1997: 159.

147. Other than, e.g., in Prov. 5.1-20; 7; Sir. 9 etc., the Matthean Jesus does *not* claim the woman has incited the man's lustful glance, e.g., by her styling or suggestive behavior.

148. In Eccl. 11.9-10 LXX, the young man (νεανίσκε) is warned that God will bring him into judgment *because* of his *heart* and *eyes*. According to Sir. 3.17-18, the *heart* is the seat of both good and evil, life and death.

149. In Mt. 18.8-9, the order is as follows: hand–foot–eye. For a comparison with Mt. 5.30, cf. Philo, *Spec. leg.* 3.176-77 (eye–hand).

150. Cf. Philo, *Spec. leg.* 3. According to him, a woman who publicly pinches a man's genitals justly gets her hand cut off.

151. Cf. Conway 2008: 25. An example for that is Plutarch's depiction of Pompey, who is so addicted to his young wife that he spends most of his time together with her in villas and gardens (i.e. within the women's realm)—and not on the agora (*Pomp.* 48.5-7). Adultery itself was considered 'unmanly' as well; cf. Conway's comment: 'In fact,

Jesus' disciples are therefore required to demonstrate their masculine self-control in refraining from the lustful glance at women.

5.5. *Divorcing One's Wife and Marrying a Divorced Woman (Matthew 5.31-32)*

The Matthean Jesus prohibits divorcing one's wife—except in the case of fornication (πορνεία), that is, if the woman commits adultery[152]—as well as marrying a divorced woman. Again, a purely male perspective dominates: whoever divorces his wife, although it is allowed in the Torah, forces her to break with her own marriage (in case she remarries), that is, the marriage with the man who divorced her. And whoever marries a divorced woman ruins the marriage of her first husband.[153]

The so-called Matthean exception clause matches this conception of marriage. Divorce is considered adultery and hence forbidden, except in the case of πορνεία (5.32; 19.9; cf. Sir. 25.26). The use of the more general term πορνεία ('fornication'), which also includes illegitimate marriages, and so on,[154] instead of μοιχεία ('adultery'), probably originates from the fact that the former term is used for women more often. In the case of πορνεία, adultery is committed and thus divorce is the necessary consequence.[155] Just like in the antithesis regarding adultery, the sanctity of marriage is emphasized. It is made clear that this sanctity is damaged irreparably when the woman has an extramarital affair.

The position of the Gospel of Matthew has internal Jewish implications. It is 'a shift from the Essene-like rejection of divorce of the Jesus tradition

---

charges of effeminacy are frequently accompanied by charges of adultery, because adultery was another case of a lack of restraint'. Chariton therefore describes the adulterer as a man whose hair shines with silk, who has perfumed curls and painted eyes, wears fine, soft clothes and many rings around his fingers (*Kallirhoe* 1.4.9). According to Artemidorus, men who dream of wearing jewelry, make-up (!) and cream, are doomed to be exposed as adulterers (*Oneir.* 81.15-17; 106.16–107.2).

152.   On that point, see Schenk 1987: 117.

153.   Schenk 1987: 113-15: γαμέω does not mean 'to marry', but 'to take a wife' (the man is the subject); μοιχεύω does not mean 'to commit adultery', but 'to become an adulteress' (an unmarried woman cannot be the object of this verb, cf. Deut. 22.22). Luz 2002a: 350, argues in the same vein.

154.   E.g. pagan intermarriages (between related persons) are illegitimate for Jews according to Lev. 18 (probably also referred to in Acts 15.20, 29); but also adultery (Sir. 23.23), incest (*Test. Rub.* 1.6), homosexual practices (*Sib.* 3.764), and so on, are covered by the term πορνεία. According to Luz 2002a: 363, a woman's extramarital sexual activity is meant here.

155.   See Schenk 1987: 117. He points out justly that the passage deals with the *observation* of adultery, not the permission of divorce. Cf. also Prov. 18.22a LXX: 'He who keeps an adulteress (μοιχαλίδα), is ignorant (ἄφρων) and godless (ἀσεβής)'.

to the clearly Shammaite position of divorce in case of adultery'.[156] Yet it is controversial whether or not the Matthean formulation implies a *commandment* for divorce in the case of adultery, as can be traced in rabbinical sources. In any case, M. Vahrenhorst, for instance, has proven a halacha from pre-rabbinic times which claims that extramarital sexual intercourse stains a married woman, so that sexual relations between the spouses become impossible.[157] The so-called exception clause therefore aims at protecting the 'cuckold' from cultic impurity by invalidating the prohibition of divorce in this particular case.

5.6. *The Prohibition of the Oath (Matthew 5.33-37)*

The fourth antithesis is concerned with speech.[158] Although not stated explicitly and although the Torah also prescribes oaths for women,[159] in the light of Mt. 5.16 the passage most likely refers to public speech, in particular that of men.[160] It remains completely open, however, whether the presumed situation is an everyday situation,[161] forensic,[162] economic,[163] political,[164] or for example, an initiation.[165] The discussion about the reach of Matthew's prohibition of oaths underlines that the text itself remains open here. We

156.   Tomson 2010: 331; cf. pp. 311-17 (on the schools of the Pharisees) and 323-26 (on Matthew). Tomson concludes from the given evidence that the Matthean ecclesia belongs to the Shammaite or at least to a Pharisaic milieu.

157.   Vahrenhorst 2002: 407-409, with reference to *m. Ned.* 11.12, *m. Sota* 5.1 and *b. Sanh.* 41A, as well as to Philo, *Abr.* 98 and others. Particularly illuminating is the reference to Mt. 1.19-20, where Joseph, the 'just man', is apparently afraid to marry his seemingly impure fiancé who must have been touched by another man.

158.   On the following, see Kollmann 2001, as well as Vahrenhorst 2002: 217-76, and Malina 2001: 41.

159.   On the so-called ordeal oath for the conviction of a woman suspected of adultery, see Num. 5.11-31.

160.   On that point, cf., e.g., Sir. 23.7-15, an instruction about talking directed at young Jews and warning them against *oaths* (vv. 9-11: ὅρκῳ μὴ ἐθίσῃς τὸ στόμα σου καὶ ὀνομασίᾳ τοῦ ἁγίου μὴ συνεθισθῇς...; cf. also 20.27 and 27.1-14). According to Xenophon, *Oec.* 11.22-25, a man has to train his speech just as his body.

161.   According to Luz 2002a: 374, the form of the warning as well as the prohibition of alternative expressions suggest this interpretation.

162.   The purification oath is found in Exod. 22.9-10; Lev. 5.20-26; the ordeal oath is found in Num. 5.11-31 (and then *Sota* 1-4); legal oaths are found in Damascus Document CDC 9.8-12 (curse in case of theft); 15.3-4.

163.   Cf. Malina and Rohrbaugh 1992: 46: 'a seller's market'. Oaths were used to advertise an article and affirm its worth (unfortunately, no primary source is given).

164.   On oaths of loyalty and the declaration of taxes (census), see Kollmann 2001: 24ff.

165.   Josephus mentions initiation oaths taken by the Essenes who normally refrain from oaths (*Bell.* 2.139-42); 1QS V 8-11 attests initiation oaths in Qumran (Kollmann 2001: 30).

have to assume that Jesus radically banned all forms of oaths,[166] and that he was motivated by the concern for the holiness of God's name as expressed in the first petition of the Our Father. Alternative formulations (such as heaven, earth, Jerusalem, one's own head) are rejected categorically as well.[167]

Just like the Jewish authors Josephus and Philo took notice of the Essenes not least because of their rejection of oaths,[168] the contemporary environment would soon perceive the speech of Jesus' disciples as different: when they speak in public they should *refrain from any form of oath* (μὴ ὀμόσαι ὅλως). With this prohibition, Jesus prevents a kind of competitive verbal 'armament' in which God himself would get involved: as God is truly bound by an oath, every vow abuses his name.[169] Thereby, Jesus' disciples also exit from 'typical village games of seeking honor by their speech'.[170] Instead of taking oaths by something out of their reach, the disciples are supposed to be recognizable by means of their unambiguous speech (ναὶ ναί, οὒ οὒ).[171]

5.7. *Provocations by the 'Evil Man' (Matthew 5.38-41)*
In the three following situations Jesus confronts his disciples with public *challenges* by other males. In each case, the initiative is not with them; rather, they are told how to *react* to these provocations. In order to classify both Jesus' demands as well as his programmatic maxim μὴ ἀντιστῆναι τῷ πονηρῷ (5.38) correctly, we have to consider each situation individually.

First of all, Jesus addresses the topic of *physical* aggression, or more precisely, a slap in the face: 'If anyone slaps you on the right cheek, turn to him the other also' (5.39).[172] The occasion, the parties involved, the

166. See Kollmann 2001: 31-32. Cf. Vahrenhorst 2002: 263-64: 'What is possible according to the Scripture, is proclaimed impossible by his [= Jesus'] halacha' (author's translation).

167. On that point, cf. also the polemics against the alternative formulations of oaths which are ascribed to the Pharisees in Mt. 23.16-22: swearing on the Temple and its gold, on the altar and its offerings, or on heaven.

168. Cf. Josephus, *Ant.* 15.371; *Bell.* 2.135 (other than with the initiation, see 2.139-42); Philo, *Quod omnis probus liber* 84. Philo also warns against the oath in *Spec. leg.* 2.2-17.

169. Cf. Luz 1997: 329.

170. Neyrey 1998: 203.

171. See Schenk 1987: 372. It is controversial whether the phrase ναὶ ναί, οὒ οὒ can be considered an assertive, and thereby an alternative formulation of an oath (see Strecker 1984: 84, as opposed to Luz 2002a: 377, who argues that the duplication of a word usually serves to intensify its meaning; see also, extensively, Vahrenhorst 2002: 269-75).

172. Even the Matthean formulation of the 'thesis' abbreviates the so-called talion principle from Exod. 21.24; Lev. 24.30 and Deut. 19.21: 'eyes' and 'teeth'; hence it is all about the *face*.

circumstances, and so on, are not specified any further. It is, however, undoubtedly certain that both the addressee as well as the aggressor are *male*. Moreover, it is obvious that the aspect of libel is much more relevant than the aspect of pain. This is further enhanced, because Matthew redactionally specifies the struck cheek as the *right* cheek (differently than Q 6.29) which insinuates a slap with the *back* of the hand.[173]

The second situation is that of an impending garnishment trial (Mt. 5.40). The man addressed as 'you' is apparently in debt and unable to repay. His creditor is about to take him to court (τῷ θέλοντι σοι κριθῆναι), although he does not have any seizable property anymore except for his 'shirt'. It is unclear whether or not the trial has already begun;[174] in any case, the garnishment will be executed publicly.

The third case could insinuate an encounter with a Roman soldier or a high officer who 'compels' (ἀγγαρεύσει) the addressee to walk with him for a mile, probably in order to carry his loads.[175] In all three situations, the confrontation between the addressee and his challenger, who each might be in a superior position, is central. Particularly for the first case, but in effect also for the other two, we can summarize that 'all of the actions against the disciple are clearly aggressive ones, which are preeminently insulting rather than painful'.[176]

Jesus' *demands* for the three exemplary cases illustrate the preceding restraint: μὴ ἀντιστῆναι τῷ πονηρῷ. Hence, it is clear that ὁ πονηρός stands for an 'evil', that is, an aggressive and violent man who challenges the other by a physical gesture, by legal remedies, or by the rights of the occupying force. In each case, the opponent is in the stronger position and does not need to fear the law; on the contrary, he can even trust that it is on his side.[177] The active semantics of ἀνθίσημι ('active resistance') can also be deduced from the context.[178]

---

173.   Cf. also Malina and Rohrbaugh 1992: 46: 'being struck on the right cheek by a backhand slap is an insult, as humiliating as being successfully sued in court or being forced to carry military gear for a mile'; likewise, Luz 2002a: 385, argues that the insult has priority over the pain (with reference to Isa. 50.6 and Lam. 3.30), and so does Wengst 2010: 118-19 (with reference to Rabbinic parallels), cf. also Malina 2001: 39.

174.   κριθῆναι could be used in the sense of 'to convict' and explicated by καὶ τὸν χιτῶνά σου λαβεῖν, meaning: 'Someone who convicts you and wants to see you deprived of your shirt...'

175.   See Schenk 1987: 6: 'forcing someone to do compulsory labor' (author's translation).

176.   Neyrey 1998: 206.

177.   See Wengst 2010: 121.

178.   See Schenk 1987: 29; Schenk interprets Mt. 5.38 as prohibition of retaliation. Likewise, Betz 1995: 280: 'Is its force more passive, as in "resist", or more active, as in "retaliate"?' For good reasons, Betz opts for the active version: do not retaliate!

Looking at the three reactions Jesus dictates to his disciples, it becomes obvious that he precisely does not want them to accept injustice or waive their rights. Remaining purely passive to these provocations would implicate the loss of manfulness (ἀνδρεία) and honor, as for example, Aristotle shows.[179] Indeed, Jesus tells his disciples *neither* to react to a provocation *passively* (and thus 'womanishly') *nor* to escalate it with violence (i.e. 'wrathfully', see above).

H.-D. Betz therefore gets the gist when he argues that the reaction to the slap in the face that Jesus recommends in 5.39 is a 'provocative invitation to receive a second strike'. This is, however, not a sign of weakness, but of moral strength: 'The gesture exposes the act of the offender as what it is: morally repulsive and improper. In addition, it doubles the renunciation of violence by the person insulted; and finally, it challenges the striker to react with comparable generosity'.[180] The exceptional dispensation with 'the coat also', provided in the second scene, is essentially a public renunciation of the subsistence minimum required by the Torah. We can assume that the addressee stands before his accuser (and the court) *naked*. It is a poignant scene in which the creditor effectively *violates the Torah*: By receiving the coat on top of the shirt, he violates Exod. 22.26-27 as well as Deut. 24.12-13, and thereby brings upon himself divine judgment.

In my opinion, J. Neyrey again misses the crucial point when he claims that Jesus prohibits 'ripostes to honor challenges'.[181] The disciples of Jesus 'not only do not challenge others (Matt. 5.21-22, 27-31), but do not give a riposte when challenged'.[182] According to him, it is all about 'nondefensive behavior'. Those disciples whose honor was challenged by other men have to suffer 'complete vulnerability and total shame'. Neyrey puts it pointedly: 'Jesus requires males to play the role of the victim, the submissive one, the person imposed upon'. Assuming that, the disciples of Jesus would no longer be 'real men' (in terms of performance)!

As H.-D. Betz correctly points out, however, the passage is precisely *not* about defeatism and resignation in the face of evil. On the contrary: the elimination of evil must actually be the purpose of the disciples' actions. The Matthean Jesus teaches that victory over evil is by no means achieved by retaliating against the 'evil man' (ὁ πονηρός) along the lines of the

---

179. Cf., programmatically, Aristotle, *Rhet.* 2.6 (1384a19f.): 'unresisting submission to them is due to unmanliness or cowardice', and this behavior is shameful (ἀπὸ ἀνανδρίας γὰρ ἢ δειλίας ἡ ὑπομονὴ καὶ τὸ μὴ ἀμύνεσθαι. ἃ μὲν οὖν αἰσχύνονται...).

180. Betz 1995: 209. See also Wengst 2010: 122.

181. On the following, see Neyrey 1998: 203-207 (quotations).

182. Neyrey 1998: 204, wrongly translates ἀνθίστημι as 'not defending one's honor'.

Mediterranean code of honor.[183] This does not mean a passive silence in the face of evil, but rather 'an aggressive move to overcome evil'.[184]

Hence, Jesus by no means wants his disciples passively to accept libel and thereby also effeminacy. Rather, he tells them to overcome the spiral of violence by provoking their opponents nonviolently.[185] Whether or not these tactics are successful and really make the aggressor see reason in any given concrete case is disputable.[186] The true intention of such actions, however, is probably to make the followers of Jesus *publicly visible* in terms of 5.16 and to display the inflicted injustice!

At the same time, the disciples' actions provided in Mt. 5.38-41 denounce the aggressors and portray their lack of self-control. Of course, the aggressor *can* strike back, take the last shirt, or force his counterpart to do more strenuous compulsory labor—but *if* he does so, he re-acts, that is, gets angry, reveals a lack of self-control, and finally appears *effeminate*.

5.8. *The Request for Aid (Matthew 5.42)*

In contrast to the three preceding situations, an *inferior* person turns to the addressee here. Again, the reader is confronted with an 'asymmetric' constellation, albeit under reversed auspices. The person addressed as 'you' is now characterized as wealthy and is asked for alms or a loan.[187] Once again, the text does not provide further descriptions of the occasion or the supplicant. As distinct from the conversation with the rich young man of Mt. 19.21-22, Jesus does not make the demand here to sell everything one possesses and give the proceeds to the poor. However, the situation itself is quite different: 5.42 is addressed to men who have already become disciples of Jesus. They should not ignore the requests imposed on them. Thus, the text apparently supposes that some disciples still have possessions which they should share generously.[188] This behavior belongs to the visible 'good works' of the followers of Jesus as well.

183.   See Betz 1995: 283-84.

184.   Betz 1995: 284. He goes on: 'The Golden Rule…requires that one takes positive action to interrupt a vicious cycle of revenge'.

185.   See Ebner 2003: 171-74, including instructive examples from Josephus.

186.   See Ebner 2003: 173; Wengst 2010: 119.

187.   Cf. Prov. 3.27-28; Sir. 4.1-10; 29.1-20; 41.20 (helping those in need as part of the sapiential male ideal). By contrast, the advice in 8.12: 'Do not lend something to someone mightier than you'.

188.   Wengst 2010: 124, justly emphasizes the connection of Mt. 5.42 with 5.38-41, redactionally composed by Matthew: Jesus gives a 'double instruction how to help infringement come to light: on the one hand by an imaginative, subversive exposure of injustice, and on the other hand by means of solidary help among those suffering from injustice' (author's translation).

5.9, *Dealing with Pursuers (Matthew 5.43-47)*

Finally, the text deals with the treatment of the 'enemy'. Matthew specified his source material from Q: the enemies are 'those who *persecute* you'. He thus connects his sixth 'antithesis' with the eighth and ninth 'beatitude' (5.10, 11) and thereby interrelates the climax of the series of macarisms with the climax of the series of antitheses. In the ninth macarism, the disciples are addressed in the second person plural as persecuted 'for my sake'. In 5.44-47, Jesus consistently addresses his disciples in the second person plural as well, but the persecution is not explicitly associated with him. Therefore, the sentence is formulated more generally and can be applied to other forms of persecution, too.

Matthew brings home to his readers the following two situations: on the one hand, the religious service of the *ecclesia* which comprises the prayer for the persecutors,[189] and on the other hand the (personal and visible) encounter with the enemy and persecutor in public. For that purpose, Jesus prompts his disciples to greet their enemies (and thereby to bless them and wish them peace!), which might coerce them into answering the greeting.[190]

Loving one's enemies is hence thought of as a concrete, social event.[191] Not least the Lukan parallels underline this assumption: according to Luke, 'loving' one's enemy means 'to do them good' (καλῶς, Lk. 6.27; ἀγαθο-ποιεῖν, Lk. 6.35), to pray for them (Lk. 6.28; cf. also Mt. 5.44), to bless them (Lk. 6.28), to lend them money (Lk. 6.34-35). Matthew in turn specifies 'love' as an intercessory prayer and applies it to the blessing at personal encounters.

The text neither suggests that this behavior turns enemies into friends nor that they should be urged to stop the persecution.[192] Enemies remain enemies, and, most of all, enemies have to be 'loved' *as enemies*.[193] The disciples' publicly visible way of dealing with their enemies (prayer instead of curse, greeting instead of aversion) should encourage others to glorify their heavenly Father.

Aristotle shows that with such behavior, a man attracts attention and thereby risks being considered 'unmanly': not only righteousness and justice are considered something good (καλόν), but also taking revenge upon one's enemies (τὸ τοὺς ἐχθροὺς τιμωρεῖσθαι) and not reconciling (καταλλάττεσ-θαι). Retaliation (ἀνταποδιδόναι) is considered just, and what is just is good.

---

189. Note the *plural* προσεύχεσθε ὑπὲρ τῶν διωκόντων ὑμᾶς—in contrast to 6.6 (σὺ δὲ ὅταν προσεύχῃ), but just like in 6.5 (ὅταν προσεύχησθε). Matthew hence refers to the *communal* prayer in the religious service.

190. According to Sir. 41.20, it is *shameful* not to react to a greeting.

191. See Sutter Rehmann 2004: 338.

192. Cf. Betz 1995: 324.

193. This even goes beyond the claims in Prov. 24.17-18; 25.21-22.

Most of all: *not succumbing stands for manfulness* (ἀνδρείου τὸ μὴ ἡττᾶσθαι).[194]

5.10. *Perfect Sons of the Father in Heaven (Matthew 5.48)*

The whole sequence is concluded by 5.48: Matthew replaces the expression γίνεσθε οἰκτίρμονες deriving from Q with ἔσεσθε οὖν ὑμεῖς τέλειοι. Again, a reference to the story of the rich young man in 19.21 catches one's eye, where Jesus says: 'If you want to be perfect (!), go, sell what you possess and give to the poor'.

Matthew aligned the story taken from Mark with his antitheses by means of the keyword τέλειος and other interpolations.[195] Here, we can detect a basic structure analogous to the antitheses: the young man (ὁ νεανίσκος) has kept all the commandments Jesus refers to as well as the command of loving one's neighbor from Lev. 19.18 (Mt. 19.18-19). In order to be 'perfect' (τέλειος), however, he must sell his possessions, give the money to the poor and follow Jesus (19.21).[196] Therefore, it is not enough to keep the commandments of the Torah, not even to love one's neighbor, if one wants to be perfect.

The Matthean Jesus hence labels a man as τέλειος if he does 'more' than just keep the commandments (including love of neighbor!). In the case of the young man of ch. 19, this means abandoning one's possessions and following Jesus; in the case of the disciples as depicted in ch. 5, it means they must love their enemies publicly, which clearly goes beyond the love of neighbor as required by the Torah.

According to 5.48, the criterion for the 'sons' is their heavenly Father who makes the 'sun rise on the evil and on the good, and sends rain on the just and on the unjust' (5.45). Thus, the focus is on the *behavior* towards the enemies.[197] The concept of God and the social situation again correspond with each other: as opposed to the 'hidden Father' of 6.1-18, here the heavenly Father, who works through sun and rain and takes effect on men

---

194.   Aristotle, *Rhet.* 1.9 (1367a20-23): 'It is noble to avenge oneself on one's enemies and not to come to terms with them: for requital is just, and the just is noble; and not to surrender is a sign of manfulness'.

195.   In particular, Matthew adds the *commandment of loving one's neighbor* (compare Mt. 19.19 and 5.43-44 with Mk 10.19) and the idea of *perfection* (compare Mt. 19.21 and 5.48 with Mk 10.21). It also bears mentioning that Mark's 'rich man' has become a 'rich *young* man' in Matthew.

196.   Another reference to the Sermon on the Mount is the image of the treasure in heaven (compare 19.21 with 6.20). Matthew 19 claims that one can accumulate a treasure in heaven by following Jesus, and in particular by selling one's earthly goods for the benefit of the poor (οἱ πτωχοί).

197.   Rightly so Davies and Allison 1991: 563: 'The emphasis is upon God's deeds, not his nature'.

'in the open air', sets the benchmark. This image has hardly been chosen randomly: according to Philo and others, the life which takes place 'in the open air' (ἐν ὑπαίθρῳ βίος) is a purely male domain (see above). In this sphere of public masculinity, the followers of Jesus can find the crucial starting point for the *imitatio Dei* required of them—by observing the weather!

Excursus:
The Composition in the Form of 'Antitheses'

In the context of his commentary on and interpretation of the Torah, the Matthean Jesus presents precisely *those* manners required in the ancient public sphere, and thereby in the *male* realm.[198] In doing so, he defines the male public sphere as a realm in which the followers of Jesus have visibly to perform God's will.

It would be beyond the scope of the present study to discuss the Matthean 'antitheses'. It should be consensus, however, that the intention for its formulation and arrangement can be traced from the programmatic texts 5.17; 5.20 and 5.48. Hence, Matthew portrays Jesus' teaching as a *fulfillment* (πληροῦν, 5.17) of the law and prophets (instead of their abolishment) and as a demand for a '*greater righteousness*', which exceeds that of the scribes and Pharisees significantly (περισσεύσῃ... πλεῖον, 5.20) as it grants access to the kingdom of heaven. This adds agonal pragmatics to the commentary: with their public behavior, the disciples compete with that of other Jewish groups.

To put it with Mt. 7.21, doing the will of the Father makes the disciples *perfect men* (τέλειοι, 5.48). As G. Röhser recently pointed out, Jesus' commentary aims both at an enhancement and fulfillment as well as at an ultimate tightening of the Torah: as the teacher of the Torah (as a 'scribe', if you like), Jesus fulfills the Torah and at the same time, he ultimately reveals God's entire will.[199]

The antithetic form strongly emphasizes Jesus' 'I' and, along with it, his *authority* which shocks the people (7.28-29): for Matthew, this statement is so distinct not because Jesus says ἐγὼ δὲ λέγω ὑμῖν, but because *Jesus* says ἐγὼ δὲ λέγω ὑμῖν. Not the form of speech, but the speaking person is decisive for him.[200] Thus, the commentary is not supposed to contrast Jesus with the Torah; it rather wants to depict his divine power as an authoritative teacher of the Law (cf. 23.8-10). In line with R. Harris, one can therefore say that the ideal of masculinity designed here is laid down as 'a divinely sanctioned command'.[201] A philosophical explanation, therefore, is missing.

198.   K. Haacker, M. Vahrenhorst *et al.* justifiably prefer to speak of the antitheses as a commentary ('Kommentarworte'). On the difficulty of the term 'antitheses', see Vahrenhorst 2002: 217-34; Röhser 2009; Wengst 2010: 77-82.

199.   Cf. Röhser 2009: 122. Elsewhere (p. 121) he advocates the model 'fulfillment of the Torah', because in contrast to the model of 'surpassing', 'fulfillment' remains in the realm of what it fulfills and does not go beyond that. Other than the model 'interpretation' it also contains the aspects of enhancement and completion as well as the ultimate aggravation.

200.   Cf. Vahrenhorst 2002: 234 n. 96. Röhser 2009: 123-24, justly criticizes a tendency towards a 'de-Christologization' which can be traced in some newer translations of Jesus' formulations.

201.   Harris 2001: 397, although he does not refer directly to the Sermon on the Mount here.

By fusing the situations of male encounters, challenges and conflicts to six comments on 'what has been said to those of old', Matthew creates exemplary 'fields' in which the followers of Jesus have to perform God's will publicly. There, in the ancient public, the light of the disciples is supposed to shine. There, in the public sphere of interpersonal, or more precisely, inter-male encounters, their 'greater righteousness' should reveal itself.

Just like in the case of the rich young man, who is not 'perfect' although he keeps the commandments—including love of one's neighbor—, in the case of the Sermon on the Mount, the commandments of the Torah do not suffice to overcome the spiral of violence and counterviolence in the depicted situations. By means of actualization and concretization based on these situations, Jesus in a way fulfills and completes the Torah which is in itself constituted by texts and exegetical traditions.[202]

6. *Conclusion*

As at all times, several competing conceptions of masculinity prevailed at the time of the Gospel of Matthew. We have tried to reconstruct the position of the Matthean Jesus within this complex framework by reading the Sermon on the Mount from a consistently androcentric perspective. In line with contemporary gender theory, masculinity is not to be understood as a biological fact, but as a cultural, social, political as well as religious *performance*.[203] At the same time, it can be regarded as the performance's instable, constantly vulnerable and aspired *result*. Thus, 'masculinity is always under construction',[204] is an 'achieved state'[205] on a 'hierarchical gender gradient or continuum',[206] and is therefore constantly endangered, exposed to challenges by other men and in need of defense.

The realm in which this takes place is the ancient public sphere. It is here that the masculinity of Jesus' disciples has to be acquired and defended—even in situations of challenge, persecution, enmity, and inner

---

202.   Formulated based on Vahrenhorst 2002: 242-43, and Röhser 2009: 121.

203.   See Butler 1990. On p. 25 Butler summarizes her conception on *performative gender identity*: gender identity itself is 'constituting the identity it is supposed to be. In this sense, gender is always a doing, though not a doing by a subject who might be said to preexist the deed... There is no gender identity behind the expressions of gender; that identity is performatively constituted by the very "expressions" that are said to be its results.' Anderson and Moore 2003: 68, bluntly state: 'anatomy alone does not make the man'.

204.   Ivarsson 2007: 166.

205.   Williams 2010: 155: 'Boys must be *made* men, while girls just *become* women. There are constant struggles involved not only in attaining masculinity—one thinks of the often painful and always challenging rites of passage by means of which boys are made men—but also in maintaining one's masculine status.' Williams refers to Maud Gleason's dictum about masculinity as an 'achieved state' (p. 156).

206.   Anderson and Moore 2003: 70-71: '...so that swift slippage from a more manly to a less manly status is an ever-present possibility even for the socially advantaged male subject'.

controversy. Hence, how can a man perform publicly as a follower of Jesus, observing 'everything I have commanded you' (Mt. 28.20, see below), without becoming effeminate?

That is why the main part of the Sermon on the Mount depicts Jesus' demands on his followers concerning their behavior in the social realm, which was considered (at least theoretically) an exclusively *male* and therefore also eminently *political* sphere in antiquity. Central parts of this text are therefore primarily concerned with the 'regulation of masculinity',[207] because it is mostly men who interact with each other in this agonal sphere—at least, according to the prevalent norm. If one defines the ancient conception of masculinity positively as 'dominance and self-mastery' and negatively as 'the opposite of effeminacy',[208] one can distinguish several ideals of masculinity based on the different importance of 'dominance' and 'self-control'. In the case of the Sermon on the Mount, we can assert on the one hand that Jesus asks his followers for 'absolute control of anger, lust, desire for revenge, pride, avarice, and anxiety'.[209] On the other hand, he also demands initiative and activeness, for example, for the purpose of reconciliation, bonding, and aid. Also, when physically assaulted, the disciples are to react in a measured way (and not simply accept being abused), while at the same time controlling their anger and refraining from becoming violent themselves.

The ideal of masculinity outlined here is parallel to several philosophical and sapiential traditions of self-control: ἐγκράτεια and σωφροσύνη, but also πραότης, and so on. Already Plato's *Gorgias* contrasts the martial ideal of masculinity with the ideal of the self-controlled and self-possessed man. The Platonic Socrates defines self-control (αὐτὸν ἑαυτοῦ ἄρχειν) with the terms 'prudent' (σώφρονα) and 'self-possessed' (ἐγκρατῆ). In his view, it signifies a mastery of one's own cravings and desires.[210] Further analogies to the ideal of masculinity of the Sermon on the Mount can be found in Stoic, as well as in Jewish-Hellenistic sapiential literature, which is usually addressed to men.[211]

---

207.   Rightly so Leutzsch 2004: 614.

208.   Ivarsson 2008: 160.

209.   Anderson and Moore 2003: 71. They go on to say, 'Mastery of one's anger and other passions is a mark of masculinity, as well as the proper attitude in regard to a brother'.

210.   Plato, *Gorgias* 491CD (ed. M. Erler). Socrates places the 'self-controlled' over those who rule the cities. The fact that his dialogue partner Callicles refers to the latter as ἀνδρειότεροι ('the more masculine ones') or ἀνδρεῖοι ('the masculine ones'), shows that the topic ultimately deals with the ideal of masculinity.

211.   This fact has often been grounds for discontent in feminist exegesis; cf., as an example, Schroer 1996. The examination of Jewish-Hellenistic literature in terms of the performance of masculinity unfortunately remains a desideratum.

The central value of self-control is increasingly recognized in recent discussions on ancient constructions of masculinity.[212] Control in general has been increasingly identified as an underlying construction principle for ancient discourses of masculinity and is often granted priority over other aspects such as the active/passive-binary.[213] This implies that ancient ideals of masculinity are more complex and heterogeneous as was often assumed particularly in older feminist-exegetical research.

To a certain extent, the ideal of masculinity presumed in the Sermon on the Mount is actually an alternative concept, but not to 'the' ancient ideal of masculinity. Rather, it opposes 'other', especially martial, ideals which were also criticized by other ancient authors (not least by those influenced by Stoics). However, Jesus clearly puts emphasis on different aspects than, for instance, Seneca.[214]

In ancient masculinity discourse, the *effeminatus* is clearly negatively connotated. Not only is he construed as passive and feminine, but also as short-tempered and unable to control his feelings and desires.[215] The ancient parallels show that neither Jesus' prohibition of anger, the lustful glance at women, divorce, or oaths, nor his demand for proactive reconciliation and peaceful yet active resistance are indicative of unmanliness. On the contrary, Jesus asks his male followers for *self-control and initiative*. The aspect of dominance is shifted entirely to one's own self. On the interpersonal level, the disciples should approach each other as *servants* (cf., on that point, Mt. 18.1-5; 20.20-28). By their public appearance, which conforms to Jesus' demands, the disciples resist a *certain* ideal of masculinity based on the dominance of others. This common ideal is, for instance, represented by the men occurring in 5.38-41. The crucial point, however, is that the disciples are precisely *not* effeminate.

212.   Cf. Williams 2010: 151-56 ('Masculinity and Self-Control'); Conway 2008: 21-29; Harris 2001: 80-87, as well as the extensive account of Nussbaum 1994.

213.   Ivarsson 2007: 165: 'Mastery is the basic criterion of masculinity'. On that point, cf. also Conway 2008: 24-25. She points out 'that by the first century and beyond, self-control appears to trump the active/passive binary when it came to defining ideal masculinity'. Regarding the 'tremendous importance placed on the notion of control in Roman ideologies of masculinity or of its absence', cf. Williams 2010: 156. At the very beginning of his work on anger, *Seneca* already notices that an angry man is *impotens sui* (*De ira* 1.1.2)! He describes overcoming one's anger as a '*fight* with oneself' (3.13.1: *pugna tecum ipse*).

214.   Throughout his entire work, he propagates an ideal of masculinity oriented at *sublimitas, quietas, tranquilitas* and *modestia* as a counter-concept to anger (*De ira* 3.6 u.ö.). Furthermore, he advises the endurance of assaults as well as injustice (3.17.4 and elsewhere: *patiebatur*), patience (3.32 and elsewhere) or reacting with humor (3.38 and elsewhere) rather than getting angry.

215.   On that point, cf. the extensive overview in Williams 2010: 137-76 ('Effeminacy and Masculinity').

Principally, the 'anomalous masculinity'[216] depicted here serves missionary purposes: according to Matthew's key phrase (5.16), the followers of Jesus are supposed to incite people to glorify their Father in heaven precisely by means of their deviating behavior in public and inter-male situations. Their behavior should render decisive contents of Jesus' 'authorized teaching' (7.28-29) *visible*—both for the Jewish as well as for the Gentile public. At the 'sight' of disciples who overcome the male spiral of violence, who take the initiative towards reconciliation and friendship, who actively and provocatively proclaim their nonresistance, who neither take oaths nor divorce their wives, who keep their gaze and tongue under control, and so on, people come to realize that these 'sons' are revealing the 'Father'.

Once Again: A Text for Men (Only)?

In his commentary on the Sermon on the Mount, Klaus Wengst takes the view that when it comes to the disciples of Jesus on the narrative level, Matthew bears in mind men only (2010: 26-27).[217] He bases his view on Matthew 28: here, 'Mary Magdalene and the other Mary' (Mt. 28.1), who belong to the group of 'many women' who 'had followed Jesus from Galilee, serving him' (27.55), are commissioned to tell the disciples to go to Galilee where they would see Jesus. They are first instructed by the angel at the tomb and then reinforced by the risen Christ himself to announce the meeting in Galilee to 'my brothers' (28.10). According to Wengst, it is evident that women do not belong to this group of 'disciples' or 'brothers' of Jesus. Helga Melzer-Keller too argues that this extremely important epiphany of the resurrected Jesus in Galilee—the scene in which the Gospel culminates and which lays the foundation both for the post-Easter reconstitution of the early Christian movement as well as for the proliferation of the faith in Christ—takes place in front of a purely male audience. Therefore, only the eleven disciples can be considered the founders of the early church. Women, by contrast, do not participate in this crucial event anymore.[218]

216.　Anderson and Moore 2003: 76: 'The gender identity narratively constructed for male disciples in Matthew amounts to an anomalous masculinity when measured by traditional Graeco-Roman standards'. Anderson and Moore even talk about 'subordinate masculinities' (p. 91).

217.　Cf. also Levine 2012: 119: 'Jesus appoints individual men; no woman is ever called to follow him' (author's translation).

218.　See Melzer-Keller 1997: 125. Levine 2012: 119, points out that the announcement the women are asked to deliver in Mt. 28.10 is restricted to people who are already part of their group. Only men receive the *great commission* (28.19-20).

Matthew 28.16-20 is also relevant for the exegesis of the Sermon on the Mount. When Matthew locates the epiphany on 'the (!) mountain' (28.16), he certainly alludes to the localization of the Sermon on the Mount (5.1). His order to teach them (i.e. the baptized nations) 'to observe all that I have commanded you' (28.20) might therefore *primarily*, yet not exclusively, *refer to the Sermon on the Mount*.[219] If that is the case, the question arises *who* the eleven disciples are supposed to teach what Jesus said.

The text reads:

28.18	d	All power in heaven and on earth has been given to me.
19	a	Go therefore
	b	and make disciples (μαθητεύσατε) of all nations,
	c	baptizing them (βαπτίζοντες αὐτούς) in the name of the Father and of the Son and of the Holy Spirit,
20	a	(and) teaching them (διδάσκοντες αὐτούς),
	b	to observe[220]
	c	everything I have commanded you.
	d	And behold,
	e	I am with you always, to the end of the age.

The structure of the decisive sentences 19a-20c is largely beyond debate: the imperative μαθητεύσατε is explicated by the two parallel participles βαπτίζοντες and διδάσκοντες[221]—'all nations' should be 'made disciples' through baptism (first) and (then) by means of instruction.

Just as K. Wengst, H. Melzer-Keller, A.J. Levine and others rightly observed, the eleven disciples are the subject of all three proceedings. Hence, it is *men* who receive the so-called great commission. However, the *object* of their actions is much more interesting: not individuals, but 'all nations' should be 'made disciples'. Since the verb 'to make disciples' (μαθητεύειν) is initially explicated with the command to baptize the nations, a restriction of the term 'disciples' to men does not seem appropriate.

Peter Wick recently and justly pointed out in another context that Mt. 28.16-20 does not focus on the evangelization of individuals, but of collectives. The priority of baptism over instruction underlines this assumption.[222] Since Matthew refers to collectives (ἔθνη) here, the differentiation between

---

219.   Especially the combination of 'the mountain' and 'teaching/to teach' in Mt. 5.1-2 and 7.28–8.1 supports this thesis. Moreover, cf. the references in Luz 2002b: 37-38 and 455.

220.   See Bauer, Aland, and Aland 1988: 1625.

221.   Cf. Luz 2002b: 429. 443.

222.   See Wick 2011: 278-79. According to Wick, the recipients are granted individual options to react in Mt. 10. This possibility is omitted in Mt. 28.16-20.

men and women is certainly not at the forefront of his thinking, although he probably thought of an instruction directed at men, especially since women were apparently not in charge of leading positions.[223]

We can therefore conclude: the message for the disciple's mission in Mt. 28.19-20 is not formulated from an androcentric perspective. It is beyond doubt that Matthew ranked women among those who should be baptized. Hence, we cannot exclude the possibility that they should also be instructed. Ulrich Luz puts it pointedly: 'For Matthew, the ecclesia is—typically Jewish!—the "school" of Jesus. He considers it the community of Jesus' disciples, both male and female, who, even after they have been baptized, constantly attend his "school" and keep his commandments by following him'.[224]

At the end of this analysis, we are left with *complex* findings for our opening question: on the one hand, the androcentric character of the Sermon on the Mount is undeniable and was probably imprinted on this text purposely by the evangelist. This assumption can be justified as central parts of the text deal with the disciple's (re)action in the public sphere. On the other hand, that does not mean that 'everything I have commanded you' holds true for men only. The disciples are supposed to teach those baptized from all nations to observe what Jesus told them. Thus, the application to several spheres, including different female realms within the ecclesia, is not excluded. Women too are able and meant to observe, meet and fulfill (τηρεῖν) Jesus' demands.

Bibliography

Anderson, Janice Capel, and Stephen D. Moore
    2003   'Matthew and Masculinity', in Anderson and Moore (eds.) 2003: 67-92.
Anderson, Janice Capel, and Stephen D. Moore (eds.)
    2003   *New Testament Masculinities* (SBL Semeia Studies, 45; Atlanta: Society of Biblical Literature):
Bauer, Walter, Kurt Aland, and Barbara Aland
    1988   *Wörterbuch zum Neuen Testament* (Berlin: W. de Gruyter, 6th edn).
Betz, Hans-Dieter
    1995   *The Sermon on the Mount: A Commentary* (Hermeneia; Minneapolis: Fortress Press).
Broer, Ingo
    1980   *Freiheit vom Gesetz und Radikalisierung des Gesetzes. Ein Beitrag zur Theologie des Evangelisten Matthäus* (SBS, 98; Stuttgart: Katholisches Bibelwerk).

223.   See Melzer-Keller 1997: 184.
224.   Luz 2002b: 454-55 (author's translation).

Burchard, Christoph
    1998   'Versuch, das Thema der Bergpredigt zu finden', in *Studien zur Theologie, Sprache und Umwelt des Neuen Testaments* (WUNT, 107; Tübingen: Mohr Siebeck): 27-50.

Butler, Judith
    1990   *Gender Trouble: Feminism and the Subversion of Identity* (New York: Routledge).

Conway, Colleen M.
    2008   *Behold the Man: Jesus and Greco-Roman Masculinity* (Oxford: Oxford University Press).

Crüsemann, F., *et al.* (eds.)
    2004   *Dem Tod nicht glauben. Sozialgeschichte der Bibel* (FS L. Schottroff; Gütersloh: Gütersloher Verlagshaus).

Davies, William D., and Dale C. Allison
    1991   *A Critical and Exegetical Commentary on the Gospel according to St. Matthew I* (ICC; Edinburgh: T. & T. Clark).

Deines, Roland
    2004   *Die Gerechtigkeit der Tora im Reich des Messias. Mt 5,13-20 als Schlüsseltext der matthäischen Theologie* (WUNT, 177; Tübingen: Mohr Siebeck).

Duff, Paul B.
    2001   'Vision and Violence. Theories of Vision and Matthew 5:27-30', in *Antiquity and Humanity: Essays on Ancient Religion and Philosophy* (FS H.-D. Betz; Tübingen: Mohr Siebeck): 63-75.

Ebner, Martin
    2003   *Jesus von Nazaret in seiner Zeit. Sozialgeschichtliche Zugänge* (SBS, 196; Stuttgart: Katholisches Bibelwerk).

Gunderson, Erik
    2000   *Staging Masculinity: The Rhetoric of Performance in the Roman World* (Ann Arbor: University of Michigan Press).

Harris, William V.
    2001   *Restraining Rage: The Ideology of Anger Control in Classical Antiquity* (Cambridge, MA: Harvard University Press).

Heiligenthal, Roman
    1983   *Werke als Zeichen. Untersuchungen zur Bedeutung der menschlichen Taten im Frühjudentum, Neuen Testament und Frühchristentum* (WUNT, 2/9; Tübingen: Mohr Siebeck).

Heinz, Marion
    2002   *Philosophische Geschlechtertheorien. Ausgewählte Texte von der Antike bis zur Gegenwart* (ed. S. Doyé, M. Heinz, and F. Kuster; Stuttgart: Reclam).

Ilan, Tal
    1995   *Jewish Women in Greco-Roman Palestine: An Inquiry into Image and Status* (TSAJ, 44; Tübingen: Mohr Siebeck).

Ivarsson, Frederic
    2007   'Vice Lists and deviant Masculinity: The Rhetorical Function of 1 Corinthians 5.10-11 and 6.9-10', in T. Penner and C.V. Stichele (eds.), *Mapping Gender in Ancient Religious Discourses* (BIS, 84; Leiden and Boston: E.J. Brill): 163-84.

2008 'Christian Identity as True Masculinity', in B. Holmberg (ed.), *Exploring Early Christian Identity* (WUNT, 226; Tübingen: Mohr Siebeck): 159-71.

Kollmann, Bernd
2001 'Erwägungen zur Reichweite des Schwurverbots Jesu (Mt. 5.34)', *ZNW* 92: 20-32.

Konstan, David
2003 'Aristotle on Anger and the Emotions: The Strategies of Status', in S. Braund and G.W. Most (eds.), *Ancient Anger: Perspectives from Homer to Galen* (Yale Classical Studies, 32; Cambridge: Cambridge University Press): 99-120.

Leutzsch, Martin
2000 'Sozialgeschichtliche Perspektiven auf die Bergpredigt', *ZNT* 12: 2-11.
2004 'Konstruktionen von Männlichkeit im Urchristentum', in Crüsemann *et al.* 2004: 600-618.

Levine, Amy-Jill
2012 'Das Matthäusevangelium: Zwischen Bruch und Kontinuität', in M. Navarro Puerto and M. Perroni (eds.), *Evangelien. Erzählungen und Geschichten* (Die Bibel und die Frauen, NT 2/1; Stuttgart: Kohlhammer): 118-39.

Liddel, Henry G., and Robert Scott
1996 *A Greek–English Lexicon* (Oxford: Clarendon Press, 9th edn).

Lohfink, Gerhard
1993 *Wem gilt die Bergpredigt?* (Freiburg: Herder).

Luz, Ulrich
1997 *Das Evangelium nach Matthäus*, vol. III (EKK; Zurich: Benzinger)
2002a *Das Evangelium nach Matthäus*, vol. I, (EKK; Zurich: Benzinger, 5th edn)
2002b *Das Evangelium nach Matthäus*, vol. II (EKK; Zurich: Benzinger, 2nd edn)

Malina, Bruce J.
2001 *The New Testament World: Insights from Cultural Anthropology* (Louisville, KY: Westminster/John Knox Press, 3rd edn).

Malina, Bruce J., and Richard L. Rohrbaugh
1992 *Social Science Commentary on the Synoptic Gospels* (Minneapolis: Fortress Press).

Melzer-Keller, Helga
1997 *Jesus und die Frauen. Eine Verhältnisbestimmung nach den synoptischen Überlieferungen* (HBS, 14; Freiburg: Herder).

Neusner, Jacob
1993 *A Rabbi Talks with Jesus: An Intermillennial, Interfaith Exchange* (New York: Doubleday).

Neyrey, Jerome, H.
1998 *Honor and Shame in the Gospel of Matthew* (Louisville, KY: Westminster/John Knox Press).
2003 'Jesus, Gender, and the Gospel of Matthew', in Anderson and Moore (eds.) 2003: 43-66.

Nussbaum, Martha C.
1994 *The Therapy of Desire: Theory and Practice in Hellenistic Ethics* (Princeton, NJ: Princeton University Press).

Rakoczy, Thomas
1996   *Böser Blick, Macht des Auges und Neid der Götter. Eine Untersuchung zur Kraft des Blickes in der griechischen Literatur* (Classica Monacensia, 13; Tübingen: Narr).

Röhser, Günther
2009   'Die "Antithesen" der Bergpredigt in neueren Bibelübersetzungen', *ThBeitr* 40: 110-24.

Schenk, Wolfgang
1987   *Die Sprache des Matthäus. Die Text-Konstituenten in ihren makro- und mikrostrukturellen Relationen* (Göttingen: Vandenhoeck & Ruprecht).

Schottroff, Luise
1994   *Lydias ungeduldige Schwestern. Feministische Sozialgeschichte des frühen Christentums* (Gütersloh: Gütersloher Verlagshaus).

Schroer, Silvia
1996   'Der eine Herr und die Männerherrschaft im Buch Jesus Sirach. Frauenbild und Weisheitsbild einer misogynen Schrift', in *Die Weisheit hat ihr Haus gebaut. Studien zur Gestalt der Sophia in den biblischen Schriften* (Mainz: Matthias-Grünewald-Verlag): 96-109.

Strecker, Georg,
1984   *Die Bergpredigt. Ein exegetischer Kommentar* (Göttingen: Vandenhoeck & Ruprecht).

Sutter Rehmann, Luzia,
2004   'Unzüchtige Rede (Mt. 5.32). Die Verwurzelung der Tora im Alltag', in Crüsemann *et al.* 2004: 333-50.

Tomson, Peter J.
2010   'Divorce Halakha in Paul and the Jesus Tradition', in R. Bieringer *et al.* (ed.), *The New Testament and Rabbinic Literature* (Leiden: E.J. Brill): 289-332.

Vahrenhorst, Martin
2002   *'Ihr sollt überhaupt nicht schwören'. Matthäus im halachischen Diskurs* (WMANT, 95; Neukirchen–Vluyn: Neukirchener Verlag).

Weidemann, Hans-Ulrich
2012   '"Vergeltet nicht dem bösen Mann!". Versuch einer konsequent androzentrischen Lektüre der Bergpredigt', in H.-U. Weidemann (ed.), *'Er stieg auf den Berg... und lehrte sie' (Mt. 5.1-2). Exegetische und rezeptionsgeschichtliche Studien zur Bergpredigt* (SBS, 226; Stuttgart: Katholisches Bibelwerk): 25-70.

Wengst, Klaus
2010   *Das Regierungsprogramm des Himmelreichs. Eine Auslegung der Bergpredigt in ihrem jüdischen Kontext* (Stuttgart: Kohlhammer).

Wick, Peter
2011   'Die Kindertaufe fordert uns heraus. Am Neuen Testament stoßen alle Tauftheorien an ihre Grenzen', *ThBeitr* 42: 264-82.

Williams, Craig A.
2010   *Roman Homosexuality* (Oxford: Oxford University Press, 2nd edn).

Zeilinger, Franz
2002   *Zwischen Himmel und Erde. Ein Kommentar zur 'Bergpredigt' Matthäus 5–7* (Stuttgart: Kohlhammer).

Zerwick, Max, and Mary Grosvenor
  1993   *A Grammatical Analysis of the Greek New Testament* (Rome: Pontifical
          Biblical Institute).
Zoepffel, Renate
  2006   'Geschlechterrollen', in *Aristoteles: Oikonomika. Schriften zu Hauswirt-
          schaft und Finanzwesen* (ed. R. Zoepffel; Aristoteles Werke in deutscher
          Übersetzung, 10/II; Darmstadt: Wissenschaftliche Buchgesellschaft): 314-
          20.

'EUNUCHS FOR THE KINGDOM OF HEAVEN': MATTHEW AND SUBORDINATED MASCULINITIES

Susanna Asikainen

1. *Introduction*

Jesus' teaching about marriage and divorce in the Gospel of Matthew (19.3-9) is followed by an enigmatic saying about eunuchs: 'For there are eunuchs who have been so from birth, and there are eunuchs who have been made eunuchs by others, and there are eunuchs who have made themselves eunuchs for the sake of the kingdom of heaven. Let anyone receive this who can' (Mt. 19.12). This puzzling saying has produced several interpretations. Halvor Moxnes suggests that the verse has been so difficult to interpret specifically because of the interpreters' presuppositions about masculinity.[1] In the present study I seek to answer two questions: (1) What does the eunuch-saying in Mt. 19.12 mean in the context of the Gospel of Matthew?[2] (2) What implications does this saying have for the ideal masculinity upheld by the Matthean community?

To answer these questions, I turn to R.W. Connell's theory of hegemonic and non-hegemonic masculinities. The theory stresses that there are several different masculinities that stand in a relation of power vis-à-vis each other. Paying attention to the diversity of masculinities can therefore illuminate the relationships existing between the masculinities of the elite male writers, the early Christian men, and the eunuchs in the ancient Greco-Roman world. After establishing a few theoretical points, I will concentrate on masculinities in the Greco-Roman antiquity, especially on eunuchs as an example of

---

1. Moxnes 2003: 74.

2. Whether the eunuch-saying comes from the historical Jesus is a complex matter that goes beyond the purposes of this article. For discussions regarding the saying's potential original context, see Moxnes 2003: 75; 2005: 30. See also Blinzler 1957; Hester 2005: 15; Loader 2007: 40; Kodell 1978: 19. Harvey (2007: 8-9) notes that commentators have too narrowly focused on the assumption that the verse has a metaphorical meaning. Even though he finds 'attractive' the suggestion that the eunuch-saying referred to Jesus and his disciples, he maintains that this interpretation 'fails to take into account the difficulties which are involved in assuming a metaphorical meaning'.

ancient subordinate masculinity. Finally, I will tackle Mt. 19.12 in some details and evaluate four existing interpretations regarding the eunuch-saying, before offering my own reading of Matthew's eunuch-saying.

2. *Theorizing Men and Masculinities*

What do we mean when we talk about 'masculinity'? It has become commonplace since the 1970s to distinguish between biological sex ('male', 'female') and socially constructed gender ('man', 'woman').[3] Maleness means how the biological make-up of males (chromosomes, hormones) affects men. Maleness is biological, whereas masculinity belongs to the realm of gender. In masculinity studies, masculinity is usually defined either as an identity or as an ideology.[4] In the present study, I will define masculinity as a gender ideology, an image of an ideal male behavior that a specific group maintains for reasons of its own.[5] Previous studies of the ideologies of masculinity have tended to stress that only one dominant ideal existed for all men; more recently it has been shown that every culture usually supports multiple ideologies of masculinity. Abercrombie and Turner, for instance, argue that no one dominant ideology is adopted by the subordinate classes or groups over against ideals of their own. In fact, the subordinate classes rarely share the ideology of the dominant class. Indeed, the dominant ideology has more significance to the internal cohesion and control of the dominant class itself.[6] It is possible, then, that each group of people has its own gender ideology and hierarchy of gender, and does not simply reflect a hierarchy imposed from outside. This view applies to antiquity as well.

The different ideologies of masculinity are not equal, but form a network of power relations. Connell's differentiation between hegemonic and non-hegemonic masculinities can usefully illuminate this network of power and privilege.[7] The *hegemonic masculinity* is the masculinity of the dominant group. It is constructed in relation to women and to other masculinities. According to Connell, hegemony means 'a social ascendancy achieved in a

3. E.g. Rubin 1975: 179: 'Gender is a socially imposed division of the sexes. It is a product of the social relations of sexuality.' These social relations 'transform males and females into "men" and "women"'.

4. E.g. Hearn and Collinson 1994: 104.

5. My definition is, then, close to that of Williams (1999: 4): '*Masculinity* refers to a complex of values and ideals that can more profitably be understood as a cultural tradition than as a biological given: the concept refers to what it is to be fully gendered as "a man" as opposed to merely having the physical features held to signify "a male"'.

6. Abercrombie and Turner 1978: 149-53.

7. A distinction originally formulated in Carrigan, Connell and Lee 1985; it was then expanded in Connell 1987: 183-86; 2005: 76-81.

play of social forces that extends beyond contests of brute power into the organization of private life and cultural process'.[8] Hegemony does not mean total cultural dominance—there are also other masculinities that have currency. Furthermore, it is important to notice that hegemonic masculinity is not a fixed character type. There is no one set of characteristics that is always and everywhere in the hegemonic position. Instead, hegemonic masculinity is the masculinity that occupies the hegemonic position in a certain configuration of gender relations. Connell emphasizes that hegemony is a currently accepted strategy, which means that its position is always contestable. Hegemony, then, can be disrupted or can disrupt itself. Thus, in certain situations new dominant groups may challenge the old hegemony and construct a new hegemony.

Hegemonic masculinity is an ideal, leaving the majority of men to struggle to meet its standards. Still, hegemonic masculinity gives the position of power to men, meaning that men in general have certain advantages over women and children. This also means that since the majority of men benefit from the hegemonic masculinity, they do not oppose it. Connell calls this *complicit masculinity*.[9] This masculinity could be characterized as a tacit agreement of the hegemony. Since the hegemonic masculinity is constructed in relation to other masculinities, there are also relations of dominance and subordination between groups of men. *Subordinated masculinities* are associated with femininity. The hegemonic masculinity defines femininity as whatever masculinity is not, and therefore the subordinated masculinities are portrayed as stereotypically effeminate. For example, since the contemporary hegemonic masculinity emphasizes heterosexuality, the key form of contemporary subordinated masculinities is homosexual masculinities.[10] In the ancient Greco-Roman world, the effeminate men were called κίναιδοι or *cinaedi*. As we will see, another group of men that were considered effeminate in antiquity were the eunuchs.

Hegemony, complicity, and subordination are relations internal to the gender order. However, gender is not independent of other social structures like class, race, and ethnicity. I would also add to the list religion, which Connell does not mention. Gender intersects with these other structures, creating further relationships between masculinities. One final gender relation that Connell introduces is *marginalized masculinities*, which intersect with other social structures mentioned above, but lack the authority or legitimation that hegemonic masculinity enjoys.[11] In the ancient Greco-Roman

8.　Connell 1987: 184.

9.　Connell 2005: 79.

10.　This does not mean that homosexuality is always necessarily subordinated in every culture. For example, in some cultures same-sex sexual behavior is ritualized.

11.　On intersectionality see, e.g., Matsuda 1990–91; Davis 2008; Kartzow 2010.

world, marginal religious groups like the Jews in diaspora or the early Christians would have had a marginal masculinity. According to Connell, some aspects of the marginalized masculinities may be authorized by the hegemonic masculinity. However, this does not yield authority to all members of the marginalized group.[12] Whereas the subordinated masculinities are the necessary 'Other' to which the hegemonic masculinity is compared, marginalized masculinities are not necessarily feminized but pushed out, ignored, or denied existence.

The strength of Connell's theory is that it acknowledges the diversity of masculinities and the intersectionality between gender and other social structures. It also takes into account the possibility of historical change: if the current hegemonic masculinity does not answer the demands of the situation, another ideal of masculinity may take its place and become hegemonic instead.

Connell's categorization is widely used in masculinity studies, but it has not escaped criticism. Wetherell and Edley, for instance, question whether there can be only one hegemonic masculinity.[13] Demetriou, too, sees the problem in Connell's theory to be its 'inability to understand the formative process of hegemonic masculinity as a reciprocal one'. He suggests that hegemonic masculinity should rather be seen as a 'hybrid bloc', a system that does not negate the 'other' but rather incorporates it by negotiation. Subordinated and marginalized masculinities thus can have some influencing capacities over the hegemonic masculinity.[14]

In spite of this critique, Connell's theory still offers a good starting point for the study of masculinities, including biblical masculinities. Critics do not question the existence of hegemonic and non-hegemonic forms of masculinity, but maintain that Connell's formulation of hegemonic masculinity should be developed further. I also think there may be several hegemonic masculinities that compete for the hegemonic position. For example, in the ancient Greco-Roman world there were several ideals circumscribing male sexual behavior. Some thought the man had to be assertive, others to be self-controlled, yet both views may have been hegemonic.

Connell also talks about complicit masculinity in the singular, but I would argue that there are several masculinities that are complicit in different ways, some more complicit than others. In other words, I do not see complicit masculinity as a category per se; rather, I would suggest that complicity

---

12.   Connell 2005: 81.

13.   Wetherell and Edley 1999: 337.

14.   Demetriou 2001: 346-47. According to Petersen (2003), in later studies that apply Connell's theory the connection between masculinities and power has disappeared, and the term 'masculinities' is used simply to depict the diversity or plurality of masculinity. Connell answers the criticisms in Connell and Messerschmidt 2005.

is a quality different masculinities can have in varying degrees. Moreover, not all marginalized and subordinated masculinities have equal status. Masculinities that are marginalized or subordinated by the hegemonic masculinity can still be complicit to hegemonic masculinity, that is, they agree with some of its ideals.[15] Thus, subordinated or marginalized masculinities are not necessarily counterhegemonic (although they can be). Furthermore, it is possible for a masculinity to be both subordinated and marginalized. Stereotyping a masculine behavior as effeminate (thus subordinate) can be used as a way of marginalizing that masculinity even more. Historically, for example, Jewish men in diaspora simultaneously have been both feminized and marginalized.[16] Some masculinity within subordinated or marginalized masculinities can be in the hegemonic position in relation to others, even though it is not in the hegemonic position in the culture overall.[17]

The hegemonic masculinity of Greco-Roman antiquity was the masculinity of members of the elite. In the first century, Christianity was not in a hegemonic position, so it could not have been the hegemonic masculinity in the society at large. On the contrary, early Christianity was marginalized by the hegemony. This marginalization does not necessarily entail active persecution, but rather ignorance of their existence. The fact that there are so few mentions of Christians in the Greco-Roman literature of the first and second centuries attests to the marginality of early Christianity. Since Christian masculinities intersect with religion, I suggest that seeing them as marginalized might be the most fruitful approach. Seeing early Christian masculinities as marginal highlights the different attitudes they had toward hegemonic masculinity.[18]

In masculinity studies, marginality has not been theorized much. In cross-cultural studies, on the other hand, it has been argued that the acculturating, marginal groups relate to the dominant culture in different ways. J.W. Berry makes the point that marginal groups may approve of certain facets of the dominant culture, even if this does not alter their marginal position.[19] The marginal group can relate to the dominant culture positively, not only negatively, and thus expose a level of complicity in the hegemonic gender system.

---

15. Connell (1991) mentions in passing that it is possible for marginalized men to be complicit to hegemonic masculinity, though he does not theorize this further.

16. Cf., e.g., Kimmel 1988: 154; Boyarin 1997.

17. Compare the Ethiopian eunuch in Acts 8.26-40 with the self-castrated eunuch of Mt. 19.12.

18. For example, Hondagneu-Sotelo and Messner (1994: 214) have argued that the standpoint of the oppressed groups should be taken as the point of departure in masculinity studies.

19. Berry 1990; 1997.

There is no reason to doubt, therefore, that some of the early Christian masculinities might have been closer and more complicit to hegemonic masculinity without becoming fully hegemonic.[20]

Dennis Duling has applied the concept of marginality to the New Testament. When studying marginality in the Gospel of Matthew, Duling differentiates between involuntary marginality and voluntary marginality. Involuntary marginality means that because of their sex, race, or ethnicity people are 'denied the opportunity to participate in roles expected of them'.[21] Voluntary marginality, on the other hand, means that people choose consciously not to 'live according to commonly accepted norms'.[22] Duling comes to the conclusion that the Gospel of Matthew has an ideology of voluntary marginality, and even uses several involuntarily marginalized groups as positive examples.[23] Although Duling does use a gender perspective, his categorization of different marginalities is illuminating for the study of masculinities as well. Marginalized masculinities can also be marginalized involuntarily or voluntarily. Using Connell's term of complicity, I would argue that voluntarily marginalized masculinities are less complicit to hegemony.[24] If Matthew's group was voluntarily marginalized, can this be seen in their masculinity ideology?

3. *Hegemonic and Subordinate Masculinities in Greco-Roman Antiquity*

In Greco-Roman antiquity, masculinity was not considered a permanent state that one could achieve irrefutably, but rather something that was always under construction and open to the scrutiny of other men. Maud Gleason describes the ancient notion of gender as 'not an absolute but a point on a sliding scale'. According to her, masculinity was an achieved state, independent of anatomical sex.[25] This also means that the mere fact

20.   I would propose that writings with apologetical purpose are more likely to be complicit to the hegemonic masculinity, since they intend to show that Christianity is not a threat to the dominant Roman order.

21.   Duling 1993: 645, 648; 2002: 521.

22.   Duling 1993: 648; 2002: 521. In his 2002 article, Duling uses the terms 'structural' and 'ideological' marginality for 'involuntary' and 'voluntary' marginality respectively (pp. 546-49).

23.   Duling 1993: 663.

24.   Involuntarily marginalized groups may be more complicit to hegemony to show that they are not a threat to the hegemony. However, they may also have a counter-reaction to their marginalization and become less complicit to the hegemony. Thus, in this case the involuntarily marginal group would be embracing their marginality.

25.   Gleason 1995: xxii, 59, 96, 159; quotation from p. 59. This is the case not only in antiquity, but in several modern-day cultures around the world; see Gilmore 1990.

that one was born with male genitalia was not enough to prove one's masculinity. There could be masculine women and effeminate men. Gleason points out that in their perfect form the categories of masculine and feminine were 'highly polarized', the exact opposites of each other.[26] The people who fell in between, for example eunuchs, were considered unclean, because they confused the categories.[27]

Masculinity was thus not an inherent part of every man. There were biological men who were not considered 'real men'. What, then, were real men like? According to Craig Williams, control and dominion were the prime directives of the ancient Greco-Roman masculinity. This means that a man had constantly to defend his masculinity by controlling both himself and his desires, as well as control those under his jurisdiction.[28] This ideal belonged to the elite writers. Even though the hegemonic masculinity was the masculinity of the elite, it did not mean that the elite operated with a unified hegemonic ideal. As mentioned above, different ideals competed for the hegemonic position. Some writers emphasized the control of others as a feature of true masculinity, others emphasized self-control.

According to Connell's definition, subordinated masculinities are associated with femininity.[29] Similarly in the Greco-Roman antiquity, the effeminate men constitute a negative paradigm to the masculine ideal: they are what the real men are not and the real men are what effeminate men are not.[30] Williams suggests that effeminacy was a failure to live up to the central imperative of Roman masculinity: control and dominion.[31] Placing excessive attention on his appearance, seeking to be dominated and to please others, and yielding to his passions were examples of the lack of control, and thus emasculated a man.[32] It was a common belief that a man could control himself much better than a woman;[33] an inability to exert control made a man effeminate.

In the ancient Greco-Roman world effeminacy was not necessarily connected with same-sex sexual behavior.[34] Instead of exclusive sexual

26. Gleason 1995: 60.

27. Gleason 1995: 133, 161.

28. Williams 1999: 141-42.

29. Connell 2005: 78-79.

30. Williams 1999: 126.

31. Williams 1999: 127.

32. Williams 1999: 139, 141; also Gleason 1995: 65; Glancy 2003: 242; Roisman 2005: 89.

33. Just 1989: 162-63.

34. Williams 1999: 7. Whether the word 'homosexual' can be used in the context of antiquity has been the subject of heated debate. See, e.g., Richlin 1993; Williams 1999; Parker 2001; Halperin 2002.

orientation, the ancient Greeks and Romans made a distinction between the insertive and receptive roles. The 'real' man was to have a penetrative, active role, whereas the 'others'—women, boys, and slaves—were the passive, penetrated. Free adult men who wanted to be penetrated were labeled as deviants and effeminate—that is, examples of subordinate masculinity.[35] Playing the passive role in sex was not the only way to acquire the label 'sexual deviant'. According to Williams, a man who played the active role could still be accused of effeminacy.[36] Thus, seeking to be penetrated was only one symptom of a greater gender deviance. Other symptoms were effeminacy, softness, and decadence.[37] Moreover, in the ancient Greco-Roman world, effeminate men were viewed as morally suspicious.[38]

Since the eunuch-saying in Mt. 19.12 is connected with Jesus' teaching of divorce and adultery, we will next look at how sexual desire and adultery featured vis-à-vis hegemonic masculinities. Concerning sexual desire, there were different ideals. There were writers who emphasized the importance of self-control. Philosophers like Epictetus and Marcus Aurelius maintained that men should strive not to desire sex.[39] These ideas were also found in the medical writings. Soranos considered permanent virginity healthful.[40] Similarly, even though Celsos argued that intercourse should not be feared too much, he maintained that it should not be desired too much either.[41] There were also writers who found sexual desire healthy and normal.[42] Williams suggests that the dominant paradigm of masculinity in ancient Rome was what he calls 'priapic masculinity'. In this paradigm, the man asserted his masculinity by dominating others.[43] Epictetus also admits that not everyone shared his ideal; on the contrary, there were some men who admired those men who 'can cajole and corrupt most women'.[44]

---

35. Williams 1999: 7. Romans called this soft, effeminate man a *cinaedus*. *Cinaedus* was a common scare-figure in several Greco-Roman texts; see, e.g., Plato, *Phaedr.* 239C-D; Epictetus, *Diatr.* 3.1. Long (1996: 71-74) offers examples of sexual accusations and effeminacy.

36. Williams 1999: 125.

37. Williams 1999: 175.

38. Hester 2005: 19.

39. Epictetus, *Diatr.* 1.18.15; 4.9.3; Marcus Aurelius 2.10; 9.40.

40. Soranus, *Gynaecology* 1.7.30-32.

41. Celsos, *De medicina* 1.1.4. Also Epicuros argued that intercourse was never beneficial; see Diog. Laert. 10.118.

42. E.g. Achilles Tatius, *Leuc. Clit.* 1.4-6; Apuleius, *Metam.* 2.8; Artemidorus Daldianus, *Onir.* 1.78. See also Diogenes of Sinope in Diog. Laert. 6.2.46, 69.

43. Williams 1999: 18, 51, 153.

44. *Diatr.* 4.9 (trans. Whitney J. Oates).

Similarly, there were different opinions concerning men's infidelity in marriage. Generally, extra-marital affairs were acceptable for men. For example, the famous dictum by Demosthenes defined three types of women: hetaerae for the sake of pleasure, concubines for the daily care of the body, and wives for legitimate children.[45] Xenophon's passing reference to the use of slaves for sexual purposes is another example of this way of thinking.[46] Thus, the priapic masculinity did not expect faithfulness in marriage on the part of the man.[47] The man could use the services of prostitutes and slaves to gratify his sexual desires. Adultery was committed only when a man had sex with another man's wife. Still, Aristotle maintained that the husband's relations to another woman were without exception shameful.[48] Later, the double standard was opposed more commonly. Both the Pythagoreans and the Stoics demanded marital faithfulness from both parties.[49] According to Musonius Rufus, the extra-marital affair harms the man himself because it shows the man's lack of self-control.[50] Like Musonius, Plutarch maintains that infidelity is due to man's lack of self-control.[51] Yet, Plutarch also argues that infidelity is wrong because it causes 'pain and disturbance' for the wife.[52] Williams, however, notes that this view was only an ideal, not the regular practice. The overwhelming majority of sources supported man's right to extra-marital affairs as long as the man's behavior was not seen as overindulging or overreaching (pursuing other men's wives) in extra-marital affairs, in which case he could be labeled 'effeminate'.[53]

4. Eunuchs as an Example of Subordinated Masculinity in Greco-Roman Antiquity

The majority of the eunuchs in the ancient Greco-Roman world were slaves or prisoners of war.[54] There were several words in Greek and Latin used for eunuch. The word used in Mt. 19.12, εὐνοῦχος, comes etymologically from

---

45. Demosthenes, *Oration* 59.122 (*Against Neaera*).
46. Xenophon, *Oec.* 10.12.
47. Williams 1999: 51.
48. Aristotle, *Pol.* 1335b40-36a1.
49. Foucault 1990: 17-18; Treggiari 1991: 312.
50. *On Sexual Indulgence* (see Lutz 1947: 84-89). Treggiari (1991: 312-13) presumes that Musonius is talking about unmarried men, because a married man would harm his wife. However, since the text continues to talk about a married man, it is plausible that the subject here is also a married man.
51. Plutarch, *Conj. praec.* 16.
52. Plutarch, *Conj. praec.* 44.
53. Williams 1999: 43, 47-48, 51-55, 143, 148.
54. Guyot 1980: 28-36; Moxnes 2003: 78.

εὐνή and ἔχειν, 'one who keeps or guards the marriage bed', hence the meaning 'chamberlain'.[55] Other words used for eunuch in Greek include σπάδων, ἐκτομίας, ἀπόκοπος, and τομίας.[56] These words derive from verbs meaning cutting off or tearing away and thus they refer to the manner of the castration. The castration was done by cutting or crushing the testicles. However, the different terms for eunuch were mostly used interchangeably, so the manner or circumstances of the castration were not significant for the choice of the terms.[57]

For the ancient Greco-Roman writers, eunuchs epitomized the lack of self-control and its supposed physiological effects. Eunuchs were not considered morally upright or virtuous.[58] This lack of self-control made them effeminate. In the ancient Greco-Roman writings, eunuchs were despised because they confused the categories of male and female. Lucian writes that 'a eunuch was neither man nor woman but something composite, hybrid, and monstrous, alien to human nature'.[59] Eunuchs were called 'half-men' (*semiviri* or *semimares*).[60] They were also described by using the feminine pronoun. For example, in Catullus' poem Attis uses the feminine pronoun to describe himself after castration.[61] In the late second and early first centuries BCE a slave was exiled from Rome after castrating himself,[62] and another eunuch was denied his inheritance on account that he was neither a man nor a woman.[63]

Accusations of sexual misconduct (blurring sexual roles) were also hurled against eunuchs. They were accused of playing both a passive role with men and an active role with women.[64] After certain kinds of postpubescent castration the possibility of penetration remains, and so eunuchs were thought to

---

55.   Beekes 2010: 481 (εὐνή); Guyot 1980: 20.

56.   For Greek and Latin terms for castration and eunuchs, see Guyot 1980: 22-23 and nn. 17-25.

57.   Guyot 1980: 24; for examples, see pp. 181-233.

58.   Hester 2005: 22. For example, Artemidorus Daldianus, *Onir.* 2.69 claims that eunuchs and castrates are unreliable.

59.   Lucian, *Eunuch.* οὔτε ἄνδρα οὔτε γυναῖκα εἶναι τὸν εὐνοῦχον λέγοντος, ἀλλά τι σύνθετον καὶ μικτὸν καὶ τερατῶδες, ἔξω τῆς ἀνθρωπείας φύσεως (trans. A.M. Harmon).

60.   Roller 1997: 550; 1999: 323 n. 57; Guyot 1980: 38-39. See, e.g., Ovid, *Fast.* 4.183; Juvenal, *Sat.* 6.513.

61.   Catullus 63.12; see also 63.27, where Attis is described as a 'fake woman' (*notha mulier*).

62.   Julius Obsequens 44A.

63.   Valerius Maximus 7.7.6.

64.   For example, Lucian (*Syr. d.* 22), Terence (*Eun.* 666), and Martial (*Epigram* 3.81) show that the eunuchs were considered having sexual relations with women. See also Guyot 1980: 59-66, esp. 63-66; Hester 2005: 22-23.

be able to have penetrative sex with women.[65] Juvenal suggests that some women waited until after puberty before castrating their slaves so that they could be used for sexual purposes.[66] Thus, eunuchs were not considered celibate in the ancient Greco-Roman world. On the contrary, as David Hester points out, they 'were universally characterized by the frequency, ease and adeptness with which they performed sex acts with both men and women'.[67] The invectives against eunuch as sexually insatiable can be found in the first and second centuries CE in the writings of Martial, Lucian, and Juvenal:[68]

> Under your rule no man shall be either eunuch or adulterer. Formerly (alas for our morals!) even a eunuch was an adulterer.[69]

> You ask why your Caelia has only eunuchs for servants,
> Pannychus? Caelia wants to be fucked and not give birth.[70]

> As a matter of fact, gentlemen, if this fellow, so smooth of jowl, effeminate in voice, and otherwise similar to a eunuch, should strip, you would find him very masculine. Unless those who talk about him are lying he was once taken in adultery, *commissis membris*, as the table of the law says.[71]

> When a soft eunuch takes to matrimony...it is hard not to write satire.[72]

Polemics against eunuchs can also be found in much later texts. Claudian's (c. 370–404 CE) invective against the eunuch consul Eutropius is another prime example of polemics directed towards eunuchs.[73] Eutropius exemplifies a eunuch who gained political power, and by the fourth century CE, non-slave eunuchs were found in influential positions in Rome.[74] This,

---

65. Hester 2005: 23; Greenstein, Plymate and Katz 1995.

66. Juvenal, *Sat.* 6.366-78.

67. Hester 2005: 18. Hester (2005: 24) concludes: 'All in all, the eunuch was seen as the embodiment of, and even the means of facilitating, sexual transgression'.

68. See also Epictetus, *Diatr.* 2.20.19: 'Even those who castrate themselves are not able to cut themselves off from the desires of men'.

69. Martial, *Epigram* 6.2: *Nec spado iam nec moechus erit te praeside quisquam: At prius—o mores!—et spado moechus erat* (trans. D.R. Schackleton Baily, LCL)

70. Martial, *Epigram* 6.67: *Cur tantum eunuchos hapeat tua Caelia, quaeris Pannyche? Volt futui Caelia nec parere* (trans. Richlin 1992: 134).

71. Lucian, *Eunuch.*: ὦ ἄνδρες δικασταί, οὑτοσὶ ὁ τὰς γνάθους λεῖος καὶ τὸ φώνημα γυναικεῖος καὶ τὰ ἄλλα εὐνούχῳ ἐοικὼς εἰ ἀποδύσαιτο, πάνυ ἀνδρεῖος ὑμῖν φανεῖται· εἰ δὲ μὴ ψεύδονται οἱ περὶ αὐτοῦ λέγοντες, καὶ μοιχὸς ἑάλω ποτέ, ὡς ὁ ἄξων φησίν, ἄρθρα ἐν ἄρθροις ἔχων (trans. A.M. Harmon).

72. Juvenal, *Sat.* 1.22, 30: *cum tener uxorem ducat spado ... difficile est saturam non scriber* (trans. G.G. Ramsay).

73. Long 1996: 122-29, 146.

74. Grayson 1995: 88; Guyot 1980.

however, did not alter the way eunuchs were perceived generally. Accusations of sexual misconduct were not the only invectives against effeminate men. Hester lists other accusations against eunuchs, like being soft, effeminate, unkind, immodest, weak, deceitful, cowardly, and incapable of virtue.[75] These were also stereotypical feminine vices.[76] Eunuchs were also ridiculed for having feminine voices.[77] Excessive concern for one's appearance was another feature that emasculated a man and was suitable for eunuchs, not for real men. Masculinity, on the other hand, was associated with uncultivated roughness.[78]

In addition to the involuntary eunuchs (slaves, prisoners), there was a group of men who voluntarily castrated themselves. These were the *galli*, the priests of a Phrygian goddess Cybele or Magna Mater.[79] The general attitude of the Romans to this cult was ambivalent. Even though the goddess herself was lauded as the savior of the state, the Romans viewed the castrated priests of Magna Mater with contempt.[80] The *galli* were also accused of sexual activities with both men and women.[81] They wore women's clothes, kept their hair long, and used perfume, all of which attracted the characterization of being effeminate.[82]

Positive remarks of eunuchs are scarce in the ancient sources. Polybius (c. 200–118 BCE) and Ammianus Marcellinus (c. 325–400 CE) mention positive examples of eunuchs, but they are mentioned specifically because they are exceptional. Ammianus, for example, calls it unbelievable that a

75. Hester 2005: 21-22.
76. Just 1989: 162-66.
77. E.g. Lucian, *Eunuch.*; Valerius Maximus 7.7.6. On voice and masculinity, see Gleason 1995: 83.
78. E.g. Ovid, *Ars* 1.505-509; Epictetus, *Diatr.* 3.1.
79. Roller 1999: 4. On the self-castration, see Roller 1999: 240. Roscoe (1996: 203) points out that it is not completely clear whether every *gallus* underwent castration and at which point in his career. On the Attis myth, see Roller 1999: 181, 240; Sawyer 1996: 120.
80. Sawyer 1996: 122. Interestingly, Lucian places the *galli* above eunuchs: τὸ δὲ τοῦ εὐνούχου καὶ τῶν βακήλων χεῖρον εἶναι: τοὺς μὲν γὰρ κἂν πεπειρᾶσθαί ποτε ἀνδρείας, τοῦτον δὲ ἐξ ἀρχῆς εὐθὺς ἀποκεκόφθαι καὶ ἀμφίβολόν τι ζῷον εἶναι κατὰ ταὐτὰ ταῖς κορώναις, αἳ μήτε περιστεραῖς μήτε κόραξιν ἐναριθμοῖντο ('whereas a eunuch was in worse case than a cut priest [βάκηλος, "eunuch in the service of Cybele, *Gallus*"], for the latter had at least known manhood once, but the former had been marred from the very first and was an ambiguous sort of creature like a crow, which cannot be reckoned either with doves or with ravens' (Lucian, *Eunuch.* [trans. A.M. Harmon]).
81. Roller 1997: 550.
82. Sawyer 1996: 122; Roller 1997: 550; 1999: 323 n. 57.

eunuch would be anything but immoral.[83] From the point of view of hegemonic masculinity, eunuchs were detestable.[84]

In Judaism, eunuchs were also scorned. The Torah prohibits castration in Deut. 23.1.[85] Commenting on this law, Philo mentions that the Law 'banishes all those who have suffered any injury or mutilation in their most important members'.[86] According to Josephus, eunuchs were to be detested, avoided, and driven away from the community, since they were comparable to the killers of children. Eunuchs had both an effeminate body and effeminate soul.[87] However, a positive evaluation of eunuchs is found in Isa. 56.3-5, where the eunuch serves as an example illustrating the miraculous nature of the new covenant. According to Wis. 3.14, being a eunuch is better than transgressing the Law. Both texts encourage the eunuch not to lament his childlessness because keeping the Law is ultimately better than having children. These sources, including the Josephus text, concentrate on the eunuch's inability to procreate. The rabbinic texts mention that eunuchs could get married; they simply could not beget children. The rabbinic texts also distinguish between two groups of eunuchs: those born a eunuch and those made a eunuch by others.[88]

---

83.   Polybius, *Histories* 22.22; Ammianus Marcellinus, *Histories* 16.7.4-9. Hester (2005: 19 n. 13) also finds very few positive examples of eunuchs. Nock (1925–26: 32 n. 9) argues that even though the *galli* often failed to receive respect, they were sometimes held in honor. Nock mentions Hippocrates' *On Airs, Waters, and Places* 22, which speaks about the popular respect of the Scythians for ᾽Αναριεῖς. However, Hippocrates argues that the Scythians are wrong in considering this disease as divine. Moreover, this mention is not about Greek views nor about *galli*. Another example Nock mentions is the last line of an inscription from Lagina which reads τῶν σεμνοτάτων τῆς θεᾶς εὐνούχων. See also Hatzfeld 1920: 84. Since this is the only line surviving of the inscription, it is not evident who erected this inscription or what its context is.

84.   Early Christian writers also used familiar rhetoric against the blurring of gender boundaries when denouncing the *galli*. See Kuefler 2001: 249. For example, the fourth-century Christian writer Firmicus Maternus writes: 'In their very temples can be seen deplorable mockery before a moaning crowd, men taking the part of women, revealing with boastful ostentation this ignominy of impure and unchaste bodies. They broadcast their crimes and confess with superlative delight the stain of their polluted bodies. They wear effeminately nursed hair and dress in soft clothes. They can barely hold their heads up on their limp necks. Then, having made themselves alien to masculinity, swept up by playing flutes, they call their Goddess to fill them with an unholy spirit so as to seemingly predict the future to idle men. What sort of monstrous and unnatural thing is this?' (Firmicus Maternus, *Err. prof. rel.* 4.2 [trans. Roscoe 1996: 195-96]). See also Augustine, *Civ.* 7.24, 26.

85.   Cf. also Lev. 21.20-21. On eunuchs in the Hebrew Bible and the ancient Near East, see Nissinen forthcoming.

86.   *Spec. leg.* 1.325 (trans. F.H. Colson). See also Eusebius, *Praep. ev.* 8.7.7.

87.   Josephus, *Ant.* 4.292.

88.   *Yeb.* 8.4-6.

From the ancient sources surveyed above we can conclude that the eunuchs were generally despised in the ancient Greco-Roman world. They were not considered an example of celibacy. The masculinity of the eunuch was a subordinated masculinity and functioned as a necessary 'Other' for the ancient Greco-Roman hegemonic masculinities. Eunuchs, together with *cinaedi* (effeminate men) and the *galli*, constituted a negative image, an anti-type against which the Roman ideal of masculinity was constructed.[89] They were ideological scare-figures for the Roman men.[90]

5. *Matthew 19.12: Eunuchs Who Have Made Themselves Eunuchs*

Turning now to Matthew's eunuch-saying in 19.12, what did it mean in the Matthean context? There are two issues that need to be considered together in order to understand the saying: (1) Jesus' teaching about divorce in vv. 3-9; and (2) the meaning of 'this word' (τὸν λόγον τοῦτον) in v. 11. For ease of access, I present the pericope here at length:

3 Καὶ προσῆλθον αὐτῷ Φαρισαῖοι πειράζοντες αὐτὸν καὶ λέγοντες· εἰ ἔξεστιν ἀνθρώπῳ ἀπολῦσαι τὴν γυναῖκα αὐτοῦ κατὰ πᾶσαν αἰτίαν; 4 ὁ δὲ ἀποκριθεὶς εἶπεν· οὐκ ἀνέγνωτε ὅτι ὁ κτίσας ἀπ' ἀρχῆς ἄρσεν καὶ θῆλυ ἐποίησεν αὐτούς; 5 καὶ εἶπεν· ἕνεκα τούτου καταλείψει ἄνθρωπος τὸν πατέρα καὶ τὴν μητέρα καὶ κολληθήσεται τῇ γυναικὶ αὐτοῦ, καὶ ἔσονται οἱ δύο εἰς σάρκα μίαν. 6 ὥστε οὐκέτι εἰσὶν δύο ἀλλὰ σὰρξ μία. ὃ οὖν ὁ θεὸς συνέζευξεν ἄνθρωπος μὴ χωριζέτω. 7 λέγουσιν αὐτῷ· τί οὖν Μωϋσῆς ἐνετείλατο δοῦναι βιβλίον ἀποστασίου καὶ ἀπολῦσαι αὐτήν; 8 λέγει αὐτοῖς ὅτι Μωϋσῆς πρὸς τὴν σκληροκαρδίαν ὑμῶν ἐπέτρεψεν ὑμῖν ἀπολῦσαι τὰς γυναῖκας ὑμῶν, ἀπ' ἀρχῆς δὲ οὐ γέγονεν οὕτως. 9 λέγω δὲ ὑμῖν ὅτι ὃς ἂν ἀπολύσῃ τὴν γυναῖκα αὐτοῦ μὴ ἐπὶ πορνείᾳ καὶ γαμήσῃ ἄλλην μοιχᾶται. 10 Λέγουσιν αὐτῷ οἱ μαθηταὶ αὐτοῦ· εἰ οὕτως ἐστὶν ἡ αἰτία τοῦ ἀνθρώπου μετὰ τῆς γυναικός, οὐ συμφέρει γαμῆσαι. 11 ὁ δὲ εἶπεν αὐτοῖς· οὐ πάντες χωροῦσιν τὸν λόγον τοῦτον ἀλλ' οἷς δέδοται. 12 εἰσὶν γὰρ εὐνοῦχοι οἵτινες ἐκ κοιλίας μητρὸς ἐγεννήθησαν οὕτως, καὶ εἰσὶν εὐνοῦχοι οἵτινες εὐνουχίσθησαν ὑπὸ τῶν ἀνθρώπων, καὶ εἰσὶν εὐνοῦχοι οἵτινες εὐνούχισαν ἑαυτοὺς διὰ τὴν βασιλείαν τῶν οὐρανῶν. ὁ δυνάμενος χωρεῖν χωρείτω.

3 Some Pharisees came to him, and to test him they asked, 'Is it lawful for a man to divorce his wife for any cause?' 4 He answered, 'Have you not read that the one who made them at the beginning "made them male and female", 5 and said, "For this reason a man shall leave his father and mother and be joined to his wife, and the two shall become one flesh"? 6 So they are no

---

89. Williams 1999: 183.

90. Williams 1999: 128, 176-77. Hester 2005: 19: 'Eunuchs were, in general, a threat to the dominant phallocentrism of patriarchy, insofar as they embodied the very loss with which men were constantly threatened'. See also Moxnes 2003: 74. Sawyer (1996: 119) calls the *galli* the 'anti-type of idealized manhood'.

longer two, but one flesh. Therefore what God has joined together, let no one separate.' 7 They said to him, 'Why then did Moses command us to give a certificate of dismissal and to divorce her?' 8 He said to them, 'It was because you were so hard-hearted that Moses allowed you to divorce your wives, but at the beginning it was not so. 9 But I say to you, whoever divorces his wife, except for unchastity, and marries another commits adultery.' 10 His disciples said to him, 'If such is the case of a man with his wife, it is better not to marry?' 11 But he said to them, 'Not everyone can receive this word, but only those to whom it is given. 12 For there are eunuchs who have been so from birth, and there are eunuchs who have been made eunuchs by others, and there are eunuchs who have made themselves eunuchs for the sake of the kingdom of heaven. Let anyone receive this who can.'[91]

Most scholars believe that v. 12 talks about celibacy.[92] The disagreement is about whether v. 12 sees celibacy as an alternative to marriage or whether celibacy is to follow a divorce. I will start by outlining and evaluating four interpretations attested in previous studies.

Interpretation # 1
Some scholars see the eunuch-saying in v. 12 to be about celibacy as an alternative to marriage.[93] After Jesus' teaching concerning the divorce, the disciples comment: it is better not to marry if it is impossible to divorce except for adultery. According to this interpretation, Jesus agrees with his disciples, but only in part: celibacy is a real alternative to marriage, but it is not for everyone. Celibacy is only a recommendation.[94] These scholars maintain that 'this word' in v. 11 refers to the disciples' objection in v. 10.[95] Keener argues that if 'this word' refers to Jesus' teaching, this would read Jesus' response in vv. 11-12 as if the disciples had not raised an objection

91. The English translation is modified from the NRSV.
92. Retief and Cilliers 2003: 73: v. 12 '*obviously* refers to celibacy'; Luz 2001: 500: '*Obviously*, as v. 12 shows, the difficulty lies in the sexual abstinence that Jesus demands after the first marriage'. Filson 1971: 207: 'But *undoubtedly* Jesus meant not a physical operation but the deliberate decision to refrain from marriage to be free to devote one's entire time to the cause of the kingdom' (emphases mine). Moxnes (2005: 28) points out that '[t]he term "of course" gives away the presuppositions of these interpreters'. Moxnes 2003: 87: 'But an interpretation of the third group of eunuchs as "unmarried" or "sexually ascetic" is far from obvious.' So also Hester 2005: 24: 'It seems odd...that the "simple and straightforward" exegesis of the eunuch logion of Matthew today would view the eunuch as a symbol of sexual chastity and celibacy'.
93. Filson 1971: 207; Hill 1972: 281; Kodell 1978: 21; Albright and Mann 1984: 227; Keener 1999: 470; Nolland 2005: 781; France 2007: 724; Evans 2012: 342.
94. Manson 1949: 215; Hill 1972: 281; Davies and Allison 1997: 21; Nolland 2005: 775; France 2007: 723.
95. Filson 1971: 207; Hill 1972: 281; Hagner 1995: 550; Davies and Allison 1997: 20; Keener 1999: 470; Nolland 2005: 776-77; France 2007: 732.

in v. 10. Instead, according to Keener, Jesus responds to the objection by replying that some would indeed be better off not marrying.[96] Jesus, in other words, agrees with his disciples. However, would Jesus accept the disciples' criticism? I will argue shortly that this is not likely.

The scholars who favor this interpretation also argue that Jesus' teaching concerning divorce in vv. 3-9 does not forbid remarriage.[97] Kodell rejects the interpretation that the eunuch-saying is about celibacy after divorce by pointing out that the word 'eunuch' means irreparable incapacity to marriage; it is not a choice.[98] The divorced, on the other hand, could get married after the first partner died. However, is it not also a matter of choice to stay single? Can celibacy, as an alternative to marriage, really be spoken of as castration? As Bernabé points out, no one called the men of Qumran 'eunuchs', even though they were not married.[99]

Moreover, if the eunuch-saying talks about celibacy as an alternative to marriage, it follows awkwardly the discussion emphasizing the permanence of marriage.[100] In this interpretation, the eunuch-saying has very little to do with Jesus' teaching in vv. 3-9.[101] This raises a question: Why did Matthew put the eunuch-saying in the context of teaching concerning divorce?

In order to interpret the eunuch-saying it is necessary to study what Matthew's Jesus teaches about divorce in vv. 3-9. The issue here is whether adultery is committed by any person who divorces and remarries, or just the person who divorces and remarries for any other reason except for *porneia*.[102] I will argue that Matthew prohibits remarriage even after divorce on account of *porneia*.

In Mt. 19.3, Jesus is approached by Pharisees who ask about the legitimate grounds for divorce. Matthew's Jesus prohibits divorce except on account of *porneia*—otherwise, divorce is adultery. The exception clause of Matthew has sometimes been understood to mean that Matthew would allow remarriage for those who have divorced because of *porneia*. However, this would mean that Jesus would be contradicting himself in succeeding

---

96. Keener 1999: 470.

97. Davies and Allison 1997: 20; Nolland 2005: 781; France 2007: 212.

98. Kodell 1978: 21.

99. Bernabé 2003: 134.

100. A similar view is put forward also by Carter 1994: 69; Wenham 1984: 98-99.

101. Luz 2001: 499.

102. The meaning of *porneia* has been debated in scholarly discussion. Some scholars argue that *porneia* in 19.9 refers to incestuous marriages (Moloney 1979: 45-49) or premarital sex (Countryman 1990: 175) and that divorce is permitted only in those cases. However, this gives *porneia* an improbably narrow meaning. See, e.g., Wenham 1986: 18; Barton 1994: 196; Carter 2000: 148. Moreover, Matthew does not want to narrow the meaning of the *porneia*; on the contrary, he wants to expand it. The same is true for other commands in the Sermon on the Mount (Mt. 5.21-48).

sentences.[103] The permanence of marriage is stressed in vv. 4-6 and 8, so allowing remarriage now would mean that Jesus is backtracking from his earlier teaching.

Matthew 19.9 is unclear as to whether second marriage is possible. However, when the readers or hearers of Matthew's Gospel reach ch. 19, they are already familiar with Jesus' teaching concerning divorce. The first time Jesus talks about divorce is in the Sermon on the Mount (5.31-32). The teaching in 19.3-9 thus needs to be read in light of this previous teaching. In 5.32a, divorce itself is called 'adultery'. In 5.32b, whoever marries a divorced woman commits adultery. The divorced woman cannot remarry, because in principle she is still married to her former husband. Similarly, a man who marries a divorced woman commits adultery, since he participates in the woman's adultery.[104] Matthew 19.9 corresponds to 5.32, where the remarriage of the woman is forbidden. This verse now expands the prohibition to the man.[105]

Moreover, Jesus' introductory formula, 'but I say to you', emphasizes that, as in the Sermon on the Mount (5.21-48), Jesus' revelation of the divine will is more authoritative than the misunderstandings of the Law by the Jewish leaders.[106] Jesus is not backtracking; rather, he is reaffirming his own teaching.[107] If 19.9 meant that Jesus permits remarriage, it would be in conflict with the emphasis of the permanence of marriage in the earlier verses.[108] In addition, Wenham argues, based on other examples of comparable expressions, that the exception clause (v. 9b) qualifies only the first conditional clause; that is, divorcing.[109] Similarly, Carter maintains that since the exception clause is placed after the mention of divorce and before 'and marries another', it refers only to the mention of divorce.[110]

Furthermore, if Jesus approves remarriage, why would the disciples be so shocked?[111] The interpretation that Jesus prohibits remarriage even in the case of *porneia* explains their reaction much better. Thus, Mt. 19.9 is an abridgement of the divorce teaching in Mt. 5.32. Divorce is permissible only in the case of *porneia*—otherwise it is adultery. Remarriage, on the other hand, is always adulterous.[112]

---

103.   Wenham 1984: 97-98.
104.   Albright and Mann 1984: 65. Cf. Mk 10.11-12 and Lk. 16.18, where remarriage is also called 'adultery'.
105.   Carter 1994: 67; 2000: 381; Luz 2001: 493.
106.   Carter 1994: 64.
107.   Wenham 1986: 18.
108.   Carter 1994: 68; 2000: 381.
109.   Wenham 1986.
110.   Carter 1994: 67; 2000: 381.
111.   Wenham 1984: 99; 1986: 18; Carter 1994: 69 n. 6; 2000: 381; Luz 2001: 493.
112.   Wenham 1984: 105; 1986: 18. See also Quesnell 1966: 336; Barton 1994: 194-95; Carter 1994: 66-71.

If Matthew therefore prohibited remarriage even after divorce on account of *porneia*, does the eunuch-saying refer to celibacy after divorce? The second interpretation argues so.[113]

Interpretation #2
Scholars who interpret the eunuch-saying as being about celibacy after divorce maintain that 'this word' in v. 11 refers to Jesus' teaching in vv. 3-9.[114] Luz argues that 'this word' cannot refer to the disciples' remark, because nowhere else in the Gospel of Matthew is the statement of disciples given that importance.[115] Gundry points out that the saying is 'given' to a select group and thus 'this word' cannot refer to what the disciples have said.[116] In addition, if the eunuch-saying was about celibacy as an alternative to marriage, it would mean that Jesus approves of what the disciples have said in v. 10. As I mentioned above, it is not likely that Jesus would agree with his disciples. According to Quesnell, the whole passage has been building up the importance and sanctity of monogamous marriage, so it would be odd if Jesus suddenly agreed with the disciples' objection.[117] Moreover, the narrative function of the disciples' speech in the Gospels is to ask questions, misunderstand, or object, but not to exemplify the Christian ideal for life. Their statements are not accepted by Jesus, but are corrected or rebuked.[118] The proponents of this interpretation argue, therefore, that 'this word' cannot refer to the disciples' objection; rather, it refers to Jesus' own teaching in vv. 3-9. The disciples' comment functions as an opportunity for Jesus to develop his teaching and underscore the permanence of marriage even more.[119]

This interpretation of the eunuch-saying as about celibacy after divorce pays attention to the permanence of marriage that Jesus emphasizes, but problems remain. According to France, if 'this word' referred to Jesus' own

113.   Even though celibacy as an alternative to marriage is the more common inter-pretation among the early Christian writers, this interpretation is attested later in Clement of Alexandria, *Strom.* 3.49-50.

114.   Luz 2001: 500; Quesnell 1966: 335, 346; Moloney 1979: 46; Carter 1994: 69; Gundry 1994: 382.

115.   Luz 2001: 500.

116.   Gundry 1994: 383.

117.   Quesnell 1966: 341-42.

118.   E.g. Mt. 8.19, 21, 25; 14.26, 30; 15.12; 16.7, 21-23; 18.1; 19.23-26. Quesnell 1966: 343; Wenham 1984: 99; Gundry 1994: 382; Luz 2001: 500.

119.   Carter 1994: 69; Luz 2001: 499. Some proponents of the celibacy interpreta-tion accept the criticism that Jesus cannot agree with the disciples and suggest that Jesus' words are a modified concession. For example, Davies and Allison (1997: 21) sug-gest that Jesus is correcting the disciples: 'v. 12 is not an endorsement of v. 10 but a qualification of it'. Instead of praising celibacy, the eunuch-saying piles up qualifications to insist that the celibacy is not for everyone.

teaching in vv. 3-9, it would mean that Jesus concedes that his teaching does not work and that not everyone is able to maintain the high standard of the permanence of marriage.[120] Thus, remarriage or divorce for other reasons than *porneia* might be permissible. Furthermore, the same question posed earlier for the first interpretation can be repeated here: can celibacy after divorce be called castration? Even though Jesus forbids remarriage, it is not likely that the eunuch-saying refers to those that stay unmarried after divorce.

The proponents of this and the preceding interpretation do not explain why the mentioning of eunuchs means celibacy. Several early Christian writers do use the term 'eunuch' as a synonym for 'celibate'.[121] Manson notices that this usage is 'unknown to classical or Hellenistic Greek', yet he argues that in 19.12 it means celibacy since it was used that way in the early Christian writings.[122] However, this usage reflects their interpretation of Mt. 19.12 and thus cannot be used to argue that it was the original meaning of the eunuch-saying.[123] Furthermore, these two interpretations do not pay attention to the social position of the eunuchs in the ancient Greco-Roman world. As we have seen in section 4 above, eunuchs were hardly considered ideal figures or even celibate.

Interpretation #3

With the rise of gender perspectives, scholars have increasingly taken into account the image of the eunuch in the Greco-Roman world. Anderson and Moore point out that Jesus' reference to the eunuch as a positive example of discipleship is striking given the negative perception of eunuchs in antiquity.[124] According to them, even though Jesus' teaching of divorce reaffirms God's original intention for marriage, alongside this appears the possibility of either celibacy as an alternative to marriage or celibacy after divorce. Anderson and Moore remark that the eunuch-saying goes against the Greco-Roman concept of hegemonic masculinity and thus represents a counter-cultural vision. Christians are urged to embrace the roles of typically subordinate masculinities: eunuchs, slaves, and children.[125]

---

120. France 2007: 732.

121. E.g. Clement of Alexandria, *Paed.* 3.4; Tertullian, *Mon.* 3; Athenagoras, *Suppl.* 33; Cyprian, *Test.* 3.32. On the interpretation of the saying by the early Christians, see Bauer 1967.

122. Manson 1949: 215.

123. So also Harvey 2007: 6.

124. Anderson and Moore 2003: 90. See also Moxnes 2005: 21.

125. Anderson and Moore 2003: 90-91; see also Moxnes 2005: 32: 'The eunuch represents a male person in a non-hegemonic position, that is, in a position similar to that of most women'.

According to Conway, the Gospel of Matthew overall is close to hegemonic masculinity, but it also has some ambiguous aspects. The eunuch-
saying is an example of such an ambiguous feature since it takes the readers
to 'the margins of gender identity in the ancient world'. Conway, like
Anderson and Moore, maintains that the eunuch figure represents a challenge to hegemonic masculinity. Conway argues, however, that Matthew
attempts to resolve the tension created by the saying, seeking to 'neutralize'
it by moving it closer to less radical ascetic practices.[126]

Hester goes furthest in arguing that the eunuchs were not considered
celibate in antiquity. According to him, the eunuchs were 'neither celibate
nor morally chaste', but highly sexual beings.[127] Hester points out that the
eunuchs 'were universally characterized by the frequency, ease and adeptness with which they performed sex acts with both men and women'.[128]
When turning to Mt. 19.12, Hester nonetheless comes to the conclusion that
'[h]ere the eunuch is a figure of sexual renunciation'.[129] In the context of the
Gospel, the saying becomes an extension to the divorce saying.[130] This
context then limits the interpretation of the saying. In v. 11 Jesus admits that
his instruction intensifies the demands of discipleship.[131] Hester mentions
both interpretations presented earlier, namely that the eunuch-saying refers
to continence after divorce or a rejection of marriage altogether. According
to Hester, Matthew thus tries to 'domesticate' the saying by placing it in a
context discussing marriage and divorce.[132]

Even though the third interpretation takes into account the social position
of eunuchs in the ancient Greco-Roman world, this interpretation still sees
the eunuchs as celibate. Thus, the third interpretation does not answer the
question: If in the ancient Greco-Roman world eunuchs were not considered
celibate, why would this saying be about celibacy? Moreover, both Conway
and Hester argue that Matthew tried to neutralize or domesticate the saying.
But is this the case? In the Gospel of Matthew in general, the traditional
honor code is turned upside down. This can be seen in the Sermon on the

126.   Conway 2008: 122-24.
127.   Hester 2005: 14, 24.
128.   Hester 2005: 18.
129.   Hester 2005: 25.
130.   Hester 2005: 16.
131.   Hester 2005: 25.
132.   Hester 2005: 30. Hester (2005: 37) argues that in its original context, however,
the saying questioned 'the privileged position of heterosexist binary paradigm of identity'. Hester (2005: 40) concludes: 'Rather than a figure that later came to reinforce conservative masculinities and their centers of privilege and power, the eunuch was a figure
that undermined and threatened male privilege'. A similar interpretation is presented also
by Moxnes (2003: 84), who maintains that the traditional interpretation of Matthew
succeeded in domesticating the saying.

Mount (chs. 5–7) as well as in the immediate context of the eunuch-saying (chs. 18–20). The disciples are, for example, exhorted not to retaliate when wronged (5.39) and not to seek public honor (6.1-18), but to become like children (18.3-5) and servants (20.26-27). Thus, when considering the entire Gospel of Matthew, it is more plausible to accept that the eunuch-saying is not neutralized.

Interpretation #4

The fourth interpretation suggests that Matthew did not try to neutralize the saying; rather, Matthew retained its radical quality. This interpretation maintains that the eunuch-saying is not about celibacy in general or celibacy after divorce, but about an alternative ideal of marriage and a new relationship between the spouses.

According to Bernabé, the eunuch-saying is about a contrast between two forms of husband–wife relationship within a marriage, traditional and alternative. The Pharisees and the disciples present the traditional, patriarchal position that gave the man unlimited freedom to divorce his wife. Jesus' reply to the Pharisees in v. 9 turns the traditional conception on its head: the husband will be the adulterer if he divorces the wife to marry another woman. In v. 10, the disciples present a traditional, androcentric position: 'If a male had to give up his privileges; if loyalty should have to be mutual; if having the type of relation Jesus proposed might result in men losing the honor and respect of other men and could even cause problems in the family, then it would be better not to marry and enter into such a relationship'.[133] Bernabé argues that Jesus does not agree with the disciples. The expression 'this word' in v. 11 does not refer to disciples' objection but to the teaching of Jesus (vv. 3-9). Instead of agreeing with the disciples, Jesus' answer to the disciples' objection both stresses and reaffirms his previous teaching.[134] Jesus insists that the men give up their honor and live in an alternative, equal marriage relationship which would have been considered 'shameful'. Giving up honor like this might lead to the disciples being called 'eunuchs', meaning that their masculinity was impugned and 'symbolically and socially denied to them'.[135]

Talbott takes a similar view but stresses more the consequences of this interpretation for women. According to Talbott, the verses seek 'to redefine social roles for women in the Jesus movement'.[136] Talbott argues that the

133.   Bernabé 2003: 133.

134.   Bernabé 2003: 128-29, 133.

135.   Bernabé 2003: 134. Dewey (1992: 114) maintains as well that the verses are about 'a countercultural understanding of the marriage relationship'.

136.   Talbott 2006: 22. Walker (2004: 243) also sees the verses as a defense of women's rights. According to Bohache (2006: 509-11), the saying is addressed to all

eunuch-saying does not justify celibacy, because that would mean either that Jesus agreed with the disciples' reaction that marriage should be abandoned if male privilege was taken away or that Jesus allowed there to be an elite class of celibate men. Instead of praising celibacy, the saying targeted male power. The verses present the ideal alternative to marriage, which would require men 'to symbolically sever their testicles as the symbolic bases of kyriarchy'.[137]

The strength of the fourth interpretation is that it pays close attention to the negative stereotypes of eunuchs found in the Greco-Roman literature and emphasizes that this saying is about male power. The saying formulates an alternative ideal, which fits in with Duling's idea of a Matthean ideology of voluntary marginality.

Nevertheless, I would argue that this saying is more about men and masculinity than about improvement of the position of women in Matthew's community. The saying is directed exclusively to men. The divorce-saying does put the wife and husband in somewhat equal positions since each must be faithful to the other.[138] However, 19.3-9 is not a defense of women's rights. Matthew 19.9 actually assigns the blame to the wife. Moreover, the impossibility of divorce for the woman actually binds the woman 'more tightly into patriarchal and androcentric patterns'.[139] Even though the ideal of mutual faithfulness can be found in the Greco-Roman literature as well, the ideal of equality in marriage is anachronistic.[140] In addition, 19.3-9 is not about the marriage relationship but about divorce. Jesus connects divorce with adultery. The eunuch-saying needs thus to be read in the light of the larger context of the divorce and adultery teaching in chs. 5 and 19.

In my view, Jesus does not allow remarriage after divorce, and I believe 'this word' (τὸν λόγον τοῦτον) in v. 11 refers to the eunuch-saying in v. 12. Quisnell argues that 'this word' cannot refer to Jesus' teaching in v. 12 because grammatically it must refer to what has already been said; that is, either to Jesus' teaching in vv. 3-9 or to the disciples' objection in v. 10.[141] However, the words from the οὗτος-group refer to what follows on several occasions in the New Testament.[142] Therefore, the expression can refer to

marginalized groups: 'Matthew 19.11-12 is one more example of Jesus' message of inclusivity toward those who were marginalized'.

137.   Talbott 2006: 39-41.

138.   So also Wenham 1984: 96; Carter 2000: 147.

139.   Carter 2000: 148.

140.   For example, even though Plutarch argues for mutual faithfulness in marriage this does not make the marriage egalitarian. Plutarch still argues that the husband should rule his wife; *Conj. praec.* 33.

141.   Quesnell 1966: 346.

142.   E.g. Mt. 10.2; Lk. 4.23; 6.3; 12.18; 13.6; 15.3; 18.9; 20.9, 17; 22.37; Jn 1.19; Acts 2.14, 16, 22; 8.32; 21.23; 23.25; 1 Cor. 9.3; Gal. 3.2, 17; Eph. 4.17. Davies and

what comes next, meaning the eunuch-saying. There are some cases when the word 'this' seems to refer both to what has been said previously and what follows.[143] In these cases, the expression refers to the same topic discussed both before and after the expression. Thus it is possible for 'this word' in v. 11 to refer both to Jesus' teaching in vv. 3-9, as well as that in v. 12. Furthermore, vv. 11 and 12 contain a similar expression using the same verb ('receive this word'), forming a sandwich structure around the eunuch-saying. Before the eunuch-saying, Jesus states 'Not everyone can receive this word' (Οὐ πάντες χωροῦσιν τὸν λόγον τοῦτον), and after the eunuch-saying, v. 12 ends with 'Let anyone receive this who can' (ὁ δυνάμενος χωρεῖν χωρείτω). It seems that both expressions refer to the same thing, that is, to the eunuch-saying. In addition, in Justin Martyr's *First Apology*, the phrase 'all cannot receive this word' follows the eunuch-saying.[144] Here 'this word' does refer to what has been said previously, but it refers to the eunuch-saying. I would then prefer the connection of 'this word' with v. 12.

How should we then translate the verb χωρέω? Some scholars translate χωρέω as 'accept'.[145] However, Ignatius uses almost the same expression as Matthew in v. 12: Ὁ χωρῶν χωρείτω.[146] In the context of Ignatius' letter, the verb does not mean that the teaching of Ignatius would be only for those who accept it. Rather, the verb means receiving, maybe in the sense of understanding, the teaching. Moreover, the expression seems to be modeled after the expression 'whoever has ears to hear, let them hear'.[147] I would argue that in 19.11-12 the verb χωρέω also means receiving or perhaps understanding the saying.[148]

Finally, I interpret the eunuch-saying as reaffirmation of Jesus' own teaching in vv. 3-9 about marriage and divorce. In order to see how the eunuch-saying is connected to the teaching on divorce, we have to recall what Matthew teaches about divorce. In 5.31-32 and 19.3-9 divorce has been likened to adultery. The divorce teaching in 5.31-32 is set in a larger context talking about *porneia*. Jesus expands the meaning of *porneia* in 5.27-30 and

Allison (1997: 20) agree that 'this word' can refer forward, although they prefer the connection with v. 10.

143.   E.g. Jn 16.16-19.

144.   Justin, *1 Apol.* 15.4: 'There are some who have been made eunuchs of men, and some who were born eunuchs, and some who have made themselves eunuchs for the kingdom of heaven's sake; but all cannot receive this word'.

145.   Evans 2012: 339, 342; Gundry 1994: 383; so also NRSV.

146.   Ignatius, *Smyrn.* 6.1.

147.   E.g. Mt. 11.15; 13.9, 43; Mk 4.9; 7.16; Lk. 8.8; 14.35. See Davies and Allison 1997: 26; Nolland 2005: 781-82.

148.   Luz (2001: 500) also mentions the possibility that the expression means 'intellectual understanding', but argues that here the expression has a broader meaning including 'agreement and willing obedience'.

argues that even looking with lust is adultery. Jesus maintains that self-mutilation is better than committing *porneia*:

> 'If your right eye causes you to sin, tear it out and throw it away; it is better for you to lose one of your members than for your whole body to be thrown into hell. And if your right hand causes you to sin, cut it off and throw it away; it is better for you to lose one of your members than for your whole body to go into hell' (5.29-30).

The connection of looking and lust was common in Judaism as well.[149] For example, a similar idea of looking and lust can be found in Philo. Philo excuses the eyes but not the hand: 'are not the hands much more to be blamed for the touch? For the eyes, being wholly at freedom, are nevertheless often constrained so as to see things which they do not wish to see; but the hands are ranked among those parts which are completely under subjection, and obey our commands, and are subservient to us.'[150] Matthew, on the other hand, condemns both the eye and the hand.

Self-mutilation to prevent sinning is also favored in Mt. 18.8-9:

> 'If your hand or your foot causes you to stumble, cut it off and throw it away; it is better for you to enter life maimed or lame than to have two hands or two feet and to be thrown into the eternal fire. And if your eye causes you to stumble, tear it out and throw it away; it is better for you to enter life with one eye than to have two eyes and to be thrown into the hell of fire.'

In the larger context of Matthew, the eunuch-saying could then be paraphrased as 'if your genitals cause you to sin, tear them out and throw them away'.[151]

Thus, the point of the whole pericope is to stress the sanctity of marriage and avoidance of adultery. The man needs to stay faithful no matter what it takes. Fidelity perhaps 'can hardly be called castration',[152] but fidelity might require it. A similar idea can be found in Philo: 'It is better to be made a eunuch than to be mad after illicit unions'.[153] Furthermore, Harvey points out that the previous metaphorical usage of the word 'eunuch' has to do with the control of sexual desire and not the renunciation of marriage.[154] For example, in Achilles Tatius' *The Adventures of Leucippe and Clitophon*,

149. Sir. 9.5, 7-9; *Test. Iss.* 7.2; on sexual desire, see also Job 31.9-10; Sir. 23.5; 41.21.

150. Philo, *Spec. leg.* 3.177 (trans. F.H. Colson).

151. Similarly, in *Acts of John* 53-54 an adulterer castrates himself. The text itself, however, opposes self-castration.

152. Nolland 2005: 781.

153. Philo, *Det. pot. ins.* 176: ἐξευνουχισθῆναί γε μὴν ἄμεινον ἢ πρὸς συνουσίας ἐκνόμους λυττᾶν (trans. F.H. Colson). In the same context Philo also says that it is better to be blinded than to see unfitting things; see Philo, *Det. pot. ins.* 175.

154. Harvey 2007: 9.

Clitophon is likened to a eunuch because he wants to stay faithful to his wife.[155] There is also an interesting inscription where εὐνοῦχος is used of a woman in the sense of 'chaste'.[156]

Self-mutilation in 5.29-30 and 18.8-9 is connected with entering life and avoiding hell. Similarly in 19.12, self-castration is done διὰ τὴν βασιλείαν τῶν οὐρανῶν. The expression is difficult to translate because the preposition διά in the expression can be understood to have a final sense ('in order to enter the kingdom' or 'in order to gain the kingdom')[157] or a causal sense ('because of the kingdom of heaven').[158] Kodell argues that Matthew uses διά in a causal sense, without excluding the possibility that the preposition could have a final sense as well.[159] Nolland, however, argues that the wider context, with its concern for entering the kingdom and having eternal life, favors the interpretation of διά in a final sense.[160] Both the previous teaching concerning divorce and adultery, and the immediate context of the eunuch-saying, talk about gaining life and avoiding hell.[161] Other scholars have made a similar connection with 19.12 and 5.29-30 and 18.8-9. For example, Nolland finds 18.8-9 the best guidance for the interpretation of 19.12.[162] The point of the sayings concerning self-mutilation is that any sacrifice is worth making to avoid sinning.[163] Harvey also argues that the self-castrated eunuchs are an example of what one should be prepared to do for the kingdom.[164] Why, then, does Matthew find it important to stress self-mutilation through-out his work? I would argue that readiness to mutilate or castrate oneself works as a sign of commitment to the Matthean community. It shows willingness to do whatever it takes to follow the commands of Jesus. Self-

155.   Achilles Tatius, *Leuc. Clit.* 5.22.5.

156.   Sijpestein (1978: 418-20) suggests that the usage reflects the actual etymology of the word εὐνοῦχος (εὐνή ἔχειν, 'one who keeps, i.e., guards the marriage bed'). See also Horsley 1983: 40-41.

157.   So Nolland 2005: 777.

158.   So Kodell 1978: 21-22; Luz 2001: 502.

159.   Kodell 1978: 21-22; so also Carter 1994: 70 n. 4.

160.   Nolland 2005: 777.

161.   Cf. Mt. 5.29-30; 18.3, 8-9; 19.16-17, 23-24, 29.

162.   Nolland 2005: 781. Nolland connects 19.12 to 19.16-29 as well, and argues that 19.12 is also a call 'to leave everything to follow Jesus'. However, 19.12 does not talk about discipleship or following Jesus. Moreover, unlike Luke, Matthew does not mention leaving wives (Mt. 19.29; cf. Lk. 14.26; 18.29).

163.   Nolland 2005: 239.

164.   Harvey 2007: 10-14. Harvey also argues that the meaning of the saying is not restricted to celibacy or sexual continence, but is 'an open metaphor for any form of radical renunciation'. However, Harvey ignores the context that talks about divorce and adultery.

mutilation and making oneself a eunuch can be seen as examples of costly-to-fake signals of commitment to the Matthean community.[165]

In sum, the eunuch-saying in 19.12 is about avoiding adultery at all costs. Avoiding lust and staying faithful to marriage may require self-mutilation, which implies that no sacrifice is too great to avoid adultery and to ensure access to the kingdom.

6. *Matthew 19.12 and the Subordinated Masculinity as the Ideal*

Finally, what implications can be derived from the eunuch-saying for the masculinity of the Matthean community? According to Connell's theory of masculinity, Greco-Roman eunuchs embody a subordinated masculinity.[166] Eunuchs were in general involuntarily marginalized slaves that did not choose to be castrated. Voluntary castration brought about shame, mockery, and accusations of effeminacy. The self-castrating eunuchs in Jesus' eunuch-saying have often been connected with the *galli*.[167] And as seen above, the *galli* were a scare-figure for hegemonic masculinity and the men who embodied that model.[168]

Jesus' eunuch-saying, therefore, requires that Christian men in Matthew's community be ready to marginalize themselves. Following Duling's idea of voluntarily marginalization in the Gospel of Matthew, it would mean that the men of this community should voluntarily accept social marginalization as part of their subordinated masculinity. The subordination of their masculinity does not necessarily make women equal to men. Thus, even though Matthew suggests that men give up some of their masculine authority, it does not mean that Matthew's ideal marriage would be completely egalitarian.

Rather than arguing that the men should stay faithful in marriage for the wife's sake, Matthew's standpoint is soteriological. The man should be willing even to castrate himself to avoid sinning and going to hell. The self-castration is a sacrifice which intends to ensure salvation and thus strengthen the vertical ties with the divinity at the expense of the horizontal ties between humans.[169] Barton argues that the marginalization of the eunuchs in

165.   The costly signaling theory (see, e.g., Sosis and Bressler 2003) can be effectively applied to this verse to underline the importance of members' real commitment to their own communities.

166.   So also Anderson and Moore 2003: 88 n. 34: 'It seems to us that even though eunuchs may occasionally have acquired a degree of elite status through serving emperors, they still represented a subordinate masculinity, since they could never fulfill the role of father'.

167.   E.g. Moxnes 2003; 2005; Harvey 2007.

168.   Williams (1999: 177) calls the *galli* the 'ultimate in unmanliness'.

169.   Cf. Launderville 2010: xxi, 486.

Greco-Roman society reflects the marginal location of the Matthean community in relation to Judaism (which in turn was marginalized in Greco-Roman society). At the same time, the Matthean community's marginality nevertheless reinforces the group's sense of being at the center of God's new order.[170] Matthew also opposes the priapic model of Greco-Roman masculinity that allowed men to have sexual relations with many women (as long as the man did not commit adultery with other men's wives). Matthew's definition of divorce and adultery is the strictest possible: the man should be faithful to his wife and even be ready to castrate himself instead of committing adultery.

Could such a man's self-control be seen as a masculine ideal? Voluntary self-castration does make Matthew compatible with one strand of ancient Greco-Roman hegemonic masculinity that recommended self-control. However, Matthew goes further than the proponents of the ideal of self-control. For example, although Plutarch argues for mutual faithfulness in marriage, in the end the man's infidelity is a minor thing the wife should forgive.[171] Matthew's marginal masculinity thus urges the Christian men to perform a masculinity that Matthew considers more perfect than the strand of hegemonic masculinity that advocates self-control.[172] But, by the same token, even though from the point of view of the ancient hegemonic masculinity adultery could effeminate a man, self-castration definitely accomplished that because it expressed a man's lack of self-control. This shows that the Matthean ideal masculinity is not complicit to the hegemonic masculinities.

Although Matthew's eunuch-saying idealizes a type of masculinity that emphasizes self-control, there exist beneath the surface an even higher ideal of male behavior implied in the text: men who do not struggle with sexual immorality and do not need castration to avoid adultery. The hierarchy that emerges when we take into consideration this type of masculinity is between the perfect man who feels no lust for other women and the man who has to castrate himself to avoid adultery. Nevertheless, it is better to be shamed than to lose salvation. Therefore the self-castrated eunuch is above sinners, like the law-abiding eunuch in Isa. 56.3-5 and Wis. 3.14. The eunuch is an example of the follower of Jesus who obeys Jesus' teaching to the extreme.

Lastly, and in conclusion, even though the image of the eunuch is utilized positively in Matthew's text, the subordinate position of eunuchs in society is hardly abandoned. The purpose of Matthew's eunuch-saying is not to

---

170.   Barton 1994: 204.
171.   Plutarch, *Conj. praec.* 16. See also Foucault 1988: 174-75.
172.   A similar idea is presented also by Conway 2008: 125.

improve the social position of eunuchs, but rather to argue that the Christian men, for the sake of the kingdom of God, should adopt the subordinate position of eunuchs and be willing to give up Greco-Roman ideals of masculinity.[173]

Bibliography

Abercrombie, Nicholas, and Bryan S. Turner
  1978   'The Dominant Ideology Thesis', *BJOS* 29: 149-70.
Albright, William Foxwell, and C.S. Mann
  1984   *Matthew: Introduction, Translation, and Notes* (AB, 26; New York: Doubleday).
Anderson, Janice C. and Stephen D. Moore
  2003   'Matthew and Masculinity', in Moore and Anderson (eds.) 2003: 67-91.
Barton, Stephen C.
  1994   *Discipleship and Family Ties in Mark and Matthew* (SNTSMS, 80; Cambridge: Cambridge University Press).
Bauer, Walter
  1967   'Matth. 19,12 und die alten Christen', in Georg Strecker (ed.), *Aufsätze und kleine Schriften* (Tübingen: Mohr): 253-62.
Beekes, Robert Stephen Paul
  2010   *Etymological Dictionary of Greek, Vol. 1* (Leiden: Brill).
Bernabé, Carmen
  2003   'Of Eunuchs and Predators: Matthew 19:1-12 in a Cultural Context', *BTB* 33: 128-34.
Berry, John W.
  1990   'Psychology of Acculturation', in John J. Berman (ed.), *Cross-Cultural Perspectives* (Current Theory and Research in Motivation, 37; Nebraska Symposium on Motivation; Lincoln, NE: University of Nebraska Press): 201-34.
  1997   'Immigration, Acculturation, and Adaptation', *Applied Psychology: An International Review* 46: 5-34.
Blinzler, Joseph
  1957   'Εἰσιν εὐνοῦχοι: Zur Auslegung von Mt 19:12', *ZNW* 48: 254-70.

---

173.   We have studied Mt. 19.12 without considering whether castration is to be taken literally or not. Cases of castration among early Christians are known, with Origen figuring here the most prominently (Eusebius, *Hist. eccl.* 6.8.1-3; Jerome, *Epist.* 84.8). Justin the Martyr also mentions a young man wanting to castrate himself but settling in the end for being unmarried (Justin, *1 Apol.* 29.2-3). *Acts of John* 53–54 tells about an adulterer who mutilates himself. The *Acts of John* text, however, opposes self-castration and regards it as Satan's doing: 'But you should have done away, not with the place of sin, but the thought which through those members showed itself harmful'. As I see it, the power of the image is such that the question of 'what if' lingers in the audience's mind. What if the masculinity Matthew advocates requires castration?

Bohache, Thomas
    2006   'Matthew', in Deryn Guest *et al.* (eds.), *The Queer Bible Commentary*
              (London: SCM Press): 487-516.
Boyarin, Daniel
    1997   *Unheroic Conduct: The Rise of Heterosexuality and the Invention of the
              Jewish Man* (Berkeley: University of California Press).
Brod, Harry, and Michael Kaufman (ed.)
    1994   *Theorizing Masculinities* (Research on Men and Masculinities Series, 5;
              Thousand Oaks, CA: Sage).
Carrigan, Tim, Bob (R.W.) Connell, and John Lee
    1985   'Toward a New Sociology of Masculinity', *Theory and Society* 14: 551-
              604.
Carter, Warren
    1994   *Households and Discipleship: A Study of Matthew 19–20* (JSNTSup, 103;
              Sheffield: JSOT Press).
    2000   *Matthew and the Margins: A Sociopolitical and Religious Reading*
              (Maryknoll, NY: Orbis Books).
Connell, R.W.
    1987   *Gender and Power: Society, the Person and Sexual Politics* (Cambridge:
              Polity Press).
    1991   'Live Fast and Die Young: The Construction of Masculinity among Young
              Working-Class Men on the Margin of the Labour Market', *Journal of
              Sociology* 27: 141-71.
    2005   *Masculinities* (Cambridge: Polity Press; 2nd edn [1st edn, 1995]).
Connell, R.W., and James W. Messerschmidt
    2005   'Hegemonic Masculinity: Rethinking the Concept', *Gender and Society*
              19: 829-59.
Conway, Colleen M.
    2008   *Behold the Man: Jesus and Greco-Roman Masculinity* (Oxford: Oxford
              University Press).
Countryman, L. William.
    1990   *Dirt, Greed and Sex: Sexual Ethics in the New Testament and Their
              Implications for Today* (Philadelphia: Fortress Press).
Davies, W.D., and Dale C. Allison
    1997   *A Critical and Exegetical Commentary on the Gospel according to Saint
              Matthew. III. Commentary on Matthew 19–28* (ICC; Edinburgh: T. & T.
              Clark).
Davis, Kathy
    2008   'Intersectionality as Buzzword: A Sociology of Science Perspective on
              What Makes a Feminist Theory Successful', *Feminist Theory* 9: 67-85.
Demetriou, Demetrakis Z.
    2001   'Connell's Concept of Hegemonic Masculinity: A Critique', *Theory and
              Society* 30: 337-61.
Dewey, Arthur J.
    1992   'The Unkindest Cut of All? Matt 19:11-12', *Foundations and Facets
              Forum* 8: 113-22.

Duling, Dennis C.
    1993   'Matthew and Marginality', in *SBL Seminar Paper, 1993* (SBLSP, 32; Atlanta, GA: Scholars Press): 642-71.
    2002   'Matthew as Marginal Scribe in an Advanced Agrarian Society', *HvTSt* 58: 520-75.
Evans, Craig A.
    2012   *Matthew* (NCBC; New York: Cambridge University Press).
Filson, Floyd Vivian
    1971   *A Commentary on the Gospel According to St. Matthew* (BNTC; London: A. & C. Black).
Foucault, Michel
    1988   *The History of Sexuality. III. The Care of the Self* (trans. Robert Hurley; New York: Vintage).
    1990   *The History of Sexuality. II. The Use of Pleasure* (trans. Robert Hurley; New York: Vintage).
France, R.T.
    2007   *The Gospel of Matthew* (NICNT; Grand Rapids, MI: Eerdmans).
Gilmore, David D.
    1990   *Manhood in the Making: Cultural Concepts of Masculinity* (New Haven: Yale University Press).
Glancy, Jennifer A.
    2003   'Protocols of Masculinity', in Moore and Anderson (eds.) 2003: 235-64.
Gleason, Maud W.
    1995   *Making Men: Sophists and Self-Presentation in Ancient Rome* (Princeton, NJ: Princeton University Press).
Grayson, A.K.
    1995   'Eunuchs in Power: Their Role in the Assyrian Bureaucracy', in Manfried Dietrich and Oswald Loretz (eds.), *Vom Alten Orient zum Alten Testament: Festschrift für Wolfram Freiherrn von Soden zum 85. Geburtstag am 19. Juni 1993* (AOAT, 240; Kevelaer: Butzon & Bercker): 85-98.
Greenstein, Alexander, Stephen R. Plymate, and P. Gary Katz
    1995   'Visually Stimulated Erection in Castrated Men', *The Journal of Urology* 153: 650-52.
Gundry, Robert Horton
    1994   *Matthew: A Commentary on His Handbook for a Mixed Church under Persecution* (Grand Rapids, MI: Eerdmans).
Guyot, Peter
    1980   *Eunuchen als Sklaven und Freigelassene in der griechisch-römischen Antike* (Stuttgart: Klett-Cotta).
Hagner, Donald A.
    1995   *Matthew 14–28* (WBC, 33B; Dallas, TX: Word Books).
Halperin, David M.
    2002   'Forgetting Foucault: Acts, Identities, and the History of Sexuality', in Martha C. Nussbaum and Juha Sihvola (eds.), *The Sleep of Reason: Erotic Experience and Sexual Ethics in Ancient Greece and Rome* (Chicago, IL: University of Chicago Press): 21-54.
Harvey, A.E.
    2007   'Eunuchs for the Sake of the Kingdom', *HeyJ* 48: 1-17.

Hatzfeld, Jean
    1920   'Inscription de Lagina en carie', *BCH* 44: 70-100.
Hearn, Jeff, and David L. Collinson
    1994   'Theorizing Unities and Differences between Men and between Masculi-
            nities', in Brod and Kaufman (eds.) 1994: 97-118.
Hester, J. David
    2005   'Eunuchs and the Postgender Jesus: Matthew 19.12 and Transgressive
            Sexualities', *JSNT* 28: 13-40.
Hill, David
    1972   *The Gospel of Matthew* (NCB; London: Oliphants).
Hondagneu-Sotelo, Pierrette, and Michael A. Messner
    1994   'Gender Displays and Men's Power: The "New Man" and the Mexican
            Immigrant Man', in Brod and Kaufman (eds.) 1994: 200-18.
Horsley, G.H.R.
    1983   *New Documents Illustrating Early Christianity*. III. *A Review of the Greek
            Inscriptions and Papyri Published in 1978* (North Ryde: Macquarie
            University).
Just, Roger
    1989   *Women in Athenian Law and Life* (London: Routledge).
Kartzow, Marianne Bjelland
    2010   '"Asking the Other Question": An Intersectional Approach to Galatians
            3:28 and the Colossian Household Codes', *BibInt* 18: 364-89.
Keener, Craig S.
    1999   *A Commentary on the Gospel of Matthew* (Grand Rapids, MI: Eerdmans).
Kimmel, Michael S.
    1988   'Judaism, Masculinity and Feminism', in Harry Brod (ed.), *A Mensch
            among Men: Explorations in Jewish Masculinity* (Freedom, CA: The
            Crossing Press): 153-56.
Kodell, Jerome
    1978   'The Celibacy Logion in Matthew 19:12', *BTB* 8: 19-23.
Kuefler, Mathew
    2001   *The Manly Eunuch: Masculinity, Gender Ambiguity, and Christian
            Ideology in Late Antiquity* (The Chicago Series on Sexuality, History, and
            Society; Chicago: University of Chicago Press).
Launderville, Dale
    2010   *Celibacy in the Ancient World: Its Ideal and Practice in Pre-Hellenistic
            Israel, Mesopotamia, and Greece* (Collegeville: Liturgical Press).
Loader, William
    2007   'Sexuality and the Historical Jesus', in Tom Holmén (ed.), *Jesus from
            Judaism to Christianity: Continuum Approaches to the Historical Jesus*
            (European Studies on Christian Origins; JSNTSup, 352; New York:
            T. & T. Clark): 34-48.
Long, Jacqueline
    1996   *Claudian's In Eutropium, or, How, When, and Why to Slander a Eunuch*
            (Chapel Hill: University of North Carolina Press).
Lutz, Cora
    1947   'Musonius Rufus: The Roman Socrates', *YCS* 10: 1-147.

Luz, Ulrich
    2001   *Matthew 8–20: A Commentary* (transl. James E. Crouch; Hermeneia; Minneapolis, MN: Fortress Press).

Manson, T.W.
    1949   *The Sayings of Jesus as Recorded in the Gospels According to St. Matthew and St. Luke* (London: SCM Press).

Matsuda, Mari J.
    1990–91   'Beside My Sister, Facing the Enemy: Legal Theory Out of Coalition', *Stanford Law Review* 43: 1183-92.

Moloney, Francis J.
    1979   'Matthew 19:3-12 and Celibacy: A Redactional and Form Critical Study', *JSNT* 2: 42-60.

Moore, Stephen D., and Janice C. Anderson (ed.)
    2003   *New Testament Masculinities* (SemeiaSt, 45; Atlanta, GA: Society of Biblical Literature).

Moxnes, Halvor
    2003   *Putting Jesus in His Place: A Radical Vision of Household and Kingdom* (Louisville: Westminster John Knox Press).
    2005   'Jesus in Gender Trouble', *Tidsskrift for kjønnsforskning* 3: 20-34.

Nissinen, Martti
  forthcoming 'Relative Masculinities in the Hebrew Bible/Old Testament', in Ilona Zsolnay (ed.), *Being a Man in Antiquity: Negotiating, Legitimating, and Maintaining Ancient Constructs of Masculinity* (London: Routledge).

Nock, Arthur Darby
    1925–26   'Eunuchs in Ancient Religion', *AR* 23: 25-33.

Nolland, John
    2005   *The Gospel of Matthew: A Commentary on the Greek Text* (NIGTC; Grand Rapids, MI: W.B. Eerdmans).

Parker, Holt N.
    2001   'The Myth of the Heterosexual: Anthropology and Sexuality for Classicists', *Arethusa* 34: 313-62.

Petersen, Alan
    2003   'Research on Men and Masculinities: Some Implications of Recent Theory for Future Work', *Men and Masculinities* 6: 54-69.

Quesnell, Quentin, S.J.
    1966   '"Made Themselves Eunuchs for the Kingdom of Heaven" (Mt 19,12)', *CBQ* 30: 335-58.

Retief, F.P., and J.F.G. Cilliers
    2003   'Congenital Eunuchism and Favorinus', *South African Medical Journal* 93: 73-76.

Richlin, Amy
    1992   *The Garden of Priapus: Sexuality and Aggression in Roman Humor* (New York: Oxford University Press).
    1993   'Not before Homosexuality: The Materiality of the *Cinaedus* and the Roman Law against Love between Men', *JHistSex* 3: 523-73.

Roisman, Joseph
    2005   *The Rhetoric of Manhood: Masculinity in the Attic Orators* (Berkeley: University of California Press).

Roller, Lynn E.
1997   'The Ideology of the Eunuch Priest', *Gender & History* 9: 542-59.
1999   *In Search of God the Mother: The Cult of Anatolian Cybele* (Berkeley: University of California Press).
Roscoe, Will
1996   'Priests of the Goddess: Gender Transgression in Ancient Religion', *HR* 35: 195-230.
Rubin, Gayle
1975   'The Traffic in Women: Notes on the "Political Economy" of Sex', in Rayna R. Reiter (ed.), *Toward an Anthropology of Women* (New York: Monthly Review Press): 157–210.
Sawyer, Deborah F.
1996   *Women and Religion in the First Christian Centuries* (Religion in the First Christian Centuries, 1; London: Routledge).
Sijpestein, P.J.
1978   'An Unpublished Greek Funeral Inscription', *Mnemosyne* 31: 418-20.
Sosis, Richard, and Eric R. Bressler
2003   'Cooperation and Commune Longevity: A Test of the Costly Signaling Theory of Religion', *Cross-Cultural Research* 37: 211-39.
Talbott, Rick Franklin
2006   'Imagining the Matthean Eunuch Community: Kyriarchy on the Chopping Block', *JFSR* 22: 21-43.
Treggiari, Susan
1991   *Roman Marriage: Iusti Coniuges from the Time of Cicero to the Time of Ulpian* (Oxford: Clarendon Press).
Walker, G.
2004   'Eunuchs for the Kingdom of Heaven: Constructing the Celibate Priest', *Studies in Gender and Sexuality* 5: 233-57.
Wenham, G.J.
1984   'Matthew and Divorce: An Old Crux Revisited', *JSNT* 22: 95-107.
1986   'The Syntax of Matthew 19:9', *JSNT* 28: 17-23.
Wetherell, Margaret, and Nigel Edley
1999   'Negotiating Hegemonic Masculinity: Imaginary Positions and Psycho-Discursive Practices', *Feminism & Psychology* 9: 335-56.
Williams, Craig A.
1999   *Roman Homosexuality: Ideologies of Masculinity in Classical Antiquity* (Oxford: Oxford University Press).

THE MAKING(S) OF AN AVERAGE JOE:
JOSEPH OF NAZARETH VS. EMPIRE, IN THREE ROUNDS*

Justin Glessner

This study maps the discursive intersection of empire and the quotidian making(s) of men in three early characterizations of Joseph of Nazareth— from the Gospels of Luke and Matthew and the *Protevangelium of James* (PJ). Although Matthew's 'just man' (δίκαιος, Mt. 1.19), Joseph was also, after all, 'just a man'—the 'average Joe'—especially when compared with other superior, if also perhaps more volatile, exemplars of early Christian masculine comportment, such as, say, the hero martyr[1] or the 'manly eunuch'.[2] Without denying the importance of analysis and critique of gender/ing in such highly visible, spectacular performances, I offer here an aligned study revealing deep instabilities inherent even (or especially) in seemingly ordinary or 'everyday'[3] citations of 'normative' masculine

*   Thanks to Reidar Aasgaard for his comments on an earlier version of this essay (Glessner 2012). Aasgaard himself has initiated critical discussion of Joseph of Nazareth's characterizations in early Christian narratives; see Aasgaard 2009b; cf. Aasgaard 2009a.
1.   See Perkins 1995; Cobb 2008.
2.   See Kuefler 2001.
3.   The varying ways in which the ostensibly straightforward notion of 'the everyday' has been put to work in the social sciences illustrate shifting concerns between research paradigms involving very different theoretical and ideological frameworks; see, e.g., Lüdtke 1995; Cuthbert 1996; Flick 1998; Gregory 1999; Seigworth 2000; Schilling 2003. Generally, the study of 'the everyday', 'daily life', and/or 'everydayness' connotes a research orientation rather than a discrete field of inquiry. By exploring the hidden worlds of ostensibly uninteresting phenomena, routines, habits, and notions of ordinary or common people (against that of elites, patriarchs, intellectuals, or experts), which tend to be neglected because their 'everydayness' makes them invisible or self-evident, different and profitable insights into social or cultural issues may be produced. As one of the key theorists on 'the everyday', Henri Lefebvre, suggests analyzing the everyday may bring out the extraordinary in the ordinary (Lefebvre 1987: 9). Furthermore, while everyday life may be familiar, this does not mean that it is understood—people do not know well how they live (Lefebvre 1959: 605)—or insignificant: 'it is the everyday that carries the greatest weight. While Power occupies the space which it generates, the everyday is the very soil on which the great architectures of politics and society rise up' (Lefebvre 1973: 85; 1976: 88-89).

While Lefebvre's concept of 'everyday life' (*la vie quotidienne*) can be seen as an application of Marx's notion of alienation to Lukács's and Heidegger's understanding of subjectivities in ancient religious narratives.[4] I read not merely for gender in the everyday but for the gendering of the everyday; in other words, how was 'everydayness' crafted into gendered experience and how was this related to early Christian group identity formation?[5] I suggest that the Josephs of Luke, Matthew, and PJ represent a number of early Christian literary attempts at crafting everyday men: paradigmatic,[6] though also unstable and at times competing, models of/for non-elite masculine subjectivity forged within multiple cultural 'contact zones' produced by imperial/colonial forces.[7]

While Luke and Matthew have been profitably read as analogues of 'ancient novels',[8] this study will treat PJ, too, as an important example of early Christian novelistic literature.[9] Though PJ is certainly shorter than

---

Alltäglickhkeit (everydayness)—the banality and conformity of decidedly *modern* everyday life, colonized as it is by capitalist forces, is such that present-day human persons are alienated (see Elden 2004: 112-13)—it should also be noted that Lefebvre himself suggested that the examination of the idea of everyday life in studies of different, premodern civilizations has often showed the *absence* of everyday life; see Lefebvre 1968b: 60; 2002b: 29; cf. Lefebvre 1970: 155. My use of the concept of the everyday is not invariably linked to Lefebvre's Marxist critique of alienation/domination in contemporary everyday life. Rather, I take 'the everyday' in a broader sense, associated with the ahistorical, pan-chronological concept of 'normality'/'everdayness' employed in ethnological sociology; see, e.g., Gullestad 1991; Niedermüller 2002: 36-38. One can thus talk about 'everydayness' equally in shamanistic societies and in Greco-Roman antiquity, as also in Lefebvre's contemporary, capitalist world of alienation.

4. See Connell 2005: 3: 'Everyday life is an arena of gender politics, not an escape from it. Gender terms are contested because the right to account for gender is claimed by conflicting discourses and systems of knowledge. We can see this in everyday situations as well as in high theory.'

5. See Peskowitz 1997: 23.

6. Ancient Greek and Roman historical biographers often taught positive or negative moral lessons by means of the characters they depicted; see, e.g., Diodorus Siculus 15.1.1; 37.4.1; see Aune 1987: 36; see Lyons 1985: 29-32.

7. Pratt 1992: 6-7. On the connections and distinctions between the concepts of 'imperialism', 'colonialism', and 'neo-colonialism', and the general applicability of postcolonial theory to the Roman imperial context of early Christian discourse, see Sugirtharajah 2002: 24-28; cf. Young 2001: 15-19, 25-29. On the intersection of the 'everyday' and 'resistance', see Scott 1990, whose interests in the 'weapons of the weak' and 'hidden scripts' highlight the importance of mundane, informal, diffuse and often individualistic responses to dominant/hegemonic ideologies.

8. See, e.g., contributions by D.R. MacDonald and J.R.C. Cousland in Brant, Hedrick, Jr., and Shea 2005: 239-54 and 255-74, respectively. As noted and discussed by Thurman (2007: 188 n. 10), 'Ancient literary theory has no single generic concept for the texts now recognized as "ancient novels," but the terms "romance" and "novel" are still preferable to others, even if somewhat anachronistic and occasionally imprecise'; see Bowersock 1994: 10-19; and Thomas 2003: 94-97, 101-104.

9. The depreciation of apocryphal infancy stories was a generally accepted fact in current Western culture until not long ago, and not an attitude specific only to traditional

other writings categorized as ancient novels,[10] it is nonetheless part of the same literary thrust that emerged out of the cultural and political dislocation produced by Roman hegemony.[11] Each of the focus texts of this study (Luke, Matthew, and PJ), then, like much of the contemporary literature produced by colonized Roman subjects, embodies creative forms of resistance, partly by telling tales that disrupt 'the "truth" or stability of any encompassing monolithic version of "history"',[12] but also by crafting symbolic boundaries of group identity and social norms across unstable terrain.

I suggest here that a constitutive part of the 'unstable terrain' traversing in these texts entails the discursive making(s) of 'everyday' men.[13] While the study of the 'everyday' in antiquity is frequently employed as 'context' enabling a fuller reading, perhaps 'thick description', of ancient texts, as the work of a number of cultural theorists makes particularly clear,[14] and as I fancy in this study, the 'everyday' is not simply a neutral label for a pre-existing, background reality, but is freighted down with layers of culturally ambivalent meanings and associations. One of these associations is, of course, the contested category of gender. Yet the conventional, nostalgic association of the 'everyday' with 'woman' or 'femininity'[15]—as also with

New Testament scholars; see the discussion in Clivaz *et al.* 2011: xv-xxv. Consideration of PJ alongside the Gospel of Matthew and is akin to the developments in the general perception/reception of Christian apocrypha (and de-privileging canonical texts) in recent work; see the collected essays in Clivaz *et al.* 2011, which attempt to consider all the stories on Jesus' infancy (including the apocrypha) in the category of 'infancy gospels'; see also Berder 2009: 211 n. 2.; Frey and Schröter 2010.

While many studies of gospel literature as ancient fiction typically address formal literary questions—see, e.g., Ehlen 2004, who employs the categories of 'point of view' and 'alternation technique' used by Tomas Hägg, and 'focalisation' used by Gérard Genette, to show that the author of PJ methodically borrowed narration techniques developed by the ancient Greek novelists of Chariton and Achilleus Tatius—I am more interested here in specific aspects of ambivalently constructed religious and cultural identities (in particular, the category of gender) that make a showing 'across *our* texts and *theirs*' (Burrus 2007: 10, emphasis original).

10. As far as length goes, PJ might more properly be categorized as an ancient novella or novelette: compare Luke (c. 19,482 words), Matthew (c. 18,345 words), and Xenophon's *Ephesian Tale* (c. 18,096 words) to PJ (c. 5,632 words).

11. Whitmarsh 2011: 6-12.

12. Burrus 2009: 145.

13. See Thurman 2012.

14. See Highmore 2002.

15. Lefebvre's Euro-centric 'critique of everyday life' in particular has remained largely undertheorized with respect to particular social relations (gender, sexuality, and race to name but a few); see McCann 1999; Blum and Nast 1996. For example, Lefebvre argues that everyday life has a more profound effect on women than men, because of the structure of societies—he is writing this in the early 1960s; see Lefebvre 1968a: 17,

the 'natural', 'authentic', 'primitive'—certainly will not do, as it promotes, among other horrors, a heroic myth of masculine transcendence.[16] Rather, conceiving of this study as an allied/pro-feminist project,[17] I quite deliberately accentuate the (fore)grounding of men (Josephs) as culturally configured bodies, embedded subjects who live, for the most part, repetitive, familiar, ordinary lives dictated by 'regulative discourses' which code and guide everyday possibilities not only of gender[18] but also of 'mutually multiplicative vectors' of subjectivity constituted by sex, sexuality, race, age, class, ethnicity, and so on.[19] The texts in which Joseph of Nazareth appears engage the context of Roman imperial rule (of the first and second century CE) with markedly dissimilar literary politics, accompanied by a range of ambivalent everyday confrontations with hegemonic patterns of masculinity—this, as I suggest below, is an important part of why we have such a spectrum of average Joes.[20] Indeed, 'the journey toward run-of-the-mill has never been so remarkable'.[21]

83-91; 2002a: 11-12, 79-87; cf. Lefebvre 1968b: 142; 2002b: 73. In fact, the initial title for the third volume—projected in 1959—was *Situation of Women in the Modern World* (Lefebvre 1959: 609), an analysis of aspects of women's lives subject to alienation, and potentially neglected by mainstream Marxist analysis (Lefebvre 1968a: 19; 2002a: 13). Lefebvre notes later that this volume was 'not without difficulties' (1975: 206, 208).

16. Not to mention that such a romantic association also promotes a long chain of gendered, ideological dichotomies, no less familiar to/in an ancient context (active/passive, subject/object, master/servant, culture/nature, society/community, public/private), which deny women's contemporaneity, self-consciousness and agency; see Felski 1999.

17. In partial answer to Tanya Modleski's crucial question regarding men's/masculinity studies, 'What's in these new developments for feminism and for women?' (1991: 5). Critique of gender inequality and mechanisms of power are at the centre of the study of masculinity, as of gender-critical studies more generally; see Kimmel 2004: 1. In the framework of men's/masculinity studies, then, while 'the *masculine* element... corresponds with Foucault's more general sense of power', 'a sustained system of domination that is enacted by and on diverse individuals in a society, male and female alike' (Vander Stichele and Penner 2009: 25, emphasis original), the 'naturalized' or 'incontrovertible' relation between men and masculinity and the implicit masculinization of power has been problematized. Halberstam 1998, offers an excellent critique of the 'natural' associations between 'men', 'masculinity', and 'power'.

18. See Butler 1990: 171-90; 1993: 95.

19. As critical feminist scholarship on 'intersectionality' has aptly demonstrated; see Crenshaw 1991; Dill and Zambrana 2009. Recently, scholars have suggested that intersectionality can provide a critical framework and lens for the critical explorations of race, gender, ethnicity, and empire in early Christian studies; see Nasrallah and Schüssler Fiorenza 2009.

20. Bowersock 1994: 29-54; Whitmarsh 2001: 78-87; Burrus 2005; Thurman 2007. I therefore carry forward some of Aasgaard's notions regarding mechanisms governing Joseph of Nazareth's characterization within and across these particular narratives— 'factors reflected in and contributing to' character changes/developments in the

Luke: Less (Joseph) Is More

Joseph is notably conspicuous in Luke's infancy account (Lk. 1.5–2.52) both by his near absence[22] and by his blithely flat characterization. Joseph's absence may be seen to promote a series of values and ideologies that adhere to Luke's overall androcentric 'social-theological logic'[23]—presumably Joseph was not the father of Jesus, 'as was supposed' (ὡς ἐνομίζετο, 3.23),[24] and, in a sense, Joseph *had* to be obscured: even to call Mary Joseph's γυνή seemed ill-matched with Luke's imperialistic notions of divine begetting and rearing (1.35; 2.49).[25] In addition, as 'the potential text is infinitely richer than any of its individual realizations',[26] Joseph's truancy may signal (perhaps unintentionally) other ideological elements as well. This is decidedly not Joseph's tale, though when he does emerge from/at the margins, he consistently holds out the center, embracing conventionally masculine traits and behaviors attendant on 'rightful', naturalized social roles. Or does he?

Luke's characterization of Joseph certainly lingers around standard indices of everyday masculinity. To begin with, Joseph is a man.[27] As a man,

---

'trajectory of the Joseph figure' (2009b: 1, 7)—highlighting in particular how contemporary views on everyday men and masculinity were shaped in part by configuring the complex relationship to Roman imperial hegemony.

21.   *Newsweek*'s book review (30 October 2005) of the bestseller Kevin O'Keefe, *The Average American: The Extraordinary Search for the Nation's Most Ordinary Citizen*, which chronicles a successfully completed nationwide search for the person (a middle-aged man) who was the most statistically average (in 140 categories) in the United States during a multi-year span starting in 2000.

22.   Indeed, 'Joseph barely appears in the narrative' (Anderson 1987: 198).

23.   I find Gabrielle Spiegel's notion of 'the social logic of the text'—a logic that attends to both the text's 'site of articulation and its discursive character as articulated "logos"'—to be a stimulating mental tool for the study of early Joseph narratives, and I also find provocative her encouragement to ferret out the 'political unconscious' of the text; see Spiegel 1990; 1997: 3-28, and discussed at length and appropriated (as 'social-theological logic') by Clark 2004: 162-65, 178-81.

24.   As Bovon notes (2002: 136), ὡς ἐνομίζετο could mean either 'he was considered to be Joseph's biological son (but I, Luke, know this is not true)' or 'he was rightfully declared to be Joseph's son (and I, Luke, agree with this)'; Bovon prefers the first option; Freed (2001: 21) suggests that this comment is a later editorial addition in any case. Elsewhere, Luke does refer to Joseph as a father: Lk. 2.33, 41, 43, 48, 51.

25.   See Billings 2009. Aside for the poorly attested 'his wife' (αὐτῷ γυναικί) in 2.5, Luke does not elsewhere speak of Mary as the γυνή of Joseph. As Satlow (2001: 72) suggests, Luke avoids the technical/legal language of 'inchoate marriage', which may have been unfamiliar to his implied readers.

26.   Iser 1974: 280.

27.   Part of what I acknowledge here and put to critical reflection in this study is that the construction of the 'everyday' in antiquity, at a basic level, occurred within

he will be properly married—Mary is betrothed (ἐμνηστευμένην) to him (1.27).[28] Whether or not Luke takes this domestic arrangement as legally binding, an inchoate marriage (likely not),[29] Joseph is portrayed without fanfare as a participant in the idealized, patriarchal institution that made wives out of daughters—even as it made men into husbands—shuttling young women from one household to the next. Luke's Joseph will, further-more, marry a virgin (παρθένος)—essentially reciting both (post-)biblical and classical banalities that real men (those who trouble over the paternity of heirs) take their maidens chaste.[30] So too, his virgin 'will conceive...and bear a son' (1.31) with or without him[31]—and, as every πατήρ is wont to do, Joseph transmits to his (perhaps adopted)[32] heir his *nomen, pecunia*, and *sacra*.[33] Luke parades Joseph's *nomen* (1.27, 32-33; 2.4) as it promotes his imperialistic agenda,[34] though the subdued citation of Joseph's *pecunia* (propertied in 'Nazareth', 1.26-27; 2.4, 39, and/or in 'Bethlehem', 2.4)[35] and *sacra* (2.22-24, 41-42) also contribute to the shape of this everyday, virgin-marrying πατήρ.

regulative discourses in which the problematic inscription of masculinity to maleness, as if it were a natural or essential quality, was one ingredient for the production of gender itself; see Cornwall and Lindisfarne 1994: 19-22; Halberstam 1998; Butler 2004: 9-11.

28.   Boyarin (1995: 168) observes with respect to rabbinic Judaism that it 'so strongly approved the married life, including the life of the sexual body, that there was virtually no escape from marriage within that culture—either for men or women'. A similar situation prevailed in Rome; see Treggiari 1991.

29.   Satlow 2001: 72.

30.   In the idealized, androcentric world of biblical and post-biblical literary texts (the degree to which they reflect actual practice is unclear), it is expected that a woman would marry as a virgin; see, e.g., Deut. 22.13-21; 4Q271 3 10-15; 4Q159; Josephus, *Ant.* 4.244; Philo, *Spec. leg.* 1.105-109; 3.51, 65-71; *m. Ket.* 1.1-2, 6; 5.2; and also the texts cited by Satlow 2001: 315 n. 141. Female virginity was akin to beauty (see Ben Sira 26.15), and, like beauty, was widely trafficked throughout the Mediterranean and Near East; see Rouselle 1988: 63-77; Treggiari 1991: 105-107.

31.   Note the ambivalence of Fitzmyer 1973: 571: 'When this account is read in and for itself—without the overtones of the Matthean annunciation to Joseph—every detail of it could be understood of a child to be born to Mary in the usual human way', with Joseph as the biological father; and later that 'the phrasing of individual verses in the [Lucan] account of Jesus' conception remains ambiguous' (Fitzmyer 1981: 61); as discussed by Schaberg 1987: 81-82.

32.   See Levin 2006.

33.   So Cicero, *de Domo* 35, discussing Roman adoption as a method of securing the continuity from father to son the principal markers of status of the adoptive father.

34.   See Horsley 1989: 32-33; Brown 1993: 415; Green 1997: 123; Rowe 2005: 285-86.

35.   Marshall 1978: 104-105; Bovon 2002: 84.

Extension of Luke's well-known 'step-parallelism' literary device,[36] juxtaposing Joseph and Zechariah, also 'apt foils for one another',[37] further reinforces the mundaneness of this male subject. Joseph, we learn, is not a priest (cf. 1.5), even of the undistinguished Judean hill-dwelling stock 'of Abijah' (1.5, 39-40).[38] He belongs rather to either the humble masses of land-working peasants or else to the even lower-ranking artisan class[39]— mirroring Mary's (un)sung 'lowly' (ταπεινούς, 1.48, 52-53) social position. Even though Joseph meets basic legal requirements (2.21, 22-24, 39, 41), he is also not exceptionally 'righteous' (δίκαιοι) or 'blameless' (ἄμεμπτοι) (cf. 1.6)—perhaps one factor which explains his failure to be included in novel events, theophanic visitations (cf. 1.8-20) or accompanying wondrous, birth signs (cf. 1.20-22, 64-66). Nor is Joseph involved in the home(l)y, domestic birth rituals of this son—swaddling, circumcising, naming (2.6-7a, 21)[40]— even when he is presumably present (2.16). Luke's Joseph generally keeps away from his home and his virgin, or indeed any other woman—he is not present with Mary at the annunciation (1.26-38), nor does he accompany her or call on her when she is away from Nazareth for three months (1.56)—a feature which also accords with the conventional binary logic of common patterns of masculinity in antiquity: to be a man is *not* to be a woman; or, put differently, to be a man is to avoid unnecessary identification or asso-ciation *with* women and women's spaces.[41]

Joseph also does not sing or prophesy (cf. 1.67-79). In fact, Luke gives us a consistently wordless Joseph throughout—a portrayal that is all the more striking when considering Luke's 'pervasive, and distinctly dialogic or hybridizing, practice of citing direct speech'.[42] The voluble speeches, songs, prophecies, and whispers of virtually *every* other figure in Luke's infancy story—Gabriel (1.13-17), Zechariah (1.67-79), Elizabeth (1.42-44, 60), Mary (1.26-55), Elizabeth's neighbors and relatives (1.61), the entire Judean-hillside community (1.66), angels (2.10-14), shepherds (2.15), Simeon (2.29-35), and even Anna (whose speech is reported indirectly, 2.38)—make

36.   See, e.g., Brown 1993: 248-53; Fitzmyer 1985: 335-36; Green 1997: 84.

37.   See Anderson 1987: 191-92, who explores contrasts produced by Luke's juxtaposition of the figures of Mary and Zechariah.

38.   Autero 2010.

39.   See Lenski 1966: 270-75, 278-79. In the handling of Mark's material (Mk 6.3), only Luke (4.23) refuses to call Jesus a τέκτων or the son of a τέκτων, as Matthew does (Mt. 13.55).

40.   Cf. the passive verbal constructions of Lk. 2.21 with the decidedly active and fully narrated involvement of Zechariah in John's birth rituals in 1.60-63. Cf. Bovon 2002: 86: 'As in 2:6-7a and 1:26-38, Joseph fades into the background in v. 21'.

41.   See the discussion of such binary tropes, the 'gender-divided world of antiquity', in Neyrey 2003: 44-53, and the sources cited therein.

42.   Burrus 2009: 148.

Joseph's silence palpable. While the silence of Joseph does not issue 'from elsewhere', as indeed Zechariah's silence does (1.20), Joseph nevertheless lends it to the vibrant 'other-tongued (heteroglossal)' linguistic ambivalence that characterizes Luke and other novelistic hybrids.[43] Joseph's silence gives voice to the masses of already-disempowered subjects performing their 'everyday' iteration of a regulatory norm[44]—the silence of Joseph is the muted, multitude bassline.

Aside from keeping his mouth wide shut, Joseph's only other (nearly)[45] autonomous act in Luke both positions Joseph as the male household head (*paterfamilias*) who 'takes care of business' and also *seemingly* naturalizes the dominant economic and political order of the Roman empire: going out of his way, literally, Luke's 'Joseph *also* went (up)...' ('Ανέβη δὲ καὶ 'Ιωσὴφ...)—that is, just like everyone else in the 'world' (οἰκουμένη)[46]—in order 'to be registered' (ἀπογράψασθαι) in a census issued by the Emperor himself with the Roman governor of neighboring Syria standing by (2.1-5). Luke's 'passing' references to both Augustus's pet census—an economically oppressive, yet patently invisible, component of the imperial regime[47]—and Quirinius's military presence at the borders of Judea, are not the only instances of Luke's reproduction of Rome's shadow. In the infancy account alone, Luke cites other local and centralized power in the forms of Herod, king of Judea (1.5), and Pontius Pilate, governor of Judea (3.1-2). Luke(–Acts) is in fact more 'politically attuned', and equivocal, than most other Second Testament writings,[48] and Joseph's act of yielding to the imperial pat down for military and financial service, too, wavers between (laudable) convention[49] and (abject) betrayal.[50]

43.　Burrus 2009: 148; citing Bakhtin 1981: 361: 'The novelistic hybrid is *an artistically organized system for bringing different languages in contact with one another, a system having as its goal the illumination of one language by means of another*, the carving out of a living image of another language' (emphasis in the original).

44.　See Glenn 2004.

45.　While the verb 'Ανέβη ('he went up', 2.4) is in fact the only active verb attributed solely to Joseph (every other verbal construction in Luke depicts Joseph and Mary acting jointly), Joseph was not alone in his movement, but σὺν Μαριάμ ('with Mary').

46.　οἰκουμένη (Lk. 4.5; 21.26) is, for Luke, the *imperium romanum*, exaggeratedly regarded as equal to the whole 'inhabited (world)', from οἰκέω, 'to dwell' (Bovon 2002: 83).

47.　Bovon (2002: 83-84) notes that such a census (ἀπογραφή) was the official registration/assessment of subjects by which a ruler would establish military service and head tax.

48.　Gilbert 2006: 84-85; Burrus 2009: 153.

49.　See the discussion of imperially mobilized rhetoric of submission by Conway 2008: 99-100; cf. Rom. 13.1-7; 1 Pet. 2.13-17.

However, the census scene (2.1-5) is further complicated, both by its highly constructed syntax—where, like the elegant, legitimating style of the prologue (1.1-4), Luke's excellent Greek shines 'like a good deed in a naughty world'[51] and signals, especially to those among Luke's implied readers 'with ears to hear', the pivotal importance of this particular narrative moment[52]—and by another set of (un)easy juxtapositions: more than an attempt at historiographical acuity, Luke fixates on the political context of first-century Judea so as to place Augustus at the foot of Jesus' manger.[53] In the capable hands of the implied author, Augustus' imperial posturing becomes a bowing to nativist prophecy fulfillment,[54] and Jesus becomes an unassuming mimic-σωτήρ ('savior') and κύριος ('lord'), heir to the 'world peace' (γῆς εἰρήνη, 2.14) that made Rome great/terrifying.[55] Meanwhile Joseph, caught between 'the totalizing claims of one empire—the Roman— [and] the totalizing claims of another—God's Kingdom',[56] becomes an emblem of Luke's 'postcolonial condition', the everyday, split subject embodying 'a highly unstable anti-imperial colonial imperialism'.[57] Not unlike Luke's Jesus' own creative resistance to Roman taxation (20.25), Joseph's fiscal pragmatism 'remains strategically veiled in ambiguity'— rendering both 'unto Caesar' (his census enrollment) and also, though unwittingly, 'unto God' (the Messiah, the son of David, in the city of David).[58]

50.   Bovon 2002: 83: 'Objection to any census in Israel had gained force, though, the minds of people had become agitated and drifted apart over this question'.

51.   Knox 1944: 9: for, just following 2.1-5, with v. 6 the narrative immediately lapses back into a 'riot of parataxis and semitic pronouns'.

52.   As Esler (1987: 184) suggests, the 'high literary style parts of Luke–Acts (Lk. 1.1-4; Acts 27) implies that its author came from the upper segment of Greco-Roman society…', and furthermore that is 'unlikely that Luke was the only member of his community with this background; there were, presumably, others capable of savoring his occasional recourse to excellent Greek'.

53.   Brent 1999: 83: 'In associating what was probably a regional or provincial census with a decree of Caesar himself, the author of Luke–Acts clearly wished to associate the birth of Jesus with Augustus'. Cf. Fitzmyer 1985: 400.

54.   Luke's Augustan census makes it possible for Joseph to bring Jesus to Bethlehem (the place where, according to Mic. 5.2, the Messiah would be born).

55.   Lk. 2.11; for implied *syncrisis* between Luke's infancy account and the stories surrounding Augustus' birth and the manner in which his subsequent reign was perceived and understood, see Billings 2009: 86-87.

56.   Burrus 2009: 139.

57.   Segovia 2009: 192.

58.   Burrus 2009: 141. As Burrus suggests, Jesus' quip to 'Return to Caesar, Caesar's stuff, and to God, God's stuff' (Lk. 20.25) either promotes 'a covert, yet thoroughgoing, denunciation of the imposed Roman monetary economy on which

What seems to me the most prudent reading of the census passage (2.1-5), then, given its highly constructed syntax and colonial funambulism, is *not* simply to resolve Luke's empire-wrestling via Joseph into a uni-vocal position supporting Zealot-dissociation (an *apologia pro ecclesia*),[59] Empire-legitimation (an *apologia pro imperio*),[60] or ruler-cult supercession.[61] Rather, Joseph's 'obedience' seems to stand as its own constitutive form of empire negotiation,[62] further suggesting that, for Luke, resistance comes in unassuming packages, veiled in 'the ideological terms of reference' or 'public transcript' by which Rome legitimated its own rule, and embodying the most threatening of critiques, as James C. Scott suggests: 'The system may have most to fear from those subordinates among whom the institutions of hegemony have been most successful'.[63] With Joseph, then, Luke soft-pedals an outwardly compliant, time-biding, menace of 'everyday' resis-tance—a form of empire negotiation that feasibly had the most cultural and political purchase with the better-to-dos of Luke's implied audience, those among the hordes of oppressed, colonial subjects who could conceivably afford to 'wait-and-see'.[64]

Joseph's understated colonial resistance is indicative of Luke's overall characterization of him. In spite of these few, sparse character cues, Luke's Joseph remains aloof, disembodied. Distance between Joseph and the implied reader is not reduced by sympathetic inside views (as we have, for example, with Mary: 1.29; 2.19, 51) or explicit, evaluative judgments. None

---

imperial exploitation is based', or, at the very least, carves out space for the salvo 'that the rightful demands of God's kingdom might conflict with those of Caesar's' (2009: 141). See also Sugirtharajah 2002: 89-90; Horsley 2003: 99.

59.   See, e.g., Moehring 1972, and sources cited therein, essentially demonstrating that Jesus' own family were model taxpaying citizens, in order to avoid any suspicions about early Christian (dis)loyalty.

60.   See, e.g., Esler 1987: 218; Walaskay 2005: 64-67; Billings 2009: 88.

61.   Bovon 2002: 83: 'the "political theology" of Augustus, supported particularly in the East by the religious worship of the ruler, is unmasked and invalidated by the christological claim'; cf. Brown 1993: 415, contrasting the advent of the *pax Augusta* with the *pax Christi*.

62.   See Gilbert 2006; Burrus 2009; cf. Carter 2001: 130-44.

63.   Scott 1990: 106-107.

64.   From the comfortable vantage of urban communities in the Hellenistic east of the Roman empire; see, e.g., Balch 1995: 223. Esler (1987: 164-200) suggests that a number of features in the text suggest that some of Luke's audience were wealthy and influential, possibly even decurions or magistrates (at the very top of the local social, economic and political hierarchy): the high literary style parts of Luke–Acts (Lk. 1.1-4; 2.1-5; Acts 27); Luke's focus upon converts of elevated status, economic position and political power (Lk. 7.1-10; 8.1-3; 23.47; Acts 8.26-39; 13.1, 7; 10.1-11; 17.12; 19.31); Luke's focus (especially in the single tradition) on warnings to the 'rich' (3.10-14; 12.13-21; 13.33; 14.12-14; 16.9, 19-31; 18.18-30).

of the other characters interact with Joseph in ways that invariably suggest either disapprobation (as we have with Zechariah in 1.18-20) or admiration, possessing God's favor (as we have, again, with Mary and the angel in 1.28, 30 and Elizabeth, inspired by the Holy Spirit in 1.42-45). Again, this is not Joseph's tale—his point-of-view is missing from Luke's narrative. What, then, are we to make of Luke's ghostly silent, pragmatically resistant, 'everyday' man?

The sparseness, remoteness of Joseph's characterization in Luke, I suggest, is precisely what made (and makes) him productively malleable as a symbol. Non-point-of-view characters can just as easily carry an author's (more implicit) ideological baggage. Unfettered by specificity, distance affords non-point-of-view characters with universal, masked appeal/applicability. With Luke's Joseph, less is more—'less Joseph' yields a high intensity of meanings and a kind of ubiquity that lends itself to repeatability in multiple, unrelated contexts. Joseph haunts the background; his timely emergence from shadowy margins reinforces select indices of conventional masculine comportment and assignment, effortlessly holding power as if he were naturally entitled to it—the virgin's platform (1.27), the tax-paying household head (2.4). Paratactic characterization, whereby the maximum possible meaning is encompassed in the minimum number of character cues, of Luke's most basic, baseline man allows the social reproduction of naturalized gender patterns to be rendered nearly invisible.[65] Luke's Average Joe: cipher of Luke's imperceptible, perhaps unconscious, recitational labors; obscured herald of ascendant myths of everyday male privilege and plenitude.

Matthew's Just Trickster

Joseph of Nazareth, 'a just man' (δίκαιος, Mt. 1.19), establishes Matthew's inaugural narrative perspective,[66] and perhaps for 'good' reason—as emblematic harbinger of the masculine-tinged, key virtue, 'righteousness' (δικαιοσύνη),[67] Joseph sets the androcentric, homosocial tone for the whole

---

65. Foucault 1980: 86: 'power is tolerable only on condition that it mask a substantial part of itself. Its success is proportional to its ability to hide its own mechanisms.'

66. Narrative perspective-taking is thought of as a relational concept between the producer and the recipient of narrative; see Bal 1997.

67. See Przybylski 1980; Olender 2008. Elsewhere in Matthew δίκαιος is similarly inflected by gender (Mt. 13.17, 43; 23.35; 27.19, 24), reciting the common Greco-Roman assumption of the association of manhood and moral excellence and the uncertainties inherent in the learned, performative and competitive nature of ancient masculinities. As Williams (1999: 27) and others have pointed out, *virtus*, often translated as 'virtue', is etymologically equivalent to 'manliness' (*vir*: 'man'). In Kuefler's words, 'Virtue was so intimately linked to maleness in the Roman universe that it is impossible to separate

of the Gospel. Joseph gets the first word in Matthew, even without open-ing his mouth:[68] spatially, readers accompany Joseph as he shrinks about (2.13-23); 'inside view' disclosures of Joseph's thoughts, plans, and emotions (1.19, 20; 2.22) establish surface-structure empathy influencing how Matthew's readers construct the meaning of narrated events, opening the way for their participatory affective responses;[69] dramatic irony based on Joseph's ignorance of narrated information (2.1-12, 16-18) creates suspense involving readers more deeply in Joseph's tale;[70] narrative pacing slows to inhabit Joseph's dream spaces (1.20-23; 2.13, 19-22); repetition of a distinctive turn of phrase consistently foregrounds Joseph's perspective—his 'rising up' (1.24; 2.13, 14, 20, 21), 'taking' of Mary and Jesus (1.24; 2.13, 14, 20, 21), and 'going' (2.13, 14, 20, 21, 22); and a number of evaluative judgments mark Joseph as an exemplary figure (especially his submission to the deity, 1.24-25; 2.14-15, 21-23, which, in each case, becomes an event of prophecy fulfillment).[71] As suggested by James H. Liu and János László with regards to prototypical in-group characters in historical narratives,[72] Joseph's point-of-view characterization in Matthew feasibly plays a key role in mediating collective memory and putative group identity, concurrently bound up with the processes of 'everyday' male self-fashioning.

Christological theorizing aside,[73] the first movement in Matthew takes the measure of Joseph's ambiguous identity as πατήρ. The Joseph of Matthew's Gospel stands ambivalently both at the foot of and also apart from the patrilineal genealogy of Jesus (1.1-17), a lineage already destabi-lized by the presence of the four women in the list.[74] In contrast to his

Roman definitions of masculinity from more general notions of ideal human behavior' (2001: 19); cf. McDonnell 2003; 2006. Similarly, righteousness or ethical virtue and male honor in Jewish thought are also closely related concepts; see e.g., Moxnes 1988.

68.   Like Luke, Matthew presents a consistently wordless Joseph—unlike Luke, however, Matthew's infancy account (Mt. 1–2) is arguably Joseph's tale; see Claudel 2011, who suggests that Matthew's representation of Joseph may be a key component of a phatic speech act designed to establish and maintain contact between the gospel writer and his recipient community: Matthew intends Joseph to represent or model to his audience the 'ideal reader'; cf. Anderson 1994, who analyzes Matthew's narrative-perspective taking (point-of-view characterization) more generally.

69.   Gerrig 1993.

70.   See Pfister 1991: 51-52.

71.   Joseph's perspective in Mt. 1–2, then, accords with each of the six point-of-view (narrative perspective) 'planes' identified by Yamasaki 2012, derived from Uspensky 1973 and Sternberg 1987.

72.   Liu and László 2007.

73.   Nolland 1996.

74.   The place of the four women (five counting Mary) in the Matthean genealogy has been much explored; the central (although not exclusive) drive of most of the investigation has been to find a common denominator between the four women, and, if

(auto-)productive forbears,[75] Joseph is, in this narrative moment, decidedly non-generative, seedless[76]—Joseph did not ἐγέννησεν Jesus (1.16)—and, according to conventional indices of masculinity, less of a man for it.[77] At the same time, Joseph resembles the model Roman πατήρ of the principate, adoptively sovereign over his lineage and distribution of familial goods.[78] While many interpreters suggest that Matthew's genealogy embodies, finally, a 'fictive' or 'spiritual' kinship arrangement,[79] Matthew's representation of Joseph's presumed adoption of Jesus also intersects with

possible, one that can embrace Mary; see Smit 2010, for summaries and a comprehensive discussion of the competing theories about Matthew's deployment of these women.

75.   Matthew apparently models the genealogy on the one found in 1 Chronicles and thus takes over the LXX translation of the *hiphil* for יָלַד in Chronicles, γεννάω ('to beget') (Erickson 2000: 40 n. 12), which, as Roland Boer has recently suggested, results in 'an endless list of men producing men', a queerly structured auto-generative formula which effaces the mother's presence by attributing the verb for giving birth to the man; see Boer 2010: 25-26.

76.   The question of what to do, then, with Matthew's later mention of Jesus' 'brothers' and 'sisters' (Mt. 12.46-50; 13.55) and whether or not these siblings are intended by Matthew to be read as the result of Joseph's later congress with Mary is a minefield that seems irresolvable by exegesis alone, although there certainly have been attempts to do so; see, e.g., Meier 1992. At the very least, Matthew does not specify Joseph as the father of Jesus' 'brothers' and 'sisters', and what I underline here is simply Matthew's citation of a conventional standard of ancient masculinity, Joseph's failure to meet that standard, and the implicit comparison between the biologically generative (inseminating) men of the genealogy who *do*.

77.   At least with Matthew's genealogy, the trope of men generating other men cites a conventional Greco-Roman assumption that males discharge the determinative function in procreation: 'to be male was to be capable of generation' (Anderson and Moore 2003: 72). Those men who did not or could not impregnate bore the marks of a subordinate or marginalized masculine identity; see Martin 2001: 83-83.

78.   The standard way to resolve the aporia of how Jesus is 'son of David, son of Abraham' (Mt. 1.1, υἱοῦ Δαυὶδ υἱοῦ Ἀβραάμ) through Joseph, if Joseph indeed did not ἐγέννησεν Jesus, is to suggest that Matthew's Jesus *becomes* Joseph's son, and so inherits his lineage, by means of *adoption*, either simply through the act of marrying Mary, naming Jesus, and raising Jesus as his own (Mt. 1.24-25), circumcising him and presenting him in the Temple (Lk. 2.21-24), protecting him from Herod (Mt. 2.13-14), traveling with him for the festivals in the Temple (Lk. 2.41-51), teaching him a vocation (Mt. 13.55), or through some unspecified legal act; see, e.g., Waetjen 1976: 227; Davies and Allison 1988–97: I, 219-20; Carter 2000: 65, 72.

79.   For example, prompted by Howard Eilberg-Schwartz's reading of Matthew's genealogy as a 'spiritual' ancestry analogous to Abraham's adoption of all peoples (1994: 233-35), Anderson and Moore (2003: 73) ask: 'What is the significance for masculinity of a patrilineal genealogy based not on a physical or literal form of descent but rather on a spiritual or fictive form of descent?'; cf. Blickenstaff 2005: 131-33.

conventional patterns of masculinity that underlie Roman legal practice, where the πατήρ reigns supreme:[80] Joseph's 'adoption of a relative…would have been only natural to a Roman',[81] Matthew sustains the typical Roman perspective on the primacy of the father–son relationship,[82] and Matthew's Joseph is ostensibly infused with *patria potestas*, 'paternal power', to reshape his household relationships, 'the most fundamental and most peculiarly Roman part of family law'.[83] Matthew's Joseph, too, like most of the Roman rulers from Caesar (49 BCE) to Marcus Aurelius (180 CE), passes on a *royal* lineage to a designated (non-biological) successor.[84] There is, of course, something queerly 'not quite'[85] about a humble craftsman (13.55) bequeathing a royal lineage to the bastard son of his betrothed—Matthew's Joseph enjoys the privilege afforded by (implied) citation of a stock aspect of the most powerful πατήρ of the empire, although he is genuinely distanced from any direct display of hegemonic power. Matthew's Joseph is a split subject, an 'almost but not quite' mimic-πατήρ—impotent, without seed, though nearly generative in another (decidedly imperial) way.

Matthew's uneven citation of conventional indices of masculinity continues in subsequent narrative movements, where Joseph first submits to the authority of his deity—in Matthew's parlance, the Father,[86] or *GodFather*[87]—over the contested field of Mary's body (1.18-24), and then, with the aid

80.   Even if Matthew does not explicitly employ one of the (two) forms of adoption (*adoptio, adrogatio*) in the Roman codes; see Aulus Gellius, *Noctes atticae* 5.19.1-16; Lindsay 2009.

81.   Levin 2006: 431.

82.   While the primacy of the father–son relationship is not something distinctly *Roman* per se, Roman discourse does view such priorities as closely linked to Roman traditions and social practice. For example, the two dominant and overlapping 'social spheres' of Roman society, politics and kinship, were ostensibly governed by the connections and relationships between fathers and sons; see Moxnes 1997: 19; Lassen 1997.

83.   Watson 1970: 37; see also Corbier 1991a, 1991b; Gardner 1998; Kunst 2005.

84.   Of all of the Roman rulers from Caesar (49 BCE) to Marcus Aurelius (180 CE), only Claudius, Vespasian and Marcus Aurelius were survived by natural sons, and Claudius's son Britannicus was murdered by Nero, Claudius's adopted son; see Lacey 1996: 227. Carter (2005: 165) suggests that Judean traditions of Abraham, David, the Christ, Jesus/Joshua, and the (new) creation evoked in relation to Jesus in Mt. 1 all 'collide with and contest Roman imperial claims'. Does Matthew further intend to position Jesus the adopted King alongside the adopted rulers of the Roman Empire? Cf. Runesson 2011: 316-20.

85.   See Bhaba 2004: 122-23

86.   See Thompson 2000: 105-14; Sheffield 2001; Viviano 2011.

87.   After the idiom of Liew 2003: 104, who refers to Mark's portrayal of the deity as 'God-Father' and Jesus as 'godfather'.

of this deity, rescues his betrothed and her son from the despotic reach of empire, embodied in the infancy account by Herod/Archelaus (2.1-23).[88] This is not a heroic rescue. This is, rather, a case of ambivalently gendered, colonial chicanery. Matthew's Joseph tale is a *con*-text.

Despite Herod's totalizing power of command—summoning (2.4, 7), sending (2.8, 16), executing (2.16)[89]—he is outmaneuvered, 'tricked' (ἐνεπαίχθη, 2.16), by the GodFather and (by association) Joseph, who together foil Herod's efforts to 'seek the child's life' (2.20) at the ghastly expenditure of the 'Innocents' (2.16-18). While it may be difficult to whitewash the GodFather's infanticide involvement,[90] it is even harder to dispense with Matthew's parallel, unflattering image of the GodFather as a trickster, who carries the salvific promise of 'the Child' (1.21) through to its incipient fulfillment by means of lithe concealment and misdirection.[91]

As with the rest of Matthew's infancy account which 'quotes' biblical prototypes, notably Moses,[92] with 'preposterous' effects,[93] Matthew's divine trickster too is inevitably engaged with and intervenes to create a revised image of portraits of the deity from the Hebrew Bible (and beyond), who secures the ancestral promise (Gen. 12.1-3; 26.4-5; 28.13-15) and defends a chosen people through equally troubling measures, including, yes, deception (2 Sam. 17.14; 1 Kgs 22.19-23; 2 Kgs 6.15-20; 7.6-7), along with the deaths of firstborn sons (Exod. 12.29), utter destruction of enemy nations

88.   While much of Matthew's narrative situates its protagonists (principally Jesus) in 'intramural' interaction with the Jewish community, it is 'extramural' interaction with Roman imperial powers that both sets the stage for Matthew's narrative (Mt. 2.1-23) and drives it inexorably toward its conclusion (Mt. 27.1-2, 11-37).

89.   Herod, too, is portrayed as 'secretly' (λάθρᾳ) plotting (Mt. 2.7), but his primary characterization is one of overt domination, utilizing his command of power.

90.   See the summary and critique of prior dealings with issue of *theodicy* in Matthew's narrative infanticide by Blickenstaff 2005: 148-53, and sources cited therein. Blickenstaff's understatement says it well: 'In the end, there is no satisfactory explanation for the deaths of these children' (p. 150). For my part, it is hard to shake Matthew's theological implication that the 'Innocents' slaughter was part of a divine trickster's master plan (Jeremiah prophesied as much), resembling perhaps the 'antipredator avoidance' strategies, which, in the natural sciences, are termed *autotomy*, self-amputation/evisceration, the shedding of a non-vital body part/fluid. But I digress.

91.   While beyond the scope of this project, it is perhaps worth noting the inchoate connection between the GodFather's preservation of 'the Child' in Matthew's nativity tale and the preservation of 'the Child' perpetuated by univocal discourses of reproductive futurity; Edelman 2004.

92.   Matthew models Jesus' nativity on that of Moses, a savior whose own saving 'requires' the deaths of many children (Exod. 1.22–2.5; 11.1-10; 12.29-32); see France 1979, 1980; Erickson 1996; and Crossan 2003. On the presence and function of intertextuality in Mt. 1–2, see Mayordomo 2011.

93.   Bal 1999.

(Deut. 7.1-2; 20.16-18; Josh. 10.40), and other sundries.[94] Similarly, the tricky collusion of Joseph and the GodFather, who maintain intimate contact throughout their tortuous plan, recites Jacob and Yahweh's collaboration in the Jacob Cycle (Gen. 27.7, 20, 28; 29.15–30.24; 30.37–31.16).[95] Matthew's Joseph, like Matthew's GodFather, is a trickster, as is already registered by Joseph's inclination to 'secretly' (λάθρᾳ) dodge his earlier problem (1.19).[96] Here lies not only an opportunity to excise 'today's warm, omnibenevolent deity' from the pages of the Second Testament,[97] but also the prospect of unpacking the 'tragicomic' performance of an everyday man's duplicitous empire negotiation. For Joseph's 'taking' of wife/mother and child (1.24; 2.13, 14, 20, 21) certainly recites conventional patterns of masculinity, but 'the cunning of a trickster is a different matter'.[98]

Trickster characters are inexorably contingent upon the cultures that shape and are shaped by them, making 'any universal statements about the function, and even the definition of this character impossible'.[99] Nonetheless, 'the structural position of the trickster hero' has been routinely harnessed in colonial contexts, as James C. Scott suggests: 'nothing illustrates the veiled cultural resistance of subordinate groups better than what have been termed trickster tales'.[100] Conventionally, Scott notes, the trickster hero charts a successful course through oppressive, dominating landscapes

94.   See Nicholas 2011: 16-25, who notes that deity in the Hebrew Bible (Yahweh) sits comfortably among the panoply of other ancient, divine tricksters: Ea/Enki, Inanna, Re, Isis, Horus, Seth, Inaras, Athena, Prometheus, Zeus, and Hermes, to name but a few.

95.   Matthews 1985.

96.   A number of interpreters have extolled Joseph's decision in Matthew 'secretly' (λάθρᾳ) to dismiss his ostensibly unfaithful betrothed, suggesting that it models and announces the theme of the 'greater' or 'more perfect' righteousness espoused by Matthew's Jesus in the remainder of the Gospel; see, e.g., Olender 2008; Allison 2005. While such manhandling of women in cases of divorce is one of the sites of Matthew's ideological struggle with other contemporary teachers of the Law—the scribes and Pharisees, Matthew's so-named doers of a 'lesser righteousness'—and so, perhaps in the context of Matthew's androcentric discourse, and compared to the divorce halakhah of other pious Jews contested by Matthew, Joseph's plan was more merciful, clement. We ought to note, however, that acts of clemency in Greco-Roman tradition and its male-centric cult of virtues, rather than being unambiguous signs of generosity or benevolence, in the hands of certain folk, could also denote tyrannical pretensions: being 'the stuff of absolute monarchy' (Leigh 1997: 65), 'ruthless violence and tender mercy were two sides of the same princely face' (Barton 2001: 175); for a discussion of the range of conno-tations *clementia* could carry in the ancient world, see Konstan 2005. I simply note here that Joseph's secret dismissal of Mary is not as effortlessly altruistic as some scholars are led to believe.

97.   Metzger 2009: 56.

98.   Haddox 2010: 11.

99.   Steinberg 1988: 4.

100.   Scott 1990: 162-63.

not by his strength but by his wit and cunning. The trickster is unable, in principle, to win any direct confrontation as he is smaller and weaker than his antagonists. Only by knowing the habits of his enemies, by deceiving them, by taking advantage of their greed, size, gullibility, or haste does he manage to escape their clutches and win victories.[101]

While here regrettably reciting Western comparative theoretical biases which mark the trickster as male[102]—eclipsing both the complex *topos* of female tricksters[103] and the trickster's more basic, gender-shifting ambiguity[104]—Scott also suitably captures the trickster hero's characteristic marginality and subversive potential.

Matthew's Joseph, like the vast majority of tricksters, subsists at the margins of his society and transgresses borderlines,[105] marked principally by his signature turn of phrase—ambivalently coupling, in three separate cases, a phallic 'rise' with a flaccid retreat[106]—but also, quite literally, by his liminal crossing over to Egypt. In the face of seemingly insurmountable forces of opposition, Joseph gets up to get down. He rises up(!)...and flees, hides away in exile, returns fearfully, only to flee once again and finally conceal himself in 'Nazareth' of all places.[107] Joseph overcomes, not by direct confrontation or 'manly' displays of strength, but by unevenly coded means of flight, concealment, guile—by crossing over and thus transgressing boundaries. He is the craven hero, the recessive redeemer, the sinful savior, and his liminality is, moreover, the source of his subversive potential.[108] Joseph's marginal status and game-changing, 'situation-inverting'[109]

101. Scott 1990: 162.

102. See Radin 1972; Babcock-Abrahams 1975; Mills 2001.

103. Fruitfully explored, for example, in the context of the Hebrew Bible; see Niditch 1987; Exum and Van Wijk-Bos 1988; Jackson 2012: 41-66.

104. Niditch 1987: 54; cf. Jurich 1999: 70.

105. Grottanelli 1983: 120: 'Tricksters are breakers of rules'; cf. Ashley 1988: 105; Bal 1988: 136.

106. Joseph 'rose up' and: (1) 'had no marital relations with her' (1.24); (2) fled 'to Egypt' (2.13); (3) returned after 'those who were seeking the child's life' were are dead, though again, hid away in 'the district of Galilee' (2.20-23).

107. Matthew's Joseph *con*-text, then, essentially corresponds to Niditch's cross-cultural, five-step structural morphology of trickster tales (1987: 44-45): (1) the hero [Joseph] has low status [under Herod's dominion], so (2) enacts a deception [flight, concealment] to improve her/his status. (3) The successful trick leads to improved status for the hero [released from Herod's reach]. (4) However, eventually the deception is revealed [Joseph returns], and (5) while surviving, the hero is returned to marginal/outsider/reduced status [settles in Nazareth]. Matthew's midrashic acrobatics employed to recuperate the ostensible ignominy of 'Nazareth' underlines the marginality of Joseph's final resting status; Davies and Allison 1988–97: I, 274.

108. According to Grottanelli 1983: 139, the 'power of breaking boundaries, of getting away with it, and of achieving salvation through sin'.

109. Hynes 1993b: 37-41.

resourcefulness—abetted of course by the divine trickster—disrupts the established social and political order, subverts power structures, and undermines the status quo.[110]

All of this is accompanied in Matthew's *con*-text by not a little bit of comedy,[111] emerging in the first place from Joseph's lowly status and ambivalently gendered, craven retreat, but also by the ironic besting of the trickster's necessary, and necessarily unstable, 'other', the fool, played by Herod. 'Seemingly in power, seemingly advantaged' (2.1-8),[112] seemingly a 'real man',[113] Matthew's Herod is at once unmasked as the fool and unmanned by his 'excessive' (λίαν), rage-filled, and ridiculously dispropor-tionate martial campaign against the 'Innocents' (2.16).[114] Here subversive comedy occurs in close proximity to tragic violence—feasibly mirroring 'real world' misfortunes of least some of Matthew's implied readership.[115] Yet in another ironic narrative reversal, rather than the child who he sought to 'destroy' (2.13), the unmanned Herod himself dies, dies, and dies again (2.19, 20, 22). By employing such 'deeply humorous negative examples' that expose social inequalities and injustices,[116] Matthew's boundary-crossing trickster creates 'imaginative breathing space in which the normal categories of order and hierarchy are less than completely inevitable',[117] and possibilities that resist those officially sanctioned become thinkable.[118]

---

110.   Niditch 1987: 49: the trickster tale possesses 'an antiestablishment quality at the very source of its being'.

111.   Grottanelli 1983: 120; Steinberg 1988: 2; Jurich 1999: 70.

112.   Jackson 2012: 47.

113.   As Anderson and Moore (2003: 69) note, a man's 'self-control/mastery' (ἐγκράτεια; LSJ 473), together with his 'temperance' (σωφροσύνη; LSJ 1751), was in classical literature held up as a supremely masculine virtue: 'Mastery of others and/or of oneself emerges as definitive of masculinity in many surviving Greco-Roman texts, the emphasis arguably shifting increasingly to self-mastery during and after the Augustan epoch', citing Foucault 1986: 84-86, 94-95; see also Foucault 1985: 65-70, 72-74; Moore and Anderson 1998: 258-59.

114.   Consistent with Herod's critical portraits elsewhere, especially Josephus, *War*, 1.437, 443-44, 550-51, 655-56, 659-60, 664-65; and *Ant.* 16.394; 17.167-69, 174-79, 187, 191; see Richardson 1999.

115.   See, e.g., Destro and Pesce 2011, who, looking primarily at evidence gleaned from Matthew's infancy narrative (Mt. 1–2), suggest that the Gospel as a whole is the expression of a persecuted minority group with a clandestine, resistance strategy of 'flight', but one that never ceases to proclaim the future defeat of those in power: it is a fugitive and antagonistic minority; cf. Carter 2000.

116.   Hynes 1993a: 207.

117.   Scott 1990: 168.

118.   Jackson 2012: 45: 'Tricksters, in exposing the deficiencies of what *is*, offer an opportunity to see what *might be*' (emphasis original); cf. Jurich 1999: 69.

Matthew's Joseph, then, as symbol of marginalization and colonial oppression, feasibly offered much to at least some of Matthew's implied readers—sharing in their lowly status and colonial misfortunes, demonstrating how to transform weakness into strength, and offering a promise that a measure of success in resistance is possible and that, at the very least, survival is probable. The average Joe fashioned at the center of this resistance *does* what other men *do*—responds to homosocial prestige threats and observes laws/norms (1.18-20),[119] 'takes' a wife, names a child,[120] and initiates conjugal relations/separation (1.24-25)[121]—but he also assumes a

119.   While Joseph's 'predicament', as many critics have noted, is covered by the decidedly androcentric laws pertaining to intercourse with a betrothed woman in Deut. 22.23-27, Schaberg (1987: 42-62) has admirably probed the legal options that Matthew's audience, conversant with contemporary Jewish law, might expect Matthew's Joseph 'to consider carefully—even agonizingly—as he reached his decision' (p. 62). But listen: in lieu of an implement of vengeance, Matthew's Joseph enters the homosocial contest brandishing his resolute, logocentric phallus (see Brenner 1997: 31-51, 175-81)—it is, notably, Joseph's righteous plan (ἐβουλήθη), presumably based on his careful reflection (ταῦτα δὲ αὐτοῦ ἐνθυμηθέντος) on traditional texts and expositions, that constitutes the obligatory response to the challenge put to him by the other man's contravention of the boundaries of his house(hold). Elsewhere in the ancient world, too, an appropriate 'manly' response to an honor challenge (insult/injury) might consist of pursuing legal action in lieu of violent reciprocity, though the manliness of such a 'passive' response needed to be proven rhetorically and not merely assumed or taken for granted; see, e.g., Demosthenes's rhetorical 'response' to Meidias's physical assault in *Against Meidias*; on which see Cohen 1991.

120.   At the very least, Matthew implicitly genders the act of naming a child in favor of the father, as is perhaps suggested by the first of Matthew's fulfillment citations ('All this took place to fulfill what the Lord had spoken by the prophet'): his gloss of Isa. 7.14, 'and they shall name him Emmanuel' (καὶ καλέσουσιν τὸ ὄνομα αὐτοῦ ʾΕμμανουήλ), not only pluralizes and thus expands/universalizes/elaborates on the import of naming in the LXX, 'and you will call his name Emmanuel' (καὶ καλέσεις τὸ ὄνομα αὐτοῦ Εμμανουηλ), but also neuters a mother's 'power to name' implicit in the MT, 'and she will call his name Emmanuel' (וְקָרָאת שְׁמוֹ עִמָּנוּ אֵל). However, the question of the power or authority to name children, at least in the Hebrew Bible and in later Jewish tradition, appears to be less straightforward. While the Hebrew Bible contains narratives which feature the naming of a child by either parent (Gen. 16.11-16; 17.19; 21.3; 29.32-30.13; 1 Sam. 1.20; 4.21; Isa. 7.14), the Torah contains no explicit commandment obligating (or authorizing) parents, let alone one of the parents (mother or father), to bestow a name upon their offspring; see Leissner 2001.

121.   Joseph's (temporary) celibacy is buttressed by wide-spread, 'procreation-alone' discourse, resembling a 'typical' form of early Jewish (religious) sexual restraint; Allison (1993) has suggested that 'both before and after Matthew's day, there were many, including many Jews, who would have considered intercourse during pregnancy inappropriate behavior' (p. 8); see, e.g., Tob. 8.7; Pseudo-Phocylides 186; Philo, *Spec. leg.* 3.2, 9, 20; *T. Iss.* 2.3; *T. Benj.* 8.2; Josephus, *Ap.* 2.202.

more ambiguously gendered posture that wavers, like his relationship to hegemonic authority itself, in the betwixt and between, interstitial spaces, belying both dominant Roman cultural codes of 'masculine' action and aggression, as well as 'feminine' passivity and submission.[122]

Protevangelium of James *'s Rodhandled Keeper*

Protevangelium of James, as a work comprising the pre-history of Jesus' family, is obsessed with Mary's purity; its core narrative is, in particular, an encomiastic 'Life of Mary' exalting Mary's virginity, perhaps for apologetic reasons.[123] However, Joseph makes a substantial appearance as well—large swaths of the story are narrated from his perspective. One of the more striking of such episodes is the tale which recounts the rhabdomantic (s)election of Joseph as Mary's keeper (PJ 8–9).[124] So the story goes, naturalizing the hegemonic fiction of 'everyday' male privilege: Mary was brought up, 'fed like a dove' (ὡσεὶ περιστερὰ νεμομένη, 8.2), in the Jerusalem Temple, and when she came of age and ostensibly posed a threat to cultic purity, the priests sought divine guidance to decide how to discharge her.[125]

Alluding to the election of Aaron in Numbers 17, an angel commanded that all the 'widowers' should be gathered together with their rods and 'the one whom the Lord God points out with a sign, she will be his wife' (PJ 8.7-8). But whereas the sign of divine favor in Numbers 17 was the budding/flowering of the rod, here the sign is somewhat different:

> Throwing down his ax, Joseph went out to meet them. And after they had gathered together with their rods, they went to the high priest. After receiving everyone's rod, the high priest went into the temple and prayed. When he was finished with the prayer, he took the rods and went out and gave them to each man, but there was no sign among them. Finally, Joseph took his rod. Suddenly, a dove came out of the rod and stood on Joseph's head (PJ 9.1-6).

The dynamic phallocentrism of the imagery is hard to miss—imagery that both recites the common conceptual metaphor in the Hebrew Bible (and beyond), where 'rod'/'staff' signals a naturalized extension of presumed

---

122. Other Jewish males from later times, too, invoked a similar gendered ambivalence, resistant to dominant cultural modes of masculinity, epitomized by the 'feminized' scholarly rabbi; see Boyarin 1997: 82; cf. Boyarin 1997, 1999.

123. See De Strycker 1964.

124. Chapter/verse divisions and translations of PJ are based on the Greek text in Hock 1995.

125. Although not stated explicitly, the priests appear to be concerned about Levitical 'blood' stipulations barring women from the sanctuary (Lev. 12.1-6; 18.19); see Fonrobert 2000.

masculine dominance and discipline,[126] and mirrors the power shifts prominently featured throughout the remainder of the scene, as we will see. What, then, of the dove—which 'Behold(!)' (ἰδοὺ) issues forth from Joseph's 'rod' (ῥάβδου), landing on his head?[127] Surely the dove signals some sort of sticky divine (s)election, standing in for the budding-rod sign from Numbers 17,[128] and perhaps echoing Gospel traditions about the appearance and authorizing sign of the dove at Jesus' baptism.[129] One recent treatment by Michael Luke Peppard positions the dove omen in Mark's account of the baptism of Jesus (Mk 1.9-11) as a colonial counter-symbol to the Roman eagle, part of his reading of this event as a divine adoption, the beginning of Jesus' accession as a 'counter-emperor' who 'will rule not in the spirit of the bellicose eagle, but in the spirit of the pure, gentle, peaceful, and even sacrificial dove'.[130] Might it be plausible to read PJ's dove scene as carrying a similar 'counter-imperial' message? The answer it seems is: *not quite*. PJ's dove scene hardly disavows the authority or methods of imperial power. PJ's dove alights not upon Jesus, but upon Joseph—a figure with considerably less subversive promise[131]—heralding not a revolutionary, divine adoption, a 'rise to power' of 'a different son of God', but the decidedly more mundane, and, for Joseph, demeaning (see below, 9.8), matter of who will *keep* the temple's dove (PJ 8.2). The temple's dove, Mary, and the dove's roost, Joseph, are in fact both bound by the naturalized authority of one group of mediating 'brokers' of imperial dominion: that of the Judean priestly elite who controlled the Jerusalem temple cult and maintained some level of independence in local matters, though who also necessarily collaborated (however

126. Like Aaron's rod (Num. 17.8; cf. Heb. 9.4), no less than the apostle Paul's stick (1 Cor. 4.21; cf. 4.14-15), or even God's rod, the Spirit (Prov. 13.24; 23.13-14).

127. Salacious imagery is not foreign to PJ; see Salome's graphic post-partum 'inspection' of Mary (PJ 20).

128. Smid 1965: 71; Davies and Allison 1988–97: I, 332: 'εὐδοκέω is the language of election and this nicely fits the theme of choice'; cf. Eusebius, *Ecc. His.* 6.29, which recounts the dove-sealed accession of Fabian to the episcopal seat of Rome (236 CE) in connection to the baptism of Jesus.

129. The dove imagery employed at Jesus' baptism is notoriously ambiguous; Davies and Allison 1988–97: I, 331-34, for example, offer sixteen ways of interpreting the dove; cf. Gero 1976.

130. Peppard 2011: 123. Peppard, too, offers a brief reading of the scene in PJ and suggests that 'the dove here marks a critical moment in the sonship of Jesus. Whereas the dove in Mark's baptism account signifies the adoption of Jesus by his divine father, the dove in the PJ signifies the earthly (non-biological) father of Jesus—an earthly succession of human sonship' (p. 123). Thus, Peppard never suggests that dove might also function similarly as an imperial counter-symbol.

131. Notice in PJ that Joseph is not even referred to as 'Son of David', perhaps one of the strongest elements of Joseph's '*counter*-imperial' characterization in the Gospels; in PJ, Mary is David's descendent (PJ 10.2-4).

ambivalently) with figures representing direct Roman power in the region—
governors and military tribunes, centurions and soldiers, and ambiguously
'Jewish' tetrarchs dependent on Roman support, who do not play a role for
the most part in PJ's narrative.[132]

While PJ does not explicitly connect its dove with the autonomous
'embodiment' (σωματικῷ εἴδει) of the Spirit from Jesus' baptism (Lk. 3.22 ‖
Mt. 3.17 ‖ Mk 1.11), it is however, another (rigid) extension of God's
power/authority, not alighting or *coming down* upon, but rather, *standing
(up)*on, erect and true, Joseph's head. The dove also signals the substantia-
tion of the high priest's oracular inquiry, summoned by the high priest's
temple prayer; following the 'dovely' eruption of Joseph's rod, we hear not
the sound of a disembodied, adoptive heavenly voice, but the sounding of a
priestly gavel swung by the local arm of imperial authority:

> And the high priest said, 'Joseph! Joseph! You have been chosen by lot to
> take the virgin of the Lord into your keeping.' (9.7)

While the angelic messenger initially declares to the high priest that Mary
will become one widower's 'wife' (γυνή), here (9.7) the high priest transmits an entirely different message: Joseph must 'take' (παραλάβαι) Mary
into his 'keeping' (τήρησιν).[133] Thus, PJ cuts against the grain of the Gospel
accounts,[134] and such a move may be read as owing to overall encomiastic
'virgin of the Lord' trajectory: the reader is continually invited to register
doubts about the *real* husband of Mary (and father of Jesus), though
ambiguities concerning that topic, especially from Joseph's perspective, play
a dramatic role in the remainder of episodes.[135]

A number of subtle shifts in the dove scene, however, hint at parallel
discourses engaged in the uneven process of the making(s) of 'everyday'
masculinities. First, in opposition to the messenger of the Lord God (8.8),
the high priest *alters* what the dove ought to portend for Joseph and Mary.[136]

132.   Though one such character, Herod [the Great], does make a showing in the later
chapters (see PJ 21–24), and, similar to Matthew's depiction, it is the high priests who
deliver the necessary information, who are depicted as collaborating with the local
embodiment of the imperial regime.

133.   LSJ 1789. The double significance of τήρησις is perhaps relevant here, for
Joseph's 'keeping' of the virgin will involve his 'safe-keeping' or guarding, custody, and
also his 'keeping' or observing the divine decree; see Wis. 6.18 (LXX); 1 Cor. 7.19.

134.   Where Mary and Joseph are eventually married: Mt. 1.25; cf. Lk. 2.41.

135.   For example, during the trial/ordeal, PJ 15–16; at the census, 17.3; and at the
birth 'inspection', 19.5-11.

136.   The significance of this shift has been relatively glossed over. Smid (1965: 72),
for example, notes the shift, but is more captivated by authorial inv/tention: 'The high
priest is here interpreting the command of the angel (8,3). So *gunè* from 8,3 is here given
the meaning: *parthenos kuriou*. In this way the author of P.J. without encroaching upon

The narrative invests the high priest with such outright authority so as to legitimate even his contorting of the significance of divine mandates! As the high priest wields power to summon the oracular sign, so too does he *interpret* that sign. He handles men's rods. He dominates the dove.[137] Mary will be, the high priest declares, not a wife but a ward. Not unlike Aaron's budding-rod in Numbers 17, then, PJ's dove functions as much to naturalize, establish and confirm priestly hegemony as it does to symbolize divine (s)election.

Here, too, PJ employs Mary as a medium of homosocial, male (dis)honor. Joseph's immediate challenge to the high priest's handling of his rod is telling:

> But Joseph objected: 'I already have sons, and I am a mature man while she is a young woman. Lest in any way I become a laughingstock among the sons of Israel!' (9.8).

Joseph's concerns about his domestic sentence—namely, his prior sons and his age—specify again a patently different character than the one depicted in either Matthew or Luke, an innovative characterization that can be read as promoting an explicit, dogmatic ideology glorifying/preserving Mary's virginity and/or purity,[138] even while it also continues to naturalize the myth of 'everyday' male privilege to 'traffic in women'.[139] In androcentric discourse such as we find in PJ, the significance accorded to a woman's presence by men involved in struggles for personal and/or familial prestige is inextricable from a consideration of her perceived impact upon male–male relations. Within and according to such naturalizing discourse, women are perceived as serving as 'a conduit of a relationship' of alliance and/or conflict between men, or as Kate Cooper puts it, in reference to the ancient (religious) milieu closer to PJ's narrative world, 'wherever a woman is mentioned a man's character is being judged—and along with it what he

---

Mt. I,20, manages to present his own opinion as the official interpretation of the priest!' Hock (1995: 49) obscures the shift with ambiguously passive terms: 'It becomes an interpretation of the heavenly messenger's order, which referred to Mary as someone's "wife" (8:8)'.

137. It is perhaps not insignificant that the Jerusalem Temple cult included a thriving system of sacrificial dove offerings (Mk 11.15).

138. So Hock 1995: 25: 'changes in Joseph's characterization are necessitated by the author's emphasis on Mary's purity'; 'Joseph will be characterized quite differently throughout this gospel from what is said about him in Matthew and Luke. The changes are due to the author's stress on the purity of Mary' (p. 49); cf. Smid 1965: 14-19.

139. A phrase taken from an influential essay by Rubin (1975: 174), who employs concepts from Levi-Strauss to explore the symbolic logic of many societies in which women are subordinate to men; see also Schwartz 1991: 47.

stands for'.[140] Mary is of course not solely an object of androcentric discourse.[141] Whatever else she stands for, PJ also constructs Mary as a different sort of *mediatrix*: part of the homosocial (dis)honor of Joseph is conveyed by her body, if also not quite (or yet)[142] located between her legs.[143]

Joseph's objections to his domestic sentence also register a moment of constitutive resistance to priestly hegemony, as seen by the high priest's riposte citing a précis of the tale of Levite uprising from Numbers 16:

> And the high priest responded, 'Joseph, fear the Lord your God and remember what God did to Dathan and Abiron and Kore, how the earth split open and swallowed them because of their rebellion. Now be afraid, Joseph, lest in any way such things happen in your house!' (PJ 9.9-10).

Without considering the details of the relationship of PJ to the cited precursor text, we might greet the high priest's reply as a 'reminder' of 'where this order is coming from'[144] or simply as 'a warning example'[145] for Joseph, and leave it at that. However, the exceptionally fluid afterlives of the Levite uprising tale should give us pause for considering its particular function here in PJ.[146] While the rendering of 'what God did to Dathan and Abiron and

---

140.   Cooper 1996: 19.

141.   It is certainly crucial to distinguish between the views of and about women in such ancient androcentric discourse, on the one hand, and the actual views of real women, on the other hand, which may or may not cohere. The question of the relationship of (actual, real) ancient historical women to the texts that discuss them is fraught with a number of difficulties—chief among them, a lack of sources by women and our inability to 'peel back layers of male rhetoric and find the 'real' woman concealed underneath' (Jacobs 2000: 720). While it is not my project, I certainly applaud the important efforts of those, such as Andrew Jacobs, who, attempting to delineate 'the space in which women could "logically" operate in the early Christian world', remind us that male-authored texts were not the products of a female-free world and that they mirror as well as create social realities (p. 722); see also Matthews 2001; Cobb 2009.

142.   Cf. PJ 13–16.

143.   See Mernissi (1982: 183), speaking broadly about 'Mediterranean men': 'The concepts of honour and virginity locate the prestige of a man between the legs of a woman. It is not by subjugating nature or by conquering mountains and rivers that a man secures his status, but by controlling the movements of women related to him by blood or by marriage, and by forbidding them any contact with male strangers.'

144.   Horner 2004: 326.

145.   Smid 1965: 74.

146.   See, for example, the spectrum of ancient receptions of the Levite uprising tale (Num. 16): cited as one of the 'historical' events demonstrating the greatness of God that all Israel is enjoined to acknowledge, with no specific action censured (Deut. 11.1-7); censured as an act of jealousy of (MT) or anger with (LXX) God's chosen leaders (Ps. 106.16-18); offered as supporting evidence of Moses' self-mastery (*4 Macc.* 2.15-17); depicted as a case of differing opinions about priestly vestment (*LAB* 16.1); traced

Kore' (9.9) as it originally appears in Numbers 16 involves, in the words of Ernest Bloch, a 'premature palace revolution' within the priestly upper class,[147] ostensibly motivated by the Levites' cooperative impulse 'not to usurp Moses but to assert that no one is superior, that all are holy before Yahweh...an assertion of a collective against an elevated ruler with some divine right',[148] this is an altogether different setting than what we find in PJ. The implied reader recalling the anterior text and drawn into the process of assigning intertextual meaning, would appreciate the differences: Joseph is not a member of the priestly upper class, he uprises alone, and his 'backtalk' (ἀντιλογία) pertains to domestic affairs (even if homosocial prestige is also at stake). The similarities, though, would also be clear enough: Joseph, like Dathan/Abiron/Kore, backtalks an established, naturalized order (signaled by the authority of the deity and his appointed man/men), which swiftly 'reacts' to preserve or assert its power. So, too, Joseph's resistance, as constitutive exception, is denied a viable space in the narrative and yet it also generates the very prospect for political and ideological *status quo* maintenance. The high priest, co-opting Joseph's phrase of imaginable, worrisome fates—

> Joseph: *lest, in any way* I become a laughingstock among the sons of Israel (μήπως ἔσομαι περίγελος τοῖς υἱοῖς Ἰσραὴλ) (9.8)
>
> High Priest: *lest, in any way* such things happen in your house... (μήπως ἔσται ταῦτα ἐν τῷ οἴκῳ σου) (9.10)

—appropriates for himself and his deity the forces of calamity, 'reacts' by (re)establishing who/why it is that Joseph *ought to* fear. As a male subject, then, and not unlike Matthew's Joseph in response to his dream annunciation (Mt. 1.18-22), Joseph is unmanned by his emotion, succumbing to the force of fearful desire that splits his will between opposition to and compliance with the dictates of the established order:[149]

to Korah's jealousy/envy of the privilege afforded to Moses/Aaron in their positions— not an 'insurrection' or 'rebellion' per se, but a 'raising of a clamor' (κατεβόα δεινὸν) (Josephus, *Ant.* 4.2.2 §14-15); described as an example of what happens to those who 'defile the flesh, reject authority, and slander the glorious ones' (Jude 11); and deployed as a warning for those who do not confess to their insidious plots of sedition (*1 Clem.* 51).

147.   Bloch 1972: 80, cited in Boer (2009: 81-82), who, elsewhere, helpfully 'disinters' Bloch's work as integral to dialectical, postcolonial critiques of biblical texts; see Boer 2007: 178.

148.   Boer 2009: 81.

149.   Cf. the similar treatment of fearful emotions and split subjectivities of Habrocomes (in Xenophon's *Ephesian Tale*) and Jesus (in the Gospel of Mark) in Thurman 2007: 202-203.

> Fearing God, Joseph took her into his own possession. And he said to her,
> 'Mary, I took you from the temple of the Lord and now I bring you into my
> house. I am going out to build houses, but I will come back to you. The Lord
> will protect you.' (9.11)

Joseph's backtalk is braced by noble soliloquy as he chooses to submit to an altered course of manly pursuits under the weight of his (now more than ever) naturalized social superiors. At the same time, Joseph alters his status from rod-handled subject to dutiful god-fearer, further naturalizing the established order while also procuring traction to presume upon the interests of the interested party: Joseph is chosen to 'take' Mary into his 'protection' (τήρησιν), but it is the Lord, Joseph says, who is *really* obligated to protect her. Actively striving to submit passively, Joseph shifts the scene from one of browbeaten to intentional submission as he employs his (yet undermined) will to distance himself from excessive association with the virgin girl, and so reclaims the autonomy that, along with his sturdy, public work ethic (his *ax*: 9.1, 12), conveys his manliness in PJ. Joseph's everyday masculinity is double.

Without denying influence of Roman imperial discourse on the construction of totalizing priestly hegemony in PJ, then, I suggest, like other contemporaneous novelistic literature, PJ is more preoccupied with the uneven processes of male self-fashioning under the weight of paternalistic, colonial rule. Rather than offering 'counter-imperial', eagle-damning resistance, PJ deals in more home(l)y gendered politics from the margins. Priests are naturalized as being 'on-top', though their scope of hegemonic influence ranges beyond the sphere of the temple cult proper, a queer pastiche of cultic correctness and imperial-toady 'manly' obligations that resist conventional generalization: attending dinner parties (6.6, 15); christening neonates (6.7, 9); attending to dependent virgins (7.7; 8.2); monitoring menarche (8.3-4); making oracular inquiries (8.5; 10.7); mustering men (8.9); yes, rod-handling (9.3-4); overseeing spinning and weaving projects (10.1, 6-7); voyeuristic surveillance (15.1-8); conducting legal proceedings (15.9–16.2); pronouncing guilt and innocence (15.16-17; 16.7); exacting physical ordeals, punishments (16.3-6); and delivering scholarly expertise for the benefit of imperial interests (21.4-6). Joseph, too, emerges from the dove scene exemplifying a split subjectivity that ruptures convention and generalization, especially the neat, polarized separation of 'manly' activity and 'feminine' passivity. PJ supplies this rod-handled, dove-shot, nobly submissive, 'everyday' man with a number of other arenas upon which to play out such an uneven masculinity—including one which positions him as a 'manly' *sotah* (PJ 16)—but that is another story.

Concluding Thoughts

Engaging in a kind of 'politics of discomfort'[150] aiming to reveal deep instabilities in seemingly 'everyday' male subjectivities produced in ancient religious narratives engaged in group identity formation under the weight of empire, I have endeavored here to bring forward that which lurks at, behind, and below the 'ground' of three novelistic characterizations of Joseph of Nazareth—from Luke, Matthew, and PJ. While gaining a better understanding of one of the 'mechanisms' governing Joseph of Nazareth's characterization within and across these particular narratives, reading this average Joe as a hybrid colonial character has also allowed us at once: to lay bare the ingredients, *the makings*, that constitute one exemplar of the 'everyday' man in early Christian novelistic writings; to expose the discursive processes and spectrum of competitive construction(s), *the making(s)*, of this common man; and to highlight a component that distinguishes one average-Joe-making endeavor from another—namely, the register of this everyday man's gendered negotiation with hegemonic authority. As I have suggested throughout, by 'thinking with'[151] these variegated average Joes and their values and practices that mark respective group identity and standing under empire.

Bibliography

Aasgaard, Reidar
    2009a   *The Childhood of Jesus: Decoding the Apocryphal Infancy Gospel of Thomas* (Eugene, OR: Cascade Books).
    2009b   'Father and Child Reunion: The Story of Joseph' (paper presented at the Christian Apocrypha Section, SBL Annual Meeting, New Orleans).
Allison, Dale
    1993   'Divorce, Celibacy and Joseph (Matthew 1.18-25 and 19.1-12)', *JSNT* 5: 3-10.
    2005   *Studies in Matthew: Interpretation Past and Present* (Grand Rapids: Baker Academic).
Anderson, Janice Capel
    1987   'Mary's Difference: Gender and Patriarchy in the Birth Narratives', *Journal of Religion* 67: 183-202.
    1994   *Matthew's Narrative Web: Over, and Over, and Over Again* (Sheffield: Sheffield Academic Press).

---

150.   See Butler 2000: 764-65: "For me, there's more hope in the world when we can question what is taken for granted, especially about what it is to be a human... What qualifies as a human, as a human subject, as human speech, as human desire? How do we circumscribe human speech or desire? At what cost? And at what cost to whom? These are questions that I think are important and that function within everyday grammar, everyday language, as taken-for-granted notions. We feel that we know the answers..."

151.   Brown 1988: 153, borrowing a phrase from Claude Lévi-Strauss.

Anderson, Janice Capel, and Stephen D. Moore
    2003   'Matthew and Masculinity', in Moore and Anderson 2003: 67-92.
Anderson, John Edward
    2011   *Jacob and the Divine Trickster: A Theology of Deception and YHWH's Fidelity to the Ancestral Promise in the Jacob Cycle* (Winona Lake, IN: Eisenbrauns).
Ashley, Kathleen M.
    1988   'Interrogating Biblical Deception and Trickster Theories: Narratives of Patriarchy or Possibility?', in Exum and Van Wijk-Bos 1988: 103-16.
Aune, David E.
    1987   *The New Testament in Its Literary Environment* (Library of Early Christianity, 8; Philadelphia: Westminster Press).
Autero, Esa
    2010   'Social Status in Luke's Infancy Narrative: Zechariah the Priest', *BTB* 41: 36-45.
Babcock-Abrahams, Barbara
    1975   '"A Tolerated Margin of Mess": The Trickster and his Tales Reconsidered', *Journal of Folklore Institute* 11: 147-86.
Bakhtin, Mikhail M.
    1981   *The Dialogic Imagination: Four Essays* (trans. C. Emerson and M. Holquist; Austin: University of Texas Press).
Bal, Mieke
    1988   'Tricky Thematics', in Exum and Van Wijk-Bos 1988: 133-55.
    1997   *Narratology: Introduction to the Theory of Narrative* (Toronto: University of Toronto Press).
    1999   *Quoting Caravaggio: Contemporary Art, Preposterous History* (Chicago: University of Chicago Press).
Balch, David L.
    1995   'Rich and Poor, Proud and Humble in Luke–Acts', in L.M. White and O.L. Yarbrough (eds.), *The Social World of the First Christians: Essays in Honor of Wayne A. Meeks* (Philadelphia: Fortress Press): 214-33.
Barton, Carlin A.
    2001   *Roman Honor: Fire in the Bones* (Berkeley: University of California Press).
Berder, Michel
    2009   'L'enfance de Jésus dans les évangiles canoniques et dans les apocryphes', in François-Marie Humann, Jacques-Noël Pérès, and Michel Berder (eds.), *Les Apocryphes chrétiens des premiers siècles. Mémoire et traditions* (Théologie à l'université, 7; Paris: Desclée de Brouwer): 211-44.
Bhaba, Homi K.
    2004   *The Location of Culture* (London; New York: Routledge).
Billings, Bradley S.
    2009   '"At the Age of 12": The Boy Jesus in the Temple (Luke 2.41-52), the Emperor Augustus, and the Social Setting of the Third Gospel', *JTS* 60: 70-89.
Blickenstaff, Marianne
    2005   *'While the Bridegroom is With Them': Marriage, Family, Gender and Violence in the Gospel of Matthew* (JSNTSup, 292; London: T. & T. Clark).

Bloch, E.
    1972   *Atheism in Christianity: The Religion of the Exodus and the Kingdom*
            (New York: Herder & Herder).
Blum, Virginia, and Heidi Nast
    1996   'Where's the Difference? The Heterosexualization of Alterity in Henri
            Lefebvre and Jacques Lacan', *Environment and Planning D: Society and
            Space* 14: 559-80.
Boer, Roland
    2007   'Marx, Postcolonialism, and the Bible', in F. Segovia and S.D. Moore
            (eds.), *Postcolonial Biblical Criticism: Interdisciplinary Intersections*
            (London: Continuum): 166-83.
    2009   *Political Myth: On the Use and Abuse of Biblical Themes* (Durham, NC:
            Duke University Press).
    2010   'Of Fine Wine, Incense and Spices: The Unstable Masculine Hegemony of
            the Book of Chronicles', in Creangă 2010: 20-33.
Bovon, François
    2002   *Luke 1: A Commentary on the Gospel of Luke 1.1–9.50* (Hermeneia; trans.
            C.M. Thomas; Minneapolis: Fortress Press).
Bowersock, Glen W.
    1994   *Fiction as History: Nero to Julian* (Berkeley: University of California
            Press).
Boyarin, Daniel
    1995   *Carnal Israel: Reading Sex in Talmudic Culture* (Berkeley: University of
            California Press).
    1997a   'Masada or Yavneh? Gender and the Arts of Jewish Resistance', in
            J. Boyarin and D. Boyarin (eds.), *Jews and Other Differences: The New
            Jewish Cultural Studies* (Minneapolis: University of Minnesota Press):
            306-29.
    1997b   *Unheroic Conduct: The Rise of Heterosexuality and the Invention of the
            Jewish Man* (Contraversions, 8; Berkeley: University of California Press).
    1999   'Virgins in Brothels: Gender and Religious Ecotypification', *Estudos de
            Literatura Oral* 5: 195-217.
Brant, Jo-Ann A., Charles W. Hedrick, and Chris Shea (eds.)
    2005   *Ancient Fiction: The Matrix of Early Christian And Jewish Narrative*
            (Atlanta: SBL).
Brenner, Athalya
    1997   *The Intercourse of Knowledge: On Gendering Desire and 'Sexuality' in
            The Hebrew Bible* (Leiden: E.J. Brill).
Brent, Allen
    1999   *The Imperial Cult and the Development of Church Order: Concepts and
            Images of Authority in Paganism and Early Christianity before the Age of
            Cyprian* (Boston: E.J. Brill).
Brown, Peter
    1988   *The Body and Society: Men, Women, and Sexual Renunciation in Early
            Christianity* (New York: Columbia University Press).
Brown, Raymond
    1993   *The Birth of the Messiah: A Commentary on the Infancy Narratives in
            Matthew and Luke* (New York: Doubleday, rev. edn).

Burrus, Virginia
    2005   'Mimicking Virgins: Colonial Ambivalence and the Ancient Romance', *Arethusa* 38: 49-88.
    2007   'Mapping as Metamorphosis: Initial Reflections on Gender and Ancient Religious Discourses', in Penner and Vander Stichele 2007: 1-10.
    2009   'The Gospel of Luke and the Acts of the Apostles', in Segovia and Sugirtharajah 2009: 133-55.
Butler, Judith
    1990   *Gender Trouble: Feminism and the Subversion of Identity* (New York: Routledge).
    1993   *Bodies That Matter: On the Discursive Limits of 'Sex'* (New York: Routledge).
    2000   'Changing the Subject: Judith Butler's Politics of Radical Resignification' (interview with Gary Olson and Lynn Worsham), *JAC* 20: 727-65.
    2004   *Undoing Gender* (New York: Routledge).
Carter, Warren
    2000   *Matthew and the Margins: A Sociopolitical and Religious Reading* (Maryknoll, NY: Orbis Books).
    2001   *Matthew and Empire: Initial Exploration*s (Harrisburg, PA: Trinity Press International).
    2005   'Matthaean Christology in Roman Imperial Key', in J. Riches and D.C. Sim (eds.), *The Gospel of Matthew in its Roman Imperial Context* (London: Continuum): 143-65.
Clark, Elizabeth
    2004   *History, Theory, Text: Historians and the Linguistic Turn* (Cambridge, MA: Harvard University Press).
Claudel, Gérard
    2011   'Joseph, Figure du Lecteur Modèle du premier Évangile', in D. Senior (ed.), *The Gospel of Matthew at the Crossroads of Early Christianity* (Leuven: Uitgeverij Peeters): 339-74.
Clivaz, Claire, *et al.* (eds.)
    2011   *Infancy Gospels: Stories and Identities* (Tübingen: Mohr Siebeck).
Cobb, L. Stephanie
    2008   *Dying to Be Men: Gender and Language in Early Christian Martyr Texts* (New York: Columbia University Press).
    2009   'Real Women or Objects of Discourse? The Search for Early Christian Women', *Religion Compass* 3: 379-94.
Cohen, David
    1991   'Demosthenes' *Against Meidias* and Athenian Litigation', in M. Gagarin (ed.), *Symposion 1990: Vorträge zur griechischen und hellenistischen Rechtsgeschichte* (Cologne: Böhlau): 155-64.
Connell, R.W.
    2005   *Masculinities* (Berkeley: University of California Press, 2nd edn).
Conway, Colleen
    2008   *Behold the Man* (Oxford: Oxford University Press).
Cooper, Kate
    1996   *The Virgin and the Bride: Idealized Womanhood in Late Antiquity* (Cambridge, MA: Harvard University Press).

Corbier, Mireille
   1991a   'Constructing Kinship in Rome: Marriage, Divorce, Filiation, and Adoption', in D.I. Kertzer and R.P. Saller (eds.), *The Family in Italy from Antiquity to the Present* (New Haven: Yale University Press): 127-44.
   1991b   'Divorce and Adoption as Roman Familial Strategies (Le divorce et l'adoption "en plus")', in B. Rawson (ed.), *Marriage, Divorce and Children in Ancient Rome* (Canberra: Humanities Research Center; Oxford: Clarendon Press): 47-78.
Cornwall, Andrea, and Nancy Lindisfarne (eds.)
   1994   *Dislocating Masculinity: Comparative Ethnographies* (London: Routledge).
Creangă, Ovidiu (ed.)
   2010   *Men and Masculinity in the Hebrew Bible and Beyond* (Sheffield: Sheffield Phoenix Press).
Crenshaw, Kimberle
   1991   'Mapping the Margins: Intersectionality, Identity Politics, and Violence against Women of Color', *Stanford Law Review* 43.6: 1241-99.
Crossan, John Dominic
   2003   'Virgin Mother or Bastard Child?', *HTS* 59.3: 663-91.
Cuthbert, David
   1996   'The Everyday Life of Cultural Studies', *University of Toronto Quarterly* 65.2: 393-403.
Davies, William D., and Dale Allison
   1988–97   *A Critical and Exegetical Commentary on the Gospel According to Saint Matthew* (3 vols.; Edinburgh: T. & T. Clark).
De Strycker, Émile
   1964   'Le Protévangile de Jacques: Problèmes critiques et exégétiques', in F.L. Cross (ed.), *Studia Evangelica III* (Texte und Untersuchungen, 88; Berlin: Akademie-Verlag): 339-59.
Destro, Adriana, and Mauro Pesce
   2011   'The Cultural Structure of the Infancy Narrative in the Gospel of Matthew', in Clivaz *et al.* 2011: 94-115.
Dill, Bonnie Thornton, and Ruth E. Zambrana (eds.)
   2009   *Emerging Intersections: Race, Class, and Gender in Theory, Policy, and Practice* (New Brunswick, NJ: Rutgers University Press).
Edelman, Lee
   2004   *No Future: Queer Theory and the Death Drive* (Durham, NC: Duke University Press).
Ehlen, Oliver
   2004   *Leitbilder und romanhafte Züge in apokryphen Evangelientexten: Untersuchungen zur Motivik und Erzählstruktur (anhand des Protevangelium Jacobi und der Acta Pilati Graec. B)* (Alterumswissenschaftliches Kolloquium, 9; Stuttgart: Steiner).
Eilberg-Schwartz, Howard
   1994   *God's Phallus and Other Problems for Men and Monotheism* (Boston: Beacon Press).
Elden, Stuart
   2004   *Understanding Henri Lefebvre: Theory and the Possible* (London: Continuum).

Erickson, Richard J.
    1996   'Divine Injustice? Matthew's Narrative Strategy and the Slaughter of the
            Innocents (Matthew 2.13-23)', *JSNT* 64: 5-27.
    2000   'Joseph and the Birth of Isaac in Matthew 1', *BBR* 10: 35-51.
Esler, Philip F.
    1987   *Community and Gospel in Luke–Acts: The Social and Political Motiva-
            tions of Lucan Theology* (Cambridge: Cambridge University Press).
Exum, J. Cheryl, and Johanna W.H. Van Wijk-Bos (eds.)
    1988   *Reasoning with the Foxes: Female Wit in a World of Male Power* (Semeia,
            42; Atlanta: SBL).
Felski, Rita
    1999   'The Invention of Everyday Life', *Cool Moves* 39: 15-31.
Fitzmyer, Joseph
    1973   'The Virginal Conception of Jesus in the New Testament', *TS* 34: 541-75.
    1981   *To Advance the Gospel: New Testament Studies* (New York: Crossroad).
    1985   *The Gospel according to Luke (I–IX): Introduction, Translation and Notes*
            (AB, 28; Garden City, NY: Doubleday).
Flick, Uwe
    1998   'Everyday Knowledge in Social Psychology', in U. Flick (ed.), *The Psy-
            chology of the Social* (Cambridge: Cambridge University Press): 41-59.
Fonrobert, Charlotte E.
    2000   *Menstrual Purity: Rabbinic and Christian Reconstructions of Biblical
            Gender* (Stanford, CA: Stanford University Press).
Foucault, Michel
    1980   *The History of Sexuality: An Introduction* (trans. R. Hurley; New York:
            Vintage).
    1985   *The History of Sexuality. II. The Use of Pleasure* (trans. Robert Hurley;
            New York: Random House).
    1986   *The History of Sexuality. III. The Care of the Self* (trans. Robert Hurley;
            New York: Pantheon).
France, Richard T.
    1979   'Herod and the Children of Bethlehem', *NovT* 21: 98-120.
    1980   'The Massacre of the Innocents—Fact or Fiction?', in E.A. Livingstone
            (ed.), *Studia Biblica 1978* (JSNTSup, 2; Sheffield: Sheffield Academic
            Press): 83-94.
Freed, Edwin D.
    2001   *The Stories of Jesus' Birth: A Critical Introduction* (St Louis, MO: Chalice
            Press).
Frey, Jörg, and Jens Schröter (eds.)
    2010   *Jesus in apokryphen Evangelienüberlieferungen: Beiträge zu ausser-
            kanonischen Jesusüberlieferungen aus verschiedenen Sprach- und
            Kulturtraditionen* (WUNT, 254; Tübingen: Mohr Siebeck).
Gardner, Jane F.
    1998   *Family and* Familia *in Roman Law and Life* (Oxford: Clarendon Press).
Gero, Stephen
    1976   'The Spirit as a Dove at the Baptism of Jesus', *NovT* 18: 17-35.
Gerrig, Richard J.
    1993   *Experiencing Narrative Worlds: On the Psychological Activities of
            Reading* (New Haven: Yale University Press).

Gilbert, Gary
    2006   'Luke–Acts and Negotiation of Authority and Identity in the Roman World', in Christine Helmer with Charlene T. Higbe (eds.), *The Multivalence of Biblical Texts and Theological Meanings* (Symposium, 37; Atlanta: SBL): 83-104.

Glenn, Cheryl
    2004   *Unspoken: A Rhetoric of Silence* (Carbondale: Southern Illinois University Press).

Glessner, Justin
    2012   'On "Being a Just Man" (Matt 1.19): Joseph of Nazareth, Gender, and Empire in the Infancy Narratives of Matthew and Luke' (paper presented at the Feminist Interpretations Section, SBL Annual International Meeting, Amsterdam).

Green, Joel B.
    1997   *The Gospel of Luke* (NICNT; Grand Rapids: Eerdmans).

Gregory, Brad S.
    1999   'Is Small Beautiful? Microhistory and the History of Everyday Life', *History and Theory* 38: 100-110.

Grottanelli, Cristiano
    1983   'Tricksters, Scapegoats, Champions, Saviors', *History of Religion* 23: 117-13.

Gullestad, Marianne
    1991   'The Transformation of the Norwegian Notion of Everyday Life', *American Ethnologist* 18.3: 480-99.

Haddox, Susan
    2010   'Favoured Sons and Subordinate Masculinities', in Creangă 2010: 2-19.

Halberstam, Judith
    1998   *Female Masculinity* (Durham, NC: Duke University Press).

Highmore, Ben
    2002   *Everyday Life and Cultural Theory* (London: Routledge).

Hock, Ronald F.
    1995   *The Infancy Gospels of James and Thomas* (Santa Rosa, CA: Polebridge Press).

Horner, Tim
    2004   'Jewish Aspects of the *Protoevangelium of James*', *JECS* 12: 313-35.

Horsley, Richard A.
    1989   *The Liberation of Christmas: The Infancy Narratives in Social Context* (New York: Crossroad).
    2003   *Jesus and Empire: The Kingdom of God and the New World Disorder* (Minneapolis: Fortress Press).

Hynes, William J.
    1993a   'Inconclusive Conclusions: Tricksters—Metaplayers and Revealers', in Hynes and Doty 1993: 202-17.
    1993b   'Mapping the Characteristics of Mythic Tricksters', in Hynes and Doty 1993: 33-45.

Hynes, William J., and William G. Doty (eds.)
    1993   *Mythical Trickster Figures: Contours, Contexts, and Criticisms* (Tuscaloosa: University of Alabama Press).

Iser, Wolfgang
    1974   *The Implied Reader: Patterns of Communication in Prose Fiction from Bunyan to Beckett* (Baltimore: The Johns Hopkins University Press).
Jacobs, Andrew S.
    2000   'Writing Demetrias: Ascetic Logic in Ancient Christianity', *Church History* 69.4: 719-48.
Jackson, Melissa
    2012   *Comedy and Feminist Interpretation of the Hebrew Bible: A Subversive Collaboration* (Oxford: Oxford University Press).
Jurich, Marilyn
    1999   'The Female Trickster—Known as Trickstar—as Exemplified by Two American Legendary Women, "Billy" Tipton and Mother Jones', *JAC* 22: 69-75.
Kimmel, Michael S.
    2004   *The Gendered Society* (Oxford: Oxford University Press).
Knox, Wilfred L.
    1944   *Some Hellenistic Elements in Primitive Christianity* (London: H. Milford).
Konstan, David
    2005   'Clemency as a Virtue', *Classical Philology* 100: 337-46.
Kuefler, Matthew
    2001   *The Manly Eunuch: Masculinity, Gender Ambiguity, and Christian Ideology in Late Antiquity* (Chicago: University of Chicago Press).
Kunst, Christiane
    2005   *Römische Adoption: zur Strategie einer Familienorganisation* (Hennef: Marthe Clauss).
Lacey, W.K.
    1996   *Augustus and the Principate: The Evolution of the System* (ARCA, 35; Leeds: Francis Cairns).
Lassen, Eva Marie
    1997   'The Roman Family: Ideal and Metaphor', in Moxnes 1997: 103-20.
Lefebvre, Henri
    1947   *Critique de la vie quotidienne* I (Paris: Grasset, 1947).
    1959   *La somme et le reste* I (Paris: La Nef de Paris).
    1968a   *Critique de la vie quotidienne. II. Fondements d'une sociologie de la quotidienneté* (Paris: L'Arche).
    1968b   *La vie quotidienne dans le monde moderne* (Paris: Gallimard).
    1970   *La fin de l'histoire* (Paris: Les Editions de Minuit).
    1973   *La survie du capitalisme: la re-production des rapports de production* (Paris: Editions Anthropos).
    1976   *The Survival of Capitalism: Reproduction of the Relations of Production* (trans. Frank Bryant; London: Allison & Busby).
    1987   'The Everyday and Everydayness', in *Everyday Life: Yale French Studies* 73: 7-11.
    1988   'Toward a Leftist Cultural Politics: Remarks Occasioned by the Centenary of Marx's Death', in Gary Nelson and Lawrence Grossberg (eds.), *Marxism and the Interpretation of Culture* (London: Macmillan): 75-88.
    1991   *Critique of Everyday Life*, I (trans. John Moore; London: Verso).
    2002a   *Critique of Everyday Life. II. Foundations for a Sociology of the Everyday* (London: Verso).

2002b   *Everyday Life in the Modern World* (trans. Sacha Rabinovitch; London: Continuum, 2nd edn).

Leigh, Matthew
1997   *Lucan: Spectacle and Engagement* (Oxford: Clarendon Press).

Leissner, Omi Morgenstern
2001   'Jewish Women's Naming Rites and the Rights of Jewish Women', *Nashim* 4: 140-77.

Lenski, Gerhard
1966   *Power and Privilege: A Theory of Social Stratification* (Chapel Hill: University of North Carolina Press).

Levin, Yigal
2006   'Jesus, "Son of God" and "Son of David": The "Adoption" of Jesus into the Davidic Line', *JSNT* 28: 415-42.

Lindsay, Hugh
2009   *Adoption in the Roman World* (Cambridge: Cambridge University Press).

Liew, Tat-Siong Benny
2003   'Re-Mark-able Masculinities: Jesus, the Son of Man, and the (Sad) Sum of Manhood?', in Moore and Anderson 2003: 93-136.

Liu, James H., and János László
2007   'Narrative Theory of History and Identity: Social Identity, Social Representations, Society and the Individual', in G. Moloney and I. Walker (eds.), *Social Representations and Identity: Content, Process, and Power* (New York: Palgrave Macmillan): 85-108.

Lüdtke, Alf
1995   *The History of Everyday Life: Reconstructing Historical Experiences and Ways of Life* (Princeton: Princeton University Press).

Lyons, George
1985   *Pauline Autobiography: Toward a New Understanding* (SBLDS, 73; Atlanta, GA: Scholars Press).

Marshall, I. Howard
1978   *The Gospel of Luke: A Commentary on the Greek Text* (NIGTC; Exeter: Paternoster).

Martin, Dale
2001   'Contradictions of Masculinity: Ascetic Inseminators and Menstruating Men in Greco-Roman Culture', in V. Finucci and K. Brownlee (eds.), *Tropes of Reproduction in Literature and History from Antiquity through Early Modern Europe* (Durham, NC: Duke University Press): 81-108.

Matthews, Shelly
2001   'Thinking of Thecla: Issues in Feminist Historiography', *JFSR* 17.2: 39-55.

Matthews, V.H.
1985   'Jacob the Trickster and Heir of the Covenant: A Literary Interpretation', *Perspectives in Religious Studies* 12: 185-95.

Mayordomo, Moisés
2011   'Matthew 1–2 and the Problem of Intertextuality', in Clivaz *et al.* 2011: 257-79.

McCann, Eugene J.
1999   'Race, Protest, and Public Space: Contextualizing Lefebvre in the US City', *Antipode* 31: 163-84.

McDonnell, Myles
2003 'Roman Men and Greek Virtue', in R.M. Rosen and I. Sluiter (eds.), *Andreia: Studies in Manliness and Courage in Classical Antiquity* (Leiden: E.J. Brill): 235-62.
2006 *Roman Manliness: 'Virtus' and the Roman Republic* (Cambridge: Cambridge University Press).

Meier, J.P.
1992 'The Brothers and Sisters of Jesus in Ecumenical Perspective', *CBQ* 54: 1-28.

Mernissi, Fatima
1982 'Virginity and Patriarchy', *Women's Studies International Forum* 5: 183-91.

Metzger, James A.
2009 'Where Has Yahweh Gone? Reclaiming Unsavory Images of God in New Testament Studies', *HBT* 31: 51-76.

Modleski, Tanya
1991 *Feminism without Women: Culture and Criticism in a 'Postfeminist' Age* (New York: Routledge).

Mills, Margaret A.
2001 'The Gender of the Trick: Female Tricksters and Male Narrators', *Asian Folklore Studies* 60: 237-58.

Moehring, Horst R.
1972 'The Census in Luke as an Apologetic Device', in D.E. Aune (ed.), *Studies in New Testament and in Early Christian Literature: Essays in Honor of Allen P. Wikgren* (Leiden: E.J. Brill): 144-60.

Moore, Stephen D., and Janic Capel Anderson
1998 'Taking it Like a Man: Masculinity in 4 Maccabees', *JBL* 117: 249-73.

Moore, Stephen D., and Janic Capel Anderson (eds.)
2003 *New Testament Masculinities* (Atlanta: SBL).

Moxnes, Halvor
1988 'Righteousness and Honor in Romans', *JSNT* 10: 61-77.
1997 'What Is Family?', in Moxnes 1997: 13-41.

Moxnes, Halvor (ed.)
1997 *Constructing Early Christian Families* (London: Routledge).

Nasrallah, Laura S., and Elisabeth Schüssler Fiorenza (eds.)
2009 *Prejudice and Christian Beginnings: Investigating Race, Gender, and Ethnicity in Early Christian Studies* (Minneapolis: Fortress Press).

Niedermüller, Peter
2002 'Europäische Ethnologie: Deutungen, Optionen, Alternativen', in Konrad Köstlin, Peter Niedermüller, and Herbert Nikitsch (eds.), *Die Wende als Wende? Orientierungen Europäischen Ethnologien nach 1989* (Veröffentlichungen des Instituts für Europäische Ethnologie der Universität Wien, 23; Vienna: Verlag des Instituts für Europäische Ethnologie): 27-62.

Neyrey, Jerome H.
2003 'Jesus, Gender, and the Gospel of Matthew', in Moore and Anderson 2003: 43-66.

Nicholas, Dean Andrew
2009 *Trickster Revisited: Deception as a Motif in the Pentateuch* (New York: Peter Lang).

Niditch, Susan
    1987   *Underdogs and Tricksters: A Prelude to Biblical Folklore* (San Francisco: Harper & Row).
Nolland, J.
    1996   'No Son-of-God Christology in Matthew 1.18-25', *JSNT* 18.3: 3-12.
Olender, Robert G.
    2008   'Righteousness in Matthew with Implications for the Declaration of Joseph's Righteousness and the Matthean Exception Clauses' (unpublished PhD diss., Southeastern Baptist Theological Seminary).
Penner, Todd, and Caroline Vander Stichele (eds.)
    2007   *Mapping Gender in Ancient Religious Discourses* (BIS, 84; Leiden: E.J. Brill).
Peppard, Michael
    2011   *The Son of God in the Roman World: Divine Sonship in its Social and Political Context* (Oxford: Oxford University Press).
Perkins, Judith
    1995   *The Suffering Self: Pain and Narrative Representation in the Early Christian Era* (London: Routledge).
Peskowitz, Miriam
    1997   *Spinning Fantasies: Rabbis, Gender, and History* (Berkeley: University of California Press).
Pfister, Manfred
    1991   *The Theory and Analysis of Drama* (Cambridge: Cambridge University Press).
Pratt, Mary Louise
    1992   *Imperial Eyes: Travel Writing and Transculturation* (London: Routledge).
Przybylski, Benno
    1980   *Righteousness in Matthew and his World of Thought* (SNTSMS, 41; Cambridge: Cambridge University Press).
Radin, Paul
    1972   *The Trickster: A Study in American Indian Mythology* (New York: Schocken Books).
Richardson, Peter
    1999   *Herod, King of the Jews and Friend of the Romans* (Minneapolis: Fortress Press).
Rouselle, Aline
    1988   *Porneia: On Desire and the Body in Antiquity* (Cambridge: Basil Blackwell).
Rowe, C. Kavin
    2005   'Luke–Acts and the Imperial Cult: A Way through the Conundrum?', *JSNT* 27: 279-300.
Rubin, Gayle
    1975   'The Traffic in Women: Notes on the "Political Economy" of Sex', in Rayna Reiter (ed.), *Toward an Anthropology of Women* (New York: Monthly Review): 157-210.
Runesson, Anders
    2011   'Giving Birth to Jesus in the Late First Century: Matthew as Midwife in the Context of Colinisation', in Clivaz *et al.* 2011: 301-27.

Satlow, Michael
    2001   *Jewish Marriage in Antiquity* (Princeton, NJ: Princeton University Press).
Schaberg, Jane
    1987   *Illegitimacy of Jesus: A Feminist Theological Interpretation of the Infancy Narratives* (San Francisco: Harper & Row).
Schilling, Derek
    2003   'Everyday Life and the Challenge to History in Postwar France: Braudel, Lefebvre, Certeau', *Diacritics* 33.1: 23-40.
Schwartz, Regina
    1992   'Adultery in the House of David: The Metanarrative of Biblical Scholarship and the Narratives of the Bible', in D. Jobling and S.D. Moore (eds.), *Poststructuralism as Exegesis* (Semeia, 54; Atlanta: SBL): 35-57.
Scott, James C.
    1990   *Domination and the Arts of Resistance: Hidden Transcripts* (New Haven: Yale University Press).
Segovia, Fernando F.
    2009   'The Gospel of John', in Segovia and Sugirtharajah 2009: 156-93.
Segovia, Fernando F., and R.S. Sugirtharajah (eds.)
    2009   *A Postcolonial Commentary on the New Testament Writings* (London: T. & T. Clark).
Seigworth, Gregory J.
    2000   'Banality for Cultural Studies', *Cultural Studies* 14.2: 268-27.
Sheffield, Julian
    2001   'The Father in the Gospel of Matthew', in A. Levine and M. Blickenstaff (eds.), *A Feminist Companion to Matthew* (The Feminist Companion to the New Testament and Early Christian Writings, 1; Sheffield: Sheffield Academic Press): 52-69.
Smid, H.R.
    1965   *Protevangelium Jacobi: A Commentary* (Apocrypha Novi Testamenti, 1; trans. G.E. van Baaren-Pape; Assen: Van Gorcum).
Smit, Peter-Ben
    2010   'Something about Mary? Remarks about the Five Women in the Matthean Genealogy', *NTS* 56: 191-207.
Spiegel, Gabrielle M.
    1990   'History, Historicism, and the Social Logic of the Text in the Middle Ages', *Speculum* 65: 59-86.
    1997   *The Past as Text: The Theory and Practice of Medieval Historiography* (Baltimore: The Johns Hopkins University Press).
Steinberg, Naomi
    1988   'Israelite Tricksters, Their Analogues and Cross-Cultural Study', in Exum and Van Wijk-Bos 1988: 1-13.
Sternberg, Meir
    1987   *The Poetics of Biblical Narrative: Ideological Literature and the Drama of Reading* (Bloomington: Indiana University Press).
Sugirtharajah, R.S.
    2002   *Postcolonial Criticism and Biblical Interpretation* (Oxford: Oxford University Press).

Thomas, Christine M.
    2003   *The Acts of Peter, Gospel Literature, and the Ancient Novel: Rewriting the Past* (New York: Oxford University Press).

Thompson, Marianne Meye
    2000   *The Promise of the Father: Jesus and God in the New Testament* (Louisville, KY: Westminster/John Knox Press).

Thurman, Eric
    2007   'Novel Men: Masculinity and Empire in Mark's Gospel and Xenophon's An Ephesian Tale', in Penner and Vander Stichele 2007: 185-230.
    2012   'Writing the Nation/Reading the Men: Some Novel Thoughts on Manliness in Mark's Gospel' (paper presented at the Jesus Traditions, Gospels, and Negotiating the Roman Imperial World Section, SBL Annual Meeting, Chicago).

Treggiari, Susan
    1991   *Roman Marriage:* Iusti Coniuges *from the Time of Cicero to the Time of Ulpian* (Oxford: Clarendon Press).

Uspensky, Boris A.
    1973   *A Poetics of Composition: The Structure of the Artistic Text and Typology of Compositional Form* (trans. V. Zavarin and S. Wittig; Berkeley: University of California Press).

Vander Stichele, Caroline, and Todd Penner
    2009   *Contextualizing Gender in Early Christian Discourse: Thinking Beyond Thecla* (London: Continuum).

Viviano, Benedict Thomas
    2011   'God as Father in the Infancy Gospels (Matthew 1 and 2, Luke 1 and 2)', in Clivaz *et al.* 2011: 390-98.

Waetjen, Herman C.
    1976   'The Genealogy as the Key to the Gospel According to Matthew', *JBL* 95: 205-30.

Walaskay, Paul W.
    2005   *'And So We Came to Rome': The Political Perspective of St Luke* (Cambridge: Cambridge University Press).

Watson, Alan
    1970   *The Law of the Ancient Romans* (Dallas: Southern Methodist University Press).

Whitmarsh, Tim
    2001   *Greek Literature and the Roman Empire: The Politics of Imitation* (New York: Oxford University Press).
    2011   *Narrative and Identity in the Ancient Greek Novel: Returning Romance* (Cambridge: Cambridge University Press).

Williams, Craig
    1999   *Roman Homosexuality: Ideologies of Masculinity in Classical Antiquity* (New York: Oxford University Press).

Yamasaki, Gary
    2012   *Perspective Criticism: Point of View and Evaluative Guidance in Biblical Narrative* (Eugene, OR: Cascade Books).

Young, Robert
    2001   *Postcolonialism: An Historical Introduction* (Oxford: Basil Blackwell).

THE FIRST CUT IS THE DEEPEST:
MASCULINITY AND CIRCUMCISION IN
THE FIRST CENTURY

Karin B. Neutel and Matthew R. Anderson

We will begin with that which is an object of ridicule among many people…, namely the circumcision of the genital organs. With similar words Philo opens his major apology for circumcision.[1] Just as in Philo's time, male circumcision is today the object of derision, defence and passionate debate. Now as then, the foreskin is a battle ground where the lines are clearly drawn. Questions emerge whether and why we distinguish between the genders when it comes to genital cutting, and what this means for our understanding of masculinity and our perceptions of the male body.

Ancient masculinity has been of interest to many and considerable gains have been made in our understanding of it.[2] Male circumcision, however, has not been included in these explorations. Nor have the insights in masculinity been brought to bear on ancient attitudes towards circumcision.[3] This chapter aims to bring these two topics together, and asks what we add to our understanding of circumcision in the ancient world if we consider ancient ideas about masculinity. The ancient ideal of masculinity included and implied a notion of the ideal male body, which inevitably informed attitudes towards the foreskin. It is therefore important to ask what explicit and implicit connections Jews and their Greek and Roman contemporaries made between masculinity and circumcision and how early Christian views fit in.

---

1. *De specialibus legibus* 1.2.

2. To name just a few that are relevant to the subject presented here: Gleason 1995; Moore and Capel Anderson 1998; Rosen and Sluiter 2003; Larson 2004; Conway 2008; Williams 2010.

3. Masculinity is absent as an interpretative category in studies of circumcision. Notable examples are Nina E. Livesey's recent discussion of Josephus, Philo, the books of the Maccabees and Paul's letters (Livesey 2010), as well as Blaschke 1998 and Barclay 1998. An exception is Niehoff 2003.

1. *Masculinity and the Male Body*

Male genitals did not an ancient man make. As Maud Gleason notes in her seminal work, 'masculinity in the ancient world was an achieved state, radically underdetermined by anatomical sex' (Gleason 1995: 59). Far from being a genetic birth right, ancient masculinity was mutable and public, a matter of perception and subject to constant challenge. It was a social construct where one's power to dominate, socially and politically, not only proved masculinity but in most practical ways actually constituted it. The benefits of being born free and male were incomparable, but the free male had constantly to prove, defend and reinforce his good fortune, or risk losing it. Courage, manner, influence, steadfastness, action, bearing, dignity, and most of all control: these were the expressions of virility. Especially on the public stage—where political, economic and social power could be most effectively demonstrated—masculinity took shape in how a man was perceived by others:

> The difficulties in achieving and maintaining masculine status may well account for the tremendous importance placed on the notion of control in Roman ideologies of masculinity, just as the intensity of Roman men's asser-tions of masculinity or of its absence may reflect the tenuousness and artifici-ality of a constructed identity in need of policing and control. In the balancing act of masculinity, one stumble can ruin the entire performance (Williams 2010: 156).

However, if masculinity was a performance, it required an instrument. Ancient masculinity may not have been determined by anatomy, but the point sometimes overlooked is that it certainly had implications for anatomy. Likewise, a man's stance and appearance were public indicators of his social status and its corollary, his masculinity. Masculinity 'was a language that anatomical males were taught to speak with their bodies' (Gleason 1995: 70).

The male ideal of the body was something that people were reminded of every day. Nude statues of heroes, athletes, and members of the imperial family gave a clear indication of what the ideal male body, including its genitals, looked like (Hallett 2005). The ideal appearance of the penis, invariably described as 'dainty' in the specialized literature, was the same in Roman as in Greek times: relatively small and covered with a foreskin tapering to a petite point. Even in rare depictions of erect penises, the glans was often still covered, signalling a man's respectability and self-control (Hodges 2001: 381). The foreskin was therefore of considerable importance, and was seen as one of nature's ornamentations of the body:

> Nature out of her abundance ornaments all the members, especially in man. In
> many parts there is manifest ornamentation, though at times this is obscured
> by the brilliance of their usefulness. The ears show obvious ornamentation,
> and so, I suppose, does the skin called the prepuce (πόσθη) at the end of the
> penis and the flesh of the buttocks (Galen, *On the Usefulness of the Parts of
> the Body* 11.13).

The process of speaking the language of masculinity with this ideal body
began at birth. It was the duty of a baby boy's nurse 'to assist, if not enforce,
the infant's physical development along appropriately "natural" lines'
(Gleason 1995: 71). Each part of the body, including the genitals, was
moulded to conform to ideal characteristics:

> If the infant is male and it looks as though it has no foreskin (λειπόδερμον),
> she should gently draw the tip of the foreskin forward (τρυφερῶς ἐπισπάσθω
> τὴν ἀκροποσθίαν) or even hold it together with a strand of wool to fasten it.
> For if gradually stretched and continuously drawn forward it easily stretches
> and assumes its normal length (τὸ κατὰ φύσιν ἀπολαμβάνει μῆκος), covers
> the glans and becomes accustomed to keep the natural good shape (τὴν
> φυσικὴν εὐμορφίαν). In addition, she should shape the scrotum from where the
> thighs meet (Soranus, *Gynaecology* 2.34).[4]

Since the foreskin was so obviously bound up with the ancient ideal of
masculinity, this connection was inevitably reflected in ancient views of
circumcision. In the next sections we will explore how masculinity and the
male body were connected in different contexts. We first examine Greco-
Roman views, and then the extensive apology for circumcision from Philo.
Finally we encounter Paul, an uncomfortable and rarely consistent bridge
between these views.

2. *Barbarian Customs: Greco-Roman Views on Circumcision*

The positive valuation of the foreskin, and its association with masculinity
defined by self-control, had its effect on attitudes towards circumcision. The
ridicule that Philo mentions can be recognized in literary sources as well as
in visual art. Even though, as noted above, the penis was usually depicted
as entirely covered, some images of a bare glans can be found, and these
images are not presented in a positive way. As Frederick Hodges concludes,
if a circumcised penis goes with a hideous face, and a long and tapered
prepuce goes with a handsome face, it is the long and tapered prepuce that
was admired (Hodges 2001: 386).

---

4. For a description of Soranus's works and his Methodist approach to medicine, see
the introduction by Owsei Temkin to Soranus 1991: xxiii-xlix.

A Laughing Matter

Literary sources confirm that circumcision was looked at with disgust, even if it could be a source of humour as well. Two of Martial's epigrams are worth quoting here, since they show that he associates circumcision with sexuality, and especially with licentiousness.[5] The subject of the first epigram is a Jewish poet (born in Solyma, meaning Jerusalem), who is repeatedly addressed as 'circumcised poet'.[6] This poet speaks disparagingly of the works of Martial while stealing from them, but more importantly, is sexually involved with the poet's beloved boy (Stern 1974: 527-28):

> Your overflowing malice, and your detraction everywhere of my books, I pardon: circumcised poet (*verpe poeta*), you are wise! This, too, I disregard, that when you carp at my poems, you plunder them: so too, circumcised poet (*verpe poeta*), you are wise! What tortures me is this, that you, circumcised poet (*verpe poeta*), although born in the very midst of Solyma, outrage my boy (*pedicas puerum meum*). There! You deny it, and swear to me by Thunderer's Temple. I don't believe you: swear, circumcised one (*verpe poeta*), by Anchialus (Martial, *Epigrams* 11.94).

This epigram plays heavily on the fact that the rival poet is circumcised, mentioning it four times.[7] Martial suggests that his colleague goes against his own Jewish principles in his relationship with the boy in question: he engages in this behaviour 'although born in the very midst of Solyma'. The lack of control already signalled for Martial by his rival's circumcision is thus confirmed in the latter's sexual actions.

The association between Jews, circumcision and lasciviousness is even more pronounced in the following epigram, aimed at criticizing the international taste in men of a woman named Caelia:

> You grant your favours to Partians, you grant them to Germans, you grant them, Caelia, to Dacians, and you do not spurn the couch of Cilicians and Capadocians; and for you from his Egyptian city comes sailing the gallant of Memphis, and the black Indian from the Red Sea; nor do you shun the lecheries of circumcised Jews (*nec recutitorum fugis inguina Iudaeorum*), and the Alan on his Sarmatian steed does not pass you by. What is your reason that, although you are a Roman girl, no Roman lewdness has attraction for you? (Martial, *Epigrams* 8.30).

---

5. A similar association can be found in *Epigrams* 7.35 and 7.82.

6. The reference to swearing to the temple of Jupiter most likely refers to the temple in Jerusalem, while the alternative is no doubt intended in a sarcastic way; see Feldman 1993: 156.

7. The term 'verpe' refers to the appearance of the circumcised penis, not to the act of circumcising; see MacKay 1994: 112. MacKay imagines the epigram to have been written in an 'exquisite frenzy of jealousy'.

Women were a frequent target for Martial, who attacked their excessive sexual desire and their lack of the chasteness which ought to characterize a Roman matron.[8] Jews appear here among a long list of foreign peoples, all of whom Caelia prefers to Romans, much to Martial's dismay. The joke, as D.S. Barrett observes, is that 'the vanquished in the field are victors in the bedroom' (Barrett 1984: 43).

Both in Greek and Roman times, barbarians were generally considered to be lacking in masculinity. This was evident in their lack of discipline and restraint, typically also in the realm of sexuality, a quality they shared with women (Hall 1989: 196; Rosivach 1999: 143). Barbarians were thus seen as effeminate, lustful, and ruled by women, whereas Greeks and Romans considered themselves to be masculine, sexually restrained, and in control of their women (Blondell 1999: 12; Schmidt 1999). As Martial's epigram makes clear, Jews could be singled out even among barbarians as especially lecherous. Since they were generally epitomized as circumcisers, Jews were especially associated with sexual depravity. However, as Shaye Cohen observes, 'sexual self-control is a quality that many cultures ascribe to themselves and deny to others' (Cohen 2005: 158).[9] Greeks and Romans were no exception in wielding this stereotype; Jews of the period threw it right back at them.

Depraved Customs
The most extensive criticism of Jews as depraved circumcisers can be found in Tacitus's famous description of Jewish customs. Jews, as a people, represent the opposite of Roman values, including those of the Roman male:[10]

> This worship, however introduced, is upheld by its antiquity; all their other customs, which are at once perverse and disgusting, owe their strength to their very badness. The most degraded out of other races, scorning their national beliefs, brought to them their contributions and presents. This augmented the wealth of the Jews, as also did the fact, that among themselves they are inflexibly honest and ever ready to shew compassion, though they regard the rest of mankind with all the hatred of enemies. They sit apart at meals, they sleep apart, and though, as a nation, they are singularly prone to lust (*proiectissima ad libidinem gens*), they abstain from intercourse with foreign women; among themselves nothing is unlawful (*inter se nihil inlicitum*). Circumcision was adopted by them as a mark of difference from other men (*circumcidere genitalia instituerunt, ut diversitate noscantur*). Those who come over to their

---

8. On this and other aspects of the epigram, see the commentary by Vioque (2002: 214-19).

9. Cohen also notes the persistence of the stereotype until modern times.

10. As D.S. Levene notes in his introduction to Tacitus's *Histories*, 'The most striking account of Tacitus' description of Jews is the notion of inversion: Jews, for him, are people who turn the familiar Roman world upside down' (Tacitus 1997: xviii).

religion adopt the practice, and have this lesson first instilled into them, to despise all Gods, to disown their country, and set at nought parents, children, and brethren (Tacitus, *Histories* 5.5.1-3).

The concept of masculinity that informs Tacitus's work centres on the notions of dominance and control. Dominance over other persons requires dominance over one's own self and self-control thus occurs in Tacitus's texts as a prerequisite for exercising power over others. Those who do not dominate but are intended to be dominated, such as non-Romans, are portrayed as lacking in self-control.[11]

Jews are a clear example of a non-Roman people lacking in self-control and therefore in masculinity. They are singularly prone to lust and consider nothing unlawful. Their circumcision serves as a mark of their inverted values: what others cover, they lay bare; what others control, they give free rein.

3. *Male Self-Control as a Jewish Defence*

It is within this understanding of circumcision as a practice that violated masculinity, that Jews explained to their neighbours and to themselves why they performed it. Most elaborate in his combat against the ridicule and antagonism is Philo. Even if he does not share their ideal of the male form, Philo does fully embrace the conception of masculinity that underlies his contemporaries' rejection of circumcision. He is, in fact, one of the most eloquent proponents of the understanding of gender as a scale on which the masculine takes up the top position, while the female is located at the opposite, inferior end. The gender gradient that is evident in his thought was the principle that supported the attitude towards male and female in his time and through much of Antiquity and the Middle Ages. Foremost was the concept that the female of the species constitutes an imperfect form, while the male has the perfected form. In his explanation as to why the Passover lamb needs to be a year-old male, Philo remarks:

> Male because male is more perfect than female—it is said by naturalists that the female is nothing else than an imperfect male (Philo, *Quaest. Exod.* 1.7; see also *Spec. leg.* 1.200-201; *Fug.* 51-52).

The male, according to Philo, is 'more complete, more dominant than the female', the female is 'incomplete and in subjection and belongs to the category of the passive rather than the active' (*Spec. leg.* 1.37). Moreover, the quality of the soul of a man and the degree of perfection that it achieves becomes visible in the body and its degree of maleness:

---

11. See Späth 2012: 437-38.

> just as bodily properties are seen in mirrors, so those of the soul (are seen) in the face and countenance. But a shameless look and an elevated neck and a continuous movement of the eyebrows and a womanish walk and not blushing at, or being ashamed of, any evil at all is the sign of a lewd soul, which clearly pictures and describes the forms of its invisible disgraces on its visible body (Philo, *Quaest. Gen.* 4.99).

From this passage we also begin to discern how readily Philo links common cultural assumptions about masculinity (or lack of it) with the state of one's soul. Again Philo describes male and female as two extremes on a continuum:

> For progress is indeed nothing else than giving up of the female genus by changing into the male, since the female kind/class is maternal, passive, corporeal and sense-perceptible while the male is active, rational, incorporeal and more akin to mind and thought (Philo, *Quaest. Exod.* 1.7).

As Coleen Conway concludes, for Philo 'becoming more pious and becoming more masculine are one and the same and both result in a move up the cosmic hierarchy toward the divine realm' (Conway 2003: 479).

Since Philo's conception of masculinity is thus entirely in line with the culturally accepted view, and his notion of gender is 'among the most consistently applied principles of his thought', it is all the more significant that he clearly deviates from these principles when discussing circumcision and addressing the question why it is customary for men but not women to be circumcised (Mattila 1996: 103).[12]

Why Should Only Males Be Circumcised?
Philo comes up with an unusual answer to the question why only men need to be circumcised:[13]

> Why orders he the males only to be circumcised? (...) the divine legislator appoints circumcision to take place in the case of the male alone for many reasons: the first of which is, that the male creature feels venereal pleasures and desires matrimonial connections more than the female, on which account the female is properly omitted here, while he checks the superfluous impetuosity of the male by the sign of circumcision (Philo, *Quaest. Gen.* 3.47).[14]

Philo explains the command that only men need be circumcised with reference to the power of male lust, which exceeds the female sexual drive.

12. Matilla is quoted with approval (although erroneously as Mattlia) by Conway (2003: 473).

13. Philo also gives a second answer, which is based on his understanding of procreation, namely that the woman provides the matter, but the male provides the form, the skill and cause. On this argument, see Cohen 2005: 145.

14. The Greek text of this work has unfortunately largely been lost, and the only extant ancient version is an Armenian translation.

While this assessment of human libido may sound very familiar to modern ears, it was extremely rare in Antiquity.[15] The licentiousness of women was a commonplace in literature and according to the well-known myth of Tiresias, women enjoy sex nine times as much as men.[16] What is more, it went against Philo's own construction of gender that saw women as associated especially with the senses, the body and sexuality.[17] The passions, Philo explains elsewhere, are by nature feminine (θήλεα δὲ φύσει τὰ πάθη), and we must practice quitting these and adopt masculine characteristics instead (*Pot.* 28).

The Jewish custom of circumcising only men thus appears to force Philo to turn his own gender construction on its head and go against the accepted view of masculine sexuality. Having made this exceptional move, Philo is then able to continue his argument by returning to the familiar ideal that men be in control of their physical desire:

> Therefore the circumcision of the skin is said to be a symbol, but as one indicating that it is proper to cut away all superfluous and extravagant desires (Philo, *Quaest. Gen.* 3.48).

It is true, as Frederick Hodges notes, that there is a wide gulf between Philo's understanding of circumcision and that of his contemporaries. According to Hodges, 'considering the antithetical nature of the Hebrews' concept that morality could be surgically engineered, it is immediately apparent why the Greeks would have viewed the circumcision of children… and the circumcised penis with antipathy' (Hodges 2001: 387-88). Yet as we have seen in the instructions given to nurses by Soranus, manipulating a boy's genitals to conform to an ideal was not an unknown concept. More importantly, Philo's moral objectives of continence and male self-control were not dissimilar to those we can assume Soranus and his contemporaries to have had, even if the idea of obtaining them through surgical means would have been foreign.

15.   Shaye Cohen notes that 'Philo here reverses the paradigm that dominates premodern western discourse on sexuality, namely, that women are more sexual, and less self-controlled and morally centered, than men' (Cohen 2005: 145).

16.   Ovid, *Metam.* 3.316-38. As Marguerite Johnson and Terry Ryan observe, 'Ironically, men were able to enjoy a variety of sexual activities within a range of culturally ordained environments and with socially specified partners, but women were regarded as more wanton' (Johnson and Ryan 2005: 3). On the licentiousness of women as a commonplace in Latin literature, see Vioque 2002: 214.

17.   Philo's understanding that the highest state, in which a person is asexual, like God, as achieved by becoming male, or by becoming a virgin, has, according to Dorothy Sly, the 'obvious implication' that the only inescapably sexual person is a woman (Sly 1990: 99). For the female as associated with the senses and the passions in Philo, see, e.g., *Cher.* 50; *Leg. All.* 3.49; *Ebr.* 54-59.

The Male, his Glans and his Heart

A second passage that shows how his understanding of masculinity informs Philo's defence of circumcision can be found in his other major discussion of it. In *Spec. leg.* 1.1-11, Philo makes four arguments for the practice of circumcision. The first two and the last seem straightforwardly physical: circumcision should take place to avoid disease, for the sake of cleanliness, and most of all, for the sake of potency and efficacy in expressing sperm and therefore having children. The third point in the series, however, contains what at first appears to be a less straightforward argument, an analogy from penis to heart:

> Thirdly, there is the resemblance of the part that is circumcised to the heart; for both parts are prepared for the sake of generation; for the breath contained within the heart is generative of thoughts, and the generative organ itself is productive of living beings. Therefore, the men of old thought it right to make the evident and visible organ, by which the objects of the outward senses are generated, resemble that invisible and superior part, by means of which ideas are formed (Philo, *Spec. leg.* 1.6).

As John Barclay notes, although Philo here makes no explicit mention of the passage, behind this third argument clearly sit the various biblical exhortations to 'circumcise your heart' or that God will 'circumcise' the hearts of believers (Deut. 10.16; 30.6; Jer. 4.3-4) (Barclay 1998: 539). With such passages in mind, it is tempting to see in this instance a break in Philo's entirely straightforward arguments in *De specialibus legibus* to explain and to justify the practice of circumcision. Far from providing a justification for no longer practicing physical circumcision, as it does for Paul, as we will see, universalizing and spiritualizing the act of circumcision for Philo creates an additional and compelling reason for the actual physical practice of circumcision. The circumcision of the heart, once accomplished, demands the taking away of the foreskin, for how else can the correspondence of material to deeper reality be expressed but in the agreement of the former to the latter?

The analogy of heart to glans is carried forward by Philo in two ways: both are generative organs, the heart giving birth to thought through the expression of breath, and the penis to human life through the expression of sperm. As if as a physical confirmation of this generative capacity, the heart looks like the end of the male penis, the glans, or as Philo puts it, 'the part that is circumcised'. There is thus no reason to think that in a series of four related arguments for circumcision in which all other elements are physical and not metaphorical, this one argument should stand out as only metaphor.[18] However, as interesting and as exegetically important as the proper

18.   Shaye Cohen also notes that this third argument should be physical, but then wonders whether it is only a question of the resemblance for Philo (Cohen 2005: 62). This

understanding of this passage may be, for our purposes the payoff of the connection between the exposed glans and the physical heart is in what it says about masculinity and in how it connects that masculinity to the act of removing the foreskin in circumcision.

We can imagine the underlying syllogism to be that if the heart is the seat of rationality, and rationality is a fundamental characteristic of ancient masculinity, then the heart is a male organ. That the fundamental correspondence between the physical heart and the exposed glans is supported in addition by a clear physical resemblance between the two simply underlines what is already proven: taking away the foreskin, for Philo, allows the male to be more purely male, that is, more purely a creature of rational thought.

In summary, the length of a foreskin may have represented an insurmountable distance between the ideal male bodies of Rome and Jerusalem, but above the belt the two visions of masculinity overlapped significantly. First-century non-Jewish Greco-Romans saw circumcision as bizarre and even offensive, but as an apologist Philo can make the point that circumcision arises out of piety and leads to modesty knowing that these masculine values will find general acceptance.

Precisely those traits that for Greco-Romans required the covering of the glans by the foreskin—modesty, self-control, and restraint—reinforced the commandment to circumcise according to Philo. While Jews saw the public exposure of penis and testes as offensive and inappropriate, the idea of exposing one's glans permanently by removing the foreskin struck Greco-Romans as forcing oneself into a permanently over-sexed and lewd display (Satlow 1997: 453).[19] In other words, the core values expected of males were the same, despite the diametrically opposed physical ways in which the communities sought to engender and to reinforce those values. Each group's standards for judgment were remarkably similar. Yet each could and did accuse the other of moral depravation.

4. *Paul's Mangled Masculinity*

As we have shown, despite their radical differences concerning the fate of the foreskin, first-century Jews and contemporary Greco-Romans shared similar ideals of masculinity. It required, then, a particular sort of genius, at least of message and person, to manage to offend both points of view at once. Insofar as we can tell from his letters, Paul appears to have done just

seems unlikely given Philo's evident knowledge of and appreciation for the passages from Deuteronomy and Jeremiah. It makes much more sense to see here a chance for Philo to link spiritual and material in a way that supports both his philosophical and his religious commitments at the same time.

19. '[For Jews] Male nakedness is an offense to the sacred' (Satlow 1997: 453).

this. We need not verify the riots reported by Acts to confirm Paul's offen-siveness, since he himself tells us often enough. In any case, the charge reported in Acts (Acts 21.21) that he was teaching Jews who 'live among the gentiles' not to circumcise their sons, whether or not it was literally true, certainly seems a reasonable inference from Paul's spiritualization of circumcision in Romans (Rom. 2.25-29) and his extended polemic against the circumcision of male gentile converts in Galatians. If the essence of Jewish manhood is expressed in the act of circumcision, Paul's challenge to the latter inevitably would have been understood as an affront to the former.

Circumcision in the End-Time

Paul was hardly the first Jew to attempt to universalize and spiritualize circumcision. Although Boyarin maintains that Paul's Hellenism was the determinative reason for his new spiritual view of circumcision, such a view seems unnecessary (Boyarin 1994: 25-29, 69-81, 86-97). After all, steps toward such spiritualization can be found already in passages from Jeremiah and Deuteronomy.

More likely the spur comes from Paul's eschatological vision. Circumci-sion for Paul is part of the previous package of ways in which God defined his people. Now that the messiah has come, the gates have been opened and non-Jews are welcomed in, not as converts, but precisely as they are: uncircumcised gentiles, whose foreskins may be intact but whose 'hearts have been circumcised'.[20] Thus the substantive difference between Paul and other Jewish Jesus-believers, at least according to Galatians and Romans, is not circumcision, which in other passages Paul seems quite proud to claim as his own state (Phil. 3.3, 5). What is at issue is what circumcision repre-sents, and what holding to its importance signifies now that the messiah has come, that is, circumcision within the larger question of what the arrival of the messiah means for Torah. In answer, Paul's opinion is clearly eschatological: 'neither circumcision nor uncircumcision is anything; but a new creation is everything!' (Gal. 6.15).

Paul, like Philo, was concerned with the importance of circumcision in relations between Jews and non-Jews, but Paul goes much further in chang-ing the basic definitions by which the debate is framed. Although both Paul and Philo engage in exegesis that can spiritualize circumcision, where they part company is in the final importance of the physical act. As Barclay notes,

20. Rom. 2.28-29. See Barclay 1998: 545. Nina Livesey agrees that Paul bases his view of gentile circumcision on the idea of the ingathering of the nations at the end time (Livesey 2010: 91-92); Paula Fredriksen argues that even though circumcision is not addressed explicitly in traditions about gentile inclusion, most sources seem to expect that gentiles will be accepted by God as gentiles (Fredriksen 1991: 547).

'social commitments...control Philo's use of allegory' (Barclay 1998: 542).[21] For Paul, God's act in the resurrection of Christ trumps all existing social commitments. In the conclusion of his discussion of circumcision in Romans, he has redefined the very notion of being a Jew: 'rather a person is a Jew who is one inwardly, and real circumcision is a matter of the heart' (Rom. 2.29). Thus among those individual and community aspects of daily life transformed by the new age, circumcision and its inevitable partner, masculinity, were of special importance to Paul.

Paul was faced with the unenviable task of trying to put into actual social practice an eschatological ideal of a community where Jews and gentiles worshiped and lived together in harmony. In doing so, outside his own small groups (and even there with difficulty) he gained none of the community status or respect that characterized the Jewish male ideal. Perhaps he identifies in more than a pastoral way with his congregation when he writes at the end of his reframing of identity that 'such a person receives praise not from others, but from God' (Rom. 2.29).

The Crucifixion of Masculinity

If Paul offended pious Jewish ideals of masculinity by spiritualizing and perhaps even implicitly abolishing circumcision, the ways in which he failed to live up to Greco-Roman forms of masculinity are every bit as clear. Whereas with other Jews it was Paul's eschatological views and his resulting insistence on the welcome of non-Jews into Israel in their natural physical state that brought judgment and conflict, with other Greco-Romans the problem was the subject of Paul's message: not only a circumcised but a deeply humiliated divine saviour. 'For I decided to know nothing among you except Jesus Christ, and him crucified', Paul writes in 1 Cor. 2.2. The problem for masculinity was that this Jesus, portrayed as crucified, embodied the opposite of the power, presence and control of others that so defined maleness:

> According to the conceptualizations of masculinity prevalent in the Roman textual tradition, a real man is in control of his own desires, fears, and passions, and he exercises dominion over others and their bodies. An effeminate man cedes control and is dominated, whether by his own desires and fears or by others' bodies—and those bodies may be male or female (Williams 2010: 170).

21. However, by contrasting Philo with Paul on this point, Barclay gives the impression that Paul had no such social commitments. In fact, Paul's social commitments to his mixed, eschatological communities were precisely what were at issue when it came to circumcision, since to circumcise gentiles would be to deny the reality of the new age.

Much can and has been said about the crucified Christ as the opposite of contemporary ideals of maleness.[22] If one is already confronted with the emasculated body of the crucified divine saviour, the foreskin may lose its relevance in terms of masculinity. Crucifixion is embodied domination, and the victim is neutered or 'feminized' by being rendered powerless in as brutal, physical, and obvious a fashion as possible (Osiek and Pouya 2010: 45). 'The connection between gender and an individual's lack of control over his or her person was summed up by Clement of Alexandria (*Paed.* 3.19.2): "to do (τὸ δρᾶν) is the mark of the man; to suffer (τὸ πάσχειν) is the mark of the woman"' (Larson 2004: 94).

Rather than attempt to deny this emasculation of Jesus, there is a kind of deconstruction of conventional masculinity implicit in Paul's description of himself, his message, and his messiah. For Paul, even at the extreme of powerlessness on the cross, Christ is still somehow the power of God (1 Cor. 1.24), through a series of textual oppositions that reverse normal human definitions of power and wisdom. Not only does Paul make this connection of Jesus' fate to the validity of cultural definitions of maleness, but through the process of imitation, Paul links this radical anti-masculinity of Jesus to his own fortunes, and the activities of those in his congregations. Jesus-followers are to imitate Paul, who imitates Christ. The reverse is not spelled out, but is nonetheless equally in effect: as the crucified Christ is radically powerless (disempowered and therefore emasculated) so is Paul and will be those who imitate him.

It is a difficult argument that Paul does not manage to employ consistently. It is somewhat ironic that to put it forward Paul so often uses the advantage-seeking language and techniques that conventional masculinity requires. Sarcasm, shaming, and threats (1 Cor. 4.21) operate best in the arena where masculinity is not a biological given but a hard-won and hardly-maintained social privilege. Whatever he might say about imitating a dominated Jesus on the cross, Paul's own rhetoric seeks to dominate his opponents (Larson 2004: 94; Osiek and Pouya 2010: 45).

One of the ways Paul does this is by tapping into the general cultural hostility to circumcision we have noted above. It is striking that he participates in the common Greco-Roman trope of circumcision as genital mutilation. In Galatians he taunts his opponents: 'I wish those agitators would castrate themselves' (ὄφελον καὶ ἀποκόψονται οἱ ἀναστατοῦντες ὑμᾶς, Gal. 5.12). In Philippians he warns his audience: 'Watch out for those dogs, watch out for those evil workers, watch out for the mutilation' (Βλέπετε τοὺς κύνας, βλέπετε τοὺς κακοὺς ἐργάτας, βλέπετε τὴν κατατομήν, Phil. 3.2).

22. Beginning with Paul himself in 1 Corinthians. See among others Larson 2004: 85-97; Conway 2008; Osiek and Pouya 2010.

While Philo tries to combat the public ridicule of circumcision, Paul actually uses such tactics. Paul ricochets between the stock assertions of both Jews and Romans, first claiming circumcision as a prized term for those who belong to God and then equating the practice with mutilation. In this light it is not surprising that it is difficult to reconstruct a consistent view of masculinity in Paul: he seems to want to have his foreskin and cut it too.

The Foreskin of the Moment

A closer look at Paul's terminology confirms his double perspective. While he divides the world, as others did, into those who are circumcised and those who are not, he does so in an unconventional way. Apart from the division into ᾽Ιουδαῖοι, 'Jews', and (ἡ) περιτομή, '(the) circumcision', on the one hand, and ῞Ελληνες, 'Greeks', and τὰ ἔθνη, 'the nations', or 'gentiles', on the other, Paul also uses the term (ἡ) ἀκροβυστία, 'the foreskin', for the latter group. The words that Greeks generally used for foreskin could be *posthe* or *posthia* (πόσθη or ποσθία), or more commonly *akroposthia* (ἀκροποσθία, Latin *praeputium*). *Akrobustia* occurs many times in the LXX, as well as in Philo and the books of the Maccabees, but does not appear to have been used by non-Jewish authors.[23] While the occurrence of the term is thus not unusual in a Jewish text, Paul's particular use of it appears to be unique. Apart from Paul, *akrobustia* does not seem to be used as shorthand for those people who are not circumcised (as Paul uses it in Rom. 2.27; 3.30; 4.9, 11; Gal. 2.7).[24] It rather refers to the literal body part, often in combination, as in the 'flesh of the foreskin' (ἡ σάρκα τῆς ἀκροβυστίας, e.g., Gen. 17.11, 14; 34.24; Jdt. 14.10). In the LXX, people who are uncircumcised are called *aperitmetos* (ἀπερίτμητος, e.g., Gen 17.14; Exod. 12.48; Judg. 14.3; 15.18; Josh. 5.7; Isa. 52.1).

Translations of Paul usually disguise his exceptional use of this term, because they not only hide the physicality and masculinity of the word, translating it as 'uncircumcised' or even 'gentile', but they also obscure the fact that Paul is doing something new here. In phrasing the opposition not in terms of circumcision–uncircumcision, but rather in terms of circumcision–foreskin, Paul retains a Jewish perspective, but seems to show awareness of

---

23. See ἀκροβυστία, *TDNT*, II, 225.

24. Few commentators make any special note of the term and many assume that Paul is following convention. Hillary Le Cornu and Joseph Shulam, for example, claim that *akrobustia* is a 'terminus technicus', for gentiles, but refer to LXX passages that only contain the word ἀπερίτμητος (Le Cornu and Shulam 2005: 106). Joel Marcus also notes the rarity of the term ἀκροβυστία but assumes that it was used by Jewish Christians in Rome as a pejorative term, who called themselves 'the circumcision' (Marcus 1989). However, the fact that Paul also uses the term in Galatians and 1 Corinthians seems to indicate that it is part of Paul's vocabulary rather than that of others.

the foreskin as a positive concept, more in line with Greco-Roman self-perception. Paul thus not only echoes the general hostility towards circumcision, in his scathing remarks about those who advocate it for gentiles. Even more in line with contemporary Greco-Roman appreciation of the male anatomy, he reconfigures the conventional Jewish nomenclature for Jews and non-Jews, reflecting the importance in the value of the foreskin.

Conclusion

It should come as no surprise that ancient constructions of masculinity can be seen to have an impact on attitudes towards male circumcision. The connection between ideals of male behaviour, the male body, and the ideal, or even acceptable, physical appearance of male genitals may seem self-evident. Yet little attention has been given to these connections in studies of circumcision, nor does there appear to be much awareness of these links in the modern debate.

To be sure, as the present study has shown, there is no straightforward line from a particular conception of masculinity to a particular attitude towards the foreskin. The ideal of masculinity as dominance of self and others shared by Philo and his Greco-Roman contemporaries leads to very different valuations of circumcision. The example of Paul shows how difficult it was to find common ground without a consistent engagement with these shared values. One of the contributions of the present study is to suggest that perhaps also in today's debates about circumcision, much may be gained by examining the constructions of masculinity underlying opposing points of view.

Bibliography

Barclay, J.M.G.
	1998	'Paul and Philo on Circumcision: Romans 2.25–9 in Social and Cultural Context', *NTS* 44: 536-56.
Barrett, D.S.
	1984	'Martial, Jews and Circumcision', *Liverpool Classical Monthly* 9/3: 42-46.
Blaschke, A.
	1998	*Beschneidung: Zeugnisse der Bibel und verwandter Texte* (Tübingen: Francke Verlag).
Blondell, R.
	1999	*Women on the Edge: Four Plays by Euripides: Alcestis, Medea, Helen, Iphigenia at Aulis* (New York: Routledge).
Boyarin, D.
	1994	*A Radical Jew: Paul and the Politics of Identity* (Berkeley: University of California Press).

Cohen, S.
    2005   *Why Aren't Jewish Women Circumcised? Gender and Covenant in Judaism* (Berkeley: University of California Press).

Conway, C.M.
    2003   'Gender and Divine Relativity in Philo of Alexandria', *JSJ* 34: 471-91.
    2008   *Behold the Man: Jesus and Greco-Roman Masculinity* (Oxford: Oxford University Press).

Feldman, L.H.
    1993   *Jew and Gentile in the Ancient World: Attitudes and Interactions from Alexander to Justinian* (Princeton, NJ: Princeton University Press).

Fredriksen, P.
    1991   'Judaism, the Circumcision of Gentiles and Apocalyptic Hope: Another Look at Galatians 1 and 2', *JTS* 42: 532-64.

Gleason, M.W.
    1995   *Making Men: Sophists and Self-Presentation in Ancient Rome* (Princeton, NJ: Princeton University Press).

Hall, E.
    1989   *Inventing the Barbarian: Greek Self-Definition through Tragedy* (Oxford: Clarendon Press).

Hallett, C.H.
    2005   *The Roman Nude: Heroic Portrait Statuary 200 BC–AD 300* (Oxford: Oxford University Press).

Hodges, F.M.
    2001   'The Ideal Prepuce in Ancient Greece and Rome: Male Genital Aesthetics and their Relation to Lipodermos, Circumcision, Foreskin Restoration, and the Kynodesme', *BHM* 75: 375-405.

Johnson, M., and T. Ryan
    2005   *Sexuality in Greek and Roman Society and Literature: A Sourcebook* (London: Routledge).

Larson, J.
    2004   'Paul's Masculinity', *JBL* 123: 85-97.

Le Cornu, Hillary, and Joseph Shulam
    2005   *A Commentary on the Jewish Roots of Galatians* (Jerusalem: Academon).

Livesey, N.E.
    2010   *Circumcision as a Malleable Symbol* (Tübingen: Mohr Siebeck).

MacKay, H.A.
    1994   *Sabbath and Synagogue: The Question of Sabbath Worship in Ancient Judaism* (Leiden: E.J. Brill).

Marcus, J.
    1989   'The Circumcision and the Uncircumcision in Rome', *NTS* 35: 67-81.

Mattila, S.L.
    1996   'Wisdom, Sense Perception, Nature, and Philo's Gender Gradient', *HTR* 89: 103-29.

Moore, S.D., and J. Capel Anderson
    1998   'Taking It like a Man: Masculinity in 4 Maccabees', *JBL* 117: 249-73.

Niehoff, M.R.
    2003   'Circumcision as a Marker of Identity: Philo, Origen and the Rabbis on Gen 17: 1-14', *JSQ* 10: 89-123.

Osiek, C., and Jennifer Pouya
  2010   'Constructions of Gender in the Roman Imperial World', in R.E. DeMaris
            and D. Neufeld (eds.), *Understanding the Social World of the New
            Testament* (London: Routledge): 44-56.
Rosen, R.M., and I. Sluiter
  2003   *Andreia: Studies in Manliness and Courage in Classical Antiquity*
            (Leiden: E.J. Brill).
Rosivach, V.J.
  1999   'Enslaving "Barbaroi" and the Athenian Ideology of Slavery', *Historia:
            Zeitschrift für Alte Geschichte* 48: 129-57.
Satlow, M.L.
  1997   'Jewish Constructions of Nakedness in Late Antiquity', *JBL* 116: 429-54.
Schmidt, T.S.
  1999   *Plutarque et les Barbares: La Rhétorique d'une Image* (Louvain: Peeters).
Sly, D.
  1990   *Philo's Perception of Women* (Atlanta: Scholars Press).
Soranus
  1991   *Soranus' Gynecology* (trans. with an introductio by Owsei Temkin;
            Baltimore: The Johns Hopkins University Press).
Späth, T.
  2012   'Masculinity and Gender Performance in Tacitus', in Victoria Emma
            Pagán (ed.), *A Companion to Tacitus* (Malden: Wiley-Blackwell): 431-57.
Stern, M.
  1974   *Greek and Latin Authors on Jews and Judaism* (Jerusalem: Israel
            Academy of Sciences and Humanities).
Tacitus
  1997   *The Histories* (trans. W.H. Fyfe; rev. and ed. D.S. Levene; Oxford: Oxford
            University Press).
Vioque, G.G.
  2002   *Martial, Book VII: A Commentary by Guillermo Galán Vioque* (Leiden:
            E.J. Brill).
Williams, C.A.
  2010   *Roman Homosexuality* (Oxford: Oxford University Press).

THECLA'S MASCULINITY
IN THE *ACTS OF (PAUL AND) THECLA*

Peter-Ben Smit

Introduction

This study traces the development of the early Christian woman Thecla of Iconium, with specific attention to her 'cross-dressing', or, rather, her change from a woman to a man. In doing so, it addresses the question of the significance of this development in Thecla's gender in the *Acts of (Paul and) Thecla*.

The *Acts of Thecla* is part of the larger corpus of the *Acts of Paul*,[1] and it ought to be dated between the middle to the end of the second century.[2] The *Acts of Thecla* has likely existed as a separate document[3] and shows traces of its own history of redaction.[4] The book probably had a broad reception among women and men in antiquity.[5] It consists of an account of the effect of Paul's preaching on a young woman, Thecla, who, in a radical way, becomes a disciple of Paul and Christ. The narrative uses a variety of motifs

1. For the text, see Rohrdorf 1997; Barrier 2010; Esch-Wermeling 2008: 311-25; parts of this paper were also published in German as 'Theologie nach dem Cultural Turn: Gender Studies am Beispiel der Theklaakten', *Salzburger Theologische Zeitschrift* 16 (2013), and are reproduced here with permission of the publisher.
2. For the dating, see Esch-Wermeling 2008: 13-15.
3. See Esch-Wermeling 2008: 13-15, and especially Geerard 1992: 119-22
4. For an overview and a largely convincing proposal, see Esch-Wermeling 2008: 71-148; the question of the development of the *Acts of Thecla* will not be of primary interest here, given that also the 'final form' of the *Acts of Thecla* should be able to make sense (on this, see also Esch-Wermeling 2008: 189-204).
5. See especially Davis 2001: 12-18, and *passim*. About the readership and the history of reception, see also, for example, Barrier 2010: 12-21, 25-30, 47-62, as well as Davies 1980: 40-96, who proposes communities of ascetic women as the original readership. See further also Johnson 2006. A more recent chapter in the history of reception of the *Acts of Thecla* is their role in the discussion about the ordination of women, for example in Orthodox theology, for which see, for example, Dunn 2010. Feminist scholarship has, naturally, had a longer interest in the *Acts of Thecla*. For a (critical) overview, see, for example, Ng 2004, and further Matthews 2001, as well as Barrier 2010: 45-47.

and strategies from Greco-Roman (romantic) novels and early Christian martyr acts. These motifs are used in the service of the book's own theological and literary interests,[6] specifically the promotion of an ascetic ideal in contrast to the ideal of marriage promoted by the Greco-Roman novels.[7]

A particularly interesting aspect of the development of the character Thecla in the course of the narrative is her 'masculinization' as part of her acceptance and embodiment of the Gospel and its values. Thecla concludes her narrative 'career' as an independent apostle. In this way, the *Acts of Thecla* may well constitute part of the history of reception of the theology of Paul that complements (and contradicts) that of the Pastoral Epistles.[8] This fact also leads to a paradox, at least for modern readers: the 'anti-sexual' *Acts of Thecla* promote the authority of a (paradigmatic) early Christian woman, while the 'family-oriented' Pastoral Epistles seek to subordinate women. In this study, however, the question that will be pursued is that of the construction, meaning, and role of Thecla's masculinity in the *Acts of Thecla*. Before turning to this question, however, something ought to be said first about 'hegemonic' or 'conventional' masculinity at the time the *Acts of Thecla* was written.

Masculinity in the Greco-Roman World and in Early Christian Martyr Acts

Even though various overviews of the characteristics of 'hegemonic' masculinity are available, the one provided by Mayordomo is particularly helpful.[9] He mentions the following seven aspects of hegemonic masculinity: (1) The conventional Greco-Roman view of gender, sex, and body was that in reality only a 'monosexual' body existed that could manifest itself as (more) masculine or (more) feminine through genitals that had either grown outwardly or inwardly. (2) Masculinity was not necessarily a fact determined by the body with which one was born, but needed to be proved constantly in the public arena, through one's appearance, behavior, and

---

6. For an overview, see, for example, Esch-Wermeling 2008: 97-136.

7. For an overview, see, for example, Barrier 2010: 1-10; Corrington Streete 2009: 76-77; Brown 1988: 156, puts it as follows: 'The Christian authors of the Apocryphal Acts had only to replace a manifest destiny to the wedding bed, with which every pagan novel had ended, with the Apostle's call to continence'. See also Lipsett 2010: 57-64, as well as the analysis of Aubin 1998 and Burrus 2005.

8. For this, see, for example, Esch-Wermeling 2008: 32-70. Barrier 2010: 31-45, however, is skeptical.

9. See Smit 2012; Mayordomo 2006, and further Leutzsch 2004; Moxnes 2007; Ivarsson 2008, and the literature referred to there.

performance. Everyone (male or female) could constantly become more or less masculine. (3) Masculinity was very closely bound up with the notions of activity and dominance; as Mayordomo puts it: 'Being a man in antiquity was very closely linked to the role of being an active agent rather than passive. Be it in politics, in sports, in war, in rhetoric or in the vast field of sexuality, what qualified an individual as a *man* was his active control of the situation.'[10] (4) Masculinity and being virtuous were closely intertwined, specifically through the cardinal virtue of ἀνδρεία and through the virtues in general (*virtutes*). (5) Self-control was an essential part of the afore-mentioned dominance: 'The most active agent would be a man who controls himself with respect to anger and all other forms of passions, especially those associated with sexuality'.[11] (6) This state of affairs also meant that, *sensu stricto*, no one was really born a man, but that even a boy needed to be educated and trained to be a proper man. (7) Finally, it should be noted that masculinity and femininity were both associated with respective social spaces, that is, outside and inside—or public and private.

These seven characteristics cover central aspects of conventional Greco-Roman masculinity. Given the literary character of the *Acts of Thecla*, however, something should be added here about masculinity in early Christian martyr acts and (other) ascetic texts. As has been remarked repeatedly in research on such texts, one of the most common ways of indicating progress or even perfection of (female) ascetics was to say that they had achieved ἀνδρεία, that is, masculinity.[12] This finding corrects the view that that early Christian ascetical literature promoted an asexual ideal; this does not seem to have been the case—rather, a change of sex was in view for both men and women, given that both that needed to become masculine, that is, attain ἀνδρεία.[13] This also means that there are close connections between ἀνδρεία/*virtus* (virile), spiritual strength, active behavior, goodness, and honor. While these features were to a limited extent tied to biologically male bodies,[14] that is to say, someone with a male body had an advantage vis-à-vis someone without such a body, this connection was anything but absolute.[15] Early Christian (and many other) texts question and undermine this connection: true ἀνδρεία can also be a characteristic of people with 'feminine' bodies (i.e. women, 'weak' men, such as old men or slaves). Typically the

10. Mayordomo 2006: 7.
11. Mayordomo 2006: 8.
12. See, for example, Aspegren 1990; Corrington Streete 2006, 2009.
13. Against, for example, Müller 2011: 155-56; see also the convincing account of Cobb 2008.
14. See Stefaniw 2010: 345.
15. See, for example, Mayordomo 2006.

embodiment of masculinity does not always lead to a change in the bodily characteristics of the protagonists involved, even though Thecla strives to achieve that.[16] 'Christianity' is in these texts presented as a road towards masculinity and redemption that is accessible to those with 'unmanly' bodies.

Thecla's Journey Towards Masculinity

Thecla develops gradually into a masculine character in the *Acts of Thecla*. This applies both to her appearance and to her role.[17] Given this development, she is in every respect a 'round character' that is increasingly initiated into her new identity as a follower of Christ and, accordingly, develops into a more and more active actor, from where she starts out as a disciple of Paul. This development has, of course, been noted by others as well; here, the change will be reviewed in greater detail from the perspective of the conventional Greco-Roman view of masculinity outlined above.

First, it is of importance to consider the first phase of Thecla's development, helpfully called 'physiotherapy' by Braun.[18] This first phase can, quite literally, be characterized as 'emancipation': Thecla emancipates herself from a number of relationships that are all characterized by the authority that others exert over her or at least carry an expectation that she will fulfil a particular social role.[19] Thecla starts out as a παρθένος,[20] that is, as a young unmarried woman (and hence also as a physically intact virgin), who is under the authority of her parents—in Thecla's case only of her mother Theocleia, her father does not play a role in the narrative at all—and who is destined for marriage and a life as matron. Thecla breaks off these various relationships when she, sitting in a window, hears a programmatic sermon of Paul in the neighboring house of Onesiphorus, where Paul stays during his visit to the city of Iconium, the setting of the first part of the narrative. The

---

16. See, for example, Stefaniw 2010 for an account of the ambivalence of the bodies of 'manly women'. Such ambivalence also applies to the bodies of other persons with 'weak bodies', such as Polycarp who is an old and hence presumably 'weak' man, but who nevertheless displays surprising masculinity (see, e.g., *Mart. Pol.* 9.1 and further 7.2; 9.2). Male adversaries are generally depicted as lacking in masculinity in these texts—Davis's remark that the 'devaluing of men' is not characteristic for literature from antiquity (2001: 10) is hence beside the point.

17. For a contribution that emphasizes the development of Thecla in the *Acts of Thecla*, see, for example, Braun 2000.

18. See Braun 2000.

19. See, for example, Braun 2000: 213.

20. As it is rightly emphasized by Misset-van de Weg 1998: 235.

sermon consists of the following beatitudes and constitutes a proclamation of the 'word of God concerning self-control and Resurrection':[21]

> Blessed are the pure in heart, for they shall see God.
>
> Blessed are those who have kept the flesh chaste, for they will be a temple of God.
>
> Blessed are the self-controlled, for God will speak to them.
>
> Blessed are they who are set apart from this world, for they will be well pleasing to God.
>
> Blessed are they who, though having a wife, are as those not having a wife, for they will inherit God.
>
> Blessed are they who have a fear of God, for they will be angels of God.
>
> Blessed are those who tremble over the words of the Lord, for they shall be comforted.
>
> Blessed are those who receive the wisdom of Jesus Christ, for they shall be called sons of the most high.
>
> Blessed are those who have kept their baptism, for they shall be refreshed by the Father and the Son.
>
> Blessed are those who have taken hold of the knowledge of Jesus Christ, for they shall be in the light.
>
> Blessed are they who have come out of the image of this world through the love of God, for they will judge angels, and they will be blessed on the right hand of God and will not see a bitter day of judgment.
>
> Blessed are the bodies of the virgins, for they shall be well pleasing to God and they will not lose the rewards of their purity, because the word of the father shall be to them a work of salvation in the day of his son, and they shall have rest forever (3.5-6).

The final macarism that refers explicitly to the bodies of 'virgins' constitutes an immediate intertextual connection with the previous description of Thecla as παρθένος. In this way, she becomes a direct addressee of the sermon of Paul.[22] Misset-van de Weg's observation concerning this is apt: the final macarism 'creates a certain amount of suspense: will she or won't she? Will she be a modest παρθένος who will soon be a wife or a chaste παρθένος as is evoked in the beatitudes?'[23] In this context, it is also worth remarking that

---

21. The translation is from Barrier 2010: 78. This and all subsequent translated quotations from the *Acts of Thecla* are taken from Barrier's translation and referred to by chapter and verse.

22. See also Ebner 2005, who, on the one hand, remarks that the macarisms are aimed at men in the first place, and, on the other hand, states the following 'Was die Makarismenreihe für Männer reklamiert, wird in den Theklaakten für Frauen adaptiert: Obwohl die Reihe eigentlich Männer anspricht, bezieht Thekla die Makarismen...sofort auf sich' ('All the things that the series of macarisms claims for men, are adapted for women in the Acts of Thecla: even though the series is aimed at men, Thekla immediately applies them to herself'; Ebner 2005: 73).

23. Misset-van de Weg 1998: 237, as well as Davis 2001: 20.

Thecla's place in a window seat does not only explain practically why she, whose place is inside the house, can hear Paul (who is in another house), albeit without seeing him, but her position in the window seat also serves narratively to express the refocusing of Thecla (away from her family and her fiancé and towards Paul),[24] while this position of Thecla also places her precisely at a spot that is at the threshold of 'inside' and 'outside'. This position fully agrees with what may be called the 'liminal' phase of the development of Thecla's identity that now begins. The question that is raised for the reader by this positioning of Thecla is: will she opt for 'inside' or 'outside', for the values of Paul or conventional social values?[25]

When Thecla hears Paul's proclamation about purity (ἀγνεία; this word can also connote autarky, i.e. active self-control and self-sufficiency, rather than passive and defensive purity), she is unable to stop listening.[26] She desires,[27] showing all signs of lovesickness,[28] a chaste life for herself. Paradoxically, Paul's sermon does indeed seduce Thecla, but to an ascetic life,[29] as that is the life to which her new—ascetic—passion (πάθος, e.g. 3.9) will lead her. That this development leads to considerable unrest immediately becomes clear from the reactions of Theocleia, Thecla's mother, from Thamyris, her fiancé (and a prominent inhabitant of the city of Iconium), and from the servant girls in Thecla's House in 3.10:

> And those in the house were weeping bitterly, Thamyris, for the loss of a wife; Theocleia, (for the loss) of a child, but the female slaves (for the loss) of a mistress.

24. See Misset-van de Weg 1998: 237.

25. See further below on liminality. Thecla's position between two worlds or two identities has a relatively long duration, as Misset-van de Weg remarks (1998: 238). However, at this point in the narrative, it goes too far to say that '[Thecla is] already detached from her family and permanently attached to the apostle and his words' (p. 238). That Thecla's seduction by Paul's message is definitive and that Thecla will remain steadfast will only become clear at the end of the story.

26. Therefore, it is not a case of 'love at first sight', given that Thecla cannot see Paul. See for a different position: Park 2004: 219. See on this issue also Esch-Wermeling 2008: 112-13, 253-54.

27. For emphasis on the desire, see especially Lipsett 2010: 55. Lipsett summarizes the paradox aptly: 'she [Thecla] is smitten with a preacher of ἐγκράτεια and sexual renunciation' (p. 55). Sexual desire is probably absent from this scene (for a different view, see, for example, Barrier 2010: 88).

28. See Bremmer 1996: 41-42; Barrier 2010: 90; and Corrington Streete 2009: 82.

29. On the erotic elements in the *Acts of Thecla*—a motif borrowed from Hellenistic novels—see, for example, Aspegren 1990: 105-107. The idea, uttered by the crowd in 3.15 that Paul has gained control over Thecla and other women by means of an erotic charm, makes an ironic impression. See Misset-van de Weg 1998: 238. For a further analysis of Thecla's desire here, see, for example, Lipsett 2010: 67-68.

This reaction is to the point: Thecla emancipates herself from the three roles of daughter, fiancée, and mistress.[30] When reading this in relation to the social conventions of the time, this refusal to fulfil the role of a (sexually available) woman meant the loss of a clearly identifiable social role and position and, with that, of the protection and security that such a role could provide. This development, however, also means a loss of honor for those that Thecla leaves behind.[31] This provides the background for the next development in the story. While Thecla's decision to become a disciple of Paul,[32] and, accordingly, to opt for ascetism and self-control, is connoted positively, from the perspective of Greco-Roman virtues,[33] it brings chaos and mourning in the (former) house of Thecla. Her mother and (former) fiancé are now obliged to take action. Theocleia indeed urges Thamyris to do so. As a prominent citizen (see 3.11, he is πρῶτος of the city) who sees his personal honor (and masculinity) threatened, not to mention the danger that Thecla's fledgling sexual and social deviance represents the social order of the *polis* (and hence for the *religio*),[34] Thamyris must act. Yet even he is unable to control the situation fully, as soon becomes clear from his failed attempts to get Paul executed (though he manages to incarcerate him and have him expelled from the city, 3.14-21).

During Paul's incarceration and subsequent banishment from Iconium at which time Thecla also takes center stage,[35] Thecla continues to develop in a decisive fashion: she begins to operate outside of the boundaries of the

30. See Misset-van de Weg 1998: 239, as well as McGinn 1995: 811.

31. See Barrier 2010: 95-96, and also Vorster 2006: 98-117, especially 106-108.

32. In the first part of the *Acts of Thecla*, Thecla is clearly depicted as Paul's disciple. On Paul and his disappearance from the narrative in the next section of the narrative, set in Antioch, see Esch-Wermeling 2008: 80-81, 205-11.

33. As an expression of σωφροσύνη, see Corrington Streete 2009: 75.

34. See, for example, Aspegren 1990: 100; Dunn 2010: 49-50; for her refusal to marry, Thecla is punished in the same way as other early Christians were punished for refusing to worship the emperor. See also the remarks of Wehn: 'The example of Thecla makes it clear that while ἐγκράτεια could mean an increased autonomy and sexual self-determination for women, it could also entail the loss of one's home and hence of protection, as well as the latent danger that non-Christian fiancés, husbands or men outside the family could exercise power by laying sexual claim to them' (Wehn 2000: 154). See also Vorster 2006. Park is right when noting that in the *Acts of Thecla* two value systems are contrasted with one another; see Park 2004: 215-16.

35. See also the following remark of Esch-Wermeling 2008: 21: 'Vor und nach dem Martyrium sucht Thekla die Anwesendheit ihres Mentors. Die Situation des Martyriums dagegen ist der Moment für sie, ihre Stärke und Standhaftigkeit ganz allein unter Beweis zu stellen' ('Both before and after her (near) martyrdom, Thecla looks for the presence of her mentor. The situation of her (near) martyrdom, however, becomes the moment at which she demonstrates her strength and steadfastness all on her own'). Steadfastness and strength are both masculine characteristics.

house and thus moves into a more masculine connoted space: the 'outside', that is, the public space. Thecla's visit to the prison where Paul dwells is a first expression of this new development (3.18). Her bribing of the jailer with her jewelry and her consequent parting with it is, in all likelihood, also an indication of distancing herself from a typically feminine identity and increased embodiment of a more ascetic and more masculine identity.[36] In prison, Thecla sits at Paul's feet and listens to his words—as a disciple, to be sure, not as a lover. These developments are met with very little enthusiasm in Iconium, as becomes clear from Theocleia's urging when Thecla, now apprehended, is made to appear before the city's governor: 'Burn the lawless one! Burn the one who is no bride in the midst of the theatre, in order that all the women who have been taught by this one might be afraid' (3.20). Dunn's analysis of this scene is to the point: 'In the eyes of her mother, if Thecla will not be a bride, she will not *be* at all'.[37] After Paul is flogged and exiled from the city (3.21), Thecla is condemned to the stake. In this context, Thecla looks for Paul as her shepherd 'like a lamb in the desert' and when she sees him, she thinks, 'As if I am not enduring, Paul gazes upon me' (3.21). Even so, the reader is told, Thecla does not really see Paul, but Christ in the shape of Paul. This brief scene could be meaningful in two ways. First, by Christ's appearance *in persona Pauli*, it might be indicated that not so much Paul, but Christ is the real point of orientation for Thecla. Second, Thecla's consideration with regard to endurance, a typically masculine characteristic, could also lead to a question on the part of the reader: will she endure or not?

When an attempt is made to execute Thecla (3.22), further aspects of her developing identity come to light. While she is standing in the arena all naked and while wood is brought together for the pyre, the governor is less impressed by her beauty as by the power that is in her (3.22).[38] This observation even makes the governor weep. This acknowledgment of Thecla's power by a person that is not *per se* amicably disposed towards her is an effective narrative means to express the developing identity of Thecla further.[39] Both the fact that there is power in Thecla and is acknowledged by a figure of authority depict her even more manly. As will become clear from the botched attempt to execute her in general (3.21-22), the very public space of the arena does not lead to her public shaming, but to a public demonstration of the divine favor towards and protection of Thecla.[40] In this

36. See, for example, Misset-van de Weg 1998: 240, as well as Esch-Wermeling 2008: 266-67.
37. Dunn 2010: 50; see also Davis 2001: 21.
38. See also Esch-Wermeling 2008: 267-68.
39. Bremmer 1996: 49.
40. See, for example, Misset-van de Weg 1998: 243.

context, Thecla herself creates an explicit connection between her faith in God and the upcoming execution by making a sign of the cross, thus underlining the connection between her faith, social deviance, and condemnation, before ascending the pyre all by herself.[41] As indicated, the attempt to execute her fails because of a divine intervention, which is in line with Thecla's association of her condemnation with her new faith.

The failure to execute her presumably leads to Thecla's release, even if the story does not say so explicitly. In any case, a reunion with Paul, who is dwelling near the city, praying and fasting, is the next development in the story. In this new context, Thecla proposes the following to Paul: 'I will cut my hair and follow you wherever you should go' (3.25). While the cutting of the hair, especially when it is done by a woman, can mean a variety of things, it seems plausible to interpret it in connection with Thecla's developing masculine identity. This line of thought is supported by Paul's response to Thecla's proposal: 'O, shameless time, and you are beautiful. May another trial not leave you worse than the first, and you might not endure but you might be cowardly' (3.25). While the reference to Thecla's beauty in relation to her suggestion to cut off her hair may well have to do with conventional notions of feminine beauty and femininity,[42] Paul's remark about behaving 'cowardly' refers directly to the danger of becoming unmasculine, given that he uses the verb δειλανδρέω. While the remark suggests, on the one hand, that Thecla's change of haircut would make her appear masculine, it also implies that Paul considers Thecla's behavior up-until-now as masculine, on the other hand. Moreover, Paul's remark also implies that he expects ἀνδρεία from his disciples.[43] Thecla's answer to Paul also refers to the possibility of future trials and her desire to become a person able to resist temptations, that is, a more masculine person: 'Only give to me the seal in the Lord, and no temptation will touch me' (3.25). Furthermore, Thecla's journey with Paul to Antioch introduces the next stage of the narrative. Whether Thecla cuts her hair on that journey, or whether she only expresses the intention to do so, what is clear is that, she leaves behind her a further aspect of her feminine identity and becomes

41. For the connection between the sign of the cross and victory, see, for example, Bremmer 1996: 49.

42. See, for example, Esch-Wermeling 2008: 234. Shepard Kraemer 2011: 136-38, also understands the cutting of Thecla's hair as a rejection of a conventional female role in society.

43. Esch-Wermeling 2008: 268; see also her remark on the same page: 'Die Musterschülerin des Paulus kann einem männlichen Ideal folgen und es auch erfüllen, da Männlichkeit nicht an die Kategorie des Körpers gebunden wird' ('The model pupil of Paul can follow a masculine ideal and also fulfill its demands, because masculinity is not attached to the category of the body').

more masculine because of it.[44] In fact, she adjusts her outwards appearance to her real identity: she has shown herself to be manly in a number of ways since first listening to Paul's sermon; hence, it is fitting for her to change her looks.

Arriving in Antioch, Techla, who has now literally left everything behind, faces the threat of further trials: Thecla is immediately accosted by a 'very strong' man by the name of Alexander (4.1). The accoster, to be sure, first enquires of Paul whether Thecla is his, but Paul denies this and disappears from the narrative for a long time.[45] Paul's behavior affirms the liminal and increasingly vulnerable position of Thecla. This position is also acknowledged by Thecla, when Alexander attempts to accost her: 'Do not force the stranger! Do not force the servant of God. I am a leading woman of the Iconians, and on account of my not wishing to marry Thamyris, I was cast out of the city' (4.1). Thecla, however, is able to defend herself and even tears apart the garment of this powerful Antiochian and takes hold of his head adornment, a sign of his prominent position.[46] The (supposedly) weak woman Thecla, who is on her own and a stranger at that, thus vanquishes the very masculine, socially and politically prominent Alexander on his own territory, that is, in public. The physical strength that Thecla suddenly displays may well be a further expression of her 'masculinization', which has its basis in her desire to follow Christ and live virtuous life. Her opponent Alexander, by contrast, who one would expect to be masculine in many ways due to his status and appearance, is anything but virtuous and lacks self-control, specifically with regard to his sexual desire and hence attacks a vulnerable stranger, a servant of God nonetheless.[47] He further displays little control over himself in his lust for revenge, as becomes clear during a veritable campaign of revenge that he starts.[48] This womanizes Alexander.

44. See Castelli 1982: 75-76. The relationship between steadfastness and baptism was already mentioned by Paul in his macarisms.

45. However one interprets Paul's disappearance, it is not an expression of ἀνδρεία in any case. His disappearance also fulfils an important narrative role: it clears the way for Thecla to develop herself independently. When Paul says that Thecla does not belong to him, this is, besides cowardice, also an indication of the truth: Thecla does not belong to him, but to herself (and to Christ). See Braun 2000: 213. For a different point of view, see Wehn 2006: 293. Esch-Wermeling 2008: 207-11, commenting on the narrative necessity of Paul's disappearance. On this topic, see also Ng 2004: 6.

46. See, for example, Dunn 2010: 52, for a lively description of Thecla's fight with Alexander. Barrier 2010: 141-42, also emphasizes the importance of the head adornment and its loss. See further the analysis of Kötzel 2005.

47. For example, Misset-van de Weg 1998: 245 n. 24, emphasizes the status of ξένη, which Thecla could claim, and the status of a(n ascetic) ἱερόδουλος.

48. See Esch-Wermeling 2008: 281, as well as Shepard Kraemer 2011: 141.

Quite in line with Thecla's public shaming of yet another prominent member of society, this time Alexander in Antioch (see 4.2; the other one was her former fiancé Thamyris in Iconium),[49] she has to appear before a governor again. This time the result is that she is condemned *ad bestias*.[50] The women of Antioch greet this condemnation with loud disapproval, calling it profane, that is, unholy (4.2). These women, often functioning as a 'chorus', will, in fact, support Thecla during her entire stay in Antioch.[51] Thecla also receives support in the shape of protective custody in order to avert a likely rape in prison. This protection is offered to her by Queen Tryphaena, a relative of the emperor.[52] In this way, Thecla retains her bodily integrity, which suits her identity: (literal) penetration would lead to a substantial loss of ἀνδρεία and also signify the end of her chastity.

Due to the protective custody that she receives, Thecla becomes something like a client of Queen Tryphaena, who, to be sure, also profits from prayers that Thecla offers on behalf of her deceased daughter Falconilla, who receives a spot at the place of the just thanks to this (4.3-4). The efficacy of Thecla's prayer—the prayer of a martyr, indeed[53]—also provides proof of her piety (εὐσέβεια), precisely the virtue that she does not have according to the powers that be: when Thecla is processed around in the πομπή together with the animals that she will have to face in the arena (the animals themselves are a generous donation of Alexander), a sign indicates her as ἱερόσυλος, that is, blasphemer (4.3), quite in spite of her self-identification as servant of God (4.1, see also 4.12 and 4.13) and the witness of the women of Antioch three times denounce Thecla's condemnation as impious (4.2, 3, 7, see also 4.8, 10).[54] Thecla's offense, it seems, can in this context be nothing else but her disregard for the social order and her place in it as an unmarried woman—due to her decision to become a disciple of

49. See, for example, Barrier 2010: 145; Shepard Kraemer 2011: 141-42; Esch-Wermeling 2008: 273. According to Corrington Streete 2009: 86, Thecla unmans Alexander.

50. Compare Dunn 2010: 52: 'This act (sc. of humiliating Alexander) is more than a personal offense to an important Antiochene, but it is an attack on the very power structures that authorize his violence against her'.

51. To be sure, not all women are depicted positively and all men negatively in the *Acts of Thecla*. See Jensen 2001: 83.

52. On the topic of the rape of women prisoners and/or their sentencing to work as prostitutes, see, for example, Jensen 1992: 185-95.

53. Rightly emphasized by Jensen 2001: 86.

54. The various comments of the women of the city that accompany many aspects of Thecla's trial are not just an expression of solidarity among women (see, for example, Dagron 1978: 37-38, and many others with him), but also associate the women with the virtues of εὐσέβεια and δικαιοσύνη.

Christ.[55] The refusal to be confined to her 'natural' roles is interpreted by the authorities as blasphemy. In the setting of the πομπή as it was just mentioned, Thecla's power and authority are further unfolded, as the following happens: 'the lioness, whom Thecla was sitting upon, was licking her feet, and all the crowd was amazed' (4.3). At the same time, Alexander continues to lose his credibility as a man: after his humiliation by Thecla, his cause is publicly opposed by the women of the city, and, when he attempts to take Thecla from the house of Queen Tryphaena to the arena, the latter opposes him and he is unable to achieve his goal (4.5). The queen also seems to turn away soldiers sent by the governor to fetch Thecla and personally conducts her to the arena instead (4.6). The arena itself has, in the meantime, become the stage of a major disagreement between various Antiochian parties, some of which agree with the execution of the blasphemer, while others consider precisely this execution a sacrilege (4.7; this may well reflect possible responses to the *Acts of Thecla* by its readership). When Thecla enters the arena, she does so largely naked as an athlete, only wearing a διαζώστρα, which could be the dress of a gladiator. Various attacks by bears and lions fail to harm her, as the lioness that was already mentioned and that is a further female supporter of Thecla, defends her until her own demise. At this point, both the (female) ruler of human beings, Queen Tryphaena, and the queen of the animals, the lioness, have chosen Thecla's side and defied all sorts of male and (supposedly) masculine figures in the process.[56] When, following the lioness' death, a further group of animals is sent to attack Thecla (4.8), Thecla prays and throws herself in a pool of water that is in the arena filled with apparently aggressive—seals.[57] This action, however, does not lead to her death, but to her baptism. In addition, she is covered with divine fire, which protects her from the animals.[58] This divine sign (the fire) also authenticates the otherwise controversial 'self-baptism'.[59] Next, when even more animals are sent into the arena, the women of the city throw spices into the arena that drug the animals. Alexander, however, who is still trying to humiliate Thecla and to regain his honor somewhat, has one further trick up his sleeve: he has Thecla bound

55. See, for example, Corrington Streete 2009: 87. For a different point of view, see Jensen 2001: 79, who argues that Thecla's allegiance to Christ constitutes the sacrilege. Both aspects are difficult to distinguish in the *Acts of Thecla*, however.

56. As Esch-Wermeling 2008: 224, rightly remarks.

57. See on this Schneider 2001.

58. See also Misset-van de Weg 1998: 249.

59. See, for example, Barrier 2010: 164. 'Self-baptism' and similar terms are only partially correct: Thecla herself states that she has been baptized by Christ (see 4.15, and compare 4.9).

between two bulls in order to let her be torn apart by them. Yet this plan also fails: the fire that was held under the genitals of the bulls in incense them also burns the ropes with which Thecla was bound to them, hence freeing her. She is even stronger than the (phallic) power of the bulls of Alexander.[60] At this point, Alexander's end is near: while the governor already lacked enthusiasm for the last attempt to kill Thecla (στυγνάσας, 4.10), Queen Tryphaena faints due to Alexander's cruelty and seems to be dead (4.11). This is more than a little upsetting for Alexander, as he must now count on the wrath of the emperor, given that he drove one of his relatives to an early death because of his sadism. He therefore gives in and immediately requests the release of Thecla, the (female) θηριομάχος. This designation is highly unusual for a woman and the combination of this masculine noun with a female article suits Thecla's developing (masculine) identity very well.[61] What this identity amounts to fundamentally, Thecla outlines in a public (!) speech in 4.12:

> I am a slave of the living God. But the things concerning me, I have placed my trust in the one whom God blessed, namely his son; on account of which not one of the beasts touched me. For this is the only way of salvation and the substance of deathless life. For to the one being stormed-tossed he is a place of refuge, a loosening to the one being oppressed, a shelter to the one who is in despair, and in general, whoever should not believe in him, shall not live but will die forever.

The central point of this speech and the preceding attempts to execute Thecla are relatively clear, as Esch-Wermeling puts it nicely: 'Die Hinrichtung der Christin endet nicht in einem Triumph der wilden Tiere, die im Dienste, die im Dienste Alexanders bzw. des römischen Staatsapparates stehen, sondern in einer Machtdemonstration Theklas bzw. des christlichen Gottes' ('The execution of this female Christian does not end with the triumph of the wild animals that serve Alexander, c.q. the Roman imperial administration, but with a demonstration of the power of Tecla, i.e. of the Christian god').[62] The speech just quoted—as such also an indication of Thecla's masculinity, given that public speaking was a male activity closely connected to the performance of ἀνδρεία—leads to Thecla's release. In the context of her release, she receives new clothes, even if she indicates that she does not need them: Christ has already clothed her through baptism. This remark also shows that her naked (female) body is no longer dishonorable.[63] In this context, Thecla's god also receives an acclamation from

60. See also Esch-Wermeling 2008: 266, 288-89.
61. See, for example, Van den Hoek and Herrmann 2001: 225, who note that a reference to a 'feminine θηριομάχος is unprecedented'.
62. Esch-Wermeling 2008: 225. On the animals, see further pp. 225-28.
63. See Shepard Kraemer 2011: 138-39.

the women of the city (4.13). Thus, Thecla and her god receive public recognition. When Queen Tryphaena recovers from her fainting, she again offers Thecla hospitality (and gives her everything she owns) and Thecla commences to teach the faith in the house(hold) of Tryphaena, thus bringing the queen and many of her servant-girls/slaves to faith (4.14). It is notable in this respect that Thecla starts her preaching again on the 'inside', that is, in the feminine sphere. While this could be evaluated as a 'test run' for her later public proclamation of the faith,[64] it can also be seen as the start of a new development, in which Thecla (again) moves from the inside to the outside, this time as a teacher of the faith, though, no longer as a disobedient daughter and fiancée.

Even while celebrating these successes in Antioch, Thecla has not forgotten her (former) mentor Paul and she begins a search for him. When she hears that he is in Myra, she travels there. She does so wearing a man's garment and accompanied by a host of followers. In this way, Thecla travels to Paul as a man, which denotes a further development in her masculinization. In the Greco-Roman culture, in which clothing expressed someone's status and identity, Thecla's decision to wear a man's garments can only mean that she now presents herself as a man. How fitting this gesture is for her becomes clearer when we consider the events that led up to this point as well as those that are to come. When finally encountering Paul again, Thecla does not behave vis-à-vis him like a disciple, but as his equal, substantiating her behavior as follows, placing herself in a relationship to God that is analogous to Paul's relationship to God: 'I took the bath, Paul; For the one who worked with you in the Gospel has even worked for me in the washing' (4.15). After Thecla has told Paul that she will travel to Iconium, Paul confirms Thecla's mission (4.16).[65] While this may well constitute an apostolic legitimation of Thecla's mission by Paul,[66] it also should be kept in mind that this does not necessarily mean that Thecla submits to Paul: when one assumes knowledge of the Acts of the Apostles, Paul has received similar legitimation without completely submitting to the authority of the Jerusalem church.[67] However one judges this matter, Thecla is at the end of the narrative a very independently operating missionary, a role she fulfils as a disciple of Paul, but even more so as a disciple of Christ, given that Christ has baptized her and equipped her to bear witness. Paul, in fact, does little more than to confirm an already existing commission and mission. After this scene in Myra, Thecla travels to Iconium to take the place of Paul, there by

64. Thus Esch-Wermeling 2008: 222.
65. See, for example, Misset-van de Weg 1998: 248.
66. Esch-Wermeling 2008: 223.
67. For a different view, see, for example, Esch-Wermeling 2008: 223, as well as Büllesbach 2003: 144. Thecla does *not* owe her authority to teach to Paul!

falling down on the floor of the house of Onesiphorus and praying to God there, just as Paul had done (4.17).[68] Even though Esch-Wermeling rightly remarks that Thecla did not sit on the floor of this house, like Paul had done, but that she throws herself on the floor and prays, this does not necessarily mean that she gives honor to Paul, but, on the contrary, and as her prayer indicates, she gives honor to God.[69] Subsequently, Thecla bears witness of her faith to her mother (Thamyris had meanwhile died) and travels to Seleucia to preach the word there. Here, she also dies (4.18).

When considering all of these developments, it becomes clear that Thecla's identity and her social role develop considerably in the course of the narrative. Three main developments can be distinguished in this respect—emancipation, masculinization, and appearance as a male apostle, as they may be called[70]—also agree with the different phases of the formation of identity as they have been identified in ritual studies. Here, a first phase is formed by the separation from a group, following a subsequent liminal phase containing the actual transformation of a person, and a third phase ('aggregation') consisting of the reintegration of the transformed person into a group again.[71] Thecla's various trials can be seen to belong to the middle, liminal phase, whereas her emancipation, that is, her leaving of her position in Iconium, agrees with the first phase, and Thecla's acceptance by Paul in her new role (and possibly also by her mother Theocleia) agrees with the phase of 'aggregation'.[72] Thus, Thecla is, in a way, trained to be a real man, which agrees with conventional Greco-Roman views on the subject of the education of a boy to become a man.[73]

The development of Thecla from a betrothed (virgin) girl to (an equally virginal) male apostle therefore contains, negatively, the negation of her social role so far and of the social structures and conventions imposed upon her life, and, positively, her embodiment of a series of characteristics denoting masculinity. Among such characteristics are self-control and abstinence (ἐγκράτεια), bodily integrity and physical strength, courage, true piety, and rhetorical performance.[74] The transformation of her looks (hair, clothes) and

---

68. With Wehn 2006: 281.

69. Lipsett 2010: 81: 'Her prayer...does not mention Paul, but recapitulates the plot, resolutely expressing praise of God and of Christ Jesus as her helper (βοηθός) at every stage of what she has endured'.

70. See for this also Braun 2000: 214-15.

71. See, for example, the overview offered by Klostergaard Pedersen 2011: 21-24; see further also Strecker 1999.

72. Dunn 2010: 48, distinguishes three more or less analogous phases in Thecla's development: catechumen, confessor, and apostle.

73. See also Shepard Kraemer 2011: 139, and in general also Connolly 2003.

74. See also, for example, Stefaniw 2010: 347.

the development of her body (strength, invisible nakedness) also echo the change in 'gender temperature'.[75] One could say that 'form follows function' here, and if so, that it would be misleading to call Thecla a transvestite: by wearing male clothing, she in fact wears clothing that suit her real status and identity.[76] Thecla, in fact, would only be a transvestite if she had worn clothing that had continued to identify her with a female role.[77] Thecla does not undergo a sex change as far as her genitals are concerned, which does not mean that her sex or gender identity is ambivalent at the end of the narrative. Every aspect of her new role as an apostle clearly indicates a masculine person and seems to prove this masculinity, *qua* ἀνδρεία, in a number of critical cases. She is even accepted in this role by her former mentor Paul.[78] One could say with confidence, then, that her genitals no longer determines her gender identity. Let us assess now the possible function of Thecla's masculinization.

Conclusions: The Function of Thecla's Masculinization

In the history of interpretation of the *Acts of Thecla*, various strategies exist to explain the masculinity of Thecla, and in particular her 'cross-dressing'. Especially the latter feature embarrassed commentators, given that it went right against cultural conventions and ecclesial norms.[79] A relatively popular explanation was to consider it as a form of protective camouflage that enabled Thecla to travel safely. However, when Thecla changes her dress, the time of her trials is over and she travels with a substantial group of disciples.[80] Apart from this, the narrative explicitly relates masculine dress and Thecla's developing identity to baptism—never to protection or camouflage. A further strategy, which is also not convincing, would be to argue that Thecla's masculine identity is an expression of her *imitatio Pauli*. This hardly applies: the more masculine Thecla becomes, the more independent

75. See Braun 2000: 212, 216.

76. See Lipsett 2010: 55: 'acquired manliness'.

77. With Di Marco 2010: 502: 'But during the torture, the virgin and martyr girl can show her naked body because she has overcome her womanliness: the body which lies without clothes in the arena is no longer a female body'.

78. This nuances Stefaniw's remark with regard to Thecla's identity, 'Here again we see maleness as parallel to or synonymous with respectable and legitimate spiritual activity, but the woman who develops maleness to pursue her spiritual vocation stays a woman with regard to the way others treat her' (Stefaniw 2010: 348). It would seem more to the point to say that those who try to treat Thecla as a (weak) women fail and that the story ends with the acceptance of Thecla's new identity by all parties involved.

79. See, for example, Castelli 1982: 75-77.

80. Anson 1974: 3.

of Paul she becomes as well.[81] Di Marco has more recently proposed something else: Thecla's changing appearance has in the end to do with being clothed with Christ in baptism, which is mentioned in 1 Cor. 15.53-54, Gal. 3.37, and Col. 3.9-10.[82] While the connection with baptism is certainly to the point, Di Marco goes beyond this and suggests that Thecla's developing identity has everything to do with remedying the femininity of women:

> Thecla's body is not the weak result of female imperfection, it is no longer the symbol of Eve's sin: martyrdom and the grace of virginity have transformed the naked female body allowing it to prefigure, on Earth, the eschatological body that Christians will dress after the Resurrection. The eschatological dimension which Thecla's body has reached implies her overcoming the original sin, cause of woman's inferiority according to Genesis. If the achievement of an eschatological dimension depends on the two martyrdoms that Thecla has suffered, as Christian witnesses cross the border between *saeculum* and afterworld in the moment the trial begins, the overcoming of Eve's inheritance is strictly linked to the *enkrateia* she embraced. Refusing marriage and motherhood, results of the first sin, and keeping her virginity, Thecla restores an Eden-like body, recovers the condition of woman before the Fall.[83]

On this basis, Di Marco also thinks that Thecla is solely a model for women, given that men do not have to overcome the deficiencies of Eve. Accordingly, Thecla demonstrates

> the possibility for women not only to act upon Christian precepts, but even to overcome that imperfection, that weakness which the Ancient thought defined as 'ontological' for women by transforming its most material evidence: the body.[84]

It seems, however, that Di Marco's perspective may well be a bit too narrow, and not only because the *Acts of Thecla* nowhere refer to the 'Fall', the ontological deficiency of women, or anything like it. While Thecla certainly undergoes a certain kind of 'physiotherapy' and physical change, it seems unlikely that this would only be a model for women. In my view, Thecla can also be understood as a representative of all who have a 'weak' body, including, but not exclusively, women. This view is, on the one hand, supported by a closer look at Paul's preaching that is not addressed to

---

81. This possibility is mentioned, but not chosen by Stefaniw 2010: 348. See also Jensen 2001: 71: 'In geen enkel ander kuisheidsverhaal zien wij een heldin die even autonoom is, nergens anders worden de belangen van vrouwen zo vastberaden verdedigd' ('In no other narrative on chastity we can find a heroine that is as autonomous [sc. as Thecla], nowhere else, the interests of women are defended so resolutely').

82. See Di Marco 2010: 500-502.

83. Di Marco 2010: 501.

84. Di Marco 2010: 502.

women only but to all (if not to men in the first place), and on the other hand, by the observation that 'weakness' is not only a problem of women in the *Acts of Thecla*: all can be weak. Alexander, for example, is a weak man, while Paul is (often, but not always) a strong or 'hard' man. Thecla develops from a weak, that is, feminine, person, to a strong, that is, masculine, one. In other early Christian (martyr) acts, such as those of Polycarp, the focus is also on weak human bodies, such as those of old men, that turn out to be real strong men in actual fact.[85] As Stefaniw puts it:

> [G]ender was understood to have far-reaching moral and spiritual implica-
> tions, such that even male persons could need to be 'made men' in order to be
> really spiritual.[86]

Stefaniw also has her own proposal for the function of the masculinization of Thecla in the *Acts of Thecla*: it is part of the development of an ascetic identity that is necessary to exercise spiritual authority as a woman.[87] While Stefaniw's observation is certainly to the point, it is—again—not correct to argue that Thecla's change of identity is only a model for women. In fact, as the *Acts of Thecla* suggests throughout, also men should show themselves to be masculine in order to be taken seriously as authority figures. While the *Acts of Thecla* uses the criterion of masculinity on the one hand to indicate who is and who is not a figure of authority, the work also shows how an unmasculine person can attain masculinity—and hence authority—through ἐγκράτεια. As Dunn puts it: 'gender is not limited by sex'.[88] Or, to put it somewhat more extensively with Esch-Wermeling: 'Die Zugehörigkeit zu einem Geschlecht läuft offensichtlich nicht über den Marker *Körper*, sondern über eine…zweite Ebene: die Tugenden' ('Having a particular gender is not determined by the marker "body', but rather by a second level: that of the virtues').[89] This agrees with a further observation by the same scholar: 'Für die Theklaakten ist nicht ausschlaggebend, ob es sich bei den in der Lehre tätigen Personen um Frauen oder Männer handelt, sondern dass man (und *Frau*) dem richtigen Lebensideal folgt—und dieses ist ein männliches Ideal' ('For the Acts of Thecla it is not decisive whether the persons that are teaching are men or women, but rather that both men and women follow the

---

85. Because of this, it is not the case that only a woman could make a transformation such as Thecla's. See, however, Lipsett 2010: 85.

86. Stefaniw 2010: 354.

87. Stefaniw 2010: 350-351.

88. Dunn 2010: 39. Esch-Wermeling 2008: 259, is probably right when she writes that the focus of the *Acts of Thecla* on a young woman serves the 'Veranschaulichung der Wirkmacht der Enthaltsamkeitslehre' ('Exemplification of the power of the doctrine of chastity').

89. Esch-Wermeling 2008: 267.

right [i.e. ideal]) life style—and this life style is masculine').[90] The point of the *Acts of Thecla*, to be sure, is that not all physical men are real men (e.g. Alexander) and that women can indeed be manly (like Thecla). The ascetic message of the *Acts of Thecla* is, therefore, not the denial of the right to exist of women *per se*, but rather the communication of a spiritual ideal that considers spiritual perfection to consist also of the liberation of suppressing, and hence emasculating, structures and roles.[91] If long hair and women's clothing had not been cultural markers for a subordinate role, Thecla would have been able to keep them; however, given the way things were, they end up contradicting the new, virtuous identity of Thecla, which, as the *Acts* show, is accessible for all, even for those with supposedly weak, unmanly bodies.

Bibliography

Anson, John
    1974   'The Female Transvestite in Early Monasticism: The Origin and Develop-
            ment of a Motif', *Viator* 5: 1-32.
Aspegren, Kerstin
    1990   *The Male Woman: A Feminine Ideal in the Early Church* (Stockholm:
            Almqvist & Wiksell).
Aubin, Melissa
    1998   'Reversing Romance? The Acts of Thecla and the Ancient Novel', in
            Ronald F. Hock, J. Bradley Chance and Judith Perkins (eds.), *Ancient
            Fiction and Early Christian Narrative* (Atlanta: Scholars Press): 257-72.
Barrier, Jeremy W.
    2010   *The Acts of Paul and Thecla* (Tübingen: Mohr Siebeck).
Braun, Willi
    2000   'Physiotherapy of Femininity in the Acts of Thecla', in S.G. Wilson and
            M. Desjardins (eds.), *Text and Artifact in the Religions of Mediterranean
            Antiquity: Essays in Honor of Peter Richardson* (Waterloo, ON: Wilfrid
            Laurier University Press): 209-30.
Bremmer, Jan N.
    1996   'Magic, Martyrdom and Women's Liberation in the Acts of Paul and
            Thecla', in Jan N. Bremmer (ed.), *The Apocryphal Acts of Paul and Thecla*
            (Kampen: Kok Pharos): 36-49.
Brown, Peter
    1988   *The Body and Society* (New York: Columbia University Press).

90. Esch-Wermeling 2008: 271.

91. If this is indeed the case, it would agree with the thesis of Cooper 1996: 20-67, that the readership of both Hellenistic novels and early Christian acts were literate men involved in shaping society.

Büllesbach, Claudia
    2003   '"Ich will mich rundherum scheren und dir folgen"—Begegnungen zwischen Paulus und Thekla in den Acta Pauli et Theclae', in Heike Omerzu and Katharina Greschat (eds.), *Körper und Kommunikation. Beiträge aus der theologischen Genderforschung* (Leipzig: Evangelische Verlagsanstalt): 125-46.

Burrus, Virginia
    2005   'Mimicking Virgins: Colonial Ambivalence and the Ancient Romance', *Arethusa* 38:49-88.

Castelli, Elisabeth
    1982   'Virginity and its Meaning for Women's Sexuality in Early Christianity', *JFSR* 2: 61-88.

Cobb, L. Stephanie
    2008   *Dying to Be Men: Gender and Language in Early Christian Martyr Texts* (New York: Columbia University Press).

Connolly, Joy
    2003   'Like the Labors of Heracles: *Andreia* and *Paideia* in Greek Culture under Rome', in Ralph. M. Rosen and Ineke Sluiter (eds.), *Andreia: Studies in Manliness and Courage in Classical Antiquity* (Leiden: E.J. Brill): 287-317.

Cooper, Kate
    1996   *The Virgin and the Bride: Idealized Womanhood in Late Antiquity* (Cambridge, MA: Harvard University Press).

Corrington Streete, Gail
    2006   'Of Martyrs and Men: Perpetua, Thecla, and the Ambiguity of Female Heroism in Early Christianity', in Richard Valantasis (ed.), *The Subjective Eye: Essays in Culture, Religion, and Gender in Honor of Margaret R. Miles* (Eugene, OR: Wipf & Stock): 254-64.
    2009   *Redeemed Bodies: Women Martyrs in Early Christianity* (Louisville, KY: Westminster/John Knox Press).

Dagron, Gilbert
    1978   *Vie et miracles de Sainte Thècle* (Subsidia haguigraphica, 62; Brussells: Société des Bollandistes).

Davies, Stevan L.
    1980   *The Revolt of the Widows: The Social World of the Apocryphal Acts* (Carbondale and Edwardsville: Southern Illinois University Press).

Davis, Stephen J.
    2001   *The Cult of Saint Thecla: A Tradition of Women's Piety in Late Antiquity* (Oxford: Oxford University Press).

Di Marco, Francesca
    2010   'Undressed: The Naked Female Body as Sign of Holiness in Apocryphal and Hagiographical Literature', *StPatr* 44: 499-508.

Dunn, David. J.
    2010   'Her that Is No Bride: St. Thecla and the Relationship between Sex, Gender, and Office', *SVTQ* 53: 37-68.

Ebner, Martin
    2005   'Paulinische Seligsprechungen à la Thekla. Narrative Relektüre der
            Makarismenreihe in ActThecl 5f.', in Ebner (ed.) 2005: 64-79.
Ebner, Martin (ed.)
    2005   *Aus Liebe zu Paulus? Die Akte Thekla neu aufgerollt* (Stuttgart:
            Katholisches Bibelwerk).
Esch-Wermeling, Elisabeth
    2008   *Thekla—Paulusschülerin wider Willen?* (Münster: Aschendorff).
Johnson, Scott Fitzgerald
    2006   *The Life and Miracles of Thekla: A Literary Study* (Cambridge, MA:
            Harvard University Press).
Geerard, Mauritius
    1992   *Clavis Apocryphorum Novi Testamenti* (Turnhout: Brepols).
Hoek, Annewies van den, and John J. Herrmann, Jr
    2001   'Thecla the Beast Fighter: A Female Emblem of Deliverance in Early
            Christian Popular Art', *SPhilo* 13: 212-49.
Ivarsson, Fredrik
    2008   'Christian Identity as True Masculinity', in Bengt Holmberg (ed.),
            Exploring Early Christian Identity (Tübingen: Mohr Siebeck): 159-71.
Jensen, Anne
    1992   *Gottes selbstbewusste Töchter: Frauenemanzipation im frühen Christen-
            tum* (Freiburg: Herder).
    2001   *Tekla—de vrouwelijke apostel naast Paulus. Een apocriefe tekst opnieuw
            ontdekt* (Baarn: Ten Have).
Klostergaard Pedersen, Anders
    2011   'Rituals of Purification, Rituals of Initiation: Phenomenological, Taxo-
            nomical and Culturally Evolutionary Reflections', in David Hellholm,
            Tor Vegge, Øyvind Nordeval, and Christer Hellholm (eds.), *Ablution,
            Initiation, and Baptism: Late Antiquity, Early Judaism, and Early Christi-
            anity* (Berlin: W. de Gruyter): 3-40.
Kötzel, Michael
    2005   'Thekla und Alexander—oder: Kleider machen Leute. Dramatische
            Ouvertüre des Antiochia-Zyklus', in Ebner (ed.) 2005: 91-109.
Leutzsch, Martin
    2004   'Konstruktionen von Männlichkeit im Urchristentum', in Frank Crüse-
            mann *et al.* (eds.), *Dem Tod nicht glauben: Sozialgeschichte der Bibel*
            (Gütersloh: Gütersloher Verlagsbuchhaus): 600-618.
Lipsett, B. Diane
    2010   *Desiring Conversion: Hermas, Thecla, Aseneth* (Oxford: Oxford Uni-
            versity Press).
Matthews, Shelly
    2001   'Thinking of Thecla: Issues in Feminist Historiography', *JFSR* 17: 39-55.
Mayordomo, Moises
    2006   'Construction of Masculinity in Antiquity and Early Christianity', *lectio
            difficilior* 2006.

McGinn, Sheila E.
1995 'The Acts of Thecla', in Elisabeth Schüssler-Fiorenza (ed.), *Searching the Scriptures*, II (New York: Crossroad, 1995): 800-28.

Misset-van de Weg, Magda
1998 'Blessed are the Bodies of the Virgins...', in Jonneke Bekkenkamp and Maaike de Haardt (eds.), *Begin with the Body: Corporeality, Religion, and Gender* (Louvain: Peeters, 1998): 233-49.

Moxnes, Halvor
2007 'Conventional Values in the Hellenistic World: Masculinity', in Per Bilde, Troels Engberg-Pedersen, Lise Hannestad and Jan Zahle (eds.), *Conventional Values of the Hellenistic Greeks* (Aarhus: Aarhus University Press): 263-84.

Müller, Barbara
2011 'Frauen in Männerdomänen', in Christine Gerber, Silke Pedersen and Wolfram Weiße (eds.), *Unbeschreiblich weiblich. Neue Fragestellungen zur Geschlechterdifferenz in den Religionen* (Berlin: LIT Verlag): 140-57.

Ng, Esther Yue L.
2004 'Acts of Paul and Thecla: Women's Stories and Precedent?', *JTS* 55: 1-29.

Park, Eung Chun
2004 'Agneia as a Sublime Form of Erōs in the Acts of Paul and Thecla', in Holly E. Hearon (ed.), *Distant Voices Drawing Near* (Collegeville, MN: Liturgical Press): 215-26.

Rohrdorf, Willy (with Pierre Cherix and Rudolphe Kasser)
1997 'Actes de Paul', in François Bovon and Pierre Geoltrain (eds.), *Écrits apocryphes chrétiens*, I (Saint Herblain: Gallimard): 1115-77.

Schneider, Horst
2001 'Thekla, und die Robben', *Vigilia Christiana* 55: 45-57.

Shepard Kraemer, Ross S.
2011 *Unreliable Witnesses: Religion, Gender and History in the Greco-Roman Mediterranean* (Oxford: Oxford University Press).

Smit, Peter-Ben
2012 'Making Men—Weakness, Justification, and *Andreia* in Romans 5:6', *lectio difficilior* 2012.

Stefaniw, Blossom
2010 'Becoming Men, Staying Women: Gender Ambivalence in Christian Apocryphal Texts and Contexts', *FemTh* 18: 341-55.

Strecker, Christian
1999 *Die liminale Theologie des Paulus: Zugänge zur paulinischen Theologie aus kulturanthropologischer Perspektive* (Göttingen: Vandenhoeck & Ruprecht).

Vorster, Johannes N.
2006 'Construction of Culture Through the Construction of a Person: The Construction of Thecla in the Acts of Thecla', in Amy-Jill Levine (ed.), *A Feminist Companion to the New Testament Apocrypha* (Feminist Companion to the New Testament and Early Christian Writings, 11; London: T. & T. Clark): 98-117.

Wehn, Beate

    2006   *"Vergewaltige nicht die Sklavin Gottes!": Gewalterfahrungen und Widerstand von Frauen in den frühchristlichen Thekla-Akten* (Königstein: Ulrike Helmer Verlag).

    2000   'Blessed are the Bodies of those Who Are Virgins: Reflections on the Image of Paul in the Acts of Thecla', *JSNT* 79: 149-64.

Part IV

FINAL REFLECTIONS

BIBLICAL MASCULINITIES:
MUSINGS ON THEORY AND AGENDA

Martti Nissinen

The issue of masculinity has taken off surprisingly late in biblical studies, considering the profusion of masculinity studies published since the 1980s. New Testament scholars have been considerably quicker than Hebrew Bible scholars in adding masculinity to their agenda, probably because masculinity in Classical Antiquity was a well-studied topic already in the 1990s, thanks to such epoch-making works as David Halperin's *One Hundred Years of Homosexuality* (1990), Maud Gleason's *Making Men* (1995), and Craig Williams's *Roman Homosexuality: Ideologies of Masculinity in Classical Antiquity* (1999/2010). The seminal volume *New Testament Masculinities* (2003), edited by Stephen Moore and Janice Anderson, has been available for a decade already, and Colleen Conway's likewise seminal *Behold the Man: Jesus and Greco-Roman Masculinity* (2008) appeared half a decade ago.

While New Testament scholars were able to build upon the work of the Classicists, Hebrew Bible scholars could not be similarly inspired by the ancient Near Eastern scholarship, for the simple reason that there was not much to rely on. At last, however, the ancient Near East and the Hebrew Bible scholars have followed suit. The first collection of essays on masculinity in the Hebrew Bible, edited by Ovidiu Creangă, appeared in 2010,[1] and the first collection of essays on ancient Near Eastern Masculinities, edited by Ilona Zsolnay, is forthcoming.[2] To be fair, though, it should be mentioned that the issue of masculinity does not appear for the first time to Hebrew Bible and ancient Near Eastern scholarship in these books. Constructions and representations of masculinity have been discussed under different rubrics ever since the mid-1990s in books exploring the Hebrew Bible and ancient Near Eastern texts from the point of view of sex and gender,[3] same-sex issues,[4] and queer studies.[5]

---

1. Creangă (ed.) 2010.
2. Zsolnay (ed.) forthcoming.
3. E.g. Parpola and Whiting (ed.) 2002.
4. E.g. Olyan 1994; Nissinen 1998.

How Are We Today Studying Biblical Masculinities?

The previous work notwithstanding, there is much truth to the estimation of David Clines, one of the first Hebrew Bible scholars to engage in masculinity studies,[6] that 'study of masculinity in the Bible is to some extent still in the stage that feminist biblical criticism was at in the 1960s and 70s, identifying and collecting the data, monitoring the language and the rhetoric of gendered discourse, and so on'.[7] Masculinity studies differ from the early phases of feminist criticism in one significant respect, though: students of biblical masculinity have from early on had a methodological toolbox at their disposal that has been developed and improved by several shifts and waves of feminist and gender studies over decades.

Indeed, the emergence of the study of masculinity can be seen as a repercussion of, and as a response to, feminist criticism which, while fore-grounding *le deuxième sexe*, questioned the self-evidence of androcentric discourse and 'othered' the male gender. According to Stephen Moore, 'masculinity studies became a thriving enterprise in literary studies because of certain fundamental changes in feminist literary studies',[8] while in biblical studies, '[m]asculinity studies…exists in a symbiotic relationship with feminist studies'.[9] That masculinity studies owe significantly to women's studies can be seen in many researchers' predilection for feminist and/or women's studies. Even in this volume, at least two writers (Ovidiu Creangă and Justin Glessner) express their pro-feminist attitudes, and I gladly join this choir with my own voice. I see no reason why masculinity studies should be introduced as an alternative or countermovement to feminist studies; I rather see both women's and men's studies operating on the common arena of gender studies or, if we prefer, gender criticism.[10]

So far, study of masculinities (rather than a uniform 'masculinity') in the Bible has not developed a specific theory or a methodological apparatus of its own. The theoretical and methodological horizons of masculinity studies are largely the same, and quite as manifold, as those of gender studies in general. Moreover, the study of biblical masculinities is informed by the larger field of masculinity studies, such as R. W. Connell's *Masculinities*[11] quoted many times in the present volume. Milena Kirova reminds us that this 'entails the application of standards to the biblical text that do not always prove adequate to the social and historical practices of the ancient

---

5. E.g. Stone (ed.) 2001.
6. See already Clines 1995 and 2002.
7. Clines 2010a: 62.
8. Moore 2010: 242.
9. Moore 2010: 241.
10. Cf. Sawyer 2009.
11. Connell 2005.

Hebrew world' (above, p. 35). I fully agree—researchers of ancient texts should be on alert when applying methodologies, let alone results, of studies concerning the modern world to their sources. Examining the life of living men in contemporary societies is not the same thing as studying textual representations of men in ancient sources. Hebrew Bible scholars, for example, should not forget that the primary object of their research is the corpus of *texts* included in the Hebrew Bible, and only secondarily *men* who once lived in 'ancient Israel', visible to us only through the keyhole provided by the Hebrew Bible.[12]

On the other hand, study of masculinities in the ancient world/ancient source materials (including the Bible) necessarily takes place on a cross-temporal and cross-cultural platform, dealing with cultural and socio-religious patterns of masculinity that vary from source to source and from time to time, including those represented by their modern interprets. What is specific for the study of masculinity in the Bible and/or the ancient Near East, I believe, is not a particular theory or methodology, but, rather, the source material. Biblical and ancient Near Eastern scholars differ from their colleagues in masculinity studies only with respect to their knowledge of their source materials. Creating a specific niche for masculinity studies—and gender studies in general, for that matter—would hardly be a wise thing to do; instead, they should be integrated into the study of related fields, depending on each researcher's academic context.[13] Biblical and ancient Near Eastern scholars are better equipped to communicate their knowledge to their colleagues in other fields if they speak a language comprehensible to their colleagues and resist the temptation of developing a scholarly dialect of their own. To my relief, I do not see this happening in the present volume.

Is It All about Hegemonic Masculinity?

The contributors to this volume come from different backgrounds, and the editors seem not to have striven for theoretical homogeneity. Nevertheless, the image of biblical masculinities emerging from the present volume is far from being incoherent. The contributors seem to be in virtual agreement

12. I owe the keyhole metaphor to Christoph Levin's inaugural lecture at the 21st congress of the International Organization for the Study of the Old Testament in Munich, 4 August 2013.

13. Athalya Brenner has recently pleaded strongly for such an integration: 'Women studies, or feminist criticism, or gender studies, is not a discipline. It is a cluster of approaches and critical practices, better than some, no worse than others. It has little to gain, apart from the creation of a very limited number of positions, from ghettoizing itself and staying isolated within and with its own converted disciples. Recognition of the non-value of inclusive exclusivity makes conversions and the attraction of neophytes much more viable' (Brenner 2013: 10).

about masculinities being configurations of gender practices that are constructed and performed within a social or literary setting,[14] and many contributors subscribe to the idea that masculinity is an achieved state, not an inborn quality.[15] In other words, masculinity is not essential but relational, and as such mutable, vulnerable, and constantly challenged. Furthermore, several authors seem to be at home with the categories of hegemonic, subordinate and marginalized masculinity (but see Kirova's criticism).

Hegemonic masculinity often appears as *the* construction of masculinity, or masculinity *per se*, against which all other subtypes of masculinity are measured. Hitherto, the scholarly construct of ideal masculinity in ancient sources, whether biblical, Greco-Roman, or Near Eastern, is characterized by hegemonic elements such as fertility and sexual potency, warfare, self-control and domination of women. These features are indeed abundantly present in ancient texts and without any doubt belong to the primary constituents of the construct of masculinity in ancient sources.

There is, however, a danger that the scholarly construct of hegemonic masculinity turns into a self-evident, unitary pattern that is all too lazily superimposed on texts under scrutiny. Fortunately, like many other powerful and useful, once-monolithic categories, even 'hegemonic masculinity' is in a constant process of reapplication and modification. In their response to the critics of the concept, R.W. Connell and James Messerschmidt disclaim its use as reflecting an essentialist and heteronormative matrix, and opt for a multidimensional and historically dynamic understanding of gender: 'We suggest, therefore, that our understanding of hegemonic masculinity needs to incorporate a more holistic understanding of gender hierarchy, recognizing the agency of subordinated groups as much as the power of dominant groups and the mutual conditioning of gender dynamics and other social dynamics'.[16] This is a very important reminder of the relationality of masculinities. Hegemonic and nonhegemonic (e.g. subordinate and marginalized) masculinities presuppose each other and unfold through mutual negotiations within the given social (or literary) space: 'Research has also documented the durability or survivability of nonhegemonic patterns of masculinity, which may represent well-crafted responses to race/ethnic marginalization, physical disability, class inequality, or stigmatized sexuality. Hegemony may be accomplished by the incorporation of such masculinities into a functioning gender order rather than by active oppression in the form of discredit or violence'.[17]

14. Cf. Connell 2005: 72, 81.

15. Cf. Gleason 1995: 59; Mayordomo 2006.

16. Connell and Messerschmidt 2005: 848. I am indebted to Brian DiPalma for turning my attention to this article.

17. Connell and Messerschmidt 2005: 848.

I think these statements of Connell and Messerschmidt are applicable to ancient sources, too. No hegemony exists without hierarchy, hence there are different degrees of hegemony corresponding to prevailing power relations in the given society. Even in ancient world, most men did probably not meet the normative standards, and everyday, non-elite masculine performance could only be 'hegemonic' within a restricted social space. Instead, gender relations were 'constituted through nondiscursive practices, including wage labor, violence, sexuality, domestic labor, and child care as well as through unreflective routinized actions'[18] in which there was a need for different kinds of gender performances.

It is gratifying to notice that in the present volume, several contributions challenge a uniform understanding of hegemonic masculinity,[19] highlighting features in the portrayal of male characters in the Bible masculinity that do not easily conform to a simplistic model of hegemonic masculinity: the weeping patriarchs (Milena Kirova), King Saul's failures (Marcel Măcelaru), Joseph, father of Jesus, as the 'Average Joe' (Justin Glessner). In these portrayals, the characteristics of the male protagonists do not appear outside the matrix of hegemonic masculinity; they rather show what can be found within its layers and fractures. This may sometimes be interpreted as subtle criticism of the dominant pattern of masculinity in the biblical writers' world. Some texts can be read as openly advocating an alternative, or at least a markedly different model of masculinity, such as the ideal male behavior as endorsed in Proverbs, consistently preferring wisdom for strength (Hilary Lipka), or the validation of subordinate masculinity by way of idealizing eunuchs in Matthew 19 (Susanna Asikainen).

The above-mentioned studies may not take hegemonic masculinity down from its pedestal, but they surely relativize the hegemony of hegemonic masculinity both in biblical texts and in scholarly theory by demonstrating that even subordinate masculinity can be valued positively in conditioning gender dynamics—and that nonhegemonic masculinity does not necessarily deprive a man of his honor. The 'anomalous masculinity' of the disciples of Jesus serves a positive missionary purpose (Hans-Ulrich Weidemann),[20] and subordinate masculinity can be a deliberate choice of those 'who can receive this word' (Asikainen).

18. Connell and Messerschmidt 2005: 842.

19. This is true also for many contributions to Creangă (ed.) 2010; cf. especially Haddox 2010, DiPalma 2010, and Creangă 2010.

20. For the 'anomalous masculinity' of the disciples in the Gospel of Matthew, see Anderson and Moore 2003: 76.

I have argued in another context[21] that the positive attitude towards eunuchs (cf. Isa. 56.3-4) is related to their 'cosmic body', that is, the body as interpreted in relation to the divine order which overrules the ideals of the physical and social body dictated by the dominant patterns of masculinity.[22] The cosmic body of a man may, thus, be physically deviant and socially disrespected or even marginalized, but still highly honorable before God, which ultimately matters the most. The cosmic body, I think, is also at stake in the case of circumcision, thoroughly discussed by Karin Neutel and Matthew Anderson in the present volume. While circumcision was a matter of public ridicule and derision in the Greco-Roman environment of Judaism, for the members of the Jewish community it was the act of constituting the cosmic body of an adult male as well as the primary signifier of his social body as the member of the community; in fact, the prerequisite of his full masculinity. Paul and Philo serve as prime examples of what kind of intellectual acrobatics was required to explain all this to contemporaries who had not internalized such a theology.

Can Women and God Be Masculine?

One way of relativizing the hegemonic pattern is to study the masculinity of women. 'Male genitals did not an ancient man make' (Neutel and Anderson; above, p. 229), and therefore, women can be masculine—this is amply demonstrated by ancient literature, of which the present volume provides two very different case studies. The first, discussed by Stuart Macwilliam, is Queen Athaliah, who 'reigned (מלכת) over the land' of Judah (2 Kgs 11.3) but was overthrown and put to death by male rivals. The second example, analyzed by Peter-Ben Smit, is Thecla, a disciple of Paul who in the *Acts of Thecla* not only attempts at male performance but actually *becomes* a man— not by way of having her physical body manipulated, but in terms of status and identity.

The drastic difference between these two cases of women's masculinity is that while Thecla's masculinity is accepted by the narrator, Athaliah becomes condemned. According to Macwilliam, the message of the (male) narrator in 2 Kings 11 is that 'Athaliah attempts to resist the necessity to perform her gender correctly and is punished for doing so' (above, p. 72). Athaliah's masculinity is an essential part of her image as an illegitimate usurper and mass murderer. Her transgressing of gender boundaries serves a wrong purpose and this is what makes her male performance condemnable. Thecla, on the other hand, appears as an admirable figure who transgresses

21. Nissinen forthcoming.
22. For physical, social, and cosmic bodies, see Launderville 2010: 252.

contemporary gender conventions only to fulfill a greater purpose, that is, to reach spiritual perfection. 'Thecla develops from a weak, that is, feminine, person, to a strong, that is, masculine, one' (Smit, above, p. 262), and there is nothing wrong with this. While Athaliah's masculinity is distinctly hege-monic, Thecla's masculinity is first and foremost related to her cosmic body.

The contrary examples of Athaliah and Thecla demonstrate that even women's masculinity does not follow a uniform pattern, and that it can appear in a positive or a negative light, depending on the narrator's view of the purpose the woman's masculinity fulfills. The Hebrew Bible knows women who are not condemned for their masculinity because their actions serve an acceptable purpose—Jael for instance, who in Judg. 4.17-22 kills Sisera, the warlord and oppressor of the Israelites. In contrast to Athaliah, Jael's masculine performance is valued positively in the ideological frame-work of the narrative and is, therefore, not rebuked.[23] The role Jael plays is that of a woman warrior, a liminal figure who shares features of both male and female performance, such as the goddess Ištar who is excessively feminine and aggressively masculine at the same time.[24]

Another example of the masculinity of a non-man is the biblical God, who can be said to be portrayed predominantly as *male* but not very often as a *man*, that is, a male human being.[25] Since God is God and not a man (כי אל אנכי ולא איש, Hos. 11.9), God's masculinity is divine masculinity that does not need to conform to the rules set for humans. On the other hand, it is God to whom those rules are ascribed, and the depictions of God often let him [*sic*] appear as 'the quintessence of masculinity',[26] even though female functions such as motherhood (e.g. Isa. 66.11-13)[27] may also be included in the image of God. In the ancient Near East, such roles typically belong to female deities, but in the monotheistic model, the one and only God has to take care of the goddesses' functions as well.

The biblical God has a body, but the divine body is not the same as the human body. Yahweh, for sure, has a face and a nose, ears and a mouth, a hand and an arm, even feet, but other body parts are mentioned only sporadi-cally.[28] The divine body is not essential but figurative and functional, and

23. Yee 2013: 180: 'She is a liminal figure and thus a threat to the dominant structures of power. In order to mitigate this threat, the author of Judges constructs Jael through syndromes—shame and sexual voracity—that reinforce his androcentric interests.'

24. For the paradoxical character of Ištar, see Bahrani 2001: 141-60.

25. On the cases of the ''*iš*-theophany' in which God is described as having a concrete human form, see Hamori 2008.

26. Clines 2010b: 239.

27. See the classic discussion of Trible 1978: 31-59. Whether these features can be read as elements of 'depatriarchalized' God or, rather, 'the ultimate finesse of a very patriarchal god' (Sawyer 2009: 5) is an issue to be discussed.

28. See the statistics in Wagner 2010: 137-38.

some body parts function better than others even in terms of masculinity. How about sexual organs? Alan Hooker discusses the masculinity of the God of the Hebrew Bible from the point of view of 'glory' (כבוד), which he interprets in phallic terms as the prime symbol of God's invincible hegemonic masculinity, manifesting his prowess in warfare, fertility, and male beauty. Even God's masculinity is not absolutely perfect, however: 'Ezekiel's Yahweh has no goddess consort, and is therefore unable to produce divine children' (Hooker, above, p. 30). Indeed, the metaphor involving a marital/sexual relationship between Yahweh and Israel in Ezekiel and elsewhere (Ezek. 16; 23; cf. Jer. 2–3; 13; Hos. 2) reveals further fractures in God's masculinity. As God has no real body, there is no real marriage between God and the people,[29] and God is no real husband but the sovereign divine autocrat whose כבוד should satisfy every desire of anyone under him. In this divine–human gender matrix, all humans are female.[30] Jerusalem's autonomous actions throw Yahweh's super-hegemonic masculinity into question, threatening his כבוד and making him fear. Yahweh's excessive reaction reveals the utmost vulnerability of his hegemonic masculinity.[31] The one who has the supreme hegemony to lose has to fear the most.

What Should We Do Next?

A crucial topic for further study of masculinity is the relationship between ancient Near Eastern and Greco-Roman sources. Stephen Moore asks whether there might be 'important continuities between ancient Near Eastern and Classical ideologies of masculinity, the Hebrew Bible being fully included in the ancient Near Eastern sources, so that the Classical sources might occasionally illuminate the Hebrew Bible on the topic of masculinity across the gulf that has traditionally separated them'.[32] Moore's point is well taken. As I mentioned earlier, the study of ancient Near Eastern masculinities has hitherto not been very extensive, even though important studies are included in a forthcoming collection of essays on the matter.[33] Therefore, many Hebrew Bible scholars (including myself) have trained their eye by reading studies written on masculinity in Classical sources, and it is my impression that the image of masculinities in the present volume is largely

---

29. Day (2008: 221) is right in contending that '*figurative* marriage and infidelity need not always conform to the laws and social norms governing *literal* marriage and infidelity in ancient Israel'.

30. Cf. Carr and Conway 2008.

31. See Schwartz 2000; Zsolnay 2010.

32. Moore 2010: 245.

33. Zsolnay (ed.) forthcoming.

informed by studies of Classical Antiquity. But can and may Greco-Roman ideals of (hegemonic) masculinity be so easily transferred to ancient Near Eastern circumstances?

I could not agree more with Moore about bridging the gulf between biblical, Greco-Roman and Near Eastern sources and studies. Knowing the methodological perils of comparative studies, we should do this by reading all source materials in their own right, knowing exactly what we are comparing. (Professor Oswald Loretz, my German *Doktorvater*, used to say: 'Herr Nissinen, Sie müssen immer wissen, *was* Sie vergleichen!') This cannot be properly done without interdisciplinary communication between specialists in ancient Near Eastern, biblical and Classical studies, including early Christianity and Judaism. No theoretical obstacles should be erected to impede this communication.

To the best of my present knowledge, many features of masculine performance that correspond to the ideal of *andreia* in Classical texts can be identified in the Near Eastern sources, such as prowess in combat, sexual virility, physical strength, and self-control.[34] Further similarities include the segregation of male and female spheres in household, as well as the division into active (male) and passive (female) sexual and societal roles, expressed in a nutshell by Clement of Alexandria (quoted in this volume by Neutel and Anderson): 'to do is the mark of the man; to suffer is the mark of the woman' (*Paed.* 3.19.2). On the other hand, both Greco-Roman and ancient Near Eastern sources recognize deviations from these ideals, such as non-married people, third gender figures,[35] eunuchs, and other people whose sexual and institutional role did not conform to conventional norms of the 'reproductive arena'.[36] The sources from both sides reflect a constant interplay between the masculine imperative and fluid gender categories, as if the former was needed to keep the latter in control.

Certainly, there are differences between the Greco-Roman and ancient Near Eastern perceptions of gender and masculinity. The ancient Near Eastern sources, including the Hebrew Bible, do not seem to have developed philosophical tools for the subordination of women. In the Hebrew Bible, the patriarchal hierarchy is presented as a divine ordinance (if not a curse, cf. Gen. 3.16) beyond further reasoning. In Mesopotamia, if Julia Asher-Greve is right, the baseline for gender configurations in the society

34. In Mesopotamia, the figure of the king represented the paragon of masculine performance; see Asher-Greve 1997: 444.

35. See Roscoe 1996 and Teppo 2008. Recently, Zsolnay (2013) has contested the consensus about the *assinnu* as representing a third-gender role everywhere in the Mesopotamian sources.

36. For 'reproductive arena' as the everyday context of gender processes, see Connell 2005: 71-74.

was the human body. There was no system of binary gender equating male with positive and female with negative values; instead, '[g]ender was the interpretation of anatomical differences and imperfections. The inscription of gender on the body was one option to structure society.'[37] Also, the dichotomy of mind and body has been considered absent in ancient Near Eastern texts and in (most of) the Hebrew Bible. The question to be asked is how absolute this dichotomy is in Greco-Roman sources, and how the mind/body pattern communicates with the concepts expressed with the Hebrew *nepeš* and the Akkadian *eṭemmu*. And was there a soul, according to ancient Near Eastern thinking?[38] How about asceticism: did the rise of the ascetic ideal in Late Antiquity have Near Eastern counterparts or precursors? I consider these matters extremely relevant for the study of masculinities. Exploring them without all too many preconceived notions about the nature of Greco-Roman *vis-à-vis* Near Eastern cultures would contribute significantly to bridging the gulf which in final analysis, as I hope and believe, turns out to exist only in the division of academic disciplines.

Taken together, this volume and its predecessor (Creangă [ed.] 2010) cover well certain parts of the Hebrew Bible, especially the Torah and the narrative literature from Joshua to Chronicles, while the prophetic literature is somewhat less represented, and wisdom literature only by the essay of Lipka on Proverbs. For further study, and also for comparative purposes, it would be rewarding to explore masculinities as represented in such biblical books as Psalms, Qoheleth, Ben Sira, and the Song of Songs. What kind of masculinities would the Psalms' different 'I's embody, whether in their distress, in their fear, or in their joy? Would Ben Sira turn out to be a fully fledged agent of hegemonic masculinity, successfully combining Jewish and Hellenistic *vir*tues into a coherent whole? Could we, between the lines, hear Qoheleth whispering to his fellow symposionists: 'Masculinity sucks!'? And if sexual initiative is a sign of virility, who is the *man* in the Song of Songs?[39]

Why Are We Today Studying Biblical Masculinities— *and Why Does It Matter?*

David Clines, in his response to the articles published in *Men and Masculinity in the Hebrew Bible and Beyond*, expresses his worry about the lack of not only theoretical refinement, but *passion* in masculinity studies in the Hebrew Bible: 'Perhaps there is no agenda in masculinity studies, other

---

37. Asher-Greve 1997: 453.
38. As suggested in several studies by Simo Parpola (e.g. Parpola 2001).
39. For a recent discussion on the man in the Song of Songs, see Exum forthcoming.

than intellectual curiosity'.[40] Ovidiu Creangă quotes this in the introductory chapter to the present volume with good reason. There is, for sure, nothing wrong with intellectual curiosity, but I do believe that there is usually more at stake when someone chooses to study such a topic as masculinity. Scholars (especially young ones who have to worry about their tenures) may be hesitant about expressing too much passion in their scholarly writings, but there is certainly an engagement involved in every contribution to the present volume, and a disengaged passion is difficult to imagine.

The passion in biblical masculinity studies may not be outspoken the same way it is expressed in feminist studies, perhaps because the study of masculinity is differently positioned with regard to the gender politics in today's world. Let me try to illustrate this with the following example: Who would introduce the study of *femininity* as a counterpart of the study of masculinity in the field of biblical studies? I have a strange feeling as if there was something wrong with this suggestion, as if it referred to something related to male domination and male gaze and, hence, cannot be considered a serious project. Another example: while 'feminist studies' refer to a cause and an agenda, and 'women's studies' to people, whether objects of research or researchers themselves, 'masculinity studies' refer to a concept or a theory.[41] This has a distancing effect, as if there was something wrong with talking about men as individuals, something that is not wrong in the case of women.

The reason for the imbalance can perhaps be found in the position of masculinity studies as a corollary of, if not a respondent to, feminist study rather than its counterpart. While feminist studies are pro-women by definition, what would be the cause for masculinity studies to advocate? Clines suggests consciousness raising, apology, and the constant definition of 'what it is about masculinity that is objectionable'.[42] I agree with every point, but still find myself asking whether masculinity, or being a man, really is void of any positive and empowering elements that could be of value when fighting injustice and struggling for a better world.

Reading ancient texts is an important tool in interpreting the modern world. It is probable that the ancient writers—and perhaps, their readers— often would not share their moral standards and societal values with their modern researchers or even with each other.[43] Neither is there one moral

40. Clines 2010b: 238.
41. The designation 'men's studies' has been used, but in the present volume it appears only once, in n. 17 of Glessner's article.
42. Clines 2010b: 238-39.
43. Sawyer 2009: 15: 'Rather, the Bible comprises multiple, contesting discourses which contradict and parody one another in a constant state of tension… This is why reading the Bible from the standpoint of gender critique broadens the lens that was first

standard among today's teachers and interpreters of the Bible that could be lived up together, but different standards depending on the (non)religious background and cultural context of each individual interpreter. This is where the real gulfs are to be found: not only the cultural distance between the ancient texts and their modern researchers but also the deep chasms dividing people in the present-day world between those who actively uphold patriarchal structures and standards and those who do every effort to challenge and change them. The ongoing debate on homosexuality (so-called) is a prime example of this.

The feedback I have received to countless public lectures on gender-related topics I have given in my home country often expresses the approval of the audiences with presenting the biblical text as a part of the literature of the ancient world. Against the background of what can be known about the ancient readers' world, even the biblical God, often so violent, erratic, and enraged, has become easier to fathom for them. I have never attempted to whitewash unpleasant features in the biblical image of God. I have only tried to communicate the idea that ancient texts were written in a cultural context that in so many ways differs from the modern reader's world, including moral standards—and that similar differences exist between people living around us here and now.

Bibliography

Anderson, Janice, and Stephen D. Moore
    2003   'Matthew and Masculinity', in Moore and Anderson (ed.) 2003: 67-91.
Asher-Greve, Julia M.
    1997   'The Essential Body: Mesopotamian Concepts of the Gendered Body', *Gender and History* 9: 432-61.
Bahrani, Zainab
    2001   *Women of Babylon: Gender and Representation in Mesopotamia* (London: Routledge).
Brenner, Athalya
    2013   'Quo Vadis Domina? Reflections on What We Have Become and Want to Be', *lectio difficilior* 2013.1.
Carr, David M., and Colleen M. Conway
    2008   'The DivineHuman Marriage Matrix and Construction of Gender and "Bodies" in the Christian Bible', in Nissinen and Uro (ed.) 2008: 275-303.
Clines, David J.A.
    1995   *Interested Parties: The Ideology of Writers and Readers of the Hebrew Bible* (JSOTSup, 205; Sheffield: Sheffield Academic Press).

introduced by feminist interpreters, allowing us to engage with ideas that are perhaps more in sympathy with the pre-modern writers who produced them, and perhaps might even allow us to gain clearer insights into the character of God who inspired them to write.'

2002 'He-Prophets: Masculinity as a Problem for the Hebrew Prophets and their Interpreters', in Alastair G. Hunter and Philip R. Davies (ed.), *Sense and Sensitivity: Essays on Reading the Bible in Memory of Robert Carroll* (JSOTSup, 348; Sheffield: Sheffield Academic Press): 311-28.

2010a 'Dancing and Shining in Sinai: Playing the Man in Exodus 32–34', in Creangă (ed.) 2010: 54-63.

2010b 'Final Reflections on Biblical Masculinity', in Creangă (ed.) 2010: 234-39.

Connell, R.W.

2005 *Masculinities* (Berkeley: University of California Press, 2nd edn).

Connell, R.W., and James W. Messerschmidt

2005 'Hegemonic Masculinity: Rethinking the Concept', *Gender and Society* 19: 829-59.

Conway, Colleen M.

2008 *Behold the Man: Jesus and Greco-Roman Masculinity* (Oxford and New York: Oxford University Press).

Creangă, Ovidiu

2010 'Variations of the Theme of Masculinity: Joshua's Gender In/stability in the Conquest Narrative (Josh. 1–12)', in Creangă (ed.) 2010: 83-109.

Creangă, Ovidiu (ed.)

2010 *Men and Masculinity in the Hebrew Bible and Beyond* (The Bible in the Modern World, 33; Sheffield: Sheffield Phoenix Press).

Day, Peggy L.

2008 'Yahweh's Broken Marriages as Metaphoric Vehicle in the Hebrew Bible Prophets', in Nissinen and Uro (ed.) 2008: 219-41.

DiPalma, Brian C.

2010 'De/Constructing Masculinity in Exodus 1–4', in Creangă (ed.) 2010: 36-53.

Exum, J. Cheryl

forthcoming 'The Man in the Song of Songs', in Claudia Camp, David Gunn, Ehud Ben Zvi and Aaron Hughes (eds.), *Poets, Prophets, Lovers and Beauty: Studies in Biblical Poetry and Prophecy in Honour of Francis Landy* (LHBOTS; London: Bloomsbury T. & T. Clark).

Gleason, Maud W.

1995 *Making Men: Sophists and Self-presentation in Ancient Rome* (Princeton: Princeton University Press).

Haddox, Susan E.

2010 'Favoured Sons and Subordinate Masculinities', in Creangă (ed.) 2010: 2-19.

Halperin, David M.

1990 *One Hundred Years of Homosexuality and Other Essays on Greek Love* (New York: Routledge).

Hamori, Esther

2008 *When Gods Were Men: The Embodied God in Biblical and Ancient Near Eastern Literature* (BZAW, 384; Berlin: de Gruyter).

Launderville, Dale

2010 *Celibacy in the Ancient World: Its Ideal and Practice in Pre-Hellenistic Israel, Mesopotamia, and Greece* (Collegeville: Liturgical Press).

Mayordomo, Moises
    2006   'Construction of Masculinity in Antiquity and Early Christianity', *lectio difficilior* 2006.2.
Moore, Stephen D.
    2010   'Final Reflections on Biblical Masculinity', in Creangă (ed.) 2010: 240-55.
Moore, Stephen D., and Janice Capel Anderson (ed.)
    2003   *New Testament Masculinities* (Semeia St, 45; Atlanta: Society of Biblical Literature).
Nissinen, Martti
    1998   *Homoeroticism in the Biblical World: A Historical Perspective* (Minneapolis: Fortress Press).
  forthcoming 'Relative Masculinities in the Hebrew Bible/Old Testament', in Zsolnay (ed.) forthcoming.
Nissinen, Martti, and Risto Uro (eds.)
    2008   *Sacred Marriages: The Divine–Human Sexual Metaphor from Sumer to Early Christianity* (Winona Lake: Eisenbrauns).
Olyan, Saul M.
    1994   '"And with a Male You Shall not Lie the Lying Down of a Woman": On the Meaning and Significance of Leviticus 18:22 and 20:13', *JHistSex* 5: 179-206.
Parpola, Simo
    2001   'Mesopotamian Precursors of the Hymn of the Pearl', in R. M. Whiting (ed.), *Mythology and Mythologies: Methodological Approaches to Intercultural Influences* (Melammu Symposia, 2; Helsinki: The Neo-Assyrian Text Corpus Project): 181-93.
Parpola, Simo, and R. M. Whiting (eds.)
    2002   *Sex and Gender in the Ancient Near East* (CRRAI, 47, Parts I–II; Helsinki: The Neo-Assyrian Text Corpus Project).
Roscoe, Will
    1996   'Priests of the Goddess: Gender Transgression in Ancient Religion', *HR* 35: 195-230.
Sawyer, Deborah F.
    2009   'Gender Criticism: A New Discipline in Biblical Studies or Feminism in Disguise', in Deborah W. Rooke (ed.), *A Question of Sex? Gender and Difference in the Hebrew Bible and Beyond* (HBM, 14; Sheffield: Sheffield Phoenix Press): 2-17.
Schwartz, Baruch J.
    2000   'Ezekiel's Dim View of Israel's Restoration', in Margaret S. Odell and John T. Strong (ed.), *The Book of Ezekiel: Theological and Anthropological Perspectives* (SBLSymS, 9: Atlanta: Society of Biblical Literature): 43-67.
Stone, Ken (ed.)
    2001   *Queer Commentary and the Hebrew Bible* (JSOTSup, 334; Sheffield: Sheffield Academic Press).
Teppo, Saana
    2008   'Sacred Marriage and the Devotees of Ištar', in Nissinen and Uro (ed.) 2008: 75-92.

Trible, Phyllis
    1978   *God and the Rhetoric of Sexuality* (OBT; Philadelphia: Fortress Press).

Wagner, Andreas
    2010   *Gottes Körper: Zur alttestamentlichen Vorstellung der Menschengestaltigkeit Gottes* (Gütersloh: Gütersloher Verlagshaus).

Williams, Craig A.
    1999   *Roman Homosexuality: Ideologies of Masculinity in Classical Antiquity* (Oxford and New York: Oxford University Press; 2nd edn, 2010).

Yee, Gale A.
    2013   'The Woman Warrior Revisited: Jael, Fa Mulan, and American Orientalism', in Athalya Brenner and Gale A. Yee (ed.), *Joshua and Judges* (Texts@Contexts; Minneapolis: Fortress Press): 175-90.

Zsolnay, Ilona
    2010   'The Inadequacies of Yahweh: A Re-examination of Jerusalem's Portrayal in Ezekiel 16', in S. Tamar Kamionkowski and Wonil Kim (ed.), *Bodies, Embodiment, and Theology of the Hebrew Bible* (LHBOTS, 465; London: T. & T. Clark): 57-74.
    2013   'The Misconstrued Role of the *Assinnu* in Ancient Near Eastern Prophecy', in Jonathan Stökl and Corrine L. Carvalho, *Prophets Male and Female: Gender and Prophecy in the Hebrew Bible, the Eastern Mediterranean, and the Ancient Near East* (Ancient Israel and Its Literature, 15; Atlanta: Society of Biblical Literature): 81-99.

Zsolnay, Ilona (ed.)
  forthcoming *Being a Man in Antiquity: Negotiating, Legitimating, and Maintaining Ancient Constructs of Masculinity* (London: Routledge).

BIBLICAL MASCULINITY MATTERS

Björn Krondorfer

'What does masculinity have to do with biblical studies?' asks Stephen Moore in his introduction to *New Testament Masculinities*. He continues: 'Almost nothing—and nearly everything; *almost nothing* until relatively recently, when studies specifically analyzing the construction of masculinity in biblical and cognate texts began to appear; ...but *nearly everything* throughout most of the history of critical biblical scholarship, when men, and men alone, almost without exception, constituted the rank and file of the discipline. Masculinity', he concludes, 'was, at once, everywhere and nowhere' (Moore 2003: 1; emphasis in original).

What Moore observed a few years ago for New Testament studies applies similarly to the study of Hebrew Scriptures. Fortunately, biblical studies is now acknowledging that masculinity matters, and this fine volume is the most recent demonstration of such recognition. Indeed, once we train our eyes on the implicit and explicit androcentric perspectives that inform biblical texts, we realize how much the once invisible male gender seems omnipresent—whether through direct portrayals of (in)famous men, through descriptions of masculine ideals (or failures to comply with them), through indirect assumptions in value-laden prescriptive passages, or through omissions and silences in the narrative structure that invite readers to fill in the gaps through acts of the imagination.

Although a few canonical passages and familiar characters make an appearance in *Biblical Masculinities Foregrounded* (Moses, Samuel, David, Paul, Jesus, and Jesus' male disciples), the contributing authors wisely avoid an approach that seeks out—and then perhaps deconstructs—male typologies and archetypes that appeal to the popular imagination. This is a welcome change to a convention that has centered on individual male heroes (or anti-heroes) in the pursuit of identifying biblical masculinities and manly virtues. Rather than seeking affirmations of patriarchal or benign-paternalistic models of men through Bible study, we now look at the 'fluid, obstinate, and unfamiliar gender conceptions' (Walz 2008: 16) that are hiding at the margins of the canon.

A few years ago, I was invited as an outside voice (that is, 'outside' to biblical studies) to respond to a SBL panel on Abraham as a key male figure in the Hebrew Scriptures.[1] To my surprise, the panelists remained closely aligned with canonical text choices in order to investigate the patriarch. Since they examined Abraham through gender-critical, feminist, and queer theoretical lenses, one could have assumed that a fresh reading of Abraham might begin at the margins, in those zones where we have to learn how to decipher the scribbles of history. I had assumed that the panelists would have investigated fragments at the edges of the corpus rather than core stories. Since this was not the case, I offered two possible explanations: the reliance on central texts either mirrors the fact that biblical research has not yet fully engaged with the area of critical men's studies; or it signals the urgency with which these scholars perceive their responsibility to enter into the fray of public controversy over biblical masculinities, and what better way than starting with familiar stories.

But why urgency? What would be urgent about biblical studies? The answer lies in the political reality that ancient holy texts remain contested in the public sphere today and continue to inform current social policies. Outside of academia, issues of gender and sexuality are still debated as 'truths' that are anchored in sacred narratives. Hence, biblical scholars may have a mandate to contribute to the public discourse, including a gender-sensitive probing of the powering figure of Abraham. We may have to acknowledge that the little attention biblical scholars receive by the general public may be better spent on stories that are culturally recognizable and familiar to the rank-and-file of Christian communities rather than investigating obscure passages and exegetical minutiae. A scholar's corrective voice may thus have a chance to counter simplified understandings of biblical masculinity that float around in the public arena.

Where does *Biblical Masculinities Foregrounded* stand in regard to those issues? For one, the contributing authors discontinue the tradition of limiting oneself to canonical text choices and to (arche)typical reconstructions of biblical male role models. Second, the contributors are well-versed with masculinity studies and its cognate fields (like feminist criticism, cultural studies, queer studies). The familiarity with these cognate fields, I suspect, has influenced the selection of themes, texts, and figures that are located more at the edges of the biblical corpus than its canonical core. Even when discussing less marginal issues, like Saul's (failed) manliness, Jesus'

---

1. 2011 Annual Meeting of the Society of Biblical Literature (SBL) in San Francisco; the SBL-session 'Feminist Hermeneutics of the Bible' hosted a panel on the theme of 'Men in Power and in Trouble: Masculinity Studies and Father Abraham', which included Ken Stone, Gregory Mobley, Bonnie Flessen, Rachel Havrelock and, as respondents, Linda Thomas and Björn Krondorfer.

Sermon on the Mount, or Philo's and Paul's understanding of circumcision, the contributors frame them in terms that are relevant to the current theoretical debate, referencing R.W. Connell's hegemonic, complicit, and subordinate masculinities, Craig Williams's priapic masculinity,[2] Judith Butler's gender performativity, and the colonial subject as part of the discourse on post/colonialism.

Third, the authors remain true to their academic trait as biblical exegetes and they delight in exegetical details. They inquire into cross-referencing of words, etymologies, sources, narrative composition, and textual deviations. For anyone not trained in biblical studies, this is, at times, hard to follow. In this sense, fourth, the chapters err on the side of arguing with exegetical minutiae rather than trying to communicate effectively with a wider audience. As a matter of fact, the language of some of the chapters would have to be 'translated' into common parlance before they would be able to be understood in a public forum on masculinity and gender relations. This is a concern that seems to be echoed in the editor's Introduction, where Ovidiu Creangă wonders whether the study of masculinities in biblical scholarship lacks 'in passion' and whether it sufficiently acknowledges that 'speaking, or refusing to speak, against certain expressions of biblical masculinity' is a 'political matter' (p. 10).

Before we return to these questions, we need to take a step back and ask what a critical men's studies approach to biblical masculinities might entail. In the general field of 'men's studies in religion',[3] we have moved away from a simple positivist reading of male figures in the Jewish and Christian traditions. We no longer approach biblical texts, or, for that matter, any sacred texts, as if they constitute prooftexts that tell us something about essential moral qualities of men (or women). Recent scholarship also no longer uses biblical stories as blueprints for creating psychological profiles of men (and that includes the technique of isolating archetypal or mytho-poetic manly core qualities or core types). Instead of putting forth a positi-vist and heteronormative reading of men's presence in religious traditions, we now engage in a critical reading of the privileged performances of male gender within those traditions. When we take the category of 'gender' and apply it to men/male identity/masculinity in religiously saturated cultural contexts, we are opening a research area that has been defined and described as 'critical men's studies in religion' (Krondorfer 2009). It is a subfield at the transdisciplinary intersection of gender studies and religious studies.

What do I mean by 'critical'? Let me focus here on three points:

---

2.   'Priapic masculinity' refers to men asserting their masculinity by dominating others (Williams 1999).

3.   See Krondorfer and Culbertson 2004; Krondorfer 2007.

1. *Critical men's studies in religion is gender-conscious and self-reflexive.* It approaches and understands 'men' as gendered beings. With the help of gender theory, including feminist theory, men are seen within their particular gendered limitations and also in their embodiments. The attention paid to embodiment also calls for self-reflexivity. Such reflexivity breaks the cycle of remaining blind to the 'everywhere' of masculinity in the field of biblical studies. It gently compels men to integrate their own genderedness into an awareness of the hermeneutical method one brings to a text. The fact that patriarchal gender codes have constructed men as normative and often disembodied beings is now understood as a historically contingent pattern—with all the repercussions which such perception had for women and men, family and society as well as modes of (religious and theological) knowing. To what extent are men—as both researching subjects and ordinary citizens—complicit in the hermeneutical and social structures within which they operate?

2. *Critical men's studies in religion requires critical and ethical analysis.* It probes, diagnoses, evaluates, and seeks explanations. It examines how and to what extent sacred texts, traditions, and institutions have to be understood as products of men. To be attentive to the visible and invisible structures of (male) power still begs an ethical stance: do we acquiesce to the sense of entitlement rooted in male privilege or, on the contrary, do we embrace with humility the limitation of male-gendered particularity? There are benefits that can be reaped and harms caused when men remain blind toward their own genderedness. What behaviors, attitudes, images, and ideals of manliness are condoned or condemned in the religious traditions, and how do we relate to them?

3. *Critical men's studies in religion is transformative.* It examines texts and traditions along the lines of shifts and frictions in the production of ideals of masculinity. It looks for locations of resistance to dominating structures. It ascertains the power of the hegemonic ideal over against the diversity of the material lives of men. It is also committed to exploring alternative visions of what it means to be religious as a man, including the critical probing of the categories of 'man' and 'religion' themselves. Where do we find traces and resources in the religious traditions that resist hegemonic ideals of masculinity and help to envision other realities?

In the following, I want to draw connections between these three rubrics regarding a critical men's studies approach in religion and the contributions to *Biblical Masculinities Foregrounded*.

To 1: Critical men's studies is gender-conscious and self-reflexive

The wide spectrum of themes covered in this volume reveals the extent to which gender-consciousness is evident in all chapters. We hear about the hidden and revealed embodied manifestations of the deity that attest to Yahweh's virility and fertility (though, paradoxically, not his offspring); we learn about the construction of masculinity through performances of male strength in Proverbs, but here with a focus on 'inner' (not physical) strength, which may constitute an alternative model of masculinity; we evaluate reasons for why Saul's masculinity is so thoroughly undermined in the narrative of Samuel, to the point of removing the 'man' out of Saul; and we contemplate the intimate experience of 'weeping' in Torah that is attested to patriarchs and prophets alike without it diminishing their masculinity. Two contributions investigate the 'manly' traits of female figures: the reviled Queen Athaliah (2 Kings) and the admired Thecla, the former usurping male royal power, the latter defying adopting a 'manly' ascetic discipline. In the chapters about the New Testament, multiple themes are addressed: the quandary of eunuchs (and how to understand Jesus' enigmatic praise for sexual self-mutilation in Mt. 19); the cost of male discipleship as outlined in the Sermon on the Mount, where the control of the passions may amount to a demand for an 'anomalous masculinity'; the accounting of ordinary masculinity of the impoverished peasant masses (and whether Joseph, the husband of Mary, can be read as the silent/silenced voice of the colonized subject); and Philo's and Paul's attitudes toward circumcision within their Hellenist context.

Throughout, traits of the male body as well as performances of male identity are investigated as sites in which power and diversity, resistance and compliance, change and continuity are negotiated. The chapters' gender consciousness and theoretical sophistication brought to bear upon biblical exegesis open up the horizon to a remarkably fresh look at the variegated mosaic of masculinities we can trace in the biblical Scriptures.

However, when we turn to 'self-reflexivity' as another feature of critical men's studies, we can observe a lack thereof in the contributions to *Biblical Masculinities Foregrounded*. Self-reflexivity may start with an awareness that biblical texts can function as mirrors: we look into them and see a part of ourselves reflected back. Self-reflexivity is the process of making conscious such mirroring effects, but the chapters in this volume are fairly silent in this regard. How, for example, does a text resonate in a male (or female) reader and scholar—culturally, personally, intellectually, viscerally? 'I have two books open as I prepare this paper', Gregory Mobley argued on a SBL panel on Abraham, 'the book of formal learning and the book of my male experience' (see n. 1, above). Tending to the latter does not imply falling into the trap of private indulgence.

Cognizant of the scholar's general fear of improper self-revelation, we may still be willing to concede a space for exploring the confluence of, on the one hand, the experience of the writing subject and, on the other, the impartiality of the examined object. The moral agency of the embodied presence of the author does not have to disappear entirely behind a dis-embodied scholarly prose.[4] The recovery of hitherto hidden aspects of complicit and subordinate masculinities in biblical texts may also be a discovery of the masculinity of the living subject in the present.

Self-reflexivity is also the awareness of how textual fragments that are passed on to us in the long line of generational readings impact us—those remembered, recalled, and half-forgotten fragments by which we have been nursed long before we developed our own hermeneutical apparatus. Biblical gender expectations that float around in the public sphere derive strength from their narrative 'truth', and scholars are not living in a vacuum. Acknowledging the power and popularity of narrative truths does not negate the task of insisting on factual and historical accuracy—it augments it.

Self-reflexivity is also about the power of memory—textual, cultural, collective, and individual. 'The stories of the Hebrew Bible', Marc Brettler writes, do not 'function as academic history...but as memory' (2001: 11). This insight applies, of course, to New Testament writings just the same.

> I will utter enigmas of the past,
> things that we have heard and known,
> that our fathers told us.
> We will not hide them from their children
> but tell to the coming generations... (Ps. 78.2-4)

Perhaps we can take Psalm 78 to heart and remember that the study of the 'enigmas of the past' comes with the entreaty to tell them to the 'coming generations.' Or to put it in another way, a prudent way to think about self-reflexivity is to realize that text-contained memory is subject to processes of mediation: narrative memory lives from being told and retold; it needs to be passed on. Such memory work requires 'imaginative investment, projection, and creation' (Hirsch 2012: 5). As a matter of fact, most contributors to *Biblical Masculinities Foregrounded* also tell a story, even when it is barely audible because it is buried beneath layers of painstaking historical and textual analysis. An exegete is also a storyteller who works with and against social and personal memories. Self-reflexivity, then, pays attention to the wisdom of cultural memory and to the (submerged) story-telling voice of the biblical scholar.

---

4.   See, for example, my study on male confessions (Krondorfer 2010).

To 2: Critical men's studies requires critical and ethical analysis

Lest we err on the side of uncritical myth-making as we investigate biblical masculinity, the second rubric of men's studies calls for critical and ethical analysis. The analytical portion is grounded both in the tools of one's professional trade as well as the theory that guides the investigation.

As mentioned above, the contributors to this volume do exceptionally well on both accounts. They summon the theoretical literature—from Lacan to Butler—and employ resourcefully biblical scholarship of the last decades. Their solidly grounded approaches leave room for disagreement among them, something that could be further explored by the discerning reader. One may ask, for example, what the conditions are that determine why and when female leaders, who have taken on 'manly' traits, virtues, and characteristics (like Thecla and Athaliah), are either condemned or condoned in the memory of a community? Why is Thecla textually praised and rescued, while Athaliah is textually ridiculed and drowned?

We can also observe, to name another example of the book's internal deviations, that the new and radical demands placed upon men in the Matthean community differ in the interpretations of two contributors. Whereas Susanna Asikainen emphasizes that Jesus' affirmative but enigmatic saying about eunuchs signals the 'costly' commitment to the Matthean community, even at the price of 'readiness to mutilate or castrate oneself' (p. 180), Hans-Ulrich Weidemann interprets Jesus' demands of his male disciples to 'overcome the male spiral of violence' and to 'provocatively proclaim their nonresistance' (p. 149). While the former puts the spotlight on male self-mutilation, the latter directs our attention to male non-violence—and this is not the same thing, especially when considering the ethical implications for men.

Inevitably, critical analysis engenders differing interpretations and conclusions; hence, the multiple and occasionally non-consensual voices that we encounter in this volume do not weaken their argumentative force. Rather, they attest to the book's intellectual integrity. What we do observe, however, is a certain reticence to making ethical judgment. A scholar of biblical criticism is, of course, not an ethicist, and those limitations ought to be respected. Yet, similar to the case about integrating moments of self-reflexivity, the 'foregrounding' of implicit ethical proclivities would strengthen a critical men's studies approach to a gendered reading of biblical texts.

It is fairly obvious, for example, that many of the authors critique patriarchy (as it manifests itself in the form of priapic, hegemonic, militant, or imperial masculinities). But it is less clear whether the same authors are ready to propose alternative ideals of masculinity, and whether they presume that biblical texts can serve to inspire and sustain alternative trajectories.

Furthermore, it is obvious that none of the contributing authors subscribe to evangelical or fundamentalist interpretations of biblical masculinities. For biblical scholars, this may be a case that needs no further justification since the reliance on the critical-historical method is seen as anathema to fundamentalism. And yet, when it comes to determining the kind of gender issues debated in the public, the fundamentalist movement is far more successful in dominating this space.

Fundamentalists have no qualms in making ethical and moral pronouncement on masculinity as derived from their reading of the biblical tradition. Focusing on questions of lifestyle (with less interest in exegetical, theological, and dogmatic controversies), they can speak straight to the anxieties and sensibilities of their audiences. Fundamentalists favour *orthopraxy* over *orthodoxy*, exhibit a 'gesetzesethischen Rigorismus [legal-ethical rigorism]' (Riesebrodt 2005: 20), and follow a theocentric view of the world: all of these features lend themselves to proclamations of eternally valid gender codes.

Responding to the insecurity and crisis that modernity has triggered among large portions of the population, fundamentalism is also an attempt to re-masculinize religion and re-patriarchalize society. Bruce Lawrence, an American religious studies scholar, claims that the driving force behind religious fundamentalism is a 'secondary male elite' (1995: 100): men who could belong to the elite based on their education and class status but who do not have, for social and political reasons (and due to religious convictions), their hands on the lever of power in secular society. Martin Riesebrodt describes them as a 'new religious elite of proletaroid intellectuals' (2005: 21).

In spite of many differences that exist within fundamentalist movements, they widely agree on gender issues, especially when it comes to pushing women out of public life and reclaiming a more militant and assertive masculinity. It is a phenomenon that can be observed equally among Jewish, Hindu, Islamic, and Buddhist fundamentalists. Among the list of extreme American fundamentalist Christians are the radical fringes of *Operation Rescue* and adherents to *Dominion Theology*, willing to set fire to abortion clinics or calling for the stoning of homosexuals and adulterers. But regardless of whether we look at the radical or moderate wings of fundamentalism, this movement offers roles to women and men that are touted as biblically anchored and eternally valid. Most of all, fundamentalism is an extraordinarily dynamic movement.

In terms of social dynamism, the contrast between fundamentalists and the male-gender conscious biblical scholars could not be greater. Hence, when Creangă amplifies David Clines's concern that masculinity studies in the field of biblical criticism is 'lacking in passion' (p. 9), we may need to take stock of a real problem. This does not invalidate or render irrelevant the scholarship of *Biblical Masculinities Foregrounded*, but it shows that the work cannot end here. The new scholarship is relevant precisely because we live in a time when simplifications rule public discourse, and not just in matters of religion. The question, then, is not one of the quality of scholarship but of effective communication. A small step toward regaining a public voice, I have suggested, is to make explicit one's ethical and moral stance toward particular behaviours, attitudes, and ideals of masculinities as they are distilled and derived from the critical study of biblical Scriptures.

To 3: Critical men's studies in religion is transformative

Questions of the formation, construction, and maintenance of male identity are present in most chapters. The contributing authors repeatedly point to the performativity of male gender and they assert the fact that masculinities are made, not begotten. Masculinities, they argue, are not stable categories but always subject to change. Scholarship on masculinity may, then, have to conceive of itself as an agent of change. In the Introduction, Creangă states explicitly that it is also 'our responsibility to offer viable models of masculinity' (p. 10), thus acknowledging that a critical men's studies approach calls for attending to transformative processes. To 'engender' such processes (both in the sense of 'creating' and 'gendering') requires, of course, an ethical commitment, as explicated above.

Philip Culbertson asks in *New Adam: The Future of Male Spirituality* (1992) whether biblical stories about men can be read as texts of terror not only for women (as Phyllis Trible had advocated back in 1984) but also for men. With regard to Abraham, for example, Culbertson points to terrifying moments in the patriarch's life, such as his paralysis, his wrestling with God, his preferential treatment of one child over another, or the often changing rules by God that destabilize Abraham's integrity. Examples of such terror are also present in *Biblical Masculinities Foregrounded*: the struggle of the colonized Joseph (Mary's husband) over against Roman imperial ideology; failing to comply with role expectations (Saul); the strain of phallic competition between a male deity and its male adherents (Aaron and Moses); the risk men take when *deviating* from normative masculinity (Jesus' male disciples), and the risk women take when *assuming* normative masculinity (Thecla; Athaliah); the always present danger of being effeminized, as, for example, through circumcision or through metaphoric or real castration (eunuchs); and the threat of inter-male violence (implicit in the Sermon on the Mount). Men, too, deserve alternative spaces that offer them well-being and protection.

In a different context, I have written that documents in the history of Christianity tell us about 'how men's lives are filled with contradictions, vagaries, indecisions, limitations, blind spots, turmoil, and unresolved business', and how these texts, 'in their partial and partisan ways, bear witness to [men's] boisterous, tarnished, and fragmented vitality' (Krondorfer 2010: 11). I believe this to be true for biblical stories as well.

Bibliography

Brettler, Marc
    2001   'Memory in Ancient Israel', in Michael Signer (ed.), *Memory and History in Christianity and Judaism* (Notre Dame: University of Notre Dame Press): 1-17.

Culbertson, Philip
    1992   *New Adam: The Future of Male Spirituality* (Minneapolis: Augsburg Fortress).

Hirsch, Marianne
    2012   *The Generation of Postmemory: Writing and Visual Culture after the Holocaust* (New York: Columbia University Press).

Krondorfer, Björn
    2007   'World Religions, Christianity,' in M. Flood, J. K. Gardiner and K. Pringle (eds.), *International Encyclopedia of Men and Masculinities* (London: Routledge): 658-60.
    2009   'Introduction', in Björn Krondorfer (ed.), *Men and Masculinities in Christianity and Judaism: A Critical Reader* (London: SCM Press): xi-xxi.
    2010   *Male Confessions: Intimate Revelations and the Religious Imagination* (Stanford: Stanford University Press).

Krondorfer, Björn, and Philip Culbertson
    2004   'Men Studies in Religion', in Lindsay Jones (ed.), *Encyclopedia of Religion* (Detroit: Macmillan, 2nd edn): IX, 5861-66.

Lawrence, Bruce
    1995   *Defenders of God: The Fundamentalist Revolt against the Modern Age* (Columbia, SC: University of South Carolina Press).

Mobley, Gregory
    2009   'Binds that Tie: Abraham and the Paradox of Patriarchy'. Unpublished paper presented at SBL Annual Meeting (San Francisco).

Moore, Stephen D.
    2003   '"O Man, Who Art Thou....?": Masculinity Studies and New Testament Studies', in Stephen D. Moore and Janice Capel Anderson (eds.), *New Testament Masculinities* (Semeia 45; Atlanta: Society of Biblical Literature): 1-22.

Riesebrodt, Martin
    2005   'Was ist religiöser Fundamentalismus?', in Clemens Six, Martin Riesebrodt, and Siegfried Haas (eds.), *Religiöser Fundamentalismus: Vom Kolonialismus zur Globalisierung* (Innsbruck: Studien Verlag): 13-32.

Trible, Phyllis
    1984   *Texts of Terror: Literary-Feminist Readings of Biblical Narratives*
              (Philadelphia: Fortress Press).
Walz, Heike
    2008   'Blinde Flecken: Warum es theologische Geschlechterdialoge queerbeet
              braucht', in Heike Walz and David Plüss (eds.), *Theologie und Geschlecht:*
              Dialoge queerbeet (Vienna/Zurich: Lit Verlag): 10-36.
Williams, Craig A.
    1999   *Roman Homosexuality: Ideologies of Masculinity in Classical Antiquity*
              (Oxford: Oxford University Press).

INDEXES

INDEX OF REFERENCES

Bellum judaicum

1.437	206
1.443-44	206
1.550-51	206
1.655-56	206
1.664-65	206
2.135	129, 139
2.139-42	138, 139

Julius
Obsequens

44A	165

Justin Martyr
1 Apologia

15.4	178
29.2-3	183

Juvenal
Satires

1.22	166
1.30	166
6.366-78	166
6.513	165

Lucian
De syria dea

22	165

Marcus Aurelius

2.10	163
9.40	163

Martial
Epigrams

3.81	165
6.2	166
6.67	166
7.35	231
7.82	231
8.30	231
11.94	231

Ovid
Ars amatoria

1.505-509	167

Fasti

4.183	165

Metamorphoses

3.316-38	235

Philo
De Abrahamo

98	138
147-55	134
154	134

De cherubim

50	235

De ebrietate

54–59	235

De fuga et inventione

51–52	233

Legum allegoriae

3.49	235

*Quod omnis probus
liber sit*

84	139

*Quaestiones et solutiones
in Exodum*

1.7	233, 234

*Quaestiones et solutiones
in Genesin*

3.47	234
3.48	235
4.99	234

*Quod deterius potiori
insidari soleat*

28	235
175	179
176	179

De specialibus legibus

1.1-11	236
1.2	228
1.6	236
1.37	233
1.105-109	194
1.200-201	233
1.325	168
2.2-17	139
5	136
3.2	207
3.9	207
3.20	207
3.51	194
3.65-71	194
3.169	117
3.170-71	117
3.172	117, 120
3.173	120
3.174	120
3.175	120
3.176-77	136
3.176	117
3.177	179

De virtutibus

19	117

Plato
Gorgias

491CD	147

Phaedrus

239C-D	163

Politeia

5.455D	118

Timaeus

16	135

Plutarch
Conjugalia praecepta

16	164, 182
44	164

INDEX OF SUBJECTS

INDEX OF AUTHORS

CPSIA information can be obtained
at www.ICGtesting.com
Printed in the USA
BVHW051235060723
666845BV00008B/234